THE
LEVERAGE OF
SEA POWER

THE LEVERAGE OF SEA POWER

The Strategic Advantage of Navies in War

Colin S. Gray

THE FREE PRESS
A Division of Macmillan, Inc.
New York

Maxwell Macmillan Canada
Toronto

Maxwell Macmillan International
New York   Oxford   Singapore   Sydney

The Free Press
A Division of Macmillan, Inc.
866 Third Avenue, New York, N.Y. 10022

Maxwell Macmillan Canada, Inc.
1200 Eglinton Avenue East
Suite 200
Don Mills, Ontario M3C 3N1

Macmillan, Inc. is part of the Maxwell Communication Group of Companies.

Printed in the United States of America

printing number
1 2 3 4 5 6 7 8 9 10

Maps by William J. Clipson

Library of Congress Cataloging-in-Publication Data

Gray, Colin S.
    The leverage of sea power: the strategic advantage of navies in war / Colin S. Gray.
        p.   cm.
    Includes bibliographical references (p.   ) and index.
    ISBN 0–02–912661–4
    1. Sea-power—History.   2. Naval history   I. Title.
V25.G73   1992
359′.03—dc20   92–22072
                                                          CIP

For the ladies in my life—Dottie, Valerie, T. J., Ciss, and Penelope—all of whom love the sea.

CONTENTS

MAPS

PROLOGUE

Great sea powers or maritime coalitions have either won or, occasionally, drawn every major war in modern history. In ancient and medieval times, when (European and Near Eastern) sea power was very short in range and dependent on the resources of the shore, great land powers tended to defeat great sea power but only by themselves taking to the sea. It has been no accident that from the defeat of Xerxes' invasion of Greece in 480–479 B.C. to the defeat of the Soviet Union in the Cold War of the late twentieth century, superior sea power has provided leverage critical for success in strategy and statecraft. Failure at sea was as fatal to the Athenians in the Peloponnesian War as it was to be for the Carthaginians in the Punic Wars, for the Arabs in their efforts to bring down the Byzantines, for Napoleon in his quest after continental security, and for the Germans and the Russians in this century.

There is a historical pattern to the repeated success of great sea powers over great land powers that defies dismissal as mere chance. My task in this book is to demonstrate how sea power has worked strategically to confer advantage or to avert or offset disadvantage. I have no brief for sea power in general, a particular navy, a particular naval strategy, or this or that class of naval weapon. I believe readers will discover that I have accorded land power its due. Indeed, my argument would lack integrity were the continental side of the strategy coin not presented fairly. As a general rule, the discussion devotes almost as much attention, and sometimes more, to what continental states could and did attempt against their maritime foes, as vice versa.

In major conflicts between maritime and continental powers or coalitions, each side must pursue a mixed strategy embracing both land and sea elements. (For a twentieth century that has seen the battle space of warfare expand below the sea, into the air, into space, and on the electromagnetic spectrum, mixed strategies become very complex.) In practice, conflicts between sea powers and land powers inexorably develop into contests to determine which side is better able to translate its original, environmentally specific, comparative advantage into success in the environment favored by the enemy. For example, the outcome of the Peloponnesian War was determined basically by the respective ability of maritime Athens to apply pressure against continentalist Sparta on land and by Sparta to menace Athens at sea. Since sea powers typically can be beaten only at sea and continental powers can be beaten only on land, struggles between great maritime and great continental states have no small proclivity to descend into a condition of stalemate.

Geography, technology, and tactics have altered radically over the centuries, but the repertoires of strategy options theoretically available to a sea power striving to defeat a land power, and to a land power seeking to bring down a sea power, have remained generally steady. Chapters 2 and 3 identify and outline these strategy repertoires and show using brief historical examples how enduring have been the ideas and the practices of strategy and statecraft.

In a series of historical case studies ranging over 2,500 years I develop the thesis that superior sea power generates a strategic leverage which enables wars to be won. The selection of cases is individual to me, but the criteria for selection are tolerably objective. First, I sought cases of conflict between a great sea power and a great land power. Second, I required that each conflict, or series of conflicts, warrant description as "major." In other words, this book is about the leverage of sea power *in major wars*.

Apart from the obvious, if perhaps unscholarly, reason that wars between strategically unlike states or coalitions (a sea power versus a land power) inherently tend to be more interesting and more richly textured, I was determined to address the subject of grand strategy and military strategy in war as a whole. I did not want to write a geostrategically truncated book about strategy for war at sea or for war on land (or in the air). Furthermore, I wanted to probe both the full range of states' strategic initiatives and responses and to maximize the likelihood that the evidence presented would cover the full scope of dangers faced by historical players. These concerns demanded the selection of cases of major wars, although much can be learned from minor conflicts.

My choice of ten historical case studies undoubtedly reflects my Anglo-American strategic culture and a large measure of Eurocentricity. So be it. I claim simply that these cases are good enough to serve my purposes, not that they are uniquely correct, as might be determined by some infallible critic. More to the point, perhaps, it is not obvious that any alternative selection of cases would yield improved understanding. My selected cases embrace all accessible historical periods and meet the tests, just specified, of a sea power versus a land power and of being unarguably a major event (or series of events) of conflict.

1. Persia and the Greeks (480–479 B.C.)
2. The Peloponnesian War (460–445, 431–404 B.C.)
3. Rome and Carthage (264–241, 219–202 B.C.)
4. The defense of the Byzantine Empire (c. 400–1453)
5. The rise and fall of Venice (c. 700–1797)
6. England and Spain (1568–1604)
7. Britain and France (1688–1815)
8. World War I (1914–18)
9. World War II (1939–45)
10. The Cold War (1947–89)

I regret being obliged to refrain from including the Crimean War, the American Civil War, and the Russo-Japanese War, but my principal criteria for selection, as well as concern for the length of the book, demanded their exclusion.

In addition to the repertoires of strategy options for sea power and land power developed in Chapters 2 and 3, certain themes, which grow to the status of conclusions, run through this analysis. Continental powers can win wars against sea powers if they are able to deny a tolerable level of sea control to their maritime-dependent enemies; that has not been accomplished in modern times, but there have been some close calls. Next, it becomes clear that although sea powers cannot win wars at sea against land powers, command of the relevant sea areas, at the least a working control, is an indispensable enabler for eventual victory in war as a whole. The historical evidence reveals that superior sea power typically functions to permit its owner to use time in the search for advantage. Sea power allows the protraction of conflict and tends to set up a frustrated continental enemy to overreach on land.

History shows that in key respects an important advantage in sea power grants the ability to control the geostrategic terms of engagement in war. Depending upon who controls the sea, water is a highway or a barrier. The continuity of the world's seas and oceans translates into a global mobility and agility for maritime forces and for merchant shipping which can have no continental parallel. That mobility and agility has been used time and time again, in all historical periods, to achieve surprise and the full strategic advantage of surprise effect. Finally, and notwithstanding the several revolutions in transportation technologies for all environments over the centuries, superior sea power has enabled its owners to knit together coalitions with a total strategic weight greatly superior to those secured by dominant continental strength.

These broad themes or conclusions are always subject to the specific details governing applicability in individual historical cases. They are generally true but can be invalidated at particular times and places. Sea power and land power are not abstractions; they are the partial expression of the strength of specific historical polities at specific times. It always matters whose sea power and land power is under examination. Sea power is not a force of nature of constant value, and neither is it a mystical generality. Rather, it matters greatly whether the sea power in question is the product of a continental-sized super state or of a small island within bombing range of even the short-legged aircraft of the Luftwaffe of 1940. Sea power and land power—and air power and space power—are always particular and relative to time, political owner, technology, and the policy issues at stake.

CHAPTER 1

THE NATURE AND USES
OF SEA POWER

The supreme test of the naval strategist is the depth of his
comprehension of the intimate relation between sea power and
land power, and of the truth that basically all effort afloat
should be directed at an effect ashore.

Dudley W. Knox, *The Naval
Genius of George Washington* (1932)

Navies fight at sea only for the strategic effect they can secure
ashore, where people live. Sea battles, naval tactics, and ship design are all means, and only means, to the gaining of strategic
leverage in conflict as a whole. Technological and therefore tactical, as well as geographical and political, conditions have changed
enormously, if typically slowly, over the past two and a half thousand years. Questions of strategy and of statecraft, however, have
endured throughout that long period.

Conditions have altered, but the leverage granted by sea power
and the strategic advantage achieved by navies is still an important
area to explore. From the Athens of the fifth century B.C., through
the Byzantine Empire, the British Empire, to the United States in
this post–Cold War decade of the 1990s, the utility of sea power
as one of the shaping influences on the course and outcome of
conflict has remained a matter of high salience for strategy and
statecraft.

Meaningful comparisons can be drawn at the levels of strategy
and high policy among the leverage gained by sea powers in different periods. If the strategic leverage accruing to the use of sea
power is the first thread, the second are the ever critical terms of

1

competition between sea power and land power or between maritime and continental states. Those terms have shifted with geography in favor of maritime states, as the arena of action expanded from the confined waters of the Mediterranean to the open ocean, for example. Nonetheless and notwithstanding changing political entities and technologies, the strategic relationship between sea power and land power, albeit modified by the emergence of air power and space power, is a subject that has integrity for the whole of recorded history, although the strategic picture has become more cluttered and the challenge to commanders more complicated. In 1900 the strategic world was strictly geophysically two-dimensional, embracing the land and the sea. As the century draws toward its close, the strategic world is now five-dimensional—with air, space, and the electromagnetic spectrum added to the land and the sea—and even that is a considerable simplification given the surface, subsurface, and overhead dimensions to naval power.

Despite the transitions from the oared galley to the sailing ship, to the steam and nuclear-driven ship and notwithstanding the appearance of aircraft, missiles, and nuclear weapons, sea power and land power have continued to be distinguishable. Defense and war has required the assembly of an ever more diverse team, but it always was a joint enterprise when approached strategically.

For reasons basically of physical and political geography, most states in most eras have had an identifiably continental or maritime inclination in their strategic orientation and culture. Sea powers and land powers are rarely only sea or land powers, but their geopolitical identity is not often in doubt. The strategic history of the past two and a half millennia lends itself to treatment as a series of competitions between sea powers and land powers for sufficient strategic effectiveness to force a favorable decision in conflict. Sea powers have had to seek to acquire land power, and land powers have had to seek to acquire sea power. Different patterns of relative advantage have manifested themselves in ancient and medieval times (in the Mediterranean), as contrasted with the modern period (of global scope). In the former era, great continental states persistently acquired the sea power necessary to defeat maritime foes. In the latter period, to the present, no sea-oriented coalition of states has lost a great conflict with a continental enemy. These truly are patterns, albeit contrasting patterns,

2

and they are the product of the conditions under which sea power and land power have functioned strategically. In some ways more telling than the ultimate victory of continental polities over maritime rivals in ancient and medieval times, however, was the persistence of the necessity for those continental powers to acquire sea power.

The idea of sea power that is commonplace today identifies an instrument of state policy and points to activities, expertise, and weapons plainly distinguishable from land power. This approach to sea power is as recent as the use of the sea for strategic purposes is of ancient lineage. Sea power, modern sea power perhaps, is the idea of an era that distinguishes piracy from state-sanctioned war on trade, naval officers from merchant seamen, and warships from merchant vessels, and it shapes its strategic visions with open ocean, rather than confined seas, in mind.

Of course, the Athenians, the Romans, the Byzantines, the Venetians, and the Ottoman Turks developed and exercised sea power also, but theirs was of a coastal, narrow-sea character, driven strategically and tactically by the constraints of geography and marine technology. As late as Elizabethan England, the idea of the sea power of the state was as alien as its physical realization was impracticable. Lack of public finance, the prevalence of shipboard diseases, the absence of overseas bases, and a shortage of naval professionalism, to cite but a handful among the limiting factors, meant that England at that time was not able to wield sea power as the navalist tracts of later centuries expected and recommended.

Is the demarcation line between sea power and land power a simple matter of physical geography, or is the division more functional and strategic? General Dwight D. Eisenhower's Allied Expeditionary Forces that landed in Normandy in June 1944 were an expression of Allied sea power (and air power), were reinforced and sustained in combat by Allied-commanded sea lines of communication, and drew next to nothing from local continental resources. Was this great continental campaign an exercise in sea power? Logic, if not common sense, suggests that the answer to this question should be "yes," with a powerful "but" appended. A different proposition is that since human endeavor is organized on behalf of land-based political units, directly or indirectly for the

3

influence of events on land, and because all of the resources that produce sea power are resources of the land, sea power can be only an exercise of land power, duly translated into instruments suitable for operation at or from the sea.

There is ample ground for dispute as to where the domains of sea power and land power should be judged to meet. The high-tide line is as commonsensical and obvious as it is unsatisfactory, given the landward reach of modern sea-based weapons and the seaward reach of modern land-based weapons. Martin Wight suggested that

> when Vasco da Gama bombarded Calicut on the Malibar coast in 1502, on his second voyage, to punish the Hindu ruler for the murder of Portuguese merchants, he began the long development of sea power that culminated on 6 August 1945, when the aeroplane *Enola Gay* set off from the island of Tinian in the Marianas for the 1,400 mile flight to Hiroshima. For this was an exercise of sea power. If the Americans had not first conquered the Pacific they could not have bombed Japan; and they too were visiting retribution on an Asiatic power for having violated Western standards of international conduct.[1]

Necessarily, sea power stems ultimately from and is directed against land power. Similarly, land power can be impotent without an adequate sea power complement or even without a sea power propellant. One maxim holds, "In a maritime form of war the army is as a bullet fired from a naval gun."[2]

Sea power is the ability to use the seas and oceans for military or commercial purposes and to preclude an enemy from the same.[3] It would be difficult to exaggerate the importance of recognizing that "the effect of sea-power upon land campaigns is in the main strategical."[4] In the timeless words of Alfred Mahan, "The first and most obvious light in which the sea presents itself from the political and social point of view is that of a great highway."[5] The power of that "obvious light" lies in Mahan's subsequent statement that "notwithstanding all the familiar and unfamiliar dangers of the sea, both travel and traffic by water have always been easier and cheaper than by land."

Marine and competing (land and air) technologies all have undergone revolutionary changes since Mahan wrote in 1890, but he pointed to a general economic truth whose validity has been

4

eroded only at the margins in the twentieth century. The basis for claims for the historical potency of sea power can be grasped by a consideration of the idea of the sea as a great highway, the enduring relative advantage in cost per ton-mile of sea transportation, and the sheer geographical extent of the maritime environment (seven-tenths of the earth's surface). Charles Callwell's argument for the "strategical," by which he meant indirect, character of sea power amounts to a definitional truism. In a political sense, enemies are always on land, so physical geography and military logic typically require that the object of policy in war be continentally defined. A country cannot physically command the seas in the same way that it might be able to command the land. *If the land of the enemy truly is commanded, the war is over.* The strategic nature of sea power is highlighted in the traditional claim that command of the sea means the control of maritime communications.[6] If, as suggested, sea power is about the ability to use the sea and to deny such use to an enemy, then plainly sea power must generate strategic leverage toward the outcome of a conflict.

Mahan identified six highly variable "principal conditions affecting the sea power of nations": geopolitical position; physical conformation, including natural production and climate; extent of territory; number of population; character of the people; and character of the government, including the national institutions.[7] Notwithstanding his avowed purpose to give sea power its due (in practice, more than its due), Mahan's discussion of "the conditions affecting the sea power of nations" was not incompatible with the dark forebodings (for insular, maritime Britain) of Sir Halford Mackinder with his announcement of the end of the maritime Columbian era of c. 1500–c. 1900.[8] The issue was not land power versus sea power, rather, it was which countries in a new age would be better positioned to develop preponderant sea power. Mackinder noted that extent of territory, population, size, and overall productive economic weight would be significant as never before because land communications (railroads) now effectively could unite the otherwise dispersed, and hence inefficient, assets of very large territories. He thus predicted that primacy in the future would belong necessarily neither to the heartland continental power nor to the maritime societies of the West (and East). He did not predict a triumph for some combination of German-Russian-Chinese land power in competition for, and with, the periphery of

Eurasia. Mackinder did not write foolishly of land power "versus" sea power. He understood that land power and sea power, strictly delimited, could not reach each other to grasp for decisive victory. Air power has not been a complication fatal to that claim, since prior to the nuclear age, it lacked the independent potency to achieve decision. In the nuclear age, the reciprocity of unquestionable potency for decision has effected a standoff by mutual nuclear deterrence. Mackinder recognized that in the immediate pre–Columbian era, the heartland forces of horse-riding steppemen did not subjugate peninsular Europe. In the Columbian era, the more and less maritime states of Western Europe never achieved territorial, or even hegemonic, imperium over the Eurasian continental heartland.

Mahan's historical writings referred to the period wherein Britain had evolved economic and strategic policy systems knit together and typically mutually well supported by sea power. The maintenance and effectiveness of that sea power was forwarded almost uniquely among nations by a fortunate geography. Mahan's strategic vision of the sources and conditions for sea power was very much a British-oriented vision, notwithstanding his U.S. nationality and his ambition to influence U.S. policy. His notion of sea power's resting upon the mutually reinforcing effects of commerce, colonies, and a navy was unduly narrow to serve as the basis for a general theory. The elements of sea power comprise merchant shipping, bases, and specialized fighting instruments, but the detailed relations among these elements have varied considerably. There is no need to belabor the obvious interdependence among maritime trade (and a skilled work force at sea and ashore that builds, repairs, and sails the ships), a navy to protect maritime commerce from state-sanctioned as well as piratical depredation in peace and war, and bases at home and overseas. In historical practice, however, the nature of sea power *and of sea powers* has been much more complicated than turn-of-the-century British-oriented navalist texts recognized.

Traditional usage has it that a sea power is a country with a maritime, as contrasted with a continental, orientation in its strategic outlook and that depends critically upon maritime communications for its economic well-being. Such a country therefore requires a healthy measure of naval control of maritime communications for national security and has an influential sea-oriented

6

community for the advancement of maritime aspects of the national interest. By way of contrast, a naval power is simply a country with a strong navy. Such a country may lack important overseas trading interests and a large mercantile marine and may not have a maritime orientation in its national strategic culture or in its defense planning.

Sea powers are not certain to prevail at sea over land powers that happen to be naval powers. A mixture of exhaustion and gross incompetence can compromise the national security of a sea power. Even if naval power is not a natural outgrowth of a maritime preoccupation in commercial matters, still it might be amassed on a scale such that a true sea power with a distinctly inferior resources base could not compete. Virtually by definition, a land power will have a relatively unfavorable geography for maritime conflict. It is the strategic meaning of national geography that suggests most powerfully whether a state must assign first priority to maritime or continental defense efforts. Land powers will lack a tradition of success against first-class maritime powers. Also, because land powers tend to be led by people unschooled in the strategic utility of sea power, it is improbable that such naval strength as can be developed will be employed wisely.

These points apply to all of recorded history. Continentalist Sparta faced geostrategic problems that for decades were of an unsolvable kind in attempting to wage war effectively against an Athens whose strategy could not obviously be assailed. The traditional Spartan continentalist way of war did not work against an Athens that had become a commercial maritime empire, protected in its access to the sea by the long walls to the port of Piraeus, and that could bear the ravaging of its farmland in Attica. For Sparta to succeed, Athens had to be weakened by plague, had to suffer irreparable losses in men and prestige in the expedition to Sicily (415–413 B.C.) and, having effected a partial recovery from these calamities, then had to commit major errors in lack of vigilance in the naval campaign for control of the Dardanelles. No less important, massive financial subsidies from Persia were required for Sparta to acquire the naval power that it needed.[9]

The more important of the handicaps under which land powers with navies typically suffer when they wage war against true sea powers are not eternal conditions, even for the course of a single war. The geopolitical conditions that require a principal focus on landward security can be improved forcibly by continental victory. Prewar disadvantages—massive distraction by hostile armies on the frontier, denial of oceanic access by a prospective enemy who controls critical choke points, and a severely limited base of resources available, and suitable, for maritime endeavor—could all be swept away by victory on land. What could not be swept away so easily would be a tradition of failure at sea and a narrowly continentalist mentality among political and military leaders. Had there been a war between the superpowers in the 1970s or 1980s, the Soviet Navy should have proved no match for a U.S. sea power that came of age in the Pacific between 1942 and 1945. The moral and strategic superiority of the U.S. Navy over the Soviet Navy should have been as great as was the superiority of the Royal Navy over the fleets that Revolutionary and Napoleonic France inherited, built, rebuilt, and sought to borrow from intimidated allies. Soviet admirals would have taken on a U.S. Navy whose sense of self-worth was defined by the victories in the Coral Sea (1942), at Midway (1942), the Philippine Sea (1944), and Leyte Gulf (1944).

There is peril unique to a recognized primacy in the prestige of particular national arms. A great continental power is not expected to lose on land and has to be very careful that its capital in credibility of land power is not discounted because of unexpected failure in the field. Nazi Germany, for example, was not willing to risk the defeat of elite elements of its land power in a hastily mounted invasion of Britain in the summer of 1940. The same point can be made for the Spartan view of their army and their reluctance to risk it in the field.[10]

Even a country with an inferior general naval tradition can enjoy brief periods of naval excellence. Furthermore, the absence of a tradition of success in great fleet actions may be offset somewhat by proficiency in the strategy and tactics suitable to a second- or third-rate naval power. Although Britain ultimately was more or less successful in every phase of its long struggle with France from 1688 to 1815 (though 1748, 1783, and 1802 had more the character of inconclusive armistices), the French Navy had brief spells of excellence, particularly in the 1680s and early 1690s and again in the 1770s, produced admirals of the first rank of competence (for example, Pierre André de Suffren, Luc-Urbain de Guichen, and François-Joseph de Grasse), and regularly built better ships. As a general rule, what Britain imposed and exploited for strategic leverage over the whole course and outcome of a conflict was what naval theorists have called *command of the sea*. Also as a general rule, the strategic value of that command has been eroded heavily in practice by enemies driven to the strategy of the weak at sea: war against mercantile shipping.

The idea of command of the sea is neutral with respect to the purposes to which it may be applied. Julian Corbett argued that the term "means nothing but the control of maritime communications, whether for commercial or military purposes."[11] This was true but misleading. Maritime communications means ships. Usefully, Corbett sought to focus attention on the purpose for which command was secured rather than on a particular means to the achievement of that purpose—specifically, battle.

Command of the sea means that fleet or squadron-size concentrations of ships dare not venture out of coastal waters because the risk of their being sunk is unacceptably high. A country enjoying maritime command or control has not swept the seas clean of all enemy shipping, but it has reduced the scale of the prudently sea-deployable naval power of the enemy to a level that can be met successfully by cruisers on trade-escort duties. The official historian of the Royal Navy in World War II has provided a useful explanation of the meaning of maritime control:

> The aim of maritime strategy is therefore not so much to establish complete control of all sea communications, which would be an ideal hardly attainable until final victory was almost won, as to develop the ability to establish zones of maritime control wherever and whenever they may be necessary for the prosecution of the war. . . . And a zone of maritime control means no more than an ability to pass ships safely across an area of water which may be quite small in extent or may cover many thousands of square miles of ocean.[12]

Save with regard to ships and what ships mean for the course and outcome of war, there is nothing at sea to be commanded, and sea lines of communication are empty. On land, in contrast, territory may be commanded by permanent garrisons, with or without prepared fortification. The sea cannot be commanded in the same way.

Command of the sea refers to a more or less geographically

extensive and porous working control of the relevant sea routes. As the reach of coastal defenses for the protection of second-class naval power increased with technological advances and as the identity of opponents changed, the tactical and operational design for the exercise of a working command at sea altered also. For example, in the eighteenth century, the Royal Navy sent frigates right into Brest Roads to check on the state of rigging of the French fleet as the key indicator of readiness to put to sea. By 1914, however, with the advent of naval mines, surface and submarine torpedo attack craft, and long-range coastal artillery, it could no longer conduct a close blockade tactically and operationally as Edward Hawke, John Jervis, and Horatio Nelson had done. The subsequent emergence of air and missile weapons confirmed the need to conduct effective blockade at some prudent distance and to approach enemy shores with great care.

The strategic geography of a particular conflict dictates where and how command of the sea most efficiently may be secured and practiced, it does not have to be exercised ubiquitously and continuously over all seas and oceans. The geographical scope of the command required varies with the purposes that sea power has to serve. In principle, the U.S. Navy in the 1980s did not concede in advance any security for the Soviet Navy in coastal bastions.[13] But in practice naval forces belonging to the North Atlantic Treaty Organization (NATO) would have been unlikely to press the Soviet Union actively in the Baltic or the Black Sea, for example. The British Royal Navy dared to send only submarines into the Baltic in the two world wars. Even in Nelson's day, the Royal Navy was exceedingly nervous of risking its line-of-battle ships in the Baltic. Certainly the Royal Navy would not proceed into that sea with a potentially unfriendly Danish fleet in its rear.

As the fighting instruments of naval power have expanded from the three classes of ship of the age of sail—the line-of-battle ship, the cruiser (or frigate), and the flotilla vessel (brig, sloop, corvette)—to encompass weapon platforms for combat in three dimensions, so the requirements for working control of the sea have altered. The First World War provides poignant illustration of this point.

On April 18, 1917, nearly a year after Jutland, Britain's Secretary of State for War, Lord Derby, wrote to the Commander in Chief of the British Expeditionary Force (BEF), Sir Douglas Haig:

10

"The state of affairs now existing is really very bad indeed, and we have lost command of the sea."[14] Germany's High Seas Fleet wisely was reposing in its harbors behind the protection of mine-fields, torpedo craft, antisubmarine nets, and coastal artillery.

In January 1917 the German High Command had decided to attempt to take Britain out of the conflict. Jutland (May 1916) had confirmed that the High Seas Fleet could not perform that task.

Germany's High Seas Fleet blundered into Britain's Grand Fleet in the failing light of a very murky May 31, 1916 off the coast of Jutland in the North Sea. Notwithstanding some material success in ships sunk, Reinhard Scheer's fleet escaped comprehensive destruction only because of its balletic skill in performing three emergency battle turns 180° away from the oncoming British battleline. The falling dusk, some appallingly bad British tactical communications among ships, and the British Admiralty's incompetence in failing to distribute intelligence information to John Jellicoe, all contributed massively to saving the Germans from being on the receiving end of the Trafalgar treatment.

Moreover, early in 1917 the German Army had yet to recover from the protracted bloodletting of 1916 at Verdun and on the Somme, and it was in no position to undertake an enormously expensive offensive against the BEF. The U-boat was the only instrument available that might remove Britain. Thus far, the German Navy had seen its U-boats principally in the role of battlefleet equalizer. That role had not been successful, and its abandonment was proof positive that German fleet strategy was bankrupt.

The Navy's promise to the Kaiser was that unrestricted U-boat warfare would render Britain *hors de combat* in six months. As the German Army had not been impressed in 1914 by the strong likelihood that the violation of Belgian neutrality would bring Britain into the war, so the German Navy was dismissive of the significance of the admitted certainty that an unrestricted U-boat campaign would add the United States to Germany's lengthening list of adversaries. There was much common reasoning in the two cases. It was asserted prior to 1914 that the war in the West would be over in six weeks, and it was noticed that Britain lacked a trained field army of more than token size (approximately 100,000 strong) for immediate insertion into continental Europe. Britain would lack the time to mobilize and train a mass army that might weigh noticeably in the balance of relevant forces, even should she attempt such an undertaking. The Royal Navy could not possibly wreak fatal damage on German military power, or even on its economic underpinnings, *given the anticipated brevity of the conflict.*

The German Navy held the certainty of U.S. intervention in 1917 to be of little strategic account because U.S. industry and agriculture already were at the service of the country that commanded the North Atlantic (a claim in imminent danger of financial invalidation by early 1917, given the terminal erosion of Britain's credit-worthiness). Moreover, the U.S. Army was in a pitiful condition for continental warfare against one of the greatest armies in world history, and there would be no time for the United States to recruit, train, and equip a mass army. In addition, the U-boat campagin would drive from the Atlantic the Allied and neutral shipping needed to transport a large U.S. expeditionary force. Germany's strategic calculations were to prove as ill founded in 1917 as they had been in 1914, and indeed as they were to prove throughout the Second World War. Nonetheless, Germany's leaders were desperate in 1917. Their vaunted Army and the High Seas Fleet had failed. Since Germany's unquenched political ambitions precluded any serious quest for a negotiated termination to the war, the unrestricted U-boat campaign was the only expedient available that appeared capable of achieving a truly strategic result against the strongest member of the enemy coalition, Great Britain.

Germany demonstrated from February to July 1917 that the *guerre de course* (commerce raiding) could make a mockery of the maritime surface command enjoyed by the British Grand Fleet that swung at its anchor chains in Scapa Flow and at Rosyth. In the first half of 1917, a technically primitive and small U-boat force (between February and April only forty-one U-boats, on average, were at sea) had shown what it could accomplish in the face of an enemy that declined to convoy merchant shipping.[15] (As early as 1673, Samuel Pepys, then Secretary of the Admiralty Office, had instituted a convoy system to protect British trade from damage by Dutch privateers.)

The strategic value of the condition of maritime command as defined and refined by Mahan and Corbett cannot be doubted. Mahan's arguments for a battlefleet strategy, however, though sound in essentials for a sea power such as Great Britain, were still considerably exaggerated. The fact has been that no matter how commanding the British position at sea, time after time *guerre de course* waged by disadvantaged or battlefleet-defeated continental powers has proved more than a minor irritant. To date, no hostile *guerre de course* in modern history has succeeded in shaping the track, let alone dictating the outcome, of war for a sea power; nonetheless, the depredations by Dutch, French, and American commerce raiders in the age of sail, and by German submarines in the steam age, were exceedingly painful. Those episodes are not proof positive that war against merchant shipping must constitute only a bearable menace to those who allegedly command the seas. In this century, the sea-commanding powers of the maritime West have enjoyed a huge measure of good fortune in the important realms of enemy technical incapacity, operational ineptitude, and policy incompetence—even rank amateurishness—in the conduct of commerce raiding.[16] It is worth noting that the war on Japanese merchant shipping prosecuted by U.S. submarines from 1941 to 1945 was the most decisive of its kind in all of maritime history.

Modern naval history teaches the lesson again and again that if strategic solutions are impractical, the only effective response to a determined *guerre de course* is the expedient of convoying in order to oblige raiders to place themselves in the way of maximum harm. From the Dutch Wars of the seventeenth century through to the close of World War II, search-and-destroy missions at sea against privateers or naval raiders were an exhausting exercise in futility, just as they tend to be in counterguerrilla operations on land. In all of its sequences of major conflict at sea over the span of three hundred years—with the Dutch, the French, and the Germans—Britain ultimately always was compelled to rediscover the magical, reliable elixir of convoy. With only a few exceptions—for well-armed East Indiamen, ships of the Hudson Bay Company, and particularly fast sailers—following the adoption of the Compulsory Convoy Act of 1798 (which strengthened the provisions of the Convoy Act of 1793), it was illegal for Britain's overseas commerce to proceed unconvoyed in wartime in the age of sail.

The state that needs to use the sea always prefers to exploit its battlefleet "command" to proceed against commerce raiders at source. From ancient times, the superior solution to piracy was not to patrol the seas, let alone to escort merchant vessels; rather was it to burn out the pirates' bases. Throughout the eighteenth century,

13

the illegal (Treaty of Utrecht, 1713) fortification of the port of Dunkirk was a litmus test issue in Anglo-French political relations, because that port traditionally was a major home to privateers.[17] During the Napoleonic Wars, the Royal Navy endeavored with fair success to alleviate its problem of commerce protection through the conquest of the overseas bases employed by French naval vessels and privateers (for example, Mauritius in the Indian Ocean was conquered very belatedly in 1810). Unfortunately, in World War II, the Western Allies lacked the technical means for wide-area submarine detection, the military means to destroy or severely disable U-boat bases (concrete U-boat "pens" were bombproof), and the strategic geography—because of Germany's conquests of Norway and France in 1940—to blockade those bases effectively. Problems of maritime command endure at the policy and strategic level through the centuries, but the identity of superior solutions alters with technology and geostrategic context. The fact that convoying generally has been necessary despite maritime command for a period of several centuries does not mean that a more offensive style of sea warfare against commerce raiders must be eternally ineffective. Convoying has been necessary, but in principle it is the last way in which a country with a superior navy would wish to protect its merchant shipping. If feasible, threats to maritime traffic should be neutralized at source. The Roman Empire showed that that could be done; the great sea powers of recent centuries have demonstrated that thus far in modern times it could not be done.

Guerre de course almost invariably has been more damaging to the countries that enjoyed battlefleet command of the sea than either navalist literature was wont to recognize or than the final outcome of a war might lead one to believe. There has always been an inverse relationship between the threat posed by raiders on and beneath the sea and the scale of threat posed by an enemy's battlefleet. The establishment and exercise of maritime command with reference to the freedom of action, even the existence, of an enemy's fleet obliges that enemy to wage the only kind of war at sea of which it is capable, the *guerre de course*. In war after war, the cream of France's skilled sailors and experienced captains transferred their labor from capital ships blockaded by the Royal Navy in Brest, Rochefort, and Toulon to the vastly more practical, enjoyable, and profitable enterprise of commerce raiding (either under naval orders or as privateers).

14

In the great wars of the past three centuries, the concepts of maritime control and even of command have been plausibly descriptive of the strategic condition enjoyed by one state or coalition for most of the time. It has been rare for a sea power at war to face no opposition at all at sea, as Britain did in the Boer War and the United States in the Korean and Vietnam wars. Far more often than not, the opposition at sea to the more maritime of the combatants has been erratic and hopeless, albeit sometimes determined. Although it is unusual for a sea power to be wholly unopposed in its uses of the sea in war, it is even more unusual for maritime control—the ability to use the sea in reasonable safety—to be very seriously in dispute.

Maritime command, or control, is thus critically important. The next issue is the style of warfare that a great sea power should follow. Should a superior navy risk itself in battle, and if so, on what terms, and for what stakes (given that it can only hazard a command that is already enjoyed)? The historical record and strategic logic yield a common story as to the necessity for an offensive slant to the naval doctrine of a sea-dependent country. A defensive doctrine of battle avoidance implies concession of the right to use the sea to an enemy, and that must mean defeat in war to a maritime coalition.

Though in support of a defensive policy goal, to restore deterrence and possibly the political status quo ante, the U.S. Navy in the 1980s proclaimed in principle that in search of strategic advantage in war, it would take the fight to the enemy as close to his coasts as operational circumstances and tactical prudence would allow. The maritime strategy was cast intentionally to emphasize offensive style and offensive operational goals for the conduct of naval warfare.[18]

The successful exercise of command of the sea is evidenced in part by unwanted events that do not occur. A state enjoying naval mastery or command typically will find that its enemy will decline to put to sea to offer itself up for destruction, although there are always exceptions to the rule that a mastered navy will decline to fight. Vice Admiral Pierre Charles de Silvestre Villeneuve knew in October 1805 that he would invite destruction if he obeyed Napoleon's peremptory order to sail from Cadiz to endeavor to join additional French ships at Cartegena and then to sail for southern

15

Italy to support Marshal André Massena's land campaign.[19] Napoleon, whose grasp of maritime realities was scarcely less uncertain than were those of Adolf Hitler or Joseph Stalin, was not a head of state to be disobeyed by a commander as pusillanimous as Villeneuve.[20] Predictably, Villeneuve's eighteen French and fifteen Spanish line-of-battle ships were detected in their sortie from Cadiz and brought to battle off Cape Trafalgar on October 21. Parallels exist between that French debacle and the banzai charge of Imperial Japan's Combined Fleet at Leyte Gulf October 23–25, 1944.[21] In both cases, the government asked the impossible of its fleet; the fleet obeyed and was duly destroyed. The Japanese campaign plan for the maritime defense of the Philippines in October 1944, SHO I, was hopeless from the outset. Aside from the error of undue complexity in operational design, SHO I was foredoomed to failure by sheer brute force. In late 1944 the U.S. armed forces enjoyed critical combat edges over their Japanese counterparts in both quantity and quality.

The influence of sea power as a strategic instrument of state policy persistently has been misunderstood. The general publics and many politicians of the Western sea powers have thought that the job of the navy was to fight sea battles. These clashes of arms at sea provide headlines, inspire writers and speakers, and forge reputation and tradition. The general public, encouraged by popular navalist tracts, has tended to treat battle as an end in itself, and with some reason. Some naval battles have decided which state subsequently would enjoy the benefits of maritime, at least of battlefleet, command. For example, the Roman naval victory off Mount Ecnomus (Sicily) in 256 B.C. in the First Punic War decided the issue of whether a Roman army could be transported to attack the Carthaginian homeland in Africa.[22] More decisive was the Roman naval victory at the Aegates Islands in 242 B.C., which decided that an economically exhausted and war-weary Carthage would not be able to run the blockade into its surviving Sicilian port base at Lilybaeum. In the long course of this war, command at sea—that is, in the area around the theater of land operations in Sicily and off the coast of North Africa—changed hands many times. Nearly two centuries prior to the Roman-Carthaginian maritime struggle for Sicily, the five naval battles in the Great Harbor of Syracuse (414–413 B.C.), again in Sicily, decided the fate of the Athenian expedition, leaving the land forces isolated from their sources of support at home and without hope of evacuation by sea.[23]

In the twentieth century, the German High Seas Fleet might have won command of the sea had it been committed determinedly to a battle for decision early in the war. But in 1914, Germany did not expect to lose on land and was nervous of risking a High Seas Fleet that might function as a diplomatic counter of great weight if and when Britain tired of the struggle. Also, Germany believed that time would work to the advantage of the fleet as U-boats and mines whittled away at the Royal Navy's battlefleet superiority. The German Navy was generally unaware of the technical, operational, and tactical deficiencies of the Royal Navy of 1914–16 and was attempting to wage war at sea in the shadow cast by the century-long spell of the maritime *Pax Britannica*. In Britain, Sir John Jellicoe was expected to be Nelson's heir; in Germany it was feared that he might be.

The side that enjoys the benefits accruing from maritime command should approach the issue of battle as a matter for choice rather than necessity. A superior fleet that functions as jailer, however, is itself in large measure restricted in its strategic utility. Such restriction is eminently bearable because friendly military transports and merchant shipping can use the sea without fear of meeting forces on a scale that must overwhelm naval escort or other covering assets. Nonetheless, command of the sea is never absolute. The naval force required to implement a close or distant blockade of the enemy's navy is not available for the direct protection of shipping against raiders (surface, subsurface, and air) or direct support of land campaigns.

Julian Corbett, writing in a heyday of British navalism that generally was unreflective on questions of strategy, criticized what he termed the "battle faith" of the Royal Navy. He caricatured the contemporary focus upon battle in the following way:

> Whatever the nature of the war in which we are engaged, whether it be limited or unlimited, permanent and general command of the sea is the condition of ultimate success. The only way of securing such a command by naval means is to obtain a decision by battle against the enemy's fleet. Sooner or later it must be done, and the sooner the better. That was the old British creed. It is still our creed [in 1911], and needs no labouring. No one will dispute it, no one will care even to discuss it, and we pass with confidence to the

17

conclusion that the first business of our fleet is to seek out the enemy's fleet and destroy it.

No maxim can so well embody the British spirit of making war upon the sea, and nothing must be permitted to breathe on that spirit. To examine its claims to be the logical conclusion of our theory of war will even be held dangerous, yet nothing is so dangerous in the study of war as to permit maxims to become a substitute for judgment.[24]

Corbett argued that since maritime warfare is about the control of sea communications, an enemy fleet blockaded in its harbors or sent to the bottom is defeated—strategically in the former case, tactically in the latter. Three years after Corbett wrote, the Royal Navy was surprised to discover that Germany's High Seas Fleet would not, and could not be compelled to, sortie from the Jade estuary to offer decisive battle for command of the North Sea, and every other sea. Imperial Germany had no great amphibious expeditions that had to be defended at almost any cost, and unlike Athens, the Dutch Republic, and other true sea powers, it had no overseas trade routes that had to be protected to ward off domestic starvation or bankruptcy. Between 1914 and 1918, there were no practicable means by which the German High Seas "fleet in being" could be reached and gripped for destruction. Nonetheless, the Royal Navy defeated Germany's High Seas Fleet strategically in the war without benefit of victory in a major fleet-to-fleet battle.

It was important—and professionally courageous—for Corbett to assail the mindless battle faith of his day. But as with most other useful correctives, the denigration of battle can be taken too far. Careful consideration is necessary of the following proposition: the state that enjoys maritime command should not risk its fleet in a sea battle that, if won, serves only to confirm that command but if lost transfers command to the enemy.

A state that decides not to hazard in battle the maritime command that accrues from superior naval power (save under circumstances so advantageous that they are most improbable ever to occur) is electing to adopt a defensive posture. The argument, from Clausewitz, that "defense is *the stronger form of waging war*," is a general truth only about land warfare.[25] Defense is the stronger form of war on land because, for example, the defending side has the advantage of intimate knowledge of the local terrain and can fortify that terrain to resist an enemy who must move and thereby expose himself. These conditions do not apply at sea, except when the defender is operating in his coastal waters.

Although a defensive posture at sea looks suitable for the state or coalition that holds maritime command, it has to make sense also in terms of overall national and coalition military strategy. For example, from 1914 to 1918, the Royal Navy functioned as the key strategic weapon of a mixed maritime-continental coalition that believed it could beat the German Army in the field. The Royal Navy was the shield to the land power sword. In 1914, the Allies expected the Grand Fleet to effect a "Trafalgar" on Germany's upstart High Seas Fleet, but they did not require such an event, nor were they greatly discomforted by its nonappearance. Typical French sentiment was expressed prewar by Georges Clemenceau, when he said to King Edward VII that "when the time came when France needed help, England's sea power would not be enough, and reminded him that Napoleon was beaten at Waterloo, not Trafalgar."[26] Whereas over 1914–18 the Royal Navy was Britain's—and after 1916, really the alliance's—last line of defense, more recently that role has been assumed by the so-called strategic forces, not by the U.S. Navy. Thinking of Winston Churchill's explanation for the caution in Admiral Jellicoe's style of fleet handling, no similar wording would have been applicable to the responsibilities of NATO's Supreme Allied Commander, Atlantic (SACLANT). Churchill wrote that "Jellicoe was the only man on either side who could lose the war in an afternoon."[27]

The Western cause in Europe and Asia during the Cold War would have foundered as a consequence of loss of command of the sea, but a Soviet maritime blockade or investment of the U.S. homeland would have had to be a very protracted operation. It would be an error to assume that maritime command, if lost, has to pass to the other side. Both belligerents may lack such command. Had the Soviet Union denied the United States a working command of the North Atlantic, it could have prevented U.S. prosecution of a ground war in Europe. But sea denial is not control or command. Soviet military power would not necessarily have been at liberty to use the oceans simply as a consequence of denying such liberty to its enemy. Of course, the United States and its allies have had an enormous strategic stake in success at sea. Much more could be asked of Cold War Western naval power to influence events on land directly and indirectly than was feasible in the British case in the First World War. The reasons for the difference are that the modern United States has had the backstop of survivable strategic nuclear forces for the ultimate protection of national values and is not a small island vulnerable to the interruption of its seaborne trade.

Inferior armed forces can get lucky. A navy committed exclusively to the protection of an existing strategic advantage will not be one seeking to create situations where new success is likely. To be unduly fearful of the risks of defeat in battle because of the scale of the strategic stakes, however, can be a recipe for disaster.

It is not obvious that Cold War NATO could have afforded a maritime strategy restricted to the local control of sea routes for the passage of men and materiel to a land battle in Europe. Should NATO have lost a ground war in Western Europe, the geostrategic context for U.S. military strategy, albeit with nuclear complications, would have been more than casually analogous to the situations in which Britain found herself after the collapse of the First, Second, and Third Coalitions against Napoleonic France and again, following the fall of France in 1940. In NATO perspective, in the 1980s, the safest prospective wartime condition for the Soviet Navy would lie in the category "sunk." So long as they existed, the fighting instruments of Soviet maritime power posed a potentially fatal threat to NATO's conduct of land campaigns. So long as an enemy's fleet is in being, it is a danger. It does not answer the case to argue that Soviet naval power confined to the Barents Sea, for example, was scarcely more of a threat than if it were consigned to the ocean floor. The Soviet Navy of the 1980s may have had operational missions more adventurous than providing a maritime buffer to Soviet land power, protecting the nuclear deterrent afloat, and generally effecting a reprise of the fleet-in-being posture of Imperial Germany.

The principal difficulty with the proposition that NATO's naval power should have confined its ambitions to a distant blockade for the defensive purpose of sea control was that it would have yielded the initiative to a powerful adversary. A blockaded navy can select the time, extent, and method for its breakout. There has never been a way in which a naval blockade could provide absolute surety against successful evasion of the blockading squadrons. The securing of a general maritime command could serve as no absolute guarantee against defeat at sea in squadron detail by a clever or lucky enemy who achieved naval superiority at the decisive point of the moment. This was a British nightmare in World Wars I and II.

Although the dominant strategic purposes of British naval power were to secure sea lines of communication and deny France the use of the sea, sea denial to the enemy was a second-class solution. That solution was secured by keeping French battleships in port, with need for a caveat concerning the commerce-raiding danger. The purpose of naval blockade frequently is misunderstood. The protracted blockade of the French Navy in Brest and Toulon was not intended to keep French ships idle in harbor. Rather, it was hoped that the enemy could not put to sea without the Royal Navy's being aware of the fact and having the option of imposing battle. The method was to effect a balance in deployment between close observation by inshore squadrons and a more distant concentration of force. The British hoped that the enemy would be tempted to try to snatch apparently unsupported British frigates, and perhaps a ship of the line of the third rate (seventy-four guns, two gun decks), ignorant of the presence of the British line-of-battle that should be within supporting distance, wind permitting. Nelson's blockade of Toulon in the period 1803–5 provides examples of every imaginable ruse to induce the French to put to sea.

In the British cases against France and then Germany, as with the United States much more recently, there was no question over the geographical focus for the principal concentration of naval force. In the wars with France (and Spain), the Royal Navy had to command the Western approaches to the English Channel. In the wars with Germany, the Royal Navy had to command the North Sea. In war with the Soviet Union, the U.S. Navy would have needed to command both the Norwegian Sea and the exits from the Sea of Japan. The geostrategic centers of gravity in naval warfare usually have been obvious. The perennial problem has been how to answer competing demands with a fleet of distinctly finite size. Strategic flexibility flows not only from sound doctrine and an open but educated mind but also from numbers; and inflexibility flows from the absence of numbers.

Again and again Britain had to decide how to deploy its naval power among pressing duties in the Channel, the Mediterranean, and the West Indies, for the blockade of enemy ports, the direct

21

protection of trade, and the support of the Army. From time to time, serious errors were committed, most notably early in the Seven Years' War, the War of the American Revolution (with France and Spain), and the War of the First Coalition against Revolutionary France. More accurately, error lay in a policy failure in peacetime to maintain the fleet in a material condition such that it could be mobilized in a hurry. Given the global geography of any large-scale East-West war, it was prudent in the 1980s to anticipate a severe potential for overstretch even in a U.S. Navy that enjoyed wholehearted Allied assistance. As with the French Navy from time to time during its wars with Britain (1689–1815) and the German Navy in 1914, the Soviet Navy of the 1970s and 1980s, while plainly inferior to the U.S. Navy and the navies of its allies on any grand assay, nonetheless was within competitive reach of U.S. strength.

An important part of the case made in the 1980s for the U.S. Navy to plan to undertake the high-risk enterprise of going after Soviet naval power early in a war lay in the high risk of not doing so. No matter what its strategy and operational design might be, the U.S. Navy would suffer attrition in war. Somehow the idea spread that the U.S. Navy could exercise a sufficient command of the sea by means of a largely passive role, guarding the exits into the open Atlantic from the Norwegian, Greenland, and Barents seas with the maritime equivalent of a Maginot Line. Jellicoe had no prudent strategic alternative other than to concede the operational initiative to Scheer, but his U.S. functional successors did have a choice. The landward reach of sea-based weapons, the value of the nuclear-powered ballistic submarine (SSBN) fleet, and the proximity of Norwegian NATO territory to base complexes on the Kola peninsula should have compelled the Soviet Navy to sortie and contest a Western maritime advance. One can speculate that Nelson and Jellicoe would have given almost anything to enjoy the strategic opportunities that beckoned the U.S. Navy in the 1980s, particularly the ability to deploy at sea in such a way that the enemy must "come out."[28] If the Soviet Union had been conceded or had seized the initiative at sea, however, it could have acted or threatened so as to encourage NATO navies to disperse their strength around the globe. The naval battle that one chooses to avoid today almost certainly will need to be fought tomorrow. This is not to endorse a reckless pursuit of battle but to suggest that there is more value in bringing an enemy's inferior fleet early to battle than often it has been fashionable to recognize.

The case for sinking the German High Seas Fleet in World War I, or the Soviet Navy in some hypothetical war in the 1970s or 1980s, was even stronger than was the case for pressing the French and Spanish navies to battle at Trafalgar in 1805. At issue was what friendly sea power could do to harass enemy land power and contribute directly and indirectly to the distraction and ultimate defeat of that land power in its own environment. Unlike the French, who could and did rebuild their fleet—albeit ineffectively with respect to its value as an actual fighting instrument, as opposed to a collection of ships in widely separated harbors—the Germans would have lacked the resources or the time to rebuild their fleet, as would the Soviet Union more recently. Nelson strove his utmost to persuade the Admiralty to send him a sufficient superiority of force that if he did engage Villeneuve, he would be able to achieve a victory of annihilation, for strategic effect. Nelson states in his dispatches that "numbers only can annihilate."[29]

A maritime power requires an offensive doctrine for the use of its sea power if it is to capitalize on its comparative advantage. This was as true for Byzantium in the tenth century as it is for the contemporary United States. There have always been limits to what sea power can accomplish, but those limits would not even be approached if a sea power restricts the ambition for its maritime operations to the more or less passive defense of sea routes and denial of use of the sea to the enemy. To derive maximum benefit from its navy, a maritime power should be willing and able to seek out the enemy's navy. Assuming no preference by the enemy for a death and glory sortie, still it may be possible to conduct operations at sea of such a menacing character to his landward interests that he will be obliged to sortie from coastal bastions and give battle. The Norwegian Sea scenario in NATO's Cold War strategy would have been an example of this, as are the Philippine Sea and Leyte Gulf battles of 1944.

History has something to say concerning the intangible, though critically important, value of the self-confidence, indeed the moral ascendancy, that flows from an offensive doctrine. The strategic defensive can encourage a professional cast of mind that is tactically defensive also. If a great sea power is too fearful of losing its precious ships to risk them in battle, save in circumstances so advantageous that any prudent enemy commander must flee from the prospect, then those ships are unlikely to provide the kind of strategic return on investment that the country has a right to expect and may need. Britain may have been fortunate in 1914–18 that Germany proved entirely as reluctant to hazard its fleet as it was itself. To commend the importance of tactical victory in battle at sea is not to subscribe foolishly to a battle faith. But, admittedly, the line can be thin between the offensive spirit and tactical boldness on the one side and reckless disregard of risks on the other. The quality of the tactical instrument will be all important. Nelson's plan of attack at the Nile, at Copenhagen, and at Trafalgar, all highly unorthodox, were justified retrospectively by success. But the risks he ran were calculated and reflected his well-founded confidence in the sailing and fighting abilities of his forces. More than a century later, Jellicoe's strategic and tactical caution reflected his knowledge of the material deficiencies of the Royal Navy and his doubts of its fighting power as a tactical instrument.

Any preponderant sea power or coalition vitally dependent on superiority at sea, whose admirals are unable to provide a contemporary variant of Nelson's "Plan of Attack" (May 1803) and subsequent detailed Trafalgar "Memorandum" (October 9, 1805), invites strategic disaster. In Nelson's words:

> The business of an English Commander-in-Chief being first to bring an Enemy's Fleet to Battle, on the most advantageous terms to himself, (I mean that of laying his ships close on board the enemy, as expeditiously as possible, and secondly, to continue them there, without separating, until the business is decided). . . .
>
> In case Signals can neither be seen nor perfectly understood, no captain can do very wrong if he places his ship alongside that of an enemy.[30]

As a superpower vitally dependent on the ability to use the sea if it is to protect distant allies and friends, the United States at war could not shrink from battle to secure command, or perhaps to dispute command, at sea. Each geophysical environment—land, sea, air, space—can be used in war potentially only over the active opposition of the enemy. A maritime-dependent power or coalition need not seek battle at sea, but if it tries to avoid battle, it concedes sea denial, *and hence the war*, to a battle-willing enemy.

* * *

In addition to understanding the nature of sea power, comprehending the importance, meaning, and implications of maritime command, and appreciating why an offensive style of war at sea can confer critical benefits for the superior navy, one needs to grasp the utility of sea power in conflict as a whole. The uses of sea power over the centuries have changed little. These uses may be presented at different levels of analysis. At the highest level, sea power is about influencing events on land in time of crisis and war. But first friendly sea power has to earn its right to function well enough in its own environment, and that is the next level of analysis. Sea power needs to secure maritime lines of communication (the ability of ships to move) for positive purposes, as well as deny enemies a reliable ability to use the sea. Also, sea power can be employed for direct military impact on land operations.

Cumulatively dramatic changes in, for example, the reach of weapons (from the Macedonian long pike to the intercontinental ballistic missile) may so change tactics in war as to have a revolutionary effect on both the absolute and the relative importance of the several uses of sea power. Even if the uses of sea power have not much altered over the centuries, perhaps the relevance of sea power itself has changed beyond plausible historical recognition. It is not difficult to register claims as to why the strategic utility of sea power might have suffered a massive decline in the course of this century in particular.

Although the United States and the Soviet Union were, respectively, primarily maritime and continental states in the politics of international security, unlike previous sea power–land power rivals, they were also nuclear, air and space powers. Additionally, the mass and potential velocity of armies in maneuver has been transformed over the past century and a half by the railroad, the internal combustion engine (and the proliferation of metaled roads), and short-haul airlift. In contrast, naval task forces and maritime expeditions, moving in the physically more resistant medium of water, have a pace of operations not dramatically different from that of their coal-fired predecessors at the turn of the century.

The vastness of the oceans that once could hide great fleets from one another today offer no hiding places on the surface from surveillance and reconnaissance from space. Indeed, speaking in 1983, Chief of Naval Operations James Watkins went so far as to

25

proclaim that "space control is sea control."[31] A fleet that wishes to hide over the horizon requires the ability to deny air and space reconnaissance to an enemy or even to a hostile-leaning neutral who might make sensor information from space available to the enemy. Back to earth, the character of fleet engagements was signaled to have changed forever by the totally over-the-horizon nature of the first carrier battle in history at the Coral Sea in May 1942.

The line-of-battle super-Dreadnoughts of 1916 that were as vulnerable to torpedoes and mines as they were largely invulnerable to each other have been superseded as capital ships first by the carrier and now, in addition, by the true submarine (nuclear powered). World War II showed that maritime surface operations were practicable only under the cover of a locally superior air power and only if the submarine threat could be contained. Witness the elaborate, critically important measures taken to keep Germany's U-boats away from the Channel during, and subsequent to, the D-Day landings on June 6, 1944.[32]

In the future, a continental enemy could offset deficiencies in naval power by using or threatening to use nuclear weapons at sea. In a long war, preponderance at sea should pose grave dangers to a continental enemy's ability to conduct operations on land successfully. A great continental power would be strongly motivated to deny the United States the ability to concentrate ships for purposes that could make a strategic difference to the course of a war. There are substantial reasons of strategic self-interest that should discourage nuclear use at sea, even by a desperate continental power, but there is no denying that the strategic world of sea power–land power relations is different when nuclear menace is introduced; that nuclear menace has to be answered in its own distinctive terms by nuclear counterdeterrence.

The enemy against whom the U.S. Navy of the Cold War planned to wage war was different in kind, not just degree, from the other enemies of offshore sea powers over the past half-millennium. The Soviet Union was considerably less dependent on overseas trade than was Nazi Germany, another great continental land power. But the military technologies and the strategic context of 1942–44 was conclusively permissive for the materially stronger Western powers, aided critically by Soviet land power in the East, to fight their way back onto the European continent. Oper-

26

ations Torch (North Africa), Husky (Sicily), Avalanche (Italy, Salerno), Overlord (Normandy), and Anvil (the South of France) would have been thoroughly impracticable in the face of German armed forces unattrited and undistracted in the East, let alone in the face of a German nuclear arsenal. One of the more persuasive lessons of history is that sea powers win wars by supporting and ultimately joining continental allies actively in the field.

Notwithstanding these points, the relative importance of sea power is scarcely less today than it was in the days of the trireme and the phalanx. Without maritime control, war cannot be waged reliably overseas. That was true for Athens's Sicilian expedition in 415–413 B.C., for Britain's ventures in Portugal and Spain in 1808–14, for the U.S. seizure of island bases for the air bombardment of the Japanese home islands in 1944–45, and for the conduct of regional war in the Persian Gulf against Iraq in 1991, and it will hold in the future for U.S. participation in any conflict in Europe and Asia that lasts longer than three to four weeks. People, but not bulk cargo, can be moved rapidly by air. Denial of the use of the sea to the Cold War Soviet Union was not an offensive mission for U.S. naval power, given the extent of continental autarky of the Soviet imperium (though this could be overstated with reference to food and fertilizers for agriculture). But the ability to control maritime communications, the passage of ships, has been and remains critical for the global maritime alliance of the West. This fact necessarily renders maritime interdiction a potential naval mission of war-winning importance to any challengers to a U.S.-guarded world order.

In 413 B.C. Athens lost a campaign in Sicily but did not lose the long-running, on-off-on war with Sparta thereby, even though defeat at sea precluded evacuation of the army. In 1940 Britain lost a campaign in Flanders but did not lose the war as a consequence. Moreover, Britain might not have lost the war even had there been no evacuation of its thirteen-division expeditionary force from Dunkirk and other French ports, though I judge that unlikely. The sea has been no less a two-way highway for strategic effect in the twentieth century than it was in the fifth century B.C. With a parallel confinement in the geostrategic scope of success for its land-bound armies, the Soviet Union of recent decades could no more have won a war against the United States in continental Europe than Revolutionary and Napoleonic France or Nazi Germany similarly could win against insular Britain. But just as Napoleonic France and Nazi Germany could change the geostrategic terms of conflict at sea by means of landward conquest, so a great Eurasian continental power or coalition in the future could use success on land for leverage at sea.

The two-way strategic effect between land power and sea power does not lack for powerful cases in every historical period. The High Middle Ages witnessed a Crusader tenure in Palestine totally dependent on control of port fortresses. Latin Palestine was doomed when it could not be reached reliably by sea. Conquest of those key ports from the landward side precluded Latin recovery. Still less well appreciated is the major maritime dimension to the Hundred Years' War of the fourteenth and fifteenth centuries between an initially all but landlocked France and an England with massive crown continental holdings. That protracted conflict was very much about the control of ports for access to, or egress from, the Continent.[33]

What could be meant by the claim that the uses of sea power have changed dramatically or are of sharply reduced strategic importance relative to the uses of other instruments of military power? U.S. naval policy in the 1990s has shelved the ideas for the conduct of global and protracted conventional war against the continental superpower foe that were embodied in the maritime strategy of the 1980s. In most respects, a hypothetical superpower World War III constituted the hardest of hard cases for the claim that the strategic utility of sea power had not diminished significantly. No matter how the new post–Cold War world finally shakes down in its security arrangements, the deletion for the time being of a hostile superstate enemy guarantees that the U.S. Navy could not be consigned to wartime strategic irrelevance because of a massive nuclear exchange. No other state could reach the United States with a war-terminating, navy-overshooting nuclear assault.

To argue in the 1980s that sea power had lost much of its relevance was to claim that a war in Europe or Asia would not last more than three to four weeks and that the United States would prefer a prompt disadvantageous armistice or a general nuclear war to the conduct of a protracted maritime conflict. It was not controversial to point out that without command at sea, NATO would lose on land. One could be reasonably sure that a Soviet Union undefeated in conventional war on land would not have been motivated to imperil its victor's inheritance by opening Pandora's nuclear box. For reasons of deterrence, U.S. and NATO policy in the 1980s held that the United States would prefer to conduct general nuclear war rather than acquiesce to defeat in Europe. This position fell woefully short of being strategically compelling or politically attractive for the United States. The traditional uses of sea power in a great war would lose much of their significance for policy and strategy only if the next such war is over quickly. Whether one was relatively optimistic or pessimistic about NATO's prospects of success in a ground and air war for peninsular Europe, the nuclear aversion evident on both sides in the 1970s and 1980s suggested strongly the policy relevance of a protracted conflict. In such a conflict, sea power would have been at a premium, though it could always have been negated by suicidal nuclear options.

A lesson of May–June 1940 is that once the continental fighting front is lost, terrible difficulties hinder the regaining of access on tolerable terms of engagement for the restoration of contact with enemy land power. But another lesson of 1940, as of 1805–7 (with the collapse of the Third Coalition against France), is that dominant sea power can recover from defeat, organize new coalitions, exploit the continental power's errors in strategy and statecraft, and eventually regain the initiative against overextended land power.

A navy's twin tasks are to secure the seas for friendly use and deny their use to the enemy. The destruction of the enemy's fleet may not be necessary to the securing of maritime control. Moreover, a dominant sea power that seeks battle recklessly may suffer such cumulative attrition to its capital ships from mines and torpedoes—and, today, from aircraft and missiles—that it will lose what had been a decisive edge in combat power. That is not in dispute. Nevertheless, the quality and assurance of working sea control enjoyed by the preponderant naval power is affected in a major way by the status of the enemy's fleet. The sound argument that battle should not be sought casually has led people repeatedly into the error of claiming not only that battle does not matter for quality of sea control but also that battle were better avoided lest the irreplaceable fleet be lost.

A continental power or coalition with a large navy can seek to avoid battle at sea. Indeed, if continental powers are not combat competitive in naval strength, they are well advised to decline to fight. If a sea power or maritime-dependent coalition seeks to avoid battle at sea, however, it risks defeat in war as a consequence of donating the naval initiative to the enemy. In practice, the issue is rarely this clear-cut. More to the point is the case where an acute caution toward battle for the excellent reasons addressed by Julian S. Corbett in 1911, and applied in practice by Jellicoe and Beatty, his successor, in 1914–18, costs the dominant sea power success that it could achieve at only moderate risk and that it forgoes along with the important benefits to strategic leverage that should accrue as a just reward for prudent boldness.

The uses of the sea, though always specific in detail to time, place, adversaries, and technology, have been quite steady over the centuries at the levels of policy and strategy. If sea power is to influence events on land, having first secured by force its right to operate tolerably freely at and from the sea, how is it to make its presence felt for strategic leverage? One may recall Mahan's purple prose:

> Amid all the pomp and circumstance of the war which for ten years to come desolated the Continent, amid all the tramping to and fro over Europe of the French armies and their auxiliary legions, there went on unceasingly that noiseless pressure upon the vitals of France, that compulsion, whose silence, when once noticed, becomes the most striking and awful mark of the working of Sea Power.[34]

30

CHAPTER 2

THE PRACTICE OF SEA POWER

The effect of sea-power upon land campaigns is in the main strategical. Its influence over the progress of military operations, however decisive this may be, is often only very indirect.

C. E. Callwell, *The Effect of Maritime Command on Land Campaigns since Waterloo* (1897)

When a sea power and a continental power wage war against each other the issue is the practice of sea power and of land power in search of strategic advantage. A sea power may seek to exhaust a continental enemy financially or deny him reliable overseas supply of critical goods and material, or it may need to commit itself to the conduct of large-scale land warfare. There is no all-purpose correct strategy or mix of strategies, but there is a useful basket of possibilities for the practice of sea power. Each of the strategies described here has been tried; the merit in each varies with time, occasion, opponent, technology, and political stakes.

In addition to the strategies just cited—financial exhaustion, supply blockade and continental commitment—the repertoire of possibilities for a sea power typically will include the conduct of peripheral raids and of warfare from the sea, the conquest of enemy territory overseas and the forging of a continental alliance. This repertoire of strategy options for a sea power or maritime coalition is introduced and illustrated in this chapter (the next chapter performs the same function for a land power or continental coalition), and then is developed as appropriate to each individual case in the extensive historical discussion which constitutes

31

the remainder of the book. These six strategies for the practice and exploitation of superior sea power, to repeat, comprise just a framework for policy, strategic and operational choices; they are not a set menu always to be attempted, albeit at a variable price.

Commonly in history, land powers and sea powers have faced great practical difficulty in coming to grips to force a decision. For example, from 1545 until 1940, a succession of continental powers pursued a variety of indirect approaches in order to attempt to transport an army to England.[1] Except through an unlikely mix of British incompetence in naval deployments, great skill on the continental side in the extraordinarily complex task of coordinating the assembly and movement of fighting ships and transports from different points, and clement weather, the task was not practicable. The record of failure in continental designs for invasion shows how great the difficulties were. Spain, France, and Germany could not grip Britain on land at home so as to snatch victory, save by the generally imprudent route of fighting for naval command of the English Channel.

Alternatively, a land power with a distinctly second-class navy can pursue the indirect approach at sea with commerce raiding. A sea power with an army second class in size, if not in quality, can pursue the indirect approach with peripheral raiding or sustained campaigns in regions far removed from the center of gravity of the strength of the continental enemy. Examples of the latter include the British campaigns in the Iberian Peninsula in 1808–14, Gallipoli in 1915, and the Western Desert in 1940–42. Raiding and campaigning on the periphery of the dominant land power has much to recommend it, and in some desperate circumstances, it has everything to recommend it. But if it is conceived as anything more potent than an adjunct or complement to the waging of war against the main land strength of the enemy, it is most likely strategically to constitute an evasion and an expensive blind alley. Two distinguished historians of different generations explained the pattern of British grand strategy in strikingly similar terms:

> When we had allies who could stand up to the enemy we sent our armies to join them. When not, we turned to theatres less crowded with triumphant foes. We didn't adopt a peripheral strategy for love of the conception, but for want of sufficiently sturdy allies. After all, the traditional British campaigning theatre was not the

32

Iberian Peninsula, or Italy, and was least of all North Africa. It was the Netherlands: the very antitype of the periphery, "the cockpit of Europe."[2]

A commitment of support to a Continental ally in the nearest available theatre, on the largest scale that contemporary resources could afford, so far from being alien to traditional British strategy, was absolutely central to it.[3]

The conquest of the coasts of Europe by land power could be vital for the conduct of a decisive campaign at sea. Similarly, the conduct of peripheral warfare around the coasts of Europe and on land in distant regions could prepare the way for a major engagement of armies. But neither of these alone can attain military decision between countries preeminent at sea and on land, at least in modern times.

By the imposition of a commercial, and in part maritime, blockade for the redirection of trade, a sea power can work to exhaust a continental foe financially. In his *Orationes Philippicae* No. V in 60 B.C., Cicero advised that "the sinews of war are infinite money." This general truth found poignant illustration in the twentieth century. In 1916 and again in 1940, Britain's ability to purchase many of the goods and services necessary for the further conduct of war was critically dependent on American credit. The Anglo-French invasion of Egypt in 1956 was outmaneuvered grand strategically by President Eisenhower's credible threat to cause a catastrophic run on sterling. More recently, the Bush administration all but demanded that its 1990–91 gendarme role in the Persian Gulf should be financed substantially by the economically better heeled among those states that stood most to benefit from the American action. It is one thing, however, to make the obvious point that finance is always important as a sinew of war; it is quite another to craft a theory and practice of war that elevates the financial exhaustion of the enemy as the most important source of leverage for victory.

As a conscious strategy for sea power in modern times, financial exhaustion enjoyed approximately a three hundred year lifespan, from the early sixteenth to the late eighteenth centuries. This strategy aimed at conducting war so that the enemy was the first to exhaust ready cash, accessible revenues, and the tolerance of creditors. War is about public finance and the administration of taxation, as well as about the activities of generals and admirals. That point was made persistently by the British Treasury in the 1930s, when it emphasized that the flow of British trade in wartime depended not only upon the strength and skill of the navy but also upon Britain's ability to finance that trade.[4] If a sea power could not pay for goods, it would be a matter of small interest whether those goods could be transported in safety by sea.

For a strategy of financial exhaustion to work, the adversary has to be at a relative disadvantage in the ability to finance hostilities. That ability is at least as much social and political as it is economic, though it can include the willingness of allies or other interested third parties to extend credit or provide subsidies. Britain, with her "fiscal-military" state in the eighteenth century,[5] repeatedly could fight France to the actual or impending exhaustion of French war finances. Synergistically, of course, the better organized the British government became in the prudent levying and efficient collection of taxes—on the value of land and as customs and excise—the better was its credit rating and hence the more easily could it borrow money against future revenue.

Financial exhaustion worked against the *anciens régimes*, which waged war for limited stakes and were unable for social and political reasons to realize anything close to the war finance potential of their countries. But this strategy failed as miserably against the American colonies as it did against Revolutionary and Napoleonic France. The Americans broke the rules of the game and merrily printed money, accepting the inevitable inflation. French and Spanish assistance to the colonists did not have to be paid for on banker's terms. France used the American Revolution as an arm of its statecraft and strategy while seeking revenge for the great defeat of 1763.

In the long struggle with Spain in the sixteenth and seventeenth centuries, English ships, waging both public and private war, could threaten to intercept the annual bullion fleet (the Flota) that sailed from Cartagena, and thereby deprive Madrid of a vital part of its purse for the payment of its war machine. Given the weakness of English sea power during this period, however, the damage wrought to Madrid's credit in the eyes of Europe's bankers was effected more by the threat of losses at sea than by the reality.

34

Immense practical difficulties precluded continuous blockade activities by English ships off the Azores, the Tagus, or Cadiz. The close blockade of French and Spanish ports, which, when feasible, was characteristic of the British way of war at sea from the late 1750s until the close of the Napoleonic Wars, rested on physical instruments, logistic understanding, and public finance, which did not exist in the 1580s and 1590s. Elizabeth I could help finance raiding expeditions by a combination of private and royal ships, but she could not wield "sea power" à la Pitt the Elder and after. John Brewer makes the point brutally when he writes that "Drake may have singed the King of Spain's beard, but he was incapable of cutting his throat."[6] English privateers seized their first Spanish treasure ship as early as 1545, but they never captured a bullion fleet at sea, a pleasure that accrued solely to the Dutchman, Piet Hein, in 1628. The strategic idea of waging maritime war systematically against the flow of Spanish treasure from the New World appears to have originated in France in 1558–59. The idea had promise, but the French, English, and Dutch military instruments of the period were not adequate to realize it. Ultimately, sea power rests on the activities of ships. The ships of the period deteriorated rapidly in tropical waters—the coppering of ships' bottoms was a late eighteenth-century innovation—as did their crews after a short cruise in any waters (scurvy was not mastered until the last quarter of the eighteenth century). Because there was no adequate victualing organization in port, Elizabeth's navy all but collapsed as a fighting force several times in the critical year of 1588.[7]

Halfhearted attempts to implement what amounted to a maritime blockade, or at least as much of a blockade as the ships, their crews, and their profit-seeking captains could tolerate, was a feature of the trade wars of the seventeenth century. But for naval power in that century to give forcible effect to a practical mercantilism, governments required a far more disciplined, professional instrument of policy than the navies of the day could approach. England, like all other European countries in the seventeenth century, lacked the technological ability to expand wealth through any significant or rapid increase in agricultural or industrial production. Only by seizing a larger share of trade from competitors could national wealth be expanded appreciably, and with each decade, this became more difficult for England as the Dutch improved their trading position.

*   *   *

If the financial exhaustion of an enemy is impracticable, it may be possible to achieve great strategic leverage by means of a maritime supply blockade—that is, denying continental enemies the materials necessary for the conduct of war. For example, by the late 1930s both the British and German governments regarded a supply blockade as the leading edge of the strategic effectiveness of sea power in its ability to influence the outcome of a war.[8] This seemed to be a principal lesson of the Great War; moreover, Germany's small navy in the 1930s precluded for the near term all options but commerce raiding. In practice, Germany turned her back on the discredited notion of seeking military command at sea. For a while at least, Hitler and his admirals were determined not to repeat the errors in policy, grand strategy, and naval strategy committed in the early years of the century. In the case of Admiral Erich Raeder, however, it was the unexpected and very unwelcome circumstance of early war that most reduced his aspiration for the building of a balanced fleet that might challenge for command at sea.[9] The Z (for *ziel*, or "target") Plan fleet endorsed on January 29, 1939, envisaged an eight-year buildup to completion in 1948, hastily revised to 1946 at Hitler's insistence. The Z Plan rested on some significant, and significantly ridiculous, assumptions. Specifically, the plan required six to eight years of peace with Britain and assumed the availability of material resources and trained people. Moreover, the plan was drafted without regard for the disadvantages of German strategic geography, an oversight that agitated naval theorist Wolfgang Wegener.[10] Furthermore, the fleet would be in a position to challenge the Royal Navy by 1946 or 1948 only if Britain neglected to take competitive corrective action against the blatant German menace in the North Sea.

The Royal Navy, though still faithful to the concept of a general maritime command, lacked for a worthy European opponent on the surface of the sea in the interwar years. The Jutland [battle] syndrome dominated a Royal Navy bereft of a European adversary with a large battlefleet. The next Jutland was expected to be waged with Japan east of the very incomplete fleet base at Singapore, not in the North Sea against Germany.[11] A large body of British opinion in the 1930s was convinced that Germany's unexpected collapse in the fall of 1918 ultimately was traceable to the Allied economic blockade.[12] If fight again she must, Britain was determined to return to a rather nostalgic and romanticized notion of its alleged traditional maritime way of war and until 1939 eschewed the kind of continental commitment that produced nearly 1 million British (Imperial) dead and 2 million wounded between 1914 and 1918. The supply blockade had been as unexpectedly effective in 1914–18 as it was overvalued in Britain in the late 1930s.

Nazi Germany was critically dependent on the foreign, including overseas, supply of raw materials.[13] But her world leadership in chemicals enabled her to invent substitute substances that worked well enough, and diplomacy enlisted the Soviet Union as a secure rearward base of supply. Furthermore, the German Army and Air Force secured by force an all but continent-wide bank of resources. That same Army and Air Force, with naval assistance in Norway, changed the geostrategic terms of engagement for the German counterblockade of Britain. To be fair, British strategic planners early in 1939 could not have predicted many of these blockade-breaking steps. Most of the threats to seaborne commerce were discounted in Britain in the 1930s on the basis of her experience in foiling the surface raiders and U-boats in World War I, of confidence in ASDIC/sonar,[14] and because of the understandable expectation that Germany would lack commerce-raiding bases on the open Atlantic. The leadership of Nazi Germany's *Kriegsmarine* entirely shared Britain's 1930s discounting of future submarine dangers to merchant shipping. Whereas Admiral Karl Dönitz insisted on April 13, 1939, that Germany required a U-boat force 300 strong in order to achieve "decisive success" against Britain, Raeder's Z Plan promised only 162 (Atlantic-capable types) by 1948.[15]

Prior to the industrial revolution and the age of mass warfare, the main purpose of a maritime blockade was to watch closely for the movement of enemy fighting ships. In war after war, the Royal Navy's blockade focused on Brest, Toulon, and Rochefort, with periodic need to add Antwerp/Flushing, Cadiz, Cartagena, Ferrol, and Corunna to the list of ports observed. The overriding objective of this naval blockade was the frustration of invasion designs. Blockade also ensured the maritime command necessary for the safe passage of British, and unsafe passage of enemy, seaborne trade. In addition, naval blockade provided strategic cover for British military expeditions on colonial or continental-peripheral ventures. Also, the blockade and actual interdiction of enemy shipping helped deny the enemy the revenue to finance military operations.

The strategic potential of supply blockade has varied widely with the differing vulnerabilities of states. Imperial Athens was as much at risk to the interruption of her seaborne supply of grain from the northern shores of the Black Sea as was twentieth-century Britain to the U-boat campaigns against her overseas food supply.[16] In modern times, however, the efficacy of supply blockade has been the product of the interaction between the raw material needs of industrial war-making economies and—in the continental case—the closing of access to landward sources of supply. It was critical to the effectiveness of the British economic blockade of Germany twice in this century that the enemy should be besieged closely on land as well as by sea. The economic blockades of Germany were effected not only at sea but also to an important degree at source and with reference to German purchasing power. Economic warfare eventually became a total enterprise in both world wars. Allied and German agents sought to control, or at least to influence markedly, the direction of trade flows from neutral countries. Strategic geography was critical, as always. Even if German economic agents could corner some market on fertilizer in a South American country, that would avail them little if they could not arrange for safe transshipment to the Reich in German or neutral bottoms.

In the Cold War era, the Soviet Union, unlike the countries of preindustrial Europe, could not have been damaged strategically significantly by a maritime blockade directed toward the financial instrument of high policy, any more than could Napoleonic France, or later, Imperial or Nazi Germany. Supply blockade, on the other hand, peaked in its effectiveness as a strategic instrument in 1918 and again in 1944–45 against insular Japan, but it had also some noteworthy promise as a tool of war against the modern Soviet imperium. With reference to post-1945 conditions, the principal granaries of the world lay overseas from Eurasia, while even a conventional war in Eurasia would have wrought massive economic damage. It follows that a Soviet Union victorious on land in Eurasia would have had severe problems feeding an expanded and politically insecure empire.

The strategic effectiveness of maritime blockade of the supply of goods, and indeed of economic warfare broadly pursued, must depend on the political, social, economic, military, and geostrategic particulars of a specific case. Economic blockade has to be viewed, as must sea power, as an instrument of grand strategy for the conduct of conflict as a whole. Rarely will blockade be independently decisive.[17] Absurdly optimistic claims for the strategic promise in economic sanctions surfaced yet again in late 1990–91 with the American debate over the prudent way to coerce Iraq to disgorge Kuwait. In permissive circumstances, however, the maritime blockade (and blockade at source) of overseas supply of critical materials can have massive multiplier effects generating strategic leverage in abundance. The leading example in modern history was the British blockade of Imperial Germany from 1914 to 1918. But even in that case the blockade worked only very slowly, necessarily by attrition, and as a contributor, a team player, to victory.

Moving from the intended indirect effect of financial and supply pressures to the realm of direct action, a sea power can engage in peripheral raiding and warfare for the purposes of imposing a debilitating dispersal in military deployment on the enemy, sustaining morale at home and among captive nations, for the encouragement of neutrals to keep their options open, and to inflict damage.

To raid the periphery of a great land power is a strategy of weakness, much as commerce raiding is a strategy of weakness for a land power unable to contest military command at sea. Nonetheless, strategies of weakness have utility. They need to be compared not, as Mahan was wont to do, with strategies of strength but rather with the costs of inaction, alternative strategies of weakness, and perhaps the price of a disadvantageous peace settlement. Time is critical in warfare. Strategies of harassment, of raiding on land and at sea, are relevant when swift favorable decision is not immediately attainable. Rarely has raiding been a preferred strategy. Some British blue-water theorists saw peripheral raiding as a vital part of the "British way in warfare."[18] Properly regarded, raiding is either a complement to the sustained application of concentrated force or a temporary expedient mandated by the inability to attempt prudently anything on a large scale of effort.

Provided it is appreciated to be only a minor strategy, raiding has a great deal to recommend it. Throughout history, seaborne mobility has been permissive of raiding or, as Julian Corbett expressed it, "coastal diversion."[19] In public debate over strategy, it is not always made clear whether the subject under discussion is a raiding strategy where the object is "ravage and destruction," or a sea-based campaign on the continental periphery where the object is "conquest and occupation."[20] The distinction between the two is fundamental. Coastal raiding is doubly hazardous for a country that does not enjoy maritime command. In addition to the standard danger that a small landing force might be overwhelmed on shore is the peril that it could be intercepted at sea. Access to an enemy's coast is a major benefit that flows from the achievement of maritime command. Of course, even when the quality of maritime command approaches the absolute, still the enemy is likely to possess some coastal patrol craft. This discussion of sea power and a peripheral raiding strategy is not meant to imply that raiding parties have to be inserted and evacuated literally across the beach. Since February 1942, with the airborne drop by Company C of the British Army's 2d Parachute Regiment on the German radar installation at Bruneval in France, it has been plain that peripheral raiding by a sea power does not have to mean raiding from the sea. In the Bruneval case, however, the 120-strong force was evacuated, almost miraculously, by sea.

The strategic geography of particular conflicts influences the feasibility of raiding. With long coastlines on the Channel, the Atlantic, and the Mediterranean, France was a particularly inviting target for raiding. The same was true for a Nazi Germany, which controlled most of the littoral of peninsular Europe. British raiding from the sea, and even more the threat of raiding, compelled an expensive dispersion in coastal deployments on France and, later, Nazi Germany. Through the threat of raids, Britain denied French and German leaders discretion over the services of tens, even hundreds, of thousands of soldiers, many of whom could have been employed much more profitably in the main field armies. Also, coastal raids could do considerable damage to local trade, coastal lines of communication on shore and just offshore (particularly important in the Mediterranean), and the political reputation of the land power. Furthermore, a raiding strategy can contribute usefully to sustenance of the offensive spirit on the part of friendly forces, and it reminds actual or potential allies that the

40

war is still on. A coastal raiding strategy is akin to a policy of aggressive patrolling in land and air warfare.

When poorly directed, raiding can become an end in itself that is unduly expensive in the high quality of military talent it attracts and requires.[21] Raiding from the sea is a class of activity ever liable to lead to small-scale military, but possibly much larger-scale political, disaster in the hands of amateurs in this highly specialized form of combat. Overenthusiastic politicians, attracted by the romance of the rugged commando mystique and the promise of quick and dramatic results, and underenthusiastic regular military organizations can function synergistically to render coastal raiding an exceedingly risky activity. Although raiding is cheap when compared with the dispatch of great expeditions charged to seize, hold, and exploit, it is not invariably cheap relative to the cost it imposes on the enemy. Although designed to achieve by surprise a decisive local tactical superiority in force, coastal raiding is a dispersal of effort. Historical experience attests to the truth that few enterprises in war are as needful of professional skill as are combined land-sea operations (today with air precursors and adjuncts), on whatever scale they are conducted. The contribution of British and Anglo-American seaborne threats, respectively, to the overthrow of Napoleonic France and Hitler's Germany rested very little on the menace or occasional reality of coastal raiding. Local damage could be effected by raids—successful (e.g., the destruction of the Normandie dock at St. Nazaire on the Loire estuary on March 28, 1942), or unsuccessful (e.g., the gallant attempt to close the U-boat exit channels at Zeebrugge and Ostend on April 23, 1918). But the threat from the sea that caused the strategic dispersal of French, and later German, military power was the threat to seize, hold, and exploit, not the threat to ravage and destroy.

Napoleon, writing in his correspondence in 1810, has been much quoted on the subject of the distractive value of threats from the sea: "With 30,000 men in transports at the Downs, the English can paralyze 300,000 of my army, and that will reduce us to the rank of a second-class Power!"[22] Although probably somewhat shaken by Britain's abortive great expedition of 1809 to Walcheren Island on the Scheldt estuary,[23] Napoleon almost certainly was aware of the logistic impracticality of the enemy's maintaining "30,000 men in transports at the Downs," or anywhere else afloat, for that matter. Amphibious operations in the Napoleonic era

41

necessarily entailed the landing of a force virtually bereft of cavalry and decisively overmatched in artillery beyond the shoreline.

On rare but vital occasions, raids have had a strategic effect out of all proportion to the scale of damage they inflicted. An all-time classic was the air raid on Tokyo commanded by Brigadier General James H. Doolittle launched from the U.S.S. *Hornet* on April 18, 1942. This raid, though militarily trivial, had a decisive effect within the Japanese government in the weight that it yielded to those arguing for the necessity of enticing the U.S. Navy's carriers into a battle of annihilation. The result was the Battle of Midway.[24]

A peripheral raiding strategy was pursued energetically by Britain as an independent source of pressure, or just as a sign of life, only when more immediately productive opportunities on land were signally absent. Generally Britain preferred to contribute modestly on land in the decisive theater of operations, most typically the Low Countries and Germany, so long as such a theater was active. Britain did not commit her army to Portugal and Spain after 1808 because she was geostrategically attracted to the remote periphery of the continent. Rather, after the Franco-Russian treaties of Tilsit in July 1807, there were no active landpower allies, operating in a geographically more central theater, whose efforts could be joined. In the Peninsular War, Britain did what she could to keep the struggle alive, with an army able to fall back on a reliably commanded sea.

Intermediate between raiding and continental commitment is what may be called peripheral warfare. This category of warfare points to the occasional ability of a sea power to exploit its comparative geostrategic advantages by way of imposing protracted combat on unfavorable terms on a continental enemy. The war in the Mediterranean from 1940 until 1945 was an example of peripheral warfare conducted by the maritime belligerent. Similarly, the expedition to the Crimea in 1854 was a clear example of a belligerent enjoying maritime command imposing geostrategic terms of conflict that the continental enemy had great difficulty meeting. Peripheral warfare shares some purposes both with raiding and with major continental commitment. Britain's on-off-on commitment to the Iberian Peninsula from 1808 to 1814 is a classic example of peripheral warfare: it was much, much more than a raid or series of raids, but also it was directed at continental territory wherein the reach and grasp of Napoleonic military power was relatively feeble (relative, that is, to the Low Countries, or to the Rhineland or lands bordering the Danube).

Raiding strategy is as old as warfare; indeed there are strategic cultures—the Bedouin, for example—wedded to raiding as the preferred style of war. Appreciation of the strategic value of raids, as well as expertise in their conduct, is the exception rather than the rule. Whether the topic is the grand expedition to Walcheren in 1809, the great raid on Sebastopol in 1854, or commando-type assaults in a dozen conflicts in the second half of the twentieth century, strategists have tended to fail to use their raiding options competently or imaginatively.[25]

In addition to peripheral raiding and warfare, maritime dominance allows a strategy of oversea conquest: taking, holding, and exploiting whatever assets a continental enemy has at risk to enemy sea power. In the age of sail, command of Europe's narrow seas meant effective control of the transoceanic routes to Britain's colonies, as well as to the overseas commercial empires of Holland, Spain, Portugal, and France. In the words of Lord Anson in 1758, "The best defence for our colonies as well as our coasts is to have such a squadron to the westward as may in all probability either keep the French in harbour or give them battle with advantage if they come out."[26]

From the time of the Battle of LaHogue-Barfleur, May 28–June 2, 1692, to the present day, any European or Eurasian continental power has had to assume that British, Anglo-American, and now U.S. naval power could close the high seas to the wartime movement of all save individual ships or small squadrons of an enemy. There have been some exceptions to this general rule. Peacetime parsimony in the maintenance of the Royal Navy (as in the early 1750s, the early 1770s, and the 1930s), exceptionally gifted or fortunate enemy admirals (like Suffren in the 1770s and 1780s), the vagaries of the weather (perennially, in the age of steam as well as sail), and relatively poor British naval leadership ashore and afloat (the 1770s and early 1790s) could yield a temporary advantage that would seem to make a mockery of Britain's pretensions to maritime command.

The strategic value of the overseas possessions or clients of the European powers has fluctuated widely by country, over time, and with changes in technology. The point is that the strategic and economic value in wartime of any maritime imperium is totally dependent on the control of the relevant sea routes. Britain's, and today the United States', enemies have had to assume that their overseas holdings would be lost in wartime sooner or later. The strategic significance of the loss of overseas territories, the trading relationships attached to them, and their utility for the logistic support of military operations against British interests has varied widely. The suffering of colonial or other maritime damage was a matter of first-order importance to a Spain able to function as a superstate in Europe in part because of a creditworthiness that rested on bankers' anticipation of reliable arrival of bullion fleets from America. The prosperity and safety of the Dutch Republic hinged entirely upon her preeminence in overseas trade. France had a sufficiency of metropolitan economic assets to hold her own as a great power without benefit of an overseas commercial empire. But Paris faced bankruptcy if she attempted to wage long land wars in Europe without regular revenue from overseas trade. By the third quarter of the seventeenth century, the period that saw the conduct of three wars with the Dutch, England had become strategically asymmetrically (in relation to France, rapidly reemerging as her major continental rival) dependent for prosperity and security on the revenue derived from overseas commerce. Although the wars with France from 1688 until 1713 had large implications for Britain's rise as a maritime great power, those wars were about the balance of power in Europe, as well as about commercial preeminence. France did not actually become a major commercial rival to Britain overseas until the 1730s, but she came to be defined as the principal threat to Britain's economic well-being by the late 1690s.

The West Indies were a principal geographical focus of the maritime dimension of the Anglo-French conflicts from 1688 to 1815. As late as the Napoleonic Wars, four-fifths of all British income from overseas investment was from that region.[27] In the eighteenth century, colonies were acquired for the profit to be derived from exclusive trade, not for national glory. This meant that national strategic interests could, and did, come into conflict with, for example, the West Indies' sugar lobby, which feared competition in price from captured French and Dutch islands. Although the motives of the various interested parties in Britain and her colonies were often divergent, a system of war emerged in the course of the hundred years of intermittent conflict with France that persisted well into the twentieth century. Maritime command was asserted as early as feasible, resting on the time-tried axiom, "When in doubt, fall back on the central fleet off Ushant, so as to cover the Channel."[28] This axiom was amended in detail in 1914 and 1939 to substitute Scapa Flow, so as to cover the northern exit from the North Sea. For the Cold War, the axiom was amended yet again so as to substitute the Greenland-Iceland-U.K. (GIUK) gap as the geographical pivot on which NATO's maritime command would rest in time of war. The strategic corollary to, and consequence of, the command pivoting off Ushant (with lesser pivots at Gibraltar and, frequently, Port Mahon in Minorca) was the dispatch of expeditions to seize whatever was seizable overseas. As a general rule, the enemy was so effectively landlocked in continental Europe that it could neither forward reinforcements for colonial warfare nor evacuate troops facing imminent destruction. This was true for the French army in Egypt in 1800–1, as it was for the Germans in Tunisia early in 1943.

British motives for overseas conquest typically embraced a need to defend colonies and trade from locally mounted French (and Spanish) expeditions and from the depredations of enemy privateers, thereby safeguarding the revenue critical to the prosecution of war in Europe. Also, Britain sought to deprive the enemy of the benefits of colonial commerce, though this advantage really was, or should be, secured by the command exercised by the Western Squadron (the Channel Fleet) off Ushant. In a fundamental sense, overseas conquest could increase British wealth and hence strengthen the sinews of war. In addition, time and again it was found that overseas acquisitions had some value as bargaining chips in peace negotiations. The colonial commerce of which continental powers were deprived was a source of income, luxury goods, and even critical naval stores.

Britain's long struggle with France was not viewed in London as a struggle to the death, at least not until Napoleon Bonaparte was crowned emperor in 1804. War was conducted with a view to the peace that would follow. The overseas possessions of France and her allies, as later of Imperial Germany, were hostages to British sea power in time of war. The challenge for British statecraft was to find, and if need be finance, a continental coalition so effective in its conduct of war on land that few of Britain's overseas conquests would have to be traded in peace negotiations for the return of French conquests on the Continent. The Hanoverian succession in Britain was a near century-long adverse complication for British statecraft, since Hanover served as a relatively easy and geostrategically quite important continental hostage. As a personal possession of the King of England, Hanover in effect deprived Britain of a small but often significant measure of her strategic insularity.

The revenue from overseas trade was much more important to the France of the *ancien régime* than it was to Republican France, which achieved near Continent-wide hegemony by 1797, again by 1801, or to an Imperial France supreme on land in 1807. For the eighteenth century, J. H. Parry reminds us that although "France and Spain were both financially exhausted in 1763 . . . too much should not be made of that." He observes:

> Eighteenth century tax systems were too inefficient, and in most countries too riddled with exemptions, for more than a small fraction of the nation's income to be collected for war or any other public purpose. A government at war could totter towards bankruptcy, as the French government did, with its subjects' wealth largely untapped. When its revenue and its credit were exhausted and its fighting men could not be paid, it had to make peace; but conversely in a relatively few years of peace it could recover sufficiently to be ready for another war of the same limited unemotional kind.[29]

Nonetheless, the West Indies were sufficiently important to Napoleon for him to order the luckless and incompetent Villeneuve to inflict damage there on British commerce in the course of executing the grand design in 1805 for the intended invasion of England. No measure of British success overseas, however, could provide adequate compensation for a great imbalance of power on land in Europe. Nonetheless, it was the commercial imperium, strengthened increasingly by the rapid rise in domestic manufacture and the efficiency of domestic agriculture, that enabled Britain to wait out Napoleon's years of continental preponderance.

Twice in the twentieth century Britain again applied the old strategic system of overseas conquest. In 1914 and 1915 Germany's lately acquired colonies were promptly conquered, with the notable and vastly expensive exception of German East Africa, where campaigning persisted throughout the war. The German colonies were of no economic importance to the Fatherland and played no strategic role in German war planning. Germany had no overseas colonies in 1939 for the Royal Navy to isolate. But following Italy's unheroic entry into the war on June 10, 1940, and in the absence of an active fighting front with Germany after the Dunkirk evacuation, Britain devoted second priority—after the defense of the home islands and their security of seaborne supply—to the eradication of the geographically impressive Italian empire in Africa. With his eyes myopically focused on continental goals, Hitler missed his first and best opportunity in 1940 to close the Mediterranean to British sea power. But in a manner that was to become familiar from Japanese operational malpractice, he was persuaded early in 1941 to send just enough air and then ground support to keep the Axis cause alive in North Africa. Hitler was paying a political debt to Mussolini; there was no geostrategic vision informing the dispatch of the Luftwaffe's Air Corps X from Norway to Sicily or of Erwin Rommel with the Afrika Korps (later Panzer Armee Afrika) to Tripolitania.

Those who argued in the 1980s that the Soviet Union had no overseas possessions or clients of great wartime importance were correct in the sense that the isolation, neutralization, and if necessary conquest of distant Soviet clients could not have served offensive Western strategic purposes. When set against the stakes in land campaigns in Europe, the Persian Gulf, or the inner Asian frontiers of China, such hostages to U.S. sea power as Cuba, Vietnam, South Yemen, and Angola would have had negligible political value. But the neutralization of the Soviet Union's extended overseas imperium might have had significant defensive importance for a global Western alliance needing to use oceanic lines of communication in a protracted war. The U.S. Navy would not have sought to discourage or remove the overseas allies of Moscow in the foolish belief that those clients had strategic value as hostages. Rather, Soviet clients would have been neutralized to prevent their providing bases for the harassment of Western shipping and other interests.

Overseas conquest, like the other strategies discussed here, rarely itself comprises the direct key to success in war. Nevertheless, the possibility of such conquest is an integral part of the structure of sea power–land power relations. That is, whatever the

47

strategic value of an enemy's overseas assets is, it must be assumed to be denied the continental belligerent. As a general rule, the conquest or other neutralization of those among a continental power's assets readily approached from the sea will be of only modest importance, but such seizure may help enable sea power to be effective in shaping the course of a war. By definition, the center of strategic gravity of a continental state or coalition will not be maritime in character or, hence, in vulnerability.

The successful practice of sea power enables continental allies to be found and sustained for the continental distraction of the enemy. Some judicious mix of financial exhaustion, supply blockade, peripheral raiding, and overseas conquest may yield noteworthy strategic leverage, but against a great continental foe, more direct pressure on land typically is required. Threats by land to a continental enemy are more menacing than is the damage wrought by the closing of sea lines of communication. Britain's principal continental enemy generally had landward, as well as maritime-colonial, ambitions. The enemy often was in scant need of diversion from effort at sea by a British policy that sought actively to foment exhausting distraction on land. The first-class naval establishment that Colbert constructed for Louis XIV, for example, could not be sustained financially in the face of Louis' determination to extend France's frontiers in the east, to unite the thrones of France and Spain, and, perennially, to conquer and hold the Low Countries.

The intensity of British need for continental allies has varied with the political character of the wars at issue, as well as with the shifting terms of the balance of power. Typically, Britain did not seek the military overthrow of its continental enemy. An exception was the Third Dutch War of the 1670s, when Charles II and Louis XIV, in unholy alliance, intended by a coordinated strategy on land and at sea to eliminate the Dutch as an independent actor. From the time of the Glorious Revolution of 1688 until the Seven Years' War (1756–63), virtually every French invasion design against England had a more or less serious politically subversive dimension to it. The British government had to worry about the menace of civil war (particularly in Ireland and Scotland) that could be triggered by a Jacobite rising. As late as 1745, Charles Edward Stuart shook the Hanoverian succession, although he landed in Scotland with only six companions. The Jacobite menace to the Protestant settlement was an instrument of convenience in French grand strategy. Anglo-French enmity in the eighteenth century was "natural," persistent, and geostrategically quite rational.[30] But neither side harbored radical policy goals against the other. Indeed, royalist France did more damage to herself politically and financially with her shortsighted support for revolution in the British Empire in North America in 1778–83 than was inflicted by Britain with her victory in 1763.

Prior to the wars of the French Revolution, the armies of Europe generally lacked the logistic reach to be instruments of decision. In the series of wars between Britain and France in the period 1688–1815, conclusive military victory on land was sought and achieved by Britain only in 1815. The France of Napoleon was as different an enemy from the France of the *ancien régime* as the scope of the militarily practicable was different between those two eras.[31] Prior to the 1790s, Britain required continental allies to keep France occupied exhaustingly in recurring campaigns on land. Those campaigns had the strategic function of emptying the French treasury and inducing war weariness. With the important exception of the interdiction of transportation of naval stores from the Baltic, British sea power could not deny preindustrial France the physical means to wage war. But British sea power could deny France important income from colonial commerce, all the while augmenting her own revenue. The successful conduct of maritime war enabled Britain to rent allies and mercenary soldiery to sustain conflicts on land that France could not afford to wage on a protracted basis. It would be a serious error to believe that Britain waged war very substantially with rented allies. Foreign subsidies peaked at 12 percent of her national war effort for the War of Austrian Succession (1740–48), while for the Wars of the French Revolution and Empire, Britain's contributions to allies averaged only 8 percent.[32] Moreover, although in principle there were usually foreigners available to be bribed to fight, in practice major allies could be hard to secure at a tolerable price, often insisted on pursuing their own political interests despite their subsidized status, and frequently suffered inconvenient defeat and as a consequence failed to perform in a strategically adequate manner.

The revolutionary expansion in the scope for operational decision on land effected by Napoleon, and sustained thenceforth—

albeit with an unanticipated hiatus in 1914–18—expanded in parallel the quantity of land power assistance Britain (and later the United States) required in her wars. The new instrument of the supply blockade was much underappreciated in advance of its thoroughgoing application in the First World War. The prewar navalist focus on battle, the evolution of an international maritime law that proscribed search and seizure of neutral ships' cargoes,[33] and the widespread anticipation that the next great war would be of brief duration conspired to blind statesmen and strategists at the turn of the century to a prescient understanding of the influence of sea power upon the course of future major conflict. This was paradoxical, given the contemporary popularity of Mahan and the strength of navalist sentiment in many countries. By the early twentieth century, maritime war appeared to have lost a considerable measure of its power to influence conflict on land. In practice, this was not to be the case. Continental allies were critically important for the distraction and overthrow of Imperial and Nazi Germany, but then Britain had always needed allies as a "continental sword" complementary to her maritime strategy. One should beware, however, of the perils of overstatement. Gerald Graham has written with particular reference to the war with France from 1778 to 1783, though with more general applicability:

> Without allied support on the Continent to divert French energies, the Royal Navy was not strong enough to ensure continuous control even in the Channel. Unless buttressed by effective alliances on the Continent, command of the sea was a delusive concept.[34]

Graham's argument is misleading on two counts. First, in the war with France, Spain, and Holland (after 1780), Britain did eventually restore a condition of maritime dominance.[35] Once fully, if belatedly, committed to naval mobilization and properly focused upon the maritime war with France and Spain, Britain demonstrated by 1782 that she could perform very well indeed without continental allies. Second, continental allies may not be available, no matter how strategically advisable their acquisition might be. In 1778, 1797, 1801, 1807, 1810, and 1940, Britain could not sign up any great power allies in Europe. A theory of war for superior sea power has to be able to cope with inconvenient geostrategic realities. It is true that the American war was both the only war in the eighteenth century that Britain lost and the only one in which Britain lacked for a continental alliance to distract Bourbon energies on land. But Britain did not lose America because she lacked continental allies. Indeed, the war that really mattered for Britain, that against France and Spain, was not lost at all. In 1783 Britain was waxing stronger, and the Bourbon powers much weaker, when domestic politics in London argued for peace.

The value of continental alliance for a sea power lends itself to overstatement. Such overstatement manifests itself in a rather casual approach to the difficulties faced by continental states in transforming land power into effective sea power, to some understatement of the proclivity of continental power to self-destruct grand strategically, and indeed—at its most basic—to a less than empathetic approach to the influence of sea power upon the course of history and the outcome of conflicts. The kinds of pressure that British sea power applied against continental enemies varied with time and technology, but the character and purposes of Britain's wars with continental states did not change in their essentials over the centuries. From the resumption of hostilities after the Peace of Amiens (March 27, 1802–August 1, 1803) until nuclear weaponry emerged on a large scale to restrict dramatically the scope of prudent war aims, Britain, and then the United States, was obliged to mobilize sufficient national and allied land power as to effect the conclusive overthrow of the threatening continental hegemon of the day. That overthrow had to be achieved in the would-be hegemon's own environment of principal strength, the land.

As a general rule, a dominant sea power cannot sustain a maritime-continental alliance unless it is prepared to make a military continental commitment itself. Such a commitment provides an earnest of serious political intention (actually hostages), it encourages by example, and it provides a "make-weight" to help maintain a balance in land power. Ever since the 1580s, British, and then U.S., strategic debate has labored to answer the question of how much of a continental commitment is required for national security. The renting of foreign armies has been only slightly less popular than has payment for the commitment of British, or U.S., soldiers to Europe.[36]

The U.S. experience with continental commitment as security organizer for the West has been similar in key respects to the lengthy British record. It was always the British preference, in sharply descending order of desirability, to wage war: for choice, strictly at sea or overseas; if necessary through token continental commitment, ideally within easy reach of coastal waters commanded by the Royal Navy; and, only as a last resort, in the face of truly unacceptable alternatives, to exert the maximum force on land that could be raised (surplus to the first priority of maritime defense). The consistency of British distaste for participation in land warfare in Europe was matched only by the consistency with which such participation was deemed essential. Moreover, that participation often was prolonged and quite large in scale. (For example, from 1809 until 1814, Britain committed virtually the whole of her disposable land forces, her only field army, totaling 47,000 men, to peripheral *but continental* war in the Iberian peninsula.) The Britain that superseded the Dutch seaborne empire and judged maritime-colonial warfare to be as profitable as land warfare in Europe was unprofitable did not commit large contingents of soldiers to fight on the Continent in war after war for frivolous reasons.

A limited maritime "British way in warfare" was contrasted by Julian Corbett and Basil Liddell Hart with a "continental way in warfare."[37] The sad history of the twentieth century has demonstrated that such a contrast must be judged the fictional reading of a strategy system evolved in a particular period. The alleged contrast betrays misunderstanding of the relationship between sea power and land power. Britain was able to pursue successfully a heavily maritime form of war with Spain, the Dutch Republic, and France for two elementary reasons. First, those countries could be damaged severely—even fatally, in the Dutch case—by the consequences of action at sea. Second, there was a balance of continental land power that preoccupied the mind, drained the purse, and attenuated the energy of the European rival of the day. There was nothing objectively strategically correct, let alone correct for all eternity, about a maritime "way in warfare" for Britain. The old system of renting continental soldiery, blockading Europe's coastal waters, and seizing sugar islands generally worked well enough for more than a hundred years, although that old system typically was supplemented opportunistically by a direct British continental commitment. Nonetheless, that continental commitment was not always feasible. Furthermore, Britain could and did survive periods, and even the entire duration of a war (1778–83 against France), without continental allies or national continental commitment.

Many reasons explain Britain's ever reluctant, often belated, and occasionally ineffectual continental commitment. Britain has sought by forward military deployments to protect distinctively British (or Hanoverian) interests that might otherwise be slighted by continental allies and to secure maximum leverage over the statecraft of allies wont to discount the strategic value of unobserved sea power. Also, Britain judged it politically necessary to provide a tangible symbol of commitment, as well as a blood hostage, to a more or less common cause and to discourage by a local military presence the defection under pressure, or offer of bribe, of land power allies. Continental commitment by the offshore sea power lent weight in the area of final decision, the center of gravity, on land, sometimes substituted for the deficient or failing power of allies, and secured the prestige and legitimacy provided only by presence on the battlefield, in order to achieve a, or the major, role in the negotiation of peace. As the British and the French demonstrated positively in the Gulf War of 1991, and the Germans and Japanese demonstrated negatively, there is no close political substitute for being there *on the ground*. A blood commitment is qualitatively different from the contribution of cash, credit, or supplies. British sea power may have wrought the circumstances that eventually overcame even Napoleon's genius for military recovery from disaster, but it was the duke of Wellington and his British soldiers at Waterloo who raised Britain's diplomatic influence to unprecedented heights in 1815. The over-the-horizon, quintessentially strategic character of maritime success will always be discounted in the minds of land-focused people.

It was a source of continental resentment that Britain, secured by maritime command against plausible danger of invasion, was able to wage land warfare abroad more at financial than at human cost and to conduct war at sea for the national profit. The maturing of long-range air and missile power, particularly when married to nuclear weapons, saw the emergence of the equality of homeland risk that continental allies always have yearned to secure as between themselves and an offshore ally. NATO found it expedient from 1967 until 1991 to adopt a strategic concept of flexible response designed to maximize perceived linkage between military events in continental Europe and the U.S. homeland.

Behind the continental commitment that is necessary for an offshore sea power if it is to lead, or even just help shape, the policy and strategy of a coalition looms the prospect of global war. The continental foe should be discouraged by the knowledge that whatever it can win promptly by operational dexterity on land, the center of gravity of the adversary coalition cannot be gripped thereby. Much as a solitary gunboat far up a Chinese river symbolized the might of imperial Britain, very limited though it was as a ship of force, so a continental commitment can be symbolic of a power that is global in reach and in scale if fully mobilized and deployed. Dominant sea power, and sea-air power, protected by an umbrella of nuclear deterrence, limits the gains of a continental aggressor to what can be achieved in but one territorial theater. There is a sense in which the waging of war by a continental-oriented coalition against a maritime alliance can become the waging of war against all but the whole world. Notwithstanding the precariousness of the Royal Navy's command of the sea from 1914 to 1918 and the inability of battlefleet command to translate into a general (including subsurface) command, Britain, France, and the United States were able to move troops around the world without loss from enemy action. As much of the extra-European world industrialized and otherwise modernized in this century, so less and less a proportion of the gross world product could be secured by continental action confined to the European peninsula. That evolving fact worked in two ways, however. Although there was relatively less for a continental power to win on land in Europe, so also offshore sea power no longer could aspire to command the oceans of the world as a direct consequence of enforcing command in European waters.

Because war is an art that varies with time, technology, and adversaries, the rich menu of strategy options for sea power cannot be reduced or combined to a single formula for success. Every war is distinctive in detail, though less so in geostrategic structure. The repertoire of strategies for dominant sea power does not vary much from one war to the next, but the weight assigned those strategies and the total complexity of the situation alters massively.

54

The practice of dominant sea power is effected in the face of the practice of dominant land power. Just as maritime preponderance has helped shape statecraft and overall military strategy, so great continental strength shapes quite distinctive paths in statecraft and strategy. The strategic leverage of sea power has to be assessed in the light of the strategic leverage of land power.

CHAPTER 3

THE PRACTICE OF LAND POWER

"Je veux conquerir la mer par la puissance de terre [I shall conquer the sea by the power of the land]."

Napoleon, quoted in J. Holland Rose, *Man and the Sea: Stages in Maritime and Human Progress* (1935)

The strategies for a sea power have to succeed in opposition to the strategies available to a land power. From Philip II to Adolf Hitler, the leading land power's recurring struggle with British sea power witnessed the employment, or attempted employment, of different mixes of an enduring repertoire of strategies. Even when complemented with land-based air power in 1940, the continental state was unable to shape a strategic context for the Narrow Seas sufficiently favorable as to render a cross-Channel invasion a practicable operation of war. An invasion of Britain in the summer of 1940 would have been less of a logistic gamble than was the invasion of the Soviet Union in 1941 or the southeastward extension of that invasion in the summer of 1942 to the Volga and the Caucasus. But like Napoleon, Hitler was the product of a continentalist culture and had only brief flashes of insight, rather than a secure grasp, on how best war should be conducted against an offshore sea power.[1] He did understand from the bitter experience of defeat in 1918 that war with maritime Britain meant war with virtually the whole world. Nonetheless, even as late as the final quarter of 1942, Hitler failed to comprehend that the Atlantic was a battleground as important for Germany's fate as was the struggle on the Volga.

A dominant continental power faces the mirror image of the grand-strategic and military strategic problems of a dominant sea power addressed in Chapter 2. As with a dominant sea power, a dominant land power in theory has a repertoire of strategy options in its search for decisive advantage. Both the sea power and the continental power strive to win the war at issue, not just the war at sea or the war on land. The heart of the strategic challenge addressed in this chapter is how superior strength on land can, or might, be translated into advantage over a sea power foe. Eight strategy options are specified and illustrated with historical examples. As with the earlier discussion of the strategy repertoire for dominant sea power, this analysis of the strategy tool-kit for land power builds the framework for strategic understanding of the historical experiences presented at length in the remainder of the book.

Dominant land power can seek to achieve and exploit continental hegemony as the basis for developing superior sea power. Less heroically, the dominant land power may aspire to construct what would amount to a continental fortress impregnable to assault or serious subversion from the sea. The proximate purpose of this strategy would be to outlast a maritime enemy and deny him a practicable theory of victory in war. Next, a dominant land power may explore the feasibility of very direct action, of amphibious invasion, no less. Much more modest is the strategy option to take continental hostages of particular value to the sea power enemy. With reference to the balance of power at sea, a dominant continental belligerent may seek to attrit the naval superiority of the foe by means of the ambush of his naval power in detail. In addition, it is a near certainty that a leading land power with a second-class (or less) navy will attempt the classic maritime strategy of the weak and wage war against seaborne commerce. A further possibility for the power dominant on land may be the strategy option of closing continental markets to the trade of the sea power. In common with the counterblockade effected by commerce raiding, this option belongs in the broad category of action of economic warfare. Finally, a great continental power frustrated at the low-tide line may seek sea power allies. As with the analysis in the previous chapter of the dilemmas facing a dominant sea power, the central issue here is how a geostrategically dissimilar enemy can be reached, grasped, and overcome.

*　　*　　*

A great land power in quest of strategic leverage for the humbling or defeat of a maritime enemy may seek to use its continental hegemony as a secure resources base, there constructing a naval strength capable of achieving maritime command, and hence the defeat of the seapower foe. The quintessential such foe, Britain, required maritime command in order to be secure against invasion and protect her seaborne trade; in short, such command was a fundamental condition of national security. Isolation from the Continent, as happened time after time during the French Revolutionary and Napoleonic Wars and again over 1940–44, was a condition fraught with both fear—that dominant land power might acquire dominant sea power—and hope—that land power would overreach itself in its own medium. Throughout the centuries of British naval ascendancy, there was always the peril that a continental hegemon that was *truly secure on land* would have the resources to build a fleet which could challenge Britain for command of the Narrow Seas. Again and again, however, this potential advantage of continental sea power over insular sea power was deflected decisively by the working of the balance of power on land. British exercise of command at sea, although annoying to European neutrals, generally was an order of magnitude less threatening to their security than was the exercise of hegemonic control on land by the leading continental power. This is not to make light of the repeated diplomatic and military difficulties that Britain brought upon herself through her conduct of maritime blockade. But it is to claim that the intrusiveness of British maritime command upon national interests, prerogatives, and pride was of an altogether lesser kind than was the overlordship on land asserted by Napoleon's or Hitler's booted legions.

In modern times command at sea has not carried with it those political seeds of its own destruction which, time and again, have brought down aspiring hegemonies on land—at least, nowhere near to the same degree. Nonetheless, the repeated threat posed by potentially dominant land power to Britain was sufficiently real as to oblige British governments, from the time of Elizabeth I, with her land commitment to the revolt against Spain in the Low Countries, to the present day, with the forward commitment of the British Army in Germany, to have an active continental policy. From time to time, including the summer of 1940, some British political leaders were tempted to come to terms with the continental super state of the day. But after the Peace of Amiens of 1802–3, the character of the continental enemy in war after war ultimately compelled London to seek that enemy's overthrow as a matter of prudence. Unbalanced continental power in the hands of Napoleon, Kaiser Wilhelm II, Adolf Hitler, or Joseph Stalin and his successors could not be trusted to confine its geostrategic ambitions to the coast of mainland Europe.

There is a contrast between theory and practice in the relationship between insular sea power and continental land power. In practice, sea power has had the geopolitical advantage because bids for imperium on land inevitably have catalyzed land power opposition that could be forged into a balancing or winning coalition by the offshore state. In theory, at least until the full maturing of the United States as a superpower, continental land power had a potential resources base that its armies might overrun or intimidate, which could serve as the secure arsenal for the building of matchless naval power. In comfortable retrospect, it is plain to see why the France of Louis XIV and Napoleon and the Germany of Kaiser Wilhelm II and Adolf Hitler were unlikely ever to achieve a complete and enduring mastery on land. Their continental achievements were never likely to be sufficiently secure as to enable them to devote themselves with the requisite consistency of effort to the wresting of maritime command from Britain. Britain's fears of continental naval power, however, were by no means unreasonable. With the certain exception of Imperial Germany, and the arguable exception of Nazi Germany,[2] the continental enemy over three and a half centuries was serious about mounting an invasion of Britain. Moreover, all of Britain's enemies over that period, had real ambitions—even, in some cases, real programs of naval construction—to build navies capable of defeating Britain at sea.

The prudential rules for imperial statecraft mandate that over-mighty continental powers aspire to mastery at sea as well as on land. For reasons of political stability and maritime security, Napoleonic France could no more concede to Britain a permanency in command of, and hence potential access from, the sea approaches to Europe than could Imperial or Nazi Germany. No matter what the geographical extent of its imperial ambitions may be—European, Eurasian, or global—a dominant continental power or coalition could never be sufficiently secure on land as to be indifferent

59

to the offshore menace of British or American sea power. For the tolerable security of its tenure on land, a dominant land power is obliged as a matter of elementary prudence to reach out to sea in order to seek a decisive grip upon an otherwise inaccessible menace.

Unlike France from the 1690s until 1815, the German Navy in the twentieth century was directed by people who understood well the idea and implications of battlefleet command. Realistically or otherwise, Grand Admiral Alfred von Tirpitz was determined to construct a navy that could accomplish more than just weigh heavily in the scales of peacetime diplomacy, let alone suffer defeat in a battle he hoped would be prohibitively expensive to the Royal Navy. The order of battle of the High Seas Fleet never approached closely the strength of the Royal Navy's Grand Fleet. Certainly Germany never succeeded in building her battleline beyond the "risk" zone of inferiority. If the second-class fleet of Imperial Germany was to accomplish anything, it had to exercise the operational initiative and shorten the odds. Unfortunately, the strategic initiative already was held by the Royal Navy as a consequence of geography, superior strength, and reputation. Even ninety or so years after the period in question, historians have difficulty explaining what Tirpitz was about with the construction of his High Seas Fleet. The formal rationales for the building of a second-class "risk" fleet appear so puerile that scholars are all but obliged to argue that Tirpitz must really have intended to oversee the development of a fleet which, one day, unquestionably would be first class. The answer to the mystery of the purpose of the High Seas Fleet may be no more subtle than Herbert Rosinski's judgment that Tirpitz was "no strategist; least of all, what his adherents never tired of acclaiming him, a statesman."[3]

Although Tirpitz had justified construction of the High Seas Fleet with the nonsense of the risk theory, there is good reason to believe that that justification was a temporary necessity. The risk theory may have said as little about Tirpitz's ambitions for German naval power as it did about Germany's potential as a naval competitor. Paul Kennedy quotes from a letter of August 30, 1914, which Tirpitz " 'censored' from his memoires," in which the admiral claimed

that "a fleet of equal strength to England's" was their "natural and single aim [which] could not be admitted in the past two decades

60

but could only be kept in mind if Germany's trade and industry and colonies expanded further."[4]

Kennedy observes:

> If *this* was his hope—and, it is fair to add, it was scarcely as pre-posterous as some writers have suggested given the German lead over Britain in population, in steel, iron, chemical, electrical and other industries, and in total national wealth by 1914—then many of the strategical inconsistencies of the "Tirpitz Plan" become much more explicable. This would also explain his devastating critique upon Bethmann Hollweg and the generals for prematurely provoking war over the Sarajevo deed.

Twice in this century Germany has gone to war on a timetable that arguably had some justification in the logic of continental land war but was fatal for the prospect of German victory at sea. On neither August 1, 1914, nor September 1, 1939, were Germany's leaders convinced that they were taking actions which must lead inexorably to a British declaration of war. The timing of both wars denied Germany the possibility of constructing a navy on a scale such that eventually it might have been able to face the Royal Navy in a fleet action with a reasonable prospect of success.

Hitler's Navy was to turn belatedly to its much underappreciated U-boat arm as the instrument of decision at sea. But that Navy, very much with the Führer's blessing, had intended to construct a balanced fleet. Such an intention was formalized in the briefly authoritative Z Plan of January 29, 1939. Reflecting on the lost opportunities that premature war with Britain meant for the German Navy, Grand Admiral Erich Raeder speculated as follows:

> By 1944–5, Germany's tally of battleships, armoured ships [pocket battleships], cruisers, aircraft carriers and submarines *would* have been enough to dispute Britain's mastery of the oceans. [Having developed a theory of battleship confrontation, he proceeded thus:] In this way—and particularly assuming the help of Japan and Italy, who would have drawn off part of the British fleet—there *would* have been every prospect of defeating the enemy's navy and closing his sea approaches. In other words, we should have found the final solution to the "British problem."[5]

Fanciful or not in their strategic aspirations, Napoleon after 1807, and Germany preceding the two world wars, attempted to build a continentally based naval power designed to challenge Britain in military excellence.[6] In so doing, France and Germany were following in the wake of such traditional land powers as Sparta, Republican Rome, the Arab Caliphate, Ottoman Turkey, and Spain.

A continental power can seek a critical leverage over a sea power foe by assaulting that foe's generally preferred strategy of coalition warfare. Continental hegemony can set the stage for the conduct of protracted conflict wherein the sea power is denied continental access all but entirely. Provided the military overthrow of offshore sea power is not an urgent war aim, a strategy aimed at the political will of sea powers to continue fighting often has found favor with dominant land powers. This may seem strange, given the apparent strength of sea power over land power in protracted conflict; conflicts protracted in time also tend to be extended in space as the belligerents seek strategically productive uses for forces that cannot otherwise immediately be employed in the search for a military decision. The construction of a continental hegemony so exclusive that the hostile sea power will despair of victory is both policy goal and policy instrument. The continental power desires to build its new order without competition on land. The more geostrategically comprehensive that new order is, the more secure it would be against subversion and challenge by balance-of-power politics organized, subsidized, and otherwise supported by offshore sea power.

This strategy is intended to deprive offshore sea powers of their continental sword. The greatest land powers of modern times—the France of the Directory and Napoleon, Imperial and Nazi Germany, and the Soviet Union of recent decades—variably hoped that *functionally* they could defeat Britain or the United States on land in continental Europe. Certainly France and Germany behaved as if Britain could be so defeated. Traditionally, Britain's ability to allocate a large scale of effort to maritime warfare depended on a healthy balance of power in the military contest on land in Europe. When that balance was upset or temporarily absent, Britain had to concentrate on her coastal waters in order to provide insurance against the danger of invasion. For example, in the summer and fall of 1940, the trade protection mission of the Royal Navy was greatly downgraded because of the need to have light forces available to command the Channel and North Sea against invasion. This direct concentration on home defense produced the first of the "happy times" of easy pickings for Admiral Karl Dönitz's U-boats on the convoy routes.

Unless long-range air and missile power are credited as a practical instrument of military decision, sea power cannot be defeated on land just as land power cannot be defeated at sea. However, war aims do not have to include the definitive overthrow of the enemy. Statecraft often has sought to achieve peace on terms favorable for the renewal of hostilities at some later date; the Treaty of Amiens of March 27, 1802 certainly had this character for the French, as—for a much more recent example—did the Paris Peace Accord of January 23, 1973, for the North Vietnamese. Land powers have aspired to be so successful in continental warfare that Britain would lack any plausible theory of how conflict might be prosecuted effectively, let alone concluded in the future on better terms than those then available. It was as true for Britain in her period as balancer of the European security system, as it was for the United States in the Cold War, that the strategic frontier of sea power was on the Danube, the Rhine, the Elbe, Niemen, or the Ussuri. Sea power could damage the war economies of continental belligerents by blockade, but that damage correlated with the effort the continental enemy was obliged to expend in war on land. Continental land power has never been entirely blockade proof. But a continent-wide hegemony and its corollary, the absence of an active fighting front on land, renders blockade from the sea more of an irritation than a threat. Moreover, economic blockade can backfire on the blockader by generating some solidarity of interests between the land power enemy and her trade-dependent continental neighbors.

French policy in the 1790s and 1800s was to knock the principal continental sword from British hands. The repeated defeats of Austria, Prussia, and Russia caused the precipitate collapse of British policy for the overthrow of France. A century later, both before and after the failure of their long prepared grand design to defeat France in a six-week campaign, the Schlieffen Plan, in August–September 1914, German leaders believed that the swift defeat of France would drive Britain out of the war or, were London still waiting on events, disincline her from entering a hopeless contest. Whether the swift defeat of France also would encompass the defeat of a 100,000-man British Expeditionary Force (BEF) was a matter of little interest in Berlin.[7] In 1917, with her third unrestricted U-boat campaign, the German Navy convinced many politicians and soldiers that it could compel Britain to leave the war within six months. Simultaneously, the U-boats would close the Atlantic to American shipping and effectively deny the United States an active war on land in Europe to which she could contribute, even if her armies could reach there.

Hitler's verbal reaction on September 3, 1939, to the shocking news of Britain's declaration of war was, "What now?"[8] The answer was provided over the next two years in moves that should have been thoroughly familiar to students of Napoleon's struggle with strategically unreachable Britain and Imperial Germany's conduct of two-fronted war over 1914–18. Following the defeat of France in May and June 1940, Hitler persuaded himself that Britain would judge the war unwinnable. Certainly Germany's victories in Scandinavia, the Low Countries, and France had effected a dramatic improvement in Germany's geostrategic position for the conduct of both *guerre de course* and air operations against the British Isles. Perhaps, after the manner of 1801–2, Britain again would elect to come to terms with the dominant, apparently unbeatable, land power. Not without reason, Hitler concluded that Churchill's Britain was fighting on in the hope that something would turn up by way of a major continental or transoceanic but continental-size ally. British reentry into land warfare in Europe would be contingent upon such an ally's turning up and proving to be effective in the prosecution of continental campaigning. This is not to suggest that the invasion of Russia on June 22, 1941, was motivated solely, or even predominantly, by the determination to beat Britain via her only potential continental ally of consequence, but there is no doubt that Hitler understood correctly that British hopes of eventual victory were tied to the prospects for a renewal of coalition warfare.

Napoleon, like Hitler, had many motives for his fatal invasion of Russia in 1812, including a determination so to complete his continental imperium that the offshore sea power would be denied any plausible hope of energizing yet another mixed continental-maritime coalition which might function as a winning combina-

64

tion.[9] Also, the origins of Napoleon's expensive commitment in Spain, his "Spanish ulcer," lay in his efforts to deny Britain economic and military access to the Continent. Britain initiated a five-year war in the Iberian Peninsula to deny Spanish naval assets to Napoleon and to benefit strategically in the maritime war from reliable access to Spanish and Portuguese metropolitan and colonial geography. From century to century and opponent to opponent, the same geostrategic logic for dominant land power has endured: deprive the offshore sea power of the practical possibility of a continental alliance and ensure that it cannot generate the strategic leverage necessary for success in war. This theory is sound; the problem has been that none of the hegemony-bound great land powers in modern times has achieved a total or lasting continental dominance. The patient sea power has always been able to find a land power ally or two.

Great land powers sensibly fearful of the strategic mischief-making potential of insular sea power have been ever attracted to the siren appeal of the amphibious invasion option. Sea powers, used to waging war abroad, are singularly sensitive to the peril of invasion. The strategic leverage of the invasion threat for a land power has been impressive indeed. Invasion threats tend to compel a defensive strategy on the part of a sea power; they ought to be able to coerce that power into a peace settlement and with successful execution can secure a military decision against hostile sea power at home.

   Until nuclear-armed strategic air and missile power rendered the issue all but irrelevant, invasion was a recurring nightmare for British governments.[10] The confidence in the Royal Navy that habitually was reaffirmed by political leaders in public frequently covered acute private anxieties. Politicians often were obliged to show an alarmed populace that they were taking the problem of home defense seriously. In practice this meant constructing coastal fortifications and encouraging the mustering of county militias.[11] Through long experience the Royal Navy evolved a system of strategic deployment that rendered successful invasion very unlikely. However, that system could not be entirely proof against the occasional fool in command or against all exigencies of weather. Furthermore, the deployment system could not be totally proof against unusual skill and luck on the part of an enemy or against British governments which might fatally underprepare the Royal Navy for war. Julian Corbett was correct when he wrote:

> The truth is, that all attempts to invade England without command of the sea have moved in a vicious circle, from which no escape was ever found. No matter how ingenious or complex the enemy's design, a determined hold on their army [blockade of the ports where transports were gathered to carry the invading army] as the primary naval objective has always set up a process of degradation which rendered the enterprise impracticable.[12]

With Olympian logic, Corbett argued that

> an invasion of Great Britain must always be an attempt over an uncommanded sea. It may be that our fleet predominates or it may be that it does not, but the command must always be in dispute. If we have gained complete command, no invasion can take place, nor will it be attempted. If we have lost it completely, no invasion will be necessary, since, quite apart from the threat of invasion, we must make peace on the best terms we can get.[13]

For four hundred years continental enemies utilized invasion threats as a vital part of a policy of coercion against Britain. On many occasions those enemies were serious about their preparations for invasion, and governments in London took the invasion danger at face value or were obliged by public opinion in the capital and in the southern counties to appear to do so. From the 1540s to 1940, there were at least twenty-four occasions when some mix of foreign invasion, foreign raids on a large scale, or foreign insertion of, and support for, rebel elements constituted a present danger to British security. The most readily identifiable years of peril were 1545, 1588, 1596, 1597, 1601, 1643, 1688, 1692, 1708, 1715, 1719, 1744, 1745–46, 1756, 1759, 1762, 1779, 1796, 1797, 1798, 1803, 1804, 1805, and 1940.[14] It was no accident that no true invasion succeeded.[15] A happy mixture of geography and judicious naval deployments rendered Britain as secure against invasion as reasonably could be asked. The navigational conditions in the Channel and the absence prior to the 1850s (when Cherbourg was deepened and fortified) of a major deep-water port on the continental littoral between Brest and Antwerp were exploited successfully by a consistently applied British maritime defense that typically was in the hands of expert naval strategists and tacticians.

At the beginning of the modern period, a French fleet of 225 ships commanded the Channel in 1545 and conducted a raid against Portsmouth and the Isle of Wight. In the Second Dutch War, the Dutch naval commander, Admiral Michiel de Ruyter, had he had an army and been so motivated, could have invaded England in the summer of 1667, since he commanded the Thames estuary for six weeks. During the Glorious Revolution, Lord Dartmouth, through ill deployment of the fleet, was unable to prevent William of Orange's invading England successfully in 1688. With an east wind, the English fleet in the Thames estuary was unable to weather the North Foreland of Kent and follow the Dutch invasion fleet into the Channel. The deeper problem, apart from political ambivalence in the fleet, was that after the fashion of a gallery of later French admirals, Dartmouth saw his fleet as a "sacred trust" that should be kept "in being" and not hazarded in an inclement season on a hazardous enterprise.

In 1690, 1779, and 1796, French naval power briefly enjoyed command in the Channel, the sufficient condition for an invasion attempt. At least in principle, Napoleon's grand design of March 2, 1805, which launched what became the Trafalgar campaign, may not have been quite as foredoomed to failure as most historians have argued.[16] In practice, however, French commanders lacked the confidence and competence to make the design work, particularly since they functioned unduly as instruments of Napoleon's territorially shaped strategic conceptions. To be fair to Napoleon, Villeneuve, the fleet commander, was all but incapable of taking bold initiatives or seizing such opportunities as fortune might bequeath. Nonetheless, hopelessly "military," at least nonmaritime, though his grand campaign design appeared to be, the seriousness of Napoleon's intent to invade England in 1804–5 cannot be doubted. He did not gather and keep in prolonged idleness 167,000 men of his projected invasion army, construct a vast flotilla of specialized invasion craft, and fortify and improve every port from Flushing to Dieppe as a bluff. Napoleon moved upon Austria in what was to become his masterly Ülm campaign only after he was convinced in early August that his navy could not play its assigned role to cover an invasion. J. Holland Rose summed up the French problem when he wrote that "he [Napoleon] and his admirals were beginners in the great game at which Barham, Nelson, Cornwallis, and Collingwood were past masters, primed with the experience of a century."[17] By the time of his death at Trafalgar on October 21, 1805, Nelson had seen no fewer than sixteen years of *wartime* service against the French.

One hundred and thirty-five years later, Hitler's highly contingent commitment to the invasion of Britain in the late summer of 1940 was rather more problematical than had been Napoleon's in 1804–5. In retrospect, Hitler's failure of nerve in the summer of 1940 ultimately proved fatal to his Third Reich, but his decision not to chance an invasion was defensible at the time. Skepticism persists over the seriousness of Hitler's invasion intentions in 1940. Israeli military historian Jehuda L. Wallach, a recent disbeliever, proceeds logically from the view that "the military and political outlook of Hitler, the foot soldier of the First World War, was confined to the continent" to the conclusion that "Hitler saw *Sea Lion* [code name for the projected invasion] as an excellent expedient [to keep "Britain quiet as long as Germany was occupied in the East"] but nothing else! Such a step fitted entirely into the framework of all Hitler's previous bluffs."[18] Wallach's logic and empathy for a continental mind-set are certainly impressive. Nevertheless, the evidence for Sea Lion's being serious business also is distinctly impressive. In by far the most persuasive analysis of Sea Lion, written by a contemporary German naval planner, the three-point case against the invasion's being a bluff virtually settles the argument:

> The senior officers of the Army and Navy were convinced that they were planning a real operation and it would have been impossible to hoodwink them to such an extent. There is the evidence of the economic disruption caused by the wholesale requisitioning of the barges of the inland water transport system which Hitler accepted. There is the wholesale commitment of the invaluable Air Force to a costly battle for air superiority. Hitler would never have used it so recklessly had he only been toying with the idea of invasion.[19]

On the rare occasions when British naval power lost command of its coastal waters, the country was saved from invasion by the limited ambitions of the enemy (to raid and coerce by the threat of further landings), by his incompetence (having secured command, what to do with it), and by the residual, if shaky, benefit of a fleet-in-being strategy. The principal danger was that an atypically bold, even reckless, continental leader would gamble on attempting an invasion over an uncommanded sea and would succeed against the odds. Even if the Royal Navy could isolate an invading force that landed in Britain, no government in London could afford to be complacent about the threat that, say, three of Napoleon's veteran army corps under Marshals Davout, Soult, and Ney would pose once ashore. The continental enemy did not require *command* of the Narrow Seas in order functionally to defeat the Royal Navy via success on land. In his correspondence, Napoleon stated rhetorically, if with great exaggeration, "Let us be masters of the Strait [Dover] for six hours and we shall be masters of the world."[20] Subsequently, he amended his time requirement for mastery of the Strait of Dover, first to three days and later to fifteen. The danger was that a sufficiently desperate Napoleon or Hitler might be willing to lose his battle fleet (and, in Hitler's case, a large fraction of his air force) as a price worth paying for tolerably safe passage for a large invasion force. Local command of the Strait of Dover for a forty-eight-hour period might have sufficed for the insertion into Britain of a continental army able to conclude the war in short order.

The lack of success of Britain's continental enemies over the centuries in their dozens of invasion designs was matched fully by the consistency of alarm that appreciation and misappreciation of those designs occasioned in Britain. Earl St. Vincent, First Lord of the Admiralty, offered in 1803 the oft-quoted assurance that the French "will not come by sea." But the responsible commander at sea (of the North Sea Fleet), Admiral Lord Keith, who was scarcely less distinguished an admiral than St. Vincent, was not quite so sanguine. In reply to questions posed by the Commander-in-Chief of the Army, the duke of York, about the practicality of a French invasion, Keith concluded a careful and detailed analysis with the following judgment:

> I therefore hazard a possible, although not a very probable, conjecture which is that a Fleet or Squadron may get out of Brest unperceived and watch an opportunity for running up the Downs and Margate Road, in which case it might be superior to our squadron long enough to cover the landing of any extent of Force from

the opposite coast; and might then escape through the North Sea or run off the Dutch Ports, and from thence protect an Embarkation of Troops to Scotland.[21]

As a hedge against the Royal Navy's being evaded, lured away from its pivot positions, caught with a temporary deficiency in force in a key blockading location,[22] or simply thwarted by contrary winds, after 1806 the British government constructed a formidable new system of fortification on the south coast.[23] Functioning synergistically with sea power, this new positional strength on land was intended to ensure that any invading force would be so delayed at the water's edge that achievement of a fleeting period of maritime command would not suffice for the purpose of throwing an army ashore. Programs of coastal fortification also were pursued later in the nineteenth century in the wake of the brief invasion panics of 1846–47, 1851, and 1859. The 1880s, 1890s, and 1900s saw reruns in Britain of the familiar debate over invasion perils. The issue was whether the solution to the menace of invasion should be entirely maritime, in the form of a Royal Navy in which entire confidence should be reposed, or whether the Navy required supplementing with energetic and expensive projects of home defense on land. As a policy matter the blue-water school of home defense repeatedly won the day. The newly created Committee on Imperial Defence (CID) studied the invasion problem three times in the years preceding the First World War—in 1903, 1908, and 1913—and thrice concluded that command at sea was virtually all of the protection that Britain required. Unsurprisingly, the 1913 study offered among its conclusions the canonical point "that if we permanently lose command of the sea, whatever may be the strength and organization of the Home force, the *position of the country would be desperate*."[24] Since the Royal Navy could not guarantee to preclude the stealthy passage of a small invading force, the CID concluded that the home defenses should be capable of dealing with an invader 70,000 strong.

The strategic leverage to the continental enemies of Britain of simulated or real invasion threats is easy to identify. Britain would be obliged to concentrate her sea and land forces at home or in home coastal waters, thereby losing the freedom of action to make offensive or defensive use of her maritime command in distant regions. As an offshore sea power, Britain was not accustomed to the conduct of war at home, at least not against invading foreigners. Long-standing enjoyment of command at sea meant that foreign wars were fought abroad. Spain, France, and Germany never succeeded in so manipulating credible threats of invasion that British policy shifted to a stance of political accommodation. England was truly strategically helpless only once in the course of four centuries—in the summer of 1667. Fortunately, the enemy that commanded the Thames and the Medway was Holland, with limited war aims.

The direct protection provided for British seaborne trade and colonies invariably was diminished by the concentration of the British battle fleet in the Narrow Seas. Of course, blockade of the enemy's principal naval bases reduced radically the scale of force that prudently he could send to sea. The enemy was watched closely off Brest, Toulon, and the Scheldt or distantly from Torbay, the Nore, or Scapa Flow (or Port Mahon), with cruiser and light flotilla forces maintaining as close a vigil off the potential invasion ports as the weather and enemy enterprise permitted. Because maritime command was ever penetrable by single ships or small squadrons and because the continental enemy was obliged to disperse in order to achieve success at sea, invasion threats encouraged commerce raiding. Although commerce raiding has never achieved decision for a continental naval power, it contributes to war weariness. That weariness is a function of the pain and expense of protracted conflict and, even more, the belief that the government lacks a plausible theory of eventual victory. It matters whether a compromise, if on balance unfavorable, peace is deemed tolerable with the particular enemy of the day. In 1801–2 and in 1940, Britain was locked in a strategic standoff with hostile land power. In 1801–2, however, the idea of peace with the first stable government Paris had seen in more than a decade (the Consulate) was popular in Britain. In 1940, by contrast, the idea of an immediate compromise peace with Nazi Germany was thoroughly politically illegitimate.

Geostrategic detail varies significantly with individual cases, but the central point advanced here applies across all of history. In theory, the continental power or coalition has the option of taking the war to the sea power enemy at home. That enemy may not be as self-evidently insular as Britain, but a virtual insularity was achieved by Athens, Byzantium, Venice, and the Netherlands. The dukes of Alba and Parma, for example, discovered in their attempted reconquest of what nominally was the Spanish Netherlands in the late 1560s, the 1570s, and the 1580s that the country comprised what amounted to a fortified archipelago.[25]

The geographical particulars are critically important. It matters greatly whether preponderant sea power is based on an island only twenty miles at the nearest point from Europe or on a continent three thousand miles distant from hostile land power. In theory, at least, the issue is the same: Can preponderant continental power achieve leverage through menaces to the sea power's homeland? The advent of long-range air and missile power married to weapons of mass destruction has provided tactical, but not strategic, solutions to the problems of transoceanic reach by continental power. Mutual deterrence negates the value of the new long-range striking power, as, increasingly, will active air and missile defenses.

If amphibious invasion is impracticable or unduly risky, given the stakes in a conflict, a dominant land power can pursue the strategy of continental hostage taking to secure leverage for bargaining in peace negotiations. This is an example of a land power's doing what it is able with its military instrument of excellence. There need be no hope that the seizing of continental hostages will yield a decisive strategic leverage vis-à-vis the maritime enemy, but such a strategy can hardly fail to be helpful. A continental power cannot overthrow a sea power by success on land, but it can perform so well that the gains of the sea power that flow from exploitation of maritime command are overmatched in relative value. The negotiating value of the benefits secured by commanding sea power varies extensively with the opponent and the historical period. A continental power would like to take to the sea and defeat the maritime enemy in that enemy's own medium. In such a favorable situation, achieved, for example, by Sparta with Persian assistance and by Rome in the First Punic War, "peace" terms (of surrender) can be dictated. More often, however, great sea and land powers in conflict have neither sought nor achieved the complete military overthrow of their enemy, at least not in a single phase in what could be a long struggle. Preponderant land power seizes what it can on the continent, while commanding sea power does the same with enemy assets that lie behind its maritime strategic frontier.

Only once in modern times did Britain negotiate a peace treaty with an enemy as powerful on land as Britain was powerful at sea: the Treaty of Amiens of 1802. Following Sir James Saumarez's brilliant victory off Algeçiras in July 1801, Britain faced no naval challenge from France or from such French allies as Spain, Holland, and Denmark. The strategic standoff between victorious French land power and victorious British sea power was comprehensive. In 1801–2 Britain wanted peace; France wanted a period of armistice for recuperation, reorganization, and naval rebuilding. The terms of the Preliminary Articles and of the Treaty of Amiens were weighted overwhelmingly in favor of France, although they were not disastrous for British national security in their overall effect. The British experience with the Peace of Amiens provides a dramatic example of the unequal value of the "hostages" that can be taken by superior land power as compared with those at risk to superior sea power, at least in the era of European domination of the international system. Britain's policy intention in all of her wars with France was to have continental allies able to perform well enough on land so that Britain would not have to disgorge much of importance among her overseas gains in the eventual peace negotiations. The preferred continental ally was Austria in the first half of the eighteenth century, Prussia in the 1750s and 1760s, and later Austria again, with Russia playing an irregularly but increasingly critical role from the later 1790s until Napoleon's final defeat. Complete failure on land by 1801 meant the defeat of Britain's traditional, mixed maritime-continental strategy. In return for the surrender of virtually all of Britain's winnings overseas, Napoleon was able to give London the appearance of peace that British public opinion demanded in what had become, of necessity, a very limited war.

The continental hostage problem for the offshore sea power that was such a perennial factor in British coalition strategy lived again in the debate over the U.S. Navy's maritime strategy in the 1980s. Some critics of the strategy suggested that the United States was preparing a very poor "exchange" of Soviet overseas clients in return for the loss of NATO-Europe.[26] Such was not the case, but the critics did emphasize accurately enough a geostrategic asymmetry of some importance. In modern times, sea power has never been able to secure overseas hostages equal in value to the whole

73

of a Europe held in thrall by temporarily matchless land power. This judgment can be applied to a range of continental powers with widely varying degrees of economic vulnerability to maritime pressure. The asymmetry of value as between maritime and continental hostages is a fact appreciated in English statecraft since the late 1560s. For example, even had English ships enjoyed major success in implementing a silver blockade against Spain in the 1580s, more than two-thirds of Spanish imperial revenue derived from Castile.[27] The remaining one-quarter to one-third was very important to Spain's solvency, but it did not equate with the full financial strength of the Habsburg Empire.

The hall of fame of statesmen sensible of the proper wartime uses of a navy has had no more distinguished a member than WIlliam Pitt the Elder. He dispatched a British army to fight in Germany in the Seven Years' War, because he realized that the profit and strategic rewards of success in maritime warfare could be more than offset by disaster on the Continent. Save rarely, and then either of necessity or in error, Britain never pursued a purely blue-water maritime strategy vis-à-vis Spain, France, or Germany, any more than did the United States vis-à-vis the Soviet Union in the Cold War. There is a persisting complementarity of maritime and continental components in military strategy. Where error creeps in is with unjustified discounting of the strategic utility of sea power *as a team player* and with the confusion of the strong desirability of a mixed continental-maritime strategy with an alleged strict necessity.

During the Cold War the Soviet Union provided no hostages in her overseas imperium remotely comparable in economic, political, or geostrategic value to the worth of Western Europe to the United States. Moreover, that imperium was not comparable in war economy value to the sugar and spice islands and the North Atlantic fisheries of France (and Spain and the Netherlands) in the eighteenth century. But the relative value of a Europe supposedly hostage to Soviet land power was vastly reduced by the facts of global economic, political, and military modernization. U.S. sea power could not have taken or otherwise neutralized (by bribe, blockade, or threats to punish) Soviet hostages overseas with a realistic view to provide a strong position for a hostage-trading exercise in negotiated war termination. But the world that U.S. sea power could have kept out of Soviet strategic reach was much

74

more important in all categories of relative power assessment than was the case in the heyday of British naval mastery. In 1801–2 French armies controlled the land world that counted in the balance of power.

An aggressive, would-be hegemonic land power virtually always seizes territory in the opening campaigns of a war, gains that have military value in the war underway and perhaps strategic value if the goal of the war is the improvement of position in a long-term struggle. In addition, territorial acquisition can acquire symbolic and prestige value for the aggressor who expended blood and treasure to acquire it.

The United States could no more have tolerated Soviet, or any other, hegemony in Europe than Britain could acquiesce either in German control of Belgium in the First World War or of German control of the coasts of France, the Low Countries, Denmark, and Norway in the Second. Then Secretary of Defense, Caspar Weinberger wrote that "the United States simply could not live in a world in which Western Europe was under Soviet domination or had become politically neutralized through Soviet intimidation."[28] In common with Republican and then Napoleonic France, and Imperial and Nazi Germany, it was prudent to assume that a Soviet Union militarily on the move in Europe was seeking to secure a lasting improvement in relative power position. Territory conquered or otherwise suborned would be a hostage only in the context of negotiations for war termination.

Territorial hostage taking by a land power obliges opposing states to attempt forcibly to retake the lost territory or to be able to exchange something for its return of comparable value to the conqueror. A sea power could choose to acquiesce in the loss of a continental interest. The more formidable is the land power that can be assembled by a maritime coalition for the opening campaign of a war, the fewer the hostages a continental enemy is likely to seize and the more tractable should be the problems of negotiating for peace.

A dominant land power may seek through maritime ambush to defeat an insular naval power that is superior overall but may be overcome sequentially in detail. The navy of a continental power will seek to avoid a full-scale fleet engagement that could only result in its precipitate destruction yet still strike aggressively to

75

engage detached units and squadrons of the enemy in circumstances of strong local advantage. With its second-class naval
power more or less well protected in coastal bastions, a land power
can entertain the hope that the sea power enemy will accept imprudent risks in order to attempt to bring on a decisive fight at sea.
The probable fact that the navy of the sea power enemy will be
heir to an offensive tradition in strategy should be key to the
prospects for success of this idea. If the commanding power at sea
declines to hazard its battle fleet in circumstances of great tactical
disadvantage, still that power may have its superiority whittled
away by the attrition suffered through overconfidence in a series of
relatively minor engagements. Poor fleet deployment and handling
or ill fortune may produce an effective equalization of material
strength. Thus can the fleet in being of a second-class naval power
pose a permanent hazard to the security of maritime command.

Prior to August 1914 the German Navy had persuaded itself
that Britain's Royal Navy, in some modern variant of Hawke's
behavior at Quiberon Bay (1759) or Nelson's at the Nile (1798)
and Copenhagen (1801), would seek decisive battle wherever the
High Seas Fleet chose to lurk.[29] The Germans harbored the comforting illusion that the material insufficiency of the battle line
with which they entered the war with Britain would decline dramatically as Admiral Jellicoe sought to establish his credentials as
a worthy successor to Nelson, Hawke, and Drake. Jellicoe was
expect to press his battle cruisers and battleships deep into the
Heligoland Bight in search of the German fleet, braving minefields,
submarine ambush lines, destroyer torpedo attacks, and fire from
long-range coastal artillery.[30] The Germans anticipated that, contrary to all contemporary tactical reason, the Royal Navy would
blow the dust off its traditional practice of close blockade and
attempt to watch the Jade, Elbe, and Ems estuaries as closely as
Brest and Toulon had been watched in centuries past. The German
misassessment of the Royal Navy's proclivity for reckless behavior
was reciprocated fully on the British side. In Arthur Marder's
words, "One thing was never in dispute. The Admiralty expected
that the High Seas Fleet would seek battle on the outbreak of war.
The British Fleet would endeavor to oblige it."[31]

In 1914, however, the Royal Navy, for all its deficiencies as a
fighting instrument, understood the implications of new technologies for the hazards to capital ships. Fleet exercises in 1901,

1902, and 1904, had suggested powerfully the growing dangers of close blockade, and by 1912, the last remains of Admiralty operational interest in the close blockade of the estuaries had evaporated. Moreover, Germany had greatly strengthened the defenses of Heligoland and had fortified the Frisian Islands, thereby denying the Royal Navy any prospect of securing a near offshore base on which to anchor close blockading squadrons.*

Lures and ambushes are possibilities both for the blockader and the blockaded. A superior naval power may leave too weak a blockading squadron off an enemy's main fleet base or may seek to lure a fleet in being to sea with the prospect of a cheap victory, only to find that superior force cannot be concentrated in time to prevent the enemy's securing an easy success. But an inferior naval power may overreach itself in its attempts to engineer ambushes at sea. The Royal Navy always recognized the possibility that a blockading fleet might be caught at a numerical disadvantage. However, as certainly was the case in August in 1805 off Brest, it was anticipated that a numerically disadvantaged British force would give so punishing an account of itself in battle that the would-be blockade-breaking enemy would be in no fit state to accomplish anything for many months thereafter. As Nelson wrote to Captain Richard Keats on August 24, 1805, "This I ventured without any fear, that if Calder got fairly close along-side them with twenty-seven or twenty-eight sail, by the time the enemy had beat our fleet soundly they would do us no harm this year."[32]

A second-class naval power in search of limited victory by stratagems is in peril to the power of uncertainty in war. Because of the success of the Royal Navy in breaking German naval codes in the First World War, the strategy of seeking to defeat isolated squadrons of the Grand Fleet by ambush was far more hazardous to the ambusher than to the intended victim. That intended victim ad-

---

* The close blockade had been a tradition since the time of Hawke's watch on Brest in 1759. For reason of lack of strength the practice was not followed in the war with France from 1778 to 1783, with disastrous consequences in North America and near-disastrous consequences for the security of Gibraltar. In modern times, the Dutch, in the 1560s, fairly effectively closed the Spanish Netherlands to maritime resupply and reinforcement. In the ancient world, close blockade was feasible only if the blockaded port also was invested on land. Blockading vessels in the days of galley warfare lacked the sea-keeping qualities necessary to maintain a vigil off a hostile shoreline—a problem that returned with the need for coal and then oil in the age of steam.

mittedly stood to lose the most at sea—surface command—a calculation critical for tolerable German safety in this dangerous game. *If*, early in the war, the Royal Navy had had a much better system for the rapid dissemination of operational intelligence; *if* it had been more competent in signaling at sea; *if* its armor-piercing shells had been less sensitive; and *if* its command style could have been more Nelsonian, German stratagems to lure British battle cruisers to destruction probably would have resulted in the replay of Trafalgar which the British public expected. This is a powerful accumulation of ifs, albeit only a short list. Nonetheless, with better intelligence, Jellicoe probably would have brought the High Seas Fleet to a definitive renewal of climactic battle on June 1, 1916 (Jutland was waged on May 31).

Maritime ambush does not have a distinguished record of accomplishment against the Royal Navy. The subject here is the strategy of ambush as a prudent means for wresting maritime command, by degree, from the preponderant sea power. The French Navy did not endorse this purpose as a general rule. It typically sought to evade sea fights in war after war from the 1680s to the 1810s, even in favorable tactical circumstances. The French sought to apply their generally inferior naval power directly to the mission of supporting military enterprises on land. This was not true of the Navy of Imperial Germany. The High Seas Fleet was trapped in the dilemma that it had a doctrine of decisive battle for command of the sea, while its enduring inferiority in practice denied it any realistic prospect of success in such a rash venture.

A second-class naval power can aspire by cunning cumulatively to erode the enemy's fighting strength at sea. The second-class naval power usually will be of a continental kind, but this is not invariably the case. In June 1942, the U.S. Navy won the most important battle in its history with the ambush of the Imperial Japanese fleet at Midway. Would-be naval ambushers have a number of tactical ploys they can try. For example, they can attempt to lure the superior navy into what that navy anticipates as a decisive fleet engagement, in tactical conditions where the inferior fleet can count upon massive equalizing assistance from what amounts to a fortified "battlefield" at sea in coastal bastions. The superior naval power would be enticed by the prospect of dealing a fatal blow to the enemy's fleet in being—into effecting the maritime equivalent of the Charge of the Light Brigade at Balaclava (October 1854), or the attack of Erich von Manstein's Fourth Panzer Army at Kursk (July 1943). The fleet in being would hope that the moral ascendancy of the superior navy would manifest itself as an imprudent disdain for the enemy's determination, skill, and position. Next, an inferior fleet can aspire to achieve a surprise concentration of force at sea against locally inferior elements of the enemy's fleet. This briefly was what Scheer believed he was doing at Jutland.

Further, a second-class fleet can try to lure the superior naval power into a dispersion of force upon distant missions, enabling the inferior navy to strike successfully at the much weakened covering forces of the enemy's blockade. In 1805 Nelson had to guess whither Villeneuve was bound and for what ultimate purpose, once he had slipped unobserved out of Toulon. In the 1914–18 war a century later, the Royal Navy, ever mindful of its overriding duty never to lose its strategic grip on the High Seas Fleet, was always reluctant to weaken the Grand Fleet in home waters in favor of distant enterprises. A second-class fleet, however, can seek to weaken the superior naval power in detail through a succession of submarine and mine (today, and air and missile) ambushes. Although the sea power of a maritime-dependent alliance rests upon a large number of naval and merchant vessels, the order of battle in capital assets is always few in numbers. By mines and submarine ambush off Scapa Flow, the Germans might have shaved Jellicoe's battle-line advantage down to a manageable challenge for the High Seas Fleet. The U.S. Navy today is at least as prudent in the tactical risks it elects to take with its fleet carriers as was Jellicoe with his battleships and battle cruisers.

Maritime ambush is an unpromising strategy for a disadvantaged continental naval power but is always a source of anxiety for the superior sea power. Through surprise, competence, and luck, a fleet in being has the potential to improve its competitive position dramatically. A maritime coalition at war will have many geographically disparate tasks for finite naval assets to perform. Enemy naval power left in being may be used unexpectedly to achieve some local success. Several local successes could result in the cumulative erosion, perhaps even the loss, of maritime surface command.

*   *   *

The classic weapon of the relatively weak at sea is the waging of war upon merchant shipping. The aim is to damage or defeat the war economy of a maritime enemy, induce war weariness, and harass, interrupt, or close the sea lines of communication. The strategy and even some of the tactics of trade warfare and trade protection have been as constant over the centuries as have the policy motives of the combatants, with one caveat: until the last century, the capture of enemy vessels at sea could be personally profitable to the captors. During the classic age of sail, naval officers were ever tempted to neglect their military duties in pursuit of personal profit. During the three Dutch wars of the seventeenth century, for example, one of the important reasons that effective blockade of the enemy's naval and privateering power was so difficult to implement was the desire of officers and men alike to become rich from taking Dutch mercantile "prizes." For the fighting men afloat, there was far greater fortune to be obtained from the capture of the enemy's commerce than there was from the protection of friendly ships.

Only rarely has a continental power begun a war firmly determined to exert pressure upon a maritime enemy's seaborne commerce as the preferred theory of victory. This is strange to note, because the nominal vulnerability of sea powers to economic and military-logistic defeat via *guerre de course* has been a permanent feature in the structure of land power–sea power competition. Trade warfare become the primary instrument of German strategy in its war against Britain, and later the United States in World War II, as the new school of German naval theorists had advocated vociferously in the interwar era.[33] But, Hitler's liking for capital ships, his basic incomprehension of sea power, and the fact that war with Britain occurred many years too soon for the maturing of the wildly ambitious Z Plan fleet meant that in 1939–40 Nazi Germany had no suitable instrument for the conduct of *guerre de course* or surface fleet that could challenge for military command. Germany turned belatedly to its U-boats to deliver victory in 1942–43. In practice, Dönitz's U-boat arm was the last shot in Germany's locker. The Luftwaffe failed in the Battle of Britain, Admiral Raeder's major surface vessels had found early in 1941 that they could be unleashed onto the North Atlantic shipping lanes only to their own destruction, and the Army failed to knock Britain's Russian sword from her hand. Fortunately for the Grand

Alliance, Hitler did not comprehend that the North Atlantic convoys comprised "the heartbeat of the war."[34]

Great land powers persistently fail to understand that a large but distinctly second-class battle fleet yields strategic benefits disproportionately small compared with the effort required for its construction and maintenance. But naval strength applied against the shipping of a maritime power or coalition yields strategic benefits disproportionately large compared with the effort committed. It has been a general truth, in the age of sail as in the age of steam, that the direct protection of maritime trade—indeed of sea lines of communication in general—requires the commitment of far greater effort than does the attack upon it.[35] This is the primary reason that the navies of dominant sea powers always have been attracted to schemes to go after a commerce-raiding foe at source.

The British record in trade protection over three centuries was unimpressive. Time and again the Royal Navy did well enough, but both naval and commercial circles persisted in committing the cardinal error of refusing to convoy or refusing to convoy on a sufficiently comprehensive basis. Even when convoying was introduced promptly with the onset of war, as in 1939, the Royal Navy dissipated scarce naval strength upon fruitless offensive sweeps rather than provide more powerful convoy escort groups. This is not to say that an offensive naval strategy was in error. On the contrary, the most cost-effective means of containing the trade protection problem was either aggressively to bring the enemy's naval strength to battle or to stop up his bases by a more or less close blockade. However, throughout its French and German wars, from the 1680s until the 1940s, the Royal Navy simply could not mount an effective blockade against the commerce raiders of continental naval power.

From the first of its modern French wars (1688–97) until the second of its German ones, the Royal Navy rarely succeeded in reducing the problem of trade protection below the level of a significant and very expensive nuisance. Indeed, on occasions losses to the merchant marine were sufficiently serious as *potentially* to imperil the steadiness of state policy. This was true, for example, in the last years of the Nine Years' War after the Battle of La Hogue-Barfleur in 1692, during the War of Spanish Succession following the Battle of Malaga (August 24, 1704), throughout the French Revolutionary and Napoleonic wars, though particularly in 1807–8 and 1810–12, in 1917, and in fall 1940, spring 1941, and much of 1942. In war after war, the security of Britain's seaborne trade reposed to an important degree on its sheer size and dispersion among many hulls. For example, although the French captured almost 11,000 British ships between 1793 and 1815, the annual average number of sailings and arrivals was on the order of 13,000 to 14,000.[36]

As a strategy for a continental power unable to achieve command at sea, commerce raiding has been as inevitable as in this century it has increased dramatically in its potential to deliver victory. It is interesting to compare what J. R. Jones has written of French limited ambitions for their *guerre de course* with Britain in the early 1690s, though his points pertain to all of the Franco-British contests, with the unlimited purposes that motivated the U-boat campaigns of this century:

> Naval historians who wrote before 1914, that is before the U-boat campaigns that twice brought Britain to the verge of defeat, tended to dismiss the French privateering war (the *guerre de course*) as futile because it was based on a fallacious strategy that could never bring victory. In fact the French never expected it to produce total victory. Their attacks were intended to provoke war-weariness and defeatism, to induce mercantile and commercial interests (which Louis, wrongly, believed to possess as much influence in England as in Holland) to put pressure on William to make peace at almost any price.[37]

Twice in this century, Germany's U-boats were promised by their service chiefs to be instruments of victory. The technological-tactical-intelligence balance that for long periods favored the U-boat, married to a war aim of military overthrow, suffice to explain the unlimited stakes in the war against seaborne commerce. The U-boats were decisively beaten in their second great campaign in the North Atlantic in World War II, in the winter of 1942–43, by a mix of factors that included Bletchley Park's (Ultra) breaking in December 1942 of the four-wheel Enigma "Shark" code used by Dönitz for the shore-based, operational control of his wolfpacks[38] and by the sheer quantity of new U.S. ship construction. The increasing provision of very long-range aerial escort of and surveillance for convoys, also was important. In addition, improved ship and airborne radar, new tactics by escort support groups, and the dilution of combat skill among U-boat crews caused by heavy losses all played parts.

Britain contributed greatly to her own good fortune in World War II. But it is well to remember that the second Battle of the Atlantic could have been lost and, with it, the war. If the 1,161 U-boats that Germany had in commission at different times from September 3, 1939, until May 7, 1945, had peaked in their availability for oceanic duty in 1940–41, instead of 1943 and had Ultra operational intelligence not been available in the spring of 1943, the Allied invasions of North Africa, Sicily, Italy and France would not have been feasible. At the beginning of the war, Dönitz had only 21 oceangoing U-boats at sea (80 percent of the total oceangoing force); early in May 1943 operational deployment peaked at 128 boats (with more than 60 of them in the North Atlantic).[39] Cajus Bekker was at least half correct when he wrote that "Germany's defeat at sea was the one which irretrievably lost her the war."[40] It would be more accurate to claim that Germany's failure to defeat Britain at sea was the one failure which irretrievably lost her the war because British sea power kept Britain in the war and led Hitler to the fatal error of waging a two-front conflict. The persistence of British belligerency also provided the offshore base through which U.S. resources could be brought to bear for the war to be reopened in the West on land and from which a strategic air offensive against the Reich could be prosecuted. Bekker's judgment from the German side was matched by these words of Winston Churchill:

> The Battle of the Atlantic was the dominating factor all through the war. Never for one moment could we forget that everything happening elsewhere, on land, at sea, or in the air, depended ultimately on its outcome, and amid all other cares we viewed its changing fortunes day by day with hope or apprehension.[41]

There is good reason to question John Terraine's judgment when he writes that "the undoubted victory at sea [over the U-boats by May 1943] did not decide the issue of the war—that had been decided already, indeed it would be said that it had been decided from the first moments of BARBAROSSA [June 22, 1941]."[42] Although ultimately Nazi Germany could be defeated on land in the East only by another great continental power, that defeat could

83

not have been contrived had the Western Allies failed to hold command at sea.

One commerce-raiding campaign did succeed against a major sea power. The Empire of Japan was a maritime power, notwithstanding the fact that her geostrategic ambitions were principally continental,[43] and she was defeated decisively in the war of attrition conducted against her mercantile marine. Japan lacked industrialization in depth; she could not replace wartime losses of shipping. Also, her material deficiencies were compounded in their potential for disaster by a faulty naval doctrine. Japan launched no new destroyer escorts between 1941 and 1943 for the protection of the inadequate merchant marine that was available, while, overall, an offensive battle-minded naval doctrine disdained such a lowly mission as the protection of mercantile shipping. The statistics of Japan's loss of merchant shipping are the statistics of national defeat:[44]

JAPAN'S MERCHANT SHIPPING (IN TONS)

Japan's merchant shipping on December 7, 1941	6,051,660
Captured from the Allies by mid-1942	1,250,000
New construction in wartime	3,293,314
	10,594,974
Lost to enemy action (all causes)	8,618,234
	2,076,740

Submarine action was the cause of 4,889,000 tons of the loss. The decision to go to war cost Japan the services of 4,000,000 tons of foreign merchant shipping, for a net loss, after captures, of 2,750,000 tons. Imperial Japan was both extraordinarily vulnerable to attrition of its seaborne commerce and was monumentally irresponsible in its operational handling of that commerce in wartime. Nonetheless, the U.S. Navy's campaign against Japanese trade stands as an object lesson in the potential for defeat at sea endemic to maritime power. Great land powers prefer to place wartime policy trust in the more traditional of their military instruments, but since maritime enemies cannot be defeated conclusively on land, continental states repeatedly have taken to the sea in the only manner militarily feasible, which is to say dispersed for the raiding of commerce. In this century to date, the *guerre de*

84

course, although applied too late and with too little, has had a strategic promise unparalleled in modern history.

If the economy of a maritime enemy cannot be defeated by commerce raiding at sea, a dominant land power can aspire to achieve the same result by the closing of continental markets to the trade of the sea power—a variant of the strategy of conquering the sea by control on land. For example, during the Napoleonic Wars, continental markets were closed to British trade and to trade carried by British ships, by ships that had submitted to British search, and by ships that had entered any British or British colonial port. These nominally draconian measures of economic warfare comprised the heart of Napoleon's Berlin and Milan Decrees (of November 21, 1806, and November 23 and December 17, 1807, respectively), known collectively as the Continental System.[45] Unfortunately for Napoleon, his landlocked continental empire could not endure in tolerable comfort in the absence of British manufactured goods or of the colonial produce access to which was controlled by the Royal Navy.

The closing of continental markets to the trade of a sea power can be only as effective a policy as the dependence of the sea power upon those markets allows and as proves to be enforceable. To work, the policy of continental exclusion requires the sea power to be unable to find extracontinental substitute markets and to be willing to settle for an unfavorable peace settlement. Also, it is important that the execution of the policy of blockade should not wreak more strategic damage upon the executor than upon the maritime enemy. Whether a bid for continental exclusion is moved in the near term by motives of military or economic strategy, to date in modern history the result has been the placing of an insupportable burden upon continental empire.

It would be wrong to suppose that the reciprocal Anglo-French economic warfare of the years after 1806 was a matter of scant significance for Britain. Nothing could be further from the truth. A combination of French policy (the Continental System) and American reaction (the Non-Intercourse Act of 1809, in particular) to Britain's response (the Orders in Council of 1807) to that French policy produced a major economic crisis for Britain in the period 1810–12, though admittedly that crisis had been slow in coming. The Continental System was not pursued rigorously until late

1807. After 1808, however, the Peninsular War opened some of Spain, most of Portugal, and all of their colonies to British trade. For a while at least, official American annoyance with Britain's practices toward her trade with the French Empire and with neutral ports in Europe was more than offset by the commercial self-interest of maritime America in cooperation with British policy. Nonetheless, 1810–12 were very bad years for Britain, marked by regional economic depression, particularly in newly industrial Lancashire, and widespread social unrest.

It was Napoleon's misfortune that, vulnerable though the British economy was to embargoes on her overseas trade, the relatively high value and low bulk of much of that trade rendered it singularly suitable for more or less clandestine entry into continental Europe. The economic warfare Napoleon had unleashed exposed more serious grand-strategic frailties on the part of his empire than on that of the maritime foe. Napoleon hoped to provoke Britain into such imperious measures of maritime control that the neutrals would do much of France's strategic job for her. For her part, Britain aspired to establish and use a maritime monopoly to foment continental revolt against France. Both aspirations were reasonable and to a degree successful. But ultimately and certainly most profoundly, "the Continental Blockade strangled the Continental System."[46]

By 1812, Napoleon believed that in order to defeat Britain on his western flank, he first had to reduce Russia to complete submission. The Continental System, like all other barrier concepts, had to be comprehensive or risk falling far short of insupportable annoyance to British commerce. In good part, the logistically impracticable Russian adventure of 1812 was a consequence of Czar Alexander I's 1810 defection from Napoleon's continental organization of anti-British economic warfare. The invasion of Spain in May 1808 similarly had been motivated substantially by the intention to enforce the closure of Spanish ports to British trade.[47] Also, both France and Britain intervened in Spain in 1808 with a view to securing the principal assets of what remained of Spanish sea power: twenty-eight ships of the line. Moreover, both sides had a large economic, and hence strategic, stake in the fate of the Spanish revolt against Joseph Bonaparte, whom Napoleon had placed on the Spanish throne as a reliable satrap. Napoleon's policy for the continental economic exclusion of Britain led inexorably to his being obliged to wage unwinnable wars at the opposite extremities of Europe. The defeat at Trafalgar obliged Napoleon to cast around for an expedient in economic policy as a means to bring Britain down.

Napoleon's armies lacked the logistic reach to defeat a Russia which could enlist space, time, and climate as vital allies. In the Iberian Peninsula the British Army—if prudently handled in the field—always could retire upon an impregnable sea power, functioned in deadly strategic synergism with Spanish guerrillas, and enjoyed a relative ease of logistic sustenance from the sea that could not be matched by a land power whose center of gravity was beyond the Pyrenees and was restricted to overland lines of supply. Judged in all the dimensions of grand strategy, the Continental System wrought more damage upon the stability of Napoleon's European imperium than it did upon Britain. Nonetheless, a commercial Venice, Dutch Republic, or Britain during a period when principal trading partners were accessible to pressure on land certainly was vulnerable to the closing of markets.

Each strategy option must be considered as just one element in a whole basket of possible measures. The case of Napoleon's Continental System is a particularly telling example of how effective an economic blockade can be—and how damaging such a choice of strategy ultimately can be. The Anglo-French experience of economic warfare over 1806–12 points to enduring lessons in policy and strategy. Economic warfare is not exactly passé. It was waged as recently as 1990–91 by the United Nations against Iraq.

It seems reasonable that a great land power desperate for strategic leverage against insular sea power would search energetically for sea power allies. The record reveals, however, the inability in modern times of the leading land power to enlist naval allies on a strategically significant scale. Germany's acquisition of Japan in December 1941 is an exception to this apparent rule, but an exception that proved fatal to the continental ally. The price paid by Germany for the securing of an ally with a first-class navy was U.S. belligerency—a status that Hitler gratuitously advanced on December 11 of that year.

Britain's continental foes generally failed to construct and execute a grand strategy of a quality comparable to that to which British statesmen persistently had successful recourse. The outcomes of the series of wars with France and then with Germany attest to the fact that at the level of grand strategy, Britain steadily outperformed her continental enemies. The France of Louis XIV and Imperial Germany, and possibly the France of Napoleon and the Germany of Hitler, had opportunities to neutralize British sea power that they neglected or were culturally unable to appreciate and pursue. Although strategy must be the servant of high policy, theoretical strategic possibilities tend to be reduced drastically by the national prism of political and strategic culture. Any great continental power that aspired to achieve hegemony in Europe might have assuaged British anxieties had it been prepared to eschew ambitions for wealth, power, and glory overseas. Instead, time after time, Britain's continental enemies indulged in the construction of naval power or sought to occupy and control the Low Countries. Those actions invariably rang alarm bells in London and triggered an all but reflexive British grand-strategic response of coalition building.

The France of Louis XIV and Napoleon, and the Germany of Kaiser Wilhelm II and Hitler, were all bidding for a continental supremacy that carried with it a long-term threat to British supremacy at sea. Nonetheless, each of those would-be hegemons undertook ill-considered campaigns on land or programs of naval construction bound to alarm Britain and drive her into irreconcilable opposition. Such opposition would have been manageable had the France or Germany of the day had a practicable solution to the security problem posed by Britain. No such solution was ever found. The history of continentalist strategies against Britain is a history of expedients that should be judged all but foredoomed to failure, even with the incomparable benefits of hindsight. The presentation of land power strategies is a discussion of abortive ideas and enterprises. Why did burgeoning continental power persistently fail to assemble a winning team to challenge British naval mastery, and hence as a consequence to attain even a lasting European empire, let alone a global imperium?

From the time of the eclipse of Dutch naval power under the pressure of continental warfare in the late 1680s and the 1690s until the early 1900s, there was only one consistently first-class navy, the British, with the French providing an irregular and typically unconvincing challenge. The fact that a rising continental power had landward gain as its principal focus of attention attenuated the effort that all continental powers were able or motivated to expend upon naval strength. As the most complex and expensive of military instruments, great navies could not be afforded save by very wealthy countries. Moreover, even relatively wealthy countries could afford strong navies only if they were not obliged simultaneously to provide large and expensive field armies or great systems of fortification.

The lapsed great naval powers of Europe, particularly Spain, Portugal, the Netherlands, and Denmark, were in a geostrategic situation where their colonial and other overseas trade was hostage to British interests or goodwill. But their political independence periodically was threatened in the most basic of ways by the armies of a continental predator. Although they could be coerced on land into coalition with France or Germany and occasionally could be moved to make common cause with the preponderant land power in resistance to the British practice of maritime blockade, typically they had a natural complementarity of strategic interests with Britain.

The geography of maritime warfare between Britain and continental Europe could be a nightmare for a Royal Navy that might, simultaneously, have to neutralize naval power from the Gulf of Riga to the Skagerrak, from the Texel to Le Havre, from Brest to Cadiz, and from Cartagena to Toulon. But the dispersed character of the continental naval threat that rendered thoroughly effective blockade a near impossibility had the paradoxical benefit of rendering the concentration of enemy naval force inordinately difficult, to the point of impracticality. Nonetheless, the British Admiralty had to establish political and geostrategic priorities for the allocation of scarce naval assets. The beginning of sound military strategy was a guiding policy and grand strategy that minimized the number of the Royal Navy's enemies. Also, time and again the British government had to decide how much effort to devote to her own continental commitment as contrasted with maritime-colonial warfare and where to apply how much of its sea-based land power among enterprises in the Mediterranean, Portugal and Spain, the Low Countries, and the Baltic. Furthermore, time and again British governments had to decide how much of a margin of safety they required in naval and land forces for the protection of the home islands.

Under the strategic conditions that have obtained thus far, aspiring hegemonic land power has carried the seeds of its own failure in maritime warfare. Failure to resolve definitively the problem of sea-threatened flanks repeatedly has resulted in the ultimate demise of land power in its own environment. Perennially continental statesmen have discounted the scale and quality of grand-strategic threat posed by an offshore sea power. Conditions of conflict have altered radically over the centuries, but the cumulatively dramatic increase in the absolute strategic power of the land has been more than offset by the increase in the absolute power of the sea. Naval mastery has come to command not only access to the wealth derived from trade in primary tropical products but also access to an entire extra-continental-European world that is industrializing. The regions that Eurasian armies cannot take by land today include in their number the principal granaries of the world, as well as the largest known deposits of many critical raw materials.

In the future a continental power may turn in a grand-strategic performance distinctly superior to that demonstrated historically by Spain, France, Germany, and the Soviet Union, as the aspiring hegemonic land powers of their day. Alternatively, nuclear folly may foreclose in a matter of hours upon what otherwise could be a protracted contest between sea and land power rivals. Nevertheless, there has been a pattern in modern times in the ultimate success of offshore sea power, and it suggests that land-oriented aspirants for continental, and eventually world, hegemony have enduring geostrategic problems that may not be resolvable in the face of competently managed sea power (and air power). While it is true that Napoleon and Hitler wrought their own destruction, it is also important to recognize that those cases of self-destruction were set up to a critical degree by the competence in grand-strategic and military-strategic method of the maritime enemy.

Continental states and coalitions have failed to win a single great war in modern times against sea-oriented foes. Contrary to some geopolitical fears expressed at the turn of the century, the transportation revolutions of the twentieth century have, if anything, strengthened the strategic-competitive position of sea power. The rise of American naval power confounded the Eurasian-focused continentalist logic of railroads, metaled highways, and the internal combustion engine. As the policy and strategic logic of sea-based power came to be more American than

British by the early 1940s, so the terms of engagement between great sea powers and great land powers persisted in disadvantaging the latter. One could argue that British, then American, sea-based power enjoyed a remarkable run of good fortune through the centuries. A point comes, though, when one is obliged to ask whether luck alone can explain why typically competent continental statesmen, generals, and admirals invariably failed to find and execute a winning formula for victory in major war against maritime enemies.

CHAPTER 4

THE AGE OF GALLEY WARFARE

Sea Power in the Mediterranean

In the last analysis control of the Mediterranean was as essential for the endurance of the Empire as the guard of the frontier, but this fact was hidden, and the Roman gentry did not love the sea.

Chester G. Starr, Jr., *The Roman Imperial Navy, 31 B.C.–A.D. 324* (1975)

For approximately 2,000 years geography and technology combined to provide an enduring geostrategic context for warfare in the narrow waters of the Mediterranean. The Byzantines and the Arabs, and later the Venetians and the Ottoman Turks, faced geostrategic and tactical-technological problems not dramatically different from those that ordered the strategies chosen by Persia, Athens, and Sparta in the fifth century B.C. or, farther west in the Mediterranean basin, by Rome and Carthage in the third century B.C. Just as there was a unity to the strategic value of sea power for England over 250 years, so the very long era of galley warfare in the Mediterranean, particularly around Greece, shows massive continuities. Indeed, given the common Mediterranean geography of conflict, together with an absence of radical innovation in marine architecture or other technical fields pertinent to sea power (gunpowder was not a factor until the fifteenth century), it is scarcely surprising that two millennia should yield a generally unified strategic story.

92

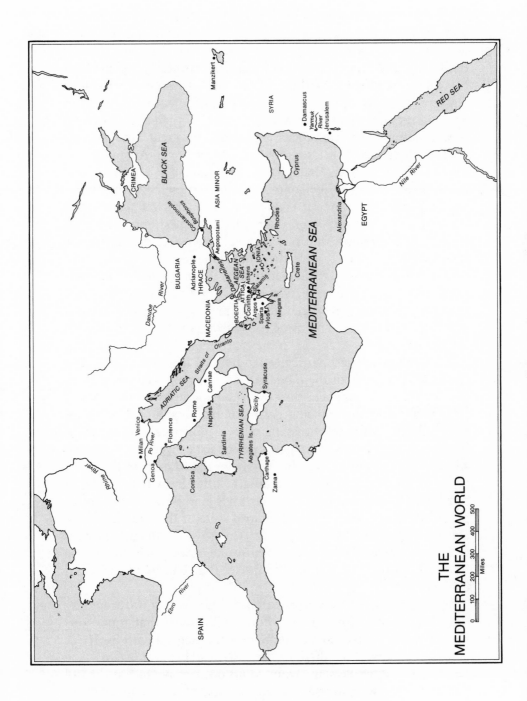

THE
MEDITERRANEAN WORLD

Modern theories of sea power do not sit well in some particulars with the history of warfare around the Mediterranean from c. 500 B.C. to c. 1500 A.D.[1] The central fact of relevance here is that dominant land power consistently had to turn to the sea in order to achieve its victory. Mediterranean conflict in the age of galley warfare is a story of strong land powers being both required and able to generate superior strength at sea rather than a story of land power dominating sea power (although the great land powers generally defeated great sea powers—Sparta over Athens, Alexander's Macedon over Persia, Rome over Carthage, Ottoman Turkey over Byzantium). The contrast between these 2,000 years and the 500-year-long modern era is not so much over the relative leverage of sea power but rather over the question of whether fundamentally continental powers could generate the sea power they needed in order to beat their maritime foes.

In modern times, maritime coalitions have translated their sea power into continental effectiveness far more efficiently than continental coalitions have been able to put to sea from a base of superior land power. The principal reason is not hard to find. In the age of galley warfare, both the maritime trunk routes and the naval instrument were critically landlocked in narrow seas. The strategic geography of the modern world has allowed for unification by naval dominance; the strategic geography of the ancient and medieval Mediterranean, given combat vessels of short range and with no ability to withstand even a moderate seaway, mandated a tactical landward dependence of sea power that had massive strategic implications.[2] Interestingly, the Mahanian theory of battle-fleet command has something to offer by way of explanation of the leverage of sea power vis-à-vis land power in the age of galley warfare, specifically, the central issue of the strategic leverage granted by superior sea power. The great continental powers ultimately tended to defeat great maritime powers over the course of this 2,000-year period, and to do so, they had to acquire first-class sea power.

The true unity of the age of galley warfare is best illustrated by the strategic similarity of the "bookend" events that frame this period. When Xerxes lost command of the Aegean with his naval defeat at Salamis in 480 B.C., he also lost his war against the Greeks. The huge Persian Army could not survive in hostile and barren Greece without the logistic support of a superior fleet. In

94

addition, the security of the Army's line of retreat back across the Hellespont (the Dardanelles) was menaced. Nineteen hundred and thirty-three years later, the Byzantine Empire's citadel capital, the city of Constantinople, fell to Sultan Mehmet II, "The Conqueror," in good part because the Turks finally had learned that without command of the sea approaches to the city, a siege could not be prosecuted successfully.

The repertoires of strategies for dominant land power and for dominant sea power introduced in the previous two chapters yield major insights to enhance the understanding of the historical cases presented here. These repertoires, or menus, are not deployed here mechanistically, but their varied contents, in ever-shifting mixes of single or compound choices, are the heart of this analysis. To cite just the case of the Peloponnesian War, we find Athens seeking a major continental ally in the polis of Argos to distract Sparta and her allies in the Peloponnese. Also, we discover that Athens sought to effect a maritime supply blockade of food (the ancient world perennially lived with the peril of starvation), engaged energetically in peripheral amphibious raiding and warfare, sought overseas conquests and made occasional continental commitments. For its part, we find that Sparta took or ravaged continental hostages, attempted maritime ambushes, and sought and found major sea power allies (or allies who would pay for a Spartan navy). When Sparta acquired a fairly robust superiority at sea, she endeavored successfully to impose a maritime supply blockade against the Athenian grain route from the Crimea.

This chapter is an affirmation of my belief that although technology, tactics, and the relevant strategic geography have changed drastically from age to age, there are massive continuities in the logic and the practice of statecraft and strategy. These pages explore the leverage of sea power in Persia's war with the Greeks in the first quarter of the fifth century B.C., in the Peloponnesian War, in the First and Second Punic Wars, in the defense of the Byzantine Empire for a millennium, and in the rise and fall of Venice.

The strategic involvement of the Persian Empire with the unruly independent city-states of mainland Greece can be explained by the dignity of empire and the legitimacy of imperial authority, as well as by the basic and enduring rules of power politics. Late in the sixth century B.C., Athens became a client of distant Persia in order to offset the menace of Sparta. But finding that it could handle the Spartan threat without Persian assistance, Athens decided to repudiate the act of its ambassadors in offering the traditional tokens of submission (Athenian earth and water) to the Great King in Susa, the Persian capital. Empires then and since could not prosper if they permitted client states to cancel relationships of formal dependency at will. This Athenian insult to the dignity of empire in 506 B.C. was a debt of dishonor in Persian eyes, to be collected when circumstances allowed. Furthermore, the Persian Empire was the very recent creation of Cyrus (reigned and ruled, 550–529), and he set a style in statecraft and in the legitimacy of rulership that mandated that the king be successful in battle.[3] To add injury to insult, Athens and other mainland Greek cities sent modest maritime assistance to their sister Greek cities in Persian-ruled Ionia, on the coast of Asia Minor, which in 500 B.C. decided to take advantage of imperial preoccupation elsewhere and revolt. That revolt flickered only briefly, but still it lent weight to the Persian determination to resolve its imperial security problem with the cities of Greece in general, and with Athens in particular.

Persia failed disastrously, though probably closely, in attempts at direct military subjugation of the troublesome Greek problem on the Aegean flank of its great continental empire. Those attempts—in 492, 490, and 480–479—came to naught because of a storm that wrecked the Persian fleet off the coast from Mount Athos (492), and because of the large errors in operational art and tactics in the latter cases, which enabled the Greek allies to win on land at Marathon (490), at sea at Salamis (480), and on land at Plataea (479) and Mycale (479). It is ironic that the strategic influence over Greece that Persia could not obtain by invasion, it was able eventually to achieve after 413–412 as a third party banking one side of the fratricidal struggle for supremacy between the Athenian Empire and Sparta's Peloponnesian League.[4] The Greek city-states were strategically self-absorbed for the better part of a century. The Peloponnesian War proper did not commence until 431, but the opening round can be dated to 460. Even the surrender of Athens in 404 was but the closing of only a chapter in a whole book of strife that was to continue until Philip II of Macedon defeated Athens and Thebes at Chaeronea in 338.

Darius and then Xerxes should have conquered Greece; they

powerfully overmatched their enemies on land and at sea, and their forces enjoyed the benefits of unity of command. However, Persian armies invading Greece were logistically dependent on maritime communications. Those communications were at hazard to the severe local storms off the European coast and to the nautical skills and local knowledge of Greek sailors in their home waters. In addition, and fatally, as in the great naval fight at Salamis, the Persians were severely at risk to the effects of an overconfidence which led to the acceptance of battle at sea in geographical circumstances that negated their numerical advantage in ships.[5] The Persians could be beaten on land, as was demonstrated incredibly at Marathon and again at Plataea and Mycale, but the essential strategic precondition for a successful Persian invasion of Greece was a secure seaward flank so that the army could be resupplied and need not fear hostile landings in its rear. Moreover, any Persian army in Greece required a safe line of retreat back through Thrace and over the Dardanelles.

Xerxes was unlucky in that the state-owned Athenian silver mines at Laurium yielded exceptionally rich deposits in the mid- to early 480s, a fortuitous development that permitted the city to build a fleet of 200 triremes of a new kind. Also it was Xerxes' misfortune that in Themistocles his Athenian foe had a statesman able to persuade his fellow citizens to spend the silver on the navy rather than to distribute it among themselves and exceptionally able in the strategic, operational, and tactical arts of war. The Persians were vulnerable in the critical interdependencies among their invading army, their merchant ships, and their fighting fleet. Only if the army controlled the shore could the ships safely beach at night for the sailors to sleep and be fed and watered. But only if the merchant ships could avoid destruction or dispersal by storms or by the enemy could the army function at all. Furthermore, the merchant shipping logistically critical for the army was itself dependent upon the war galleys for protection. As a recent study has noted, "this web of interdependence was a major weakness of the Persian strategic plan."[6] The freedom of action of the army, the merchant marine, and the fighting ships thus was constrained. Moreover, and potentially fatally, a breakdown by any one of these three interdependent elements meant the collapse of the whole invasion effort.

The naval defeat at Salamis, where 300 to 400 Greek war galleys defeated 700 to 1,400 (estimates vary widely) in waters so narrow that the Persians' ships could not deploy and use their great numerical advantage, obliged Xerxes to retreat back to Asia with most of his army. Quite literally, Athenian-led sea power saved all of Greece from Persian conquest. It would be difficult to find a more straightforward example of sea power's producing a strategic leverage fatal for the invader. In the following year, 479, the Persian general Mardonius led a much smaller landward invasion of mainland Greece, only to be defeated by the superior tactical skill of the Greeks at the Battle of Plataea. Across the Aegean, Greek forces completed the temporary frustration of Persian ambition by winning a battle on land (Mycale) that had the direct effect of allowing seizure of the Persian fleet.

The Persians' Greek problem of imperial security was alleviated most effectively and economically by the conduct of an agile balance-of-power policy among rival Greek polities. The Greeks' Persian problem could not be resolved all the while they quarreled in deadly fashion among themselves. Alexander of Macedon was to demonstrate in 334 B.C. how the Persian menace most effectively could be extirpated, as opposed to merely held at bay until it reappeared: he took the enemy's naval bases and shipyards from the landward side, precluding even the possibility of hostile sea power. The later Roman occupation and organization of the entire shoreline of the Mediterranean necessarily had the same benign effect of securing a monopoly for friendly sea power.

Alexander solved the Greeks' Persian problem with outright conquest in 334–330. Imperial Rome was not able to repeat Alexander's definitive achievement, but it did succeed in keeping Persian military power away from the Mediterranean (until the second decade of the seventh century A.D.), and hence away from a geostrategic condition wherein it could take a naval form.

Seventy-five years on from her defeat and humiliation at Salamis, Persia secured revenge by subsidizing the final Spartan naval victory over the beached Athenian fleet at Aegospotami on the Dardanelles in 405. Those intervening years witnessed the on-off fratricidal balance-of-power and ideological struggle known to history as the Peloponnesian War. The consequence of that was was a permanent weakening of the city-states of Greece which in the near term allowed Persian wealth to become the true arbiter of

Greek affairs, in the medium term enabled the barbarous Macedonians to establish a continental empire over all of Greece and then over much of the known world, and in the long run facilitated the Roman conquest.

The leverage of sea power that in 480 had doomed Xerxes' invasion of Greece was shown in the great Peloponnesian War between the Athenian Empire (formerly the Delian League) and the Peloponnesian League led by Sparta again to be critical. The war, which sputtered from 460 until 445 (concluded as a draw), flared in earnest from 431 until 421 (Athenian victory), and then saw its climactic phase from 413 until 404 (Spartan victory), was about the political leadership of Greece and the fortunes of rival theories of good governance. In grim practice, the war was also about the strategic utility of military dominance on land versus the strategic utility of military dominance at sea.[7] Oligarchic, agrarian, slave-holding, and continentalist Sparta—the traditional leader of the Hellenes in times of foreign peril prior to 479—was pitted against populist-democratic, commercial, imperial, and maritime Athens. The respective military strengths of the two polities were as different as their strategic dilemmas mirrored each other. For Sparta, the problem was how to wage war so that her dominance on land would offset Athens's apparently unmatchable prowess at sea and yield the strategic leverage necessary for victory. For Athens, the problem was how to wage war so that her maritime superiority would offset Sparta's apparently unmatchable prowess on land. These interlocking dilemmas or challenges have been repeated so often since the fifth century B.C. as to warrant description as a pattern. The stakes—which include the long-term relative weight of Greek ideas in the basket of Western civilization—could hardly have been higher.

In the view of envious and fearful rivals, the commercial maritime empire of Athens threatened to become an unacceptably hegemonic actor in Greek security affairs, a view that persisted from the 460s until at least the 410s.[8] Athens overreached her strength and skills disastrously in the 450s and 440s when in vain she sought to dominate Egypt (459–454) and then to acquire lasting continental empire in Greece with the conquest of Boeotia (457–446). In the 420s, a restored, even potentially dominant, Athens that was devastated by a recurring plague (430–429, 427) and by an unresolved geostrategic conundrum, sought for five years to

99

wage protracted war for the negative aim of persuading Sparta that she could not win. The plain failure of this Periclean strategy encouraged new Athenian leaders to attempt a bolder maritime design of coastal raiding, peripheral warfare based upon sea-supported defensible coastal enclaves. Luck as well as judgment produced success for Athens. Boldness became gross imprudence, however, when Athens sought empire in the west with her abominably mishandled Sicilian expedition of 415–413; to some degree she recovered yet again but finally was brought down by a Persian-subsidized Spartan fleet under Lysander's command at Aegospotami in 405. The strategic story of the Peloponnesian War is a story of the *superiority of land power as a basis for success at sea*. Sparta and Athens were all but self-parodies of polities with contrasting continentalist and maritime approaches to security and the conduct of war. As a land power, notwithstanding both her small population of males available and eligible to fight and her acute need to guard at home against slave (helot) revolts, Sparta was in a class by herself in fifth century B.C. Greece. The identical claim is appropriate for Athens as a sea power. M. I. Finley advises that in sixth and fifth century Greece, Sparta had (perhaps was) a "professional army in a world of citizen militias." Nonetheless, Sparta never committed to battle numbers more than the 5,000 men who fought at Plataea (479). Sparta was politically exceptionally vulnerable to pressure when numbers of her citizen-professional soldiers were taken prisoner-hostage.[9]

When in 479 Sparta declined to step up to the role of leading "the Greeks" (those in the Hellenic alliance of 481 formed to resist Persia) in defense of the Greek Ionian cities again in revolt against Persia, Athens was the natural and inevitable substitute. Athens had a genuinely geographically more expansive view of the domain of the Greeks, and unlike Sparta and most of her Peloponnesian ally-clients, had excellent reasons for favoring defending Greece a long way north of the isthmus of Corinth. Justly or not, in the last months of the war against Persia whose course had been turned by the great naval victory of Salamis, many of the Greek city-states not already closely allied to Sparta in the Peloponnesian League became increasingly suspicious of Spartan motives. They noticed that the Spartan war leader (the regent Pausanias) was treating with the Persian foe, and they registered negatively the Spartan objections to Greek cities' building or rebuilding fortifi-

100

cations. The rebuilding by Athens of its city walls after their destruction by Xerxes' Persians was an important irritant to a Sparta who feared, correctly, that such physical defenses on land might defeat its continental strategy. The long walls to the port of Piraeus were constructed at Pericles' insistence in the late-450s. If Thucydides is to be believed, in 478 a Spartan embassy had the temerity to propose "that not only should Athens refrain from building her own fortifications, but that she should join them in pulling down all the fortifications which still existed in cities outside the Peloponnese."[10] City walls could keep the Spartan army out. The upshot was that in 478 or 477, by invitation, Athens became the leader of a new, essentially maritime alliance of Greek city-states, the Delian League.

There is no question that Athens transformed the Delian League into the Athenian Empire. There is some question, however, over the degree to which Athens exploited her "allies," as there is over the issue of whether Athens set out ruthlessly to build an empire or was more the opportunist, driven inadvertently to empire building as a consequence of the need to deter and resist defection from the League. Similarly, the traditional view of the principal cause of the Peloponnesian War, Thucidydes' claim that it was Sparta's fear of the growth of Athenian power, is prone to mislead. The security context that Sparta favored was the traditional one wherein she would remain the unquestioned leader of the Greeks. Spartans would lead their fellow Greeks in such a way that everything north of the isthmus of Corinth would function as a defensive glacis for the citadel of the Hellenes, the Peloponnese within which Sparta and her principal security clients happened to reside. In an age when siegecraft lacked both science and engineering, strong city walls could be overcome reliably only by sickness and hunger among the besieged. Greek cities bereft of walls were open to intimidation by the Spartan army.

Much about the war between Sparta and Athens is uncertain because of the scanty and undoubtedly prejudiced literary evidence available. Thucydides may well rank as the world's greatest historian, but he was not wholly impartial—he was a disgraced Athenian general—his account does not cover the crucial last years of the struggle, he has a powerful interpretation of events which colors his narrative, and no matter how plausible one finds his argument, a single contemporary source is no basis upon which to construct fine-grained interpretation of obscure happenings. None-theless, the central geostrategic and military strategic facts and the general course of political events are not in serious doubt.

On balance, our knowledge of Greek affairs in the Fifth Century B.C. suggests that although rivalry between Athens and Sparta was inevitable, a great war probably could have been avoided. Also, it is reasonably obvious that either side could have won. Indeed, both sides did win different phases of the struggle. Whether or not the war is judged avoidable, it would certainly appear to have been the case that there was little active antagonism between Athens and Sparta from the heroic days of 480–479 until the late 460's. In fact, there is no historical dispute over the fact that hostility between Athens and Sparta was triggered in this period only by the events in 462. In that year Athens, by Spartan request, sent a force of possibly 4,000 heavy infantry (hoplites) under its very pro-Spartan general, Cimon, to assist Sparta put down a revolt of its helots in Messenia (in the southwestern Peloponnese). Before they could accomplish anything (they had been summoned for their skill in siegecraft), the large Athenian force was peremptorily dismissed by the Spartans. Furious, Athens renounced her treaty of 481 (against the Persians) with Sparta and secured an alliance with the Peloponnesian, distinctly continental, polis of Argos.

Argos was an implacable traditional foe of Sparta. More to the point, in addition to fielding a small but superb hoplite army, Argos was located as it were in Sparta's "front yard." If an Argive force was in the field, the Spartans could hardly dare venture with much of their army beyond the Peloponnese. To complete the grand design of land-locking Sparta in the Peloponnese, Athens proceeded to secure a new alliance with the geostrategically critical polis of Megara. Megara was located north of Corinth literally athwart the Corinthian isthmus, and hence blocked entry into the Athenian homeland of Attica. To compound Spartan difficulties, also in 462 Athens allied with the state of Thessaly, acquiring thereby both the services of an outstanding cavalry force, and an ally on the other side of the traditionally hostile region of Boeotia. Just as Argos in the Peloponnese was Sparta's traditional enemy, so Thebes in Boeotia was Athens'. In 457 Athens sought definitively to revolve its security problem in the north by the conquest of Boeotia (at the battle of Oenophyta). That substantial venture was successful and endured for a decade, but this bid for enhanced security via extensive continental empire was demonstrated in 446 to be thoroughly unwise. Most of the cities in Boeotia revolted, as did the cities on the island of Euboea, and as did Megara. Judiciously, Athens decided to save her maritime empire at the expense of her more recent continental holdings. The so-called First Peloponnesian War was concluded in 445 on terms that amounted to Spartan confirmation of the Athenian maritime empire and Athenian eschewal of continental imperium.

Argos and Sparta had concluded a Thirty Years' Peace in 451—the same year in which Athens and Sparta agreed to a Five Years' Truce—that, taken in context with the strategic loss of Megara and of Boeotia in 446, amounted to a prospect of enormous peril for Athens. In short, the way into Attica no longer was barred by continental barrier allies (Argos and Megara), and almost the whole of Athens' northern frontier with Boeotia could be a springboard for invasion. Fortunately a peace, the Peace of Callias, had been negotiated with Persia (probably) in 449, reducing thereby the list of active Athenian commitments. Athens had been taught severe lessons about the limitations of her power, notwithstanding the new level of core security guaranteed by the long walls to the sea.

The shape of the principal phases of the Peloponnesian War (that is, after 431) was driven by the Athenians' construction in 459–57 of the long walls connecting their city walls to the fortified port of Piraeus. In the words of Donald Kagan, "the completion of this construction would in effect turn Athens into an island unassailable by land and invincible so long as it retained command of the sea."[11] The Spartan army, excellent though it generally was, could not succeed directly against the new Athenian fortifications. When the war renewed in 431, the Spartans were obliged to design and implement a strategy to answer the challenge posed by Athens' long walls. It took the better part of twenty years and a critical amount of almost incredible folly on the part of Athens for Sparta to identify a theory of victory and be able to execute it. Even having found the winning formula, it still took six to seven years to achieve total, albeit brief and disappointing, success.

Sparta's initial theory of victory envisaged the repeated ravagement of the unwalled continental assets of Athens and her more accessible allies, until the pain inflicted compelled either a negotiated peace of surrender or an Athenian acceptance of battle (and hence of defeat, albeit of honorable defeat). For Athens's part, her imperial leader, Pericles, designed a strategy of balanced maritime offense and severely constrained continental defense. Sparta would be denied access to Athens's urban center of gravity by the city walls, and the long parallel walls to the ports of Piraeus and Phaleron would enable the city to survive by maritime resupply and trade. That, of course, is a theory of defense, not of victory—at least it is if the maritime offense is largely retaliatory and highly episodic in character.

Periclean strategy was to outlast the Spartan strategy of ravagement on land by raiding from the sea against vulnerable Spartan coastal assets. The dominant idea was expressed thus by a contemporary of these events: "A power dominant by sea can do certain things which a land power is debarred from doing; as, for instance, ravage the territory of a superior, since it is always possible to coast along to some point, where either there is no hostile force to deal with or merely a small body."[12] Athens raided and ravaged and even, after 427, established small coastal bases in Spartan territory (especially at Pylos) that could be sustained by sea. The problem was how to generate sufficient effectiveness via this peripheral variation of maritime strategy as to achieve the goals of policy. The Spartans faced the same dilemma. Whatever they could reach on land that was not well fortified, they could capture or destroy. But the citizens of Athens and their principal commercial assets were impregnable behind high walls. Athens had learned from her failure at continental empire building in Boeotia in 457–46 that she would rely only upon those things that her naval power could defend.

Pericles has been much criticized down the centuries for adhering to a strategy of peripheral pressure that failed to apply a decisive intensity of pain upon Sparta and her allies. In other words, Pericles had devised a strategy for Athens not to lose, but he had not devised a strategy for victory.[13] Because of the Argives' Thirty Years' Truce with the Spartans of 451, and the hostility to Athens of Corinth, Megara and most of Boeotia, Pericles in 431 lacked even for the plausible shadow of the continental strategy that had discouraged Spartan ventures beyond the Peloponnese in the 450s. If Sparta was to be landlocked south of the isthmus of Corinth this time, it would only be because Athens posed major threats either of amphibious ravagement, or to stir up and support revolt among the very numerous helots in Sparta's own backyard. In principle at least, the landward gateway into Attica was open after 431.

By the mid to early 420s, it was evident that both Sparta and Athens had failed to discover a vulnerability in each other's strategy that could be exploited to decisive effect. On balance and in some respects, wealthy Athens with maritime access to most of the known world was better able to endure a protracted and apparently indecisive conflict than was Sparta. But the other side of the ledger records the unpleasant facts that Pericles' "island-city" theory of protracted war meant a vastly overcrowded populace fatally at risk to infectious disease. A terrible plague wrought havoc in besieged Athens in the years 430–429 and 427. Also, it was very bad for public morale, not to mention the economic interests of many citizens, rich and poor, to witness uncontested Spartan despoliation of Athens's crops. Five times the Spartans invaded Attica: in 431, 430, 428, 427 and 425. It was revolutionary for a Greek polis to plan on evacuation of most of its territory—the plain implication of the long walls to the sea—rather than to stand and fight an invader.[14] Greek military tradition was heroic in kind. Athens in the 450's was not ready for such a scheme, and it was fortunate that Sparta did not press hard upon Attica in that decade. Pericles' success in implementing his extreme continental defensive in the war which began in 431 was a great personal achievement; the question remains, was it a critical part of an adequate theory of success in war as a whole?

After 427 (Pericles had died of the plague in 429) Athenian policy, led by Cleon, altered in favor of the offensive against Spartan assets or interests. Cleon's strategy was to seize and hold or to threaten Spartan assets remote from Attica, so distracting Spartan land power that it could no longer invade Athenian territory at will. The new theory was sound in principle, almost incredibly lucky in initial practice, and risked inviting the sin of continentalist adventure for an Athens that should have learned its lesson about the folly of empire on land in the 440s in Boeotia. The good luck was the capture in 425 of 120 Spartan soldiers at Pylos who served as hostages against near-term repetition of the traditional pattern of the all but annual Spartan invasion of Attica. This success also over-encouraged the Athenians in the belief that they could compete on land as well as at sea. The result was Athenian overextension on land (as usual, an attempt to conquer Boeotia) and a stalemate registered in 421 as the Peace of Nicias, formally providing for fifty years of peace, but in actuality merely an armistice while both sides reconsidered their grand and military strategies and restored their war-making resources as best they could. Although both Athens and Sparta had suffered severely in the warfare of the previous decade, there is no serious doubt that Athens and her allies both deserved and received the better terms of peace.[15]

In 415 Athens dispatched a great force, initially of 134 triremes (100 Athenian) and 5,100 (2,000 Athenian) hoplites, plus many lightly armed soldiers, and then reinforced failure with a further 73 triremes and 5,000 hoplites, to subdue Syracuse and hence dominate Sicily. *This entire force was lost in 413.* Much encouraged by this self-inflicted Athenian strategic wound—which was a reprise of the disastrous expedition to Egypt of the 450s—the Persians provided Sparta with the money to build, and rebuild several times, a fighting fleet capable of challenging Athens at sea. The strategic center of gravity for Athens was her maritime grain supply from the Crimea.[16] Sparta persisted in contesting the passage of Athenian grain at the maritime defile, the choke point, of the Dardanelles, until eventually Athens's last fleet was taken in 405. Writing about the 410s and 400s, Kagan observes,

> To win, each had to acquire the capacity to fight and succeed on the other's favorite domain. The Athenian defeat in Sicily gave the Spartans the opportunity to succeed by making an alliance with Persia. After many failures, they won the war by defeating the Athenian fleet [Aegospotami, 405]. There was no other way to win. To win a true victory rather than a Periclean stand-off, the Athenians would have had to find a way to defeat the Spartans on land.[17]

Kagan believes that after 421, Athens could have assembled the continental power from allies necessary to beat Sparta on land but declined to make the attempt with the necessary commitment. By contrast, Sparta committed itself eventually to defeating Athens at sea. Considering the typical absence of strategic excellence about the Spartan way of war and statecraft, as well as the great economic strength of Athens, it is somewhat surprising that Sparta emerged as the clear victor of the Peloponnesian War. The explanation lies in the heroic scale of incompetence with which Athens conducted her expedition to Sicily in 415–413, in the readiness and ability of Persia to fund a client Sparta, and in the contrasting qualities of war leadership with which the rivals irregularly were cursed and blessed in those years.

The centerpiece of the story is the Athenian disaster in Sicily. It would be geostrategically satisfying to believe that Athens's great expedition to Syracuse was motivated by the rational purpose of cutting off at source the principal grain supply to Sparta and her allies. This proposition provides an agreeable symmetry with Spartan strategy in the 400s. Unfortunately, and notwithstanding Thucydides' mention of the importance to Athens (in 427–424) of menacing the Peloponnesians' grain supply,[18] it is far from certain that that supply was of critical significance for the Peloponnesian League. It is not good enough to say that "it can only be assumed that Sicily as a source of supply was as important to the Spartans and Corinthians as the Ukraine was to the Athenians, and the command of the strait of Messina was as vital to the first two as the command of the Hellespont was to the latter."[19]

On balance, Athens's decision to hazard in excess of 30,000 men and more than 200 ships on its Sicilian venture must be judged to lack a strategic rationale suitable to the risks it represented. The expedition was launched by a popular democracy temporarily bedazzled by the style and rhetoric of the brilliant, if unsound, young general, Alcibiades. At best the strategic purpose or purposes of the expedition were somewhat vague. The reality was the dispatch of a great armament which, even if successful, could not wreak the ruin of Sparta but which had the plain potential to weaken Athens critically in the event of failure. Hindsight threatens to distort our judgment. Strategically dubious though the enterprise was, there was no good reason that it had to end in military catastrophe. For a very powerful fleet from the greatest navy of the period to allow itself to be blockaded and eventually outfought in the confined waters of Syracuse harbor was an outcome far beyond the skill of the enemy alone to organize and execute. Apparently, the Syracusans, taking their cue from the Corinthians, greatly strengthened the anchor-blocks in the bows of their ships, a development that gave them a crucial advantage over the Athenians in the prow-to-prow confrontation that could be enforced in the narrow waters of Syracuse harbor.[20]

The Athenian expedition beat itself. By divided and pusillanimous command in the hands of a leader who had opposed the
venture all along (Nicias), the expedition wrote its own death
warrant by delay. The consequences of the half-hearted Athenian
attempts to take Syracuse were that the city recovered its political
courage, enhanced its physical strength as the Athenians failed to
implement comprehensive siege-lines on the landward side of city,
and effected a truly land- and water-tight countersiege of the besiegers. Politically, in terms of human loss, and materially, the
disaster at Syracuse ruined the Athenian cause in the great protracted war with Sparta. There was, however, a great deal of ruin
left in Athens, as the mixed military fortunes of 413–404 attest.

Of utmost importance to Athens was her grain supply through
the Dardanelles from the Crimea. In the 420s, in the closing years
of the Archidamian War phase of the struggle, the Spartan general,
Brasidas, had sought to strike at this Athenian vulnerability with
a land campaign against Athenian colonies and allies in Thrace.
But at the time, Sparta was not prepared to hazard the men and the
wealth necessary to press for a clear decision in that region so far
from the Peloponnese to the north. The reinforcement of troops in
the region was all but impossible because of Athens's command of
the sea and because her continental Thessalian allies in central
Greece opposed the passage of Spartan soldiers. Also, in general
and overall, the Peloponnese was suffering badly from the war. In
short, Sparta was war weary and pessimistic about her prospects
for bringing down the Athenian Empire. It was principally political, strategic, and tactical errors on the part of the Athenians in
the 410s that changed Sparta's prospects for eventual success. In
the next decade, as a result of Persian gold, Athenian exhaustion,
and a properly focused *maritime* strategy, Sparta defeated her
chief rival.

So intense and enduring were the rivalries among the Greek
city-states that, in the context of the very limited resources of each
of those states and with Persia playing the age-old game of divide
and influence, it is scarcely surprising that none of the leading
actors in the internal Greek wars of the fifth and fourth centuries
achieved a stable and lasting preponderance. The Peloponnesian
War certainly ruined Athens's bid for a lasting great imperium, but
the succeeding hegemony of Sparta lasted for barely thirty years.[21]
Athenian prestige at sea was shattered by the naval defeats in

Syracuse harbor, which sealed the fate of its expeditionary force to Sicily, and by Lysander of Sparta at Aegospotami. The reputation of Spartan land power, for its part, was to be shattered by Thebes at the Battle of Leuctra in 371. The period of Theban ascendancy was even briefer than had been that of Sparta. Athens and Sparta in rare alliance, together with defecting former members of the Theban-led Arcadian League, were beaten on land at the Battle of Mantinea (362) by Thebes. But the political-military aftermath was a chaos in the security order, which Philip II's Macedon was only too willing to exploit. The fact that Sparta was a land power should not obscure the significance of the necessity of her settling upon a naval solution to the strategic problem posed by maritime imperial Athens. Spartan's purely continental strategy failed dismally in the early 420s, but—it must be admitted—so too did the less-than-rigorous, purely maritime strategy pursued by Athens in the same period. Yet again a land power would defeat a sea power in the narrow waters of the Mediterranean, as Rome and Carthage contested for supremacy and even just for survival in the third century B.C. But yet again the victorious land power that was Rome would be able to secure that victory only by becoming supreme at sea.

If Sparta in the fifth century B.C. had shown how a land power could reach successfully for sea power in order to bring down a maritime enemy, Rome in the third century B.C. provided a yet more dramatic example of the same strategic phenomenon. The three Punic Wars between Rome and Carthage (264–21, 219–202, 149–46) could hardly have been designed to show more clearly the strategic leverage granted by superior sea power. Notwithstanding the familiar problem of an acute shortage of sources and the biased nature of the ones that are available, still the strategic framework and general course of Rome's three-round struggle with Carthage is plain. In the First Punic War continentalist Rome acquired dominant sea power to defeat Carthaginian maritime strategy *overseas* (in Sicily); in the Second Punic War, formerly maritime Carthage adopted a wholly continental strategy against newly sea power preponderant Rome. The Third Punic War some half-century later was a brutally definitive tidying up by Rome of its unfinished Carthagian business. By her total destruction of Carthage in 146, Rome bequeathed to history the ironic content and phrase, a "Carthaginian and peace." Rome won these wars because of superior strategy, superior material and human strength, and much superior political will to persevere and sacrifice for eventual victory.

In its wars with Carthage, Rome for the first time in its history faced the necessity of fighting overseas. In geostrategic terms in the 260s, the expanding power of agricultural, land-oriented Rome and the expanding power of maritime Carthage, met in and about the Strait of Messina and Eastern Sicily. Carthaginian political and, particularly, commercial leaders by no means thought steadily in geostrategic terms, however. Chary though one must be of simple explanations for victory and defeat, nonetheless it is persuasive to argue that the most important Roman advantage in these wars lay in her civic virtue. Two generations of Punic leaders were to discover that Rome was an enemy unlike any other their state had faced.[22] The military details of the struggle were important, but Rome's ultimate military triumphs in the First and Second Punic Wars stemmed from the unwillingness of Romans to accept defeat.

A clash between two very different political cultures, the Punic Wars saw both sides misunderstand the character of war the enemy was waging. The Romans may perhaps be excused misreading Carthaginian purpose and style, particularly with reference to the Second War, because in Hannibal Barca they faced a thoroughly and disconcertingly "Roman" enemy. The victor of Cannae (216 B.C.) would have made a perfect Roman of the imperial republic of that era. He waged war for revenge for the defeat and dishonor suffered in the First War, for love of military glory, and with a persistence and operational and tactical skill that for many years his enemy could not begin to match. It was fortunate for Rome that Hannibal was less skilled in grand and military strategy than he was in operational art and tactics.[23] Above all else, Rome benefited from the fact that *his* war against her was not steadily endorsed by the politicians at home.

In the First and the Second Wars, the Carthaginians were obliged by circumstances and by their own folly in statecraft to wage a war that maximized the strategic relevance of Rome's superior domestic political assets. Carthage was a commercial empire devoted to the safety and expansion of trade and heavily reliant on mercenaries. In the political will to fight, it could not hope to outlast a republic of citizen soldiers which identified wealth primarily with

110

the profits from landholding. In both 264 and in 219, Carthage went to war far too lightly against an enemy profoundly different in political and strategic culture. As a source of enhanced state security as well as personal glory and wealth (plunder), war was very much a way of life for third-century Rome. In the chilling words of William V. Harris:

> One of the most striking features of Roman warfare is its regularity—almost every year the legions went out and did massive violence to someone—and this regularity gives the phenomenon a pathological character.[24]

Moreover,

> Few others [among nonprimitive ancient peoples] are known to have displayed such an extreme degree of ferocity in war while reaching such a high level of political culture.

In 264 the Romans had no naval tradition and were not a sea power in the broadest of senses.[25] Until that time the enemies of Rome had been other land powers, and the strategic object of Roman policy was restricted to the consolidation of continental security in Italy. Carthage was a new kind of enemy for Rome as, fatally, Rome was to prove a novel challenge for Carthage. In terms more than a little reminiscent of Dutch statesman Jan de Witt's adverse judgment on the willingness of his commercially minded countrymen to fund adequate maritime defense preparations in peacetime[26]—a judgment also leveled frequently at the British and American peoples—Brian Caven has written of the Carthaginians:

> They had, indeed, remained unchallenged for so long that they had come to regard the command of the sea as theirs by prescriptive right; yet the same anti-militarist and commercialist attitudes of mind that tended to make them dilatory in their reaction to military threats also led them to spend no more on their navy—upon whose efficiency their whole commercial empire outside of Africa ultimately rested—than was absolutely necessary.[27]

In the First Punic War, the Carthaginians would appear to have discounted thoroughly the danger of a Roman fleet. In the starkest of terms, Carthage lost the war because Rome adopted a superior strategy and had the strength and the will to provide, and replace time after time, the physical means to make the strategy work. On at least five occasions, continental-minded Rome built and rebuilt a fleet which, notwithstanding the most awful disasters at sea in the entire history of war, enabled Carthaginian power in Sicily ultimately to be isolated and to wither through logistic strangulation.[28] Having secured command of the maritime passage from Sicily to Africa, Rome invaded Carthage proper in 256. Although this was a strategically sound venture directed at the continental center of gravity of the enemy, it met with operational disaster in the Battle of Tunes (255) at the hands of a Carthaginian army led by Xanthippus, a Spartan soldier of genius. The remnants of the Roman land forces were evacuated by a relief expedition, only to meet a disaster in a storm at sea.

The Romans constructed and fought their fleets so as to neutralize the tactical advantages in battle which the Carthaginians might have derived from superior nautical skills. The Roman solution to Carthaginian excellence in ship handling was the *corvus,* or crow, a heavy spiked and pivoted gangway mounted on the prow of war galleys for the purpose of literally "nailing" two ships together. Suitably "nailed," the ships would become platforms for infantry combat, the style of war in which Rome excelled. Unfortunately for Roman soldiers and sailors, the *corvus* which enabled Rome to win command at sea in great battles at Mylae (off the north coast of Sicily) in 260 and Ecnomus (off the south coast of Sicily) in 256 turned galleys with poor sea-handling capability into veritable death traps. The doyen of historians of Roman sea power judges that "between battles and storms about 600 Roman warships and 1000 transports were sunk; probably no naval war in history has seen such casualties by drowning."[29] Within ten years of its introduction, the *corvus* was abandoned as being unduly hazardous to the seaworthiness of ships.

Roman naval mastery generally isolated the theater of war in Sicily and denied Carthage the access that it needed to that island in order to wage war there effectively. Having tried and failed to reach Carthage on land in North Africa, Rome settled for the strategy of denying her enemy the ability to fight effectively in Sicily. This sound strategy was accomplished neither cheaply nor quickly. The Roman disasters on land and at sea in 255 in the abortive blow at North Africa enabled Carthage to stage a note-worthy recovery. Carthage reinforced her garrisons in Sicily and, after mixed fortunes in land warfare, inflicted a major defeat on the Roman navy at the Battle of Drepanum in 249. That battle, and a storm that succeeded it, effectively deprived Rome of her sea power for the fourth time in this war. Seven years later, Rome returned for the last time in the conflict with a powerful fleet and seized the last major Carthaginian strongholds in Western Sicily (Lilybaeum and Drepanum) in 242. In the following year, the Roman navy defeated a large Carthaginian fleet off Western Sicily in the Battle of the Aegates Islands. The Carthaginians crucified Hanno, their unsuccessful admiral, and accepted a peace which yielded Rome both a modest financial indemnity and her first overseas province, in Western Sicily.

In this First Punic War, both Rome and Carthage attempted to bring pressure to bear upon the other close to home. Rome actually invaded North Africa, though with disastrous results on land and at sea in 256–255, and Hamilcar Barca raided the coasts of Roman-allied Italy over the years 247–242 when Roman sea power was in temporary eclipse. In this war, neither side's thrusting for leverage on land close to the enemy's home even came close to achieving a critical weight. The story would be different next time.

The First Punic War had the geostrategic effect of preventing the western Mediterranean from becoming a Carthaginian lake. In the Second Punic War, Rome functioned as a full-fledged maritime power, enabled critically by its effective command at sea to direct the "general course and character" of the war,[30] notwithstanding Hannibal's long string of operational and tactical successes on land in Italy. Naval historians, Mahan in particular, have fallen victim to a familiar level-of-analysis problem and exaggerated the significance of Roman command at sea as the *prima mobile* in the downfall of Carthage.[31] It is true that Roman naval mastery enabled her to wage to ultimate victory what amounted to six quasi-autonomous wars, often in parallel. In addition to opposing Hannibal's sixteen-year campaign in Italy, Rome waged a twelve-year war in Spain, conducted a nine-year war against Macedon, conducted a four-year war in Sicily, opposed Hannibal's brother, Mago, in a three-year war in the north of Italy, and waged war for two years in Africa.[32] Nevertheless Carthage, with a great, if recently forcibly lapsed, maritime tradition and with the finest field army in the world led by a general who sustained for sixteen years a deserved reputation for invincibility in the field, could not assemble a sufficient concentration of force to deal Rome a fatal blow. The reason, at one level, is Roman sea power. At the level of state policy, however, the answer is the unwillingness of Carthage to pay the price of waging war *à outrance* against Rome.

The story of the Second Punic War is succinctly told in its strategic essentials. Carthage recovered quickly from the damage to her trade and wealth wrought by Rome in the First War, and in the 230s she began to acquire and consolidate a new continental empire in Spain south of the Ebro. For a commercial city never enthusiastic for the military costs of prosperity, let alone greatness, the new Spanish imperium had the benefits of being both self-financing and a convenient repository for adventurous spirits. In 221, twenty-six-year-old Hannibal Barca all but "inherited" the Carthaginian empire in Spain and was at liberty to make what trouble he would with the Rome that he hated. In 218 Hannibal invaded Italy from Spain by land, proceeded to inflict defeat upon defeat on the armies of Rome—most notably at Cannae in 216—and remained unchallenged in the field in Italy until 203. In 203 Hannibal returned to a North Africa that had been invaded by the Romans from Sicily and met his Wellington and his Waterloo in the person of Scipio (Africanus) at the Battle of Zama in 202.

Hannibal's study of the first war with Rome had taught him that the Roman center of strategic gravity was her Italian material and human strength. Rome had won in 242–241 by being able and willing to build one more fleet than were the Carthaginians. Hannibal believed that by invading Italy, he could ally with the anti-Roman Gaulish tribes of the Pô valley and, by defeating Roman arms in the field, create a bandwagon effect of former Roman allies and clients deserting their previous allegiance. Unfortunately for Hannibal, his theory of victory was only as good as was its assumption about the fragility of the Roman alliance system. In practice, the Italian allies of Rome did not defect to Hannibal, notwithstanding his smashing battlefield successes in 218, 217, and 216. Rome was a good and reliable friend and an exceedingly bad enemy, as the exemplary punishment in 211 of the citizens of defecting Capua demonstrated unarguably. (By systematic execution, enslavement, and expulsion of the Capuans judged guilty of

114

treason—they were Roman citizens—Rome sought to discourage defection by other allies.) Moreover, having learned at long and painful last, after three catastrophes in the field, not to offer battle to Hannibal, the Romans were able to defeat the Carthaginian strategy. Roman armies in being deprived Hannibal of the ability to disperse his forces widely to exert pressure for defection from the Roman alliance. He lacked the strength to lay siege to well-fortified cities, and his need to keep his relatively small forces concentrated also meant that plunder for payment of the troops was not easy to acquire. The absence of a maritime dimension of his—one can hardly say Carthage's—strategy, married to the lack of wholehearted support for his war on the part of profit-minded Carthaginians, meant that the failure of his continental strategy in Italy left him stranded.

Had Carthage decided that the focus of the war should be Hannibal's campaign in Italy, it would have stood a good chance of winning. But in contrast to its most prominent, wayward, if brilliant general, Carthage was waging a limited war to secure the new economic base in Spain and, if possible, to regain its lost commercial imperium over Sardinia and Sicily.[33] Carthage repeatedly declined to commit itself to the expensive prospect of building a battle fleet that could challenge Rome for command at sea. Such a fleet could have enabled that flexibility in the concentration of force on land that was needed if the war was to be won.

Hannibal's entire strategy was unsound. He attempted the overthrow of an enemy of extraordinary resilience on the basis of a commitment to his Italian adventure by the politicians at home that was unsteady and tepid. Campaigns in Spain and Sicily, because they touched most closely upon what the Carthaginian government thought the war was about, translated into a dispersal of rival Carthaginian efforts that Rome could afford but a logistically embarrassed Hannibal could not. Moreover, with unchallenged command at sea, Rome could be far more sure and agile in its shifting foci of force concentration among geographically disparate regions than could Carthage. Carthaginian generals overwhelmingly were dependent on continental lines of communication or upon the furtive insertion of "fugitive" squadrons.[34] Indeed, Hannibal's situation in Italy in 218–203 is more than casually reminiscent of Field Marshal Erwin Rommel's dilemmas in North Africa more than two thousand years later. In 1941–42 Rommel could outfight every British general and British army that dared to challenge him, except for the final one, but his government at home was not committed to the African adventure. Moreover, in common with Hannibal's problem in Italy and over much the same stretch of water, British strength at sea and in the air increasingly deprived Rommel of maritime reinforcements and resupply.

The Second Punic War demonstrated the folly of Carthage—though not Hannibal, who had the definitive defeat of Rome in mind—attempting to wage a limited war for limited purposes of commercial security against an enemy that did not direct its policy according to a culturally comprehensive cost-gain calculus. Also, the means employed to pressure Rome to come to terms were certain to stimulate the enemy to a dogged resistance if they failed to achieve decisive military success promptly. Preeminent among those means was Hannibal's unilateral decision to campaign in Italy, anchored on a Gaulish alliance in the north. Carthage failed to appreciate that having aroused the maximum hostility of Rome and having failed to wreak its prompt political-military unraveling, there could be no evading the necessity of building a fleet to challenge for command at sea. The protraction of the war, as Hannibal campaigned victoriously but ultimately indecisively for sixteen years in Italy, provided the time and experience for Rome to find a general of unusual excellence. As the French and German armies of modern times have trained their enemies in the necessary skills of war and as British or Anglo-American sea power and Russian depth of territory and severity of climate has extended conflicts in duration, so Romans supreme at sea were able to improve their land power over time and find in C. Cornelius Scipio "Africanus" a commander who could win battles and campaigns reliably.[35]

The critical Carthaginian failure was in the strategic realm of a sea power lamentably deficient for the support of a war that embraced virtually the whole of the littoral of the western Mediterranean. The reasons for that failure had everything to do with a policy that misunderstood the nature of the war and a society that was unwilling to commit very large resources, time and again, to bid realistically for victory. The most remarkable aspect of the Second Punic War was Carthage's persistence in strategic error. Carthage failed to attempt to reinforce Hannibal in Italy on a large scale from 218 until 207 (when his brother, Hasdrubal, was defeated in the Battle of the Metaurus), and no realistic endeavor was made to change strategic course. By 211–210 at the latest, it should have been apparent that the Carthaginian continentalist theory of victory against Rome had failed. Hannibal could keep winning battles but could not exert decisive leverage on land with the forces available to him in Italy. With unchallenged supremacy at sea, Rome could project her legions into Sicily, Spain, and eventually North Africa and certainly could deny to Carthage the ability to use the sea to combine her disparate military efforts. The Carthaginian weakness at sea denied Hannibal the reinforcements that might have enabled him to conclude the war on land in Italy.

Land minded though they were, the Romans demonstrated an admirably swift grasp of the leverage of sea power. It was by the creation from scratch of a great navy and by its replacement five times in the face of huge natural and some military disasters that the First War with Carthage for, and principally in and around, Sicily was waged and won. It was by the maintenance of naval supremacy that Carthage was confined to a fatally flawed continentalist (via Spain and Gaul) strategy in her Second War with Rome. To wage war successfully across and around the Mediterranean required preponderance at sea or, at the least, a superior continental strategy. The Carthaginian error was the belief that in its field army under Hannibal, it had an instrument of military decision. Behind the inability of Carthage to make a vital midwar course correction in favor of an intelligent mixed continental-maritime strategy was a fundamental ambivalence over war aims and a lack of societal commitment to the waging of total war against Rome.

The Roman Empire of Augustus and long after is rightly regarded as very much a continental entity, famous for its roads and its general landward focus. Nonetheless, despite being "a landbound folk . . . these same Romans developed the control and organs of sea power to their highest refinement in antiquity."[36] It can be easy to forget that the Mediterranean provided the interior lines of (maritime) communication for the empire, at least in all seasons except winter. Secure use of the Mediterranean was essential for the efficient running and defense of an empire that totally girdled it. It is true that until the fifth century A.D. the Roman Empire succeeded in keeping enemies away from the sea, so there could be

117

no naval threats in the Mediterranean (or the Black Sea). But it is no less true to claim that the use of the Mediterranean and of such rivers as the Rhine and the Danube critically helped the empire to deploy and supply her military power on threatened frontiers. A glance at a map of the Roman Empire shows the strategic leverage conveyed by effective exploitation of sea lines of communication around and across the Mediterranean, from Gaul to Britain, and up the frontier rivers in Germany and the Balkans and Central Europe.

The Byzantine Empire, anchored by its fortress-capital on the Bosporus, was the principal bulwark of Christian Europe for a thousand years against invasion from the East. In that role Byzantium was the successor to Athens and Sparta. It is well recognized that the desperate resistance of the Byzantine capital of Constantinople in 674–678 and again in 717–718 was critical in stemming the floodtide of militant Islam.[37] It is less well recognized that even in the course of her lengthy decline in the thirteenth through mid-fifteenth centuries, the presence, unconquered, of what amounted only to the city "empire" of Byzantium in the Turkish *rear* on the extreme eastern littoral of the Balkans served as a brake upon the Ottoman surge toward central Europe.[38]

The Byzantine experience in statecraft and strategy thus speaks to stakes wholly in line with those at issue in the wars between Persia and Greece, between the Athenian and Spartan alliances, and between Rome and Carthage. What is more, the strategic history of the Byzantine Empire could hardly speak more eloquently to the vital leverage for high policy, indeed for the basic survival of state and society, of sea power. On no fewer than three occasions in less than a century, the Byzantine Navy saved Constantinople (respectively from the Avars, Slavs, and Persians in 626, and the Arabs in 674–678 and again in 717–718) from capture. Although the empire did survive the loss of its capital for a fifty-seven-year period (1204–61) to the Latin adventurers of the Fourth Crusade, it is no great exaggeration to equate the Eastern Roman, later Byzantine, Empire with its capital city.

Founded in 324 by the Emperor Constantine on the site of the ancient Greek colony of Byzantium, Constantinople stood at the crossroads of Asia and Europe on a promontory of the European shore of the Bosporus: it guarded East-West communications between Asia Minor and the Balkans, as well as traffic between the Mediterranean and the Black seas. The site of the city was as uniquely favorable for local defense, as its geostrategic situation was ideal for the protection of the empire as a whole. Constantinople was built approximately in the shape of a triangle with a blunted apex. The great land walls extended across the base of the triangle for four miles, and sea walls protected the city facing the Sea of Marmora for five and a half miles and the Golden Horn for three and a half miles. Strong currents and shoals rendered attack from the Sea of Marmora impracticable, and assault direct from boats against the sea wall on the Golden Horn required the prior securing of full naval and military control of that narrow body of water.[39]

Enemy after enemy of Byzantium came to realize that they could not compete strategically unless they acquired first-class naval power. In addition, if war with Byzantium was to be pressed to a conclusion, the imperial capital had to be besieged and taken. Constantinople could be captured by main force, as opposed to treachery, only by the combined efforts of land power and sea power. The military history of the Byzantine Empire is a history of successive foes of distinctively continentalist strategic culture taking to the sea. Over the course of a millennium, the Avars, the Arabs, and the Turks[40] all had to acquire a naval complement to their continentalist preference in order to attempt to seal Constantinople off from relief and resupply by sea. The Byzantines, for their part, built and rebuilt their naval strength in cases of acute need.[41] In the early sixth century, the empire built a navy so that power could be projected into North Africa, Italy, and Spain. In the seventh and eighth centuries, the navy was rebuilt to thwart the Avars, Persians, and Arabs, and in the ninth and tenth centuries, Byzantine naval strength was reconstituted as a vital support to the imperial revival on land and for the purpose of retaking the islands which provided bases either to attack or to protect Christian maritime commerce (Cyprus, Crete, Rhodes, Sicily). In the eleventh and twelfth centuries, a periodically revived Byzantine navy opposed the burgeoning threat posed by land and loot-hungry Normans from southern Italy and Sicily, and both supported and helped constrain the crusader thrusts into the eastern Mediterranean.

As with the other cases, the long strategic record of the defense of the Byzantine Empire is a mixed story of the implications of land power and sea power for each other. Unlike Imperial Rome, Imperial Constantinople was magnificently defensible and capable of resisting assault *unless* the attacker was supreme at sea and suitably equipped for siegecraft. Relative to Rome, Constantinople was well situated to support the forward defense of the empire's vulnerable continental marches—along the Danube and in Eastern Anatolia—to serve as a citadel for military regrouping and recovery in the face of disaster on land in Europe or Asia and as a fortress-barrier to the extension of disaster from Europe to Asia or vice versa. For example, in the late 440s Attila's Huns ravaged across the Danube into Thrace, as had the Visigoths and the Ostrogoths following their victory over Emperor Valens at Adrianople in 378, but they could neither capture Constantinople nor cross the Bosporus to reach the continental heartland of the empire in Asia Minor.[42] In 626, the imperial navy prevented the Persians from joining their barbarian allies across the Bosporus to join in the assault on Constantinople.

Byzantium's strategic challenge may best be characterized as the agile management of periodic, but always renewed, menaces from the East (Persians, Arabs, Turks) and from the West and North (Goths, Slavs, Avars, Bulgars, "Russians," Normans, Italians). Also the empire had difficulty surviving her own bids for restoration of universal rule (in the sixth and again in the late tenth century)[43] and from the domestic focus of religious and class interest. From the fifth through the ninth centuries, religious controversy had periodically dire consequences for imperial security. Most dramatic, perhaps, a deep religious dispute (over the nature of Christ) between the majority of people in the eastern provinces of the empire and orthodox opinion in the western provinces and in the capital contributed massively to the Byzantine cities of Palestine, Syria and Egypt essentially opening their gates without sustained resistance to the Islamic flood in the 640s. Scarcely less dramatic or unfortunate was the consequence for imperial security of the long-festering hatred between the great landowners (the military aristocracy or "border barons") of Anatolia and the centralized state bureaucracy in Constantinople. It would be too simple to assert that conflict between court and country alone fatally undermined the defenses of the empire in the half-century following the death of the greatest of Byzantine emperors, Basil II

120

(*Bulgaroctonus,* or "Bulgar Slayer"), but it would be true to claim that the Byzantine battlefield disaster at Manzikert in 1071 and its consequences were largely self-inflicted wounds. Hans Delbrück was persuasive when he argued that

> the principal reason for the longevity of that portion of the Roman Empire that was transplanted onto Greek soil was a geographical one, that is, the incomparable military situation of Constantinople.[44]

He noted that

> because the capital withstood all attacks, it served as a base time and again for the restoration of the empire, and in those periods when the enemies showed weaknesses, the capital city even led the empire again to victory and conquest.

The fortifications of Constantinople were the most formidable in medieval Europe. The city was taken by assault only three times over the course of a thousand years: in 1203 and 1204 to the Fourth Crusade and in 1453 to the Ottoman Turks. In 1204 the critical breach was effected by Venetian ships attacking from across the Golden Horn, and in 1453 breaches were battered by the greatest artillery train in the world at that time (including a super-bombard that threw a ball of 800 pounds), in conjunction with a maritime assault.[45] In the tradition of all of the more competent besiegers of Constantinople over the centuries, Mehmet II had recognized that the city, even in the parlous state to which it was reduced in 1453 (with only 8,000 active defenders), could be taken only by a combined land-sea operation in the presence of a naval blockade against any effort at maritime relief.[46] The table shown here, which summarizes the record of the sieges of Constantinople from its founding in 324 until its fall in 1453, both overstates and understates the resilience of the fortifications and strategic location of the city. The events noted in the table vary from repeated assaults carried through with the utmost determination to attacks that were little more than demonstrations against the walls. To balance the account, however, the table omits cases where one can infer that would-be attackers were deterred by the strength of the city from initiating an assault (eg, Attila and the Huns in 441–443 and possibly 447, the Bulgars in 813, and the Arabs in 904). So great was the confidence reposed by the Byzantines in both the physical strength of their capital's defenses and in the quality of divine protection extended by the Virgin for "her" city[47] that the emperor Heraclius was able to continue his ultimately decisive campaigning against the Persian Empire in 626, even when Constantinople was under intense siege far in his rear.

SIEGES OF CONSTANTINOPLE (617–1453)

DATE	BESIEGER	DATE	BESIEGER
UNSUCCESSFUL			
617	Avars	924	Bulgars
626	Avars, Slavs	941	Russians
669	Arabs, Persians	978	Byzantines (civil war)
672–678	Arabs	988	Byzantines (civil war)
717–718	Arabs	1043	Russians
813	Bulgars	1047	Byzantines (civil war)
821–823	Byzantines (civil war)	1090–91	Turks (Patzinaks)
907	Russians	1235–36	Bulgars, Russians
913	Bulgars	1376	Byzantines (civil war)
921	Bulgars	1411	Turks
922	Bulgars	1422	Turks
SUCCESSFUL			
1203	Latin Crusaders	1453	Turks
1204	Latin Crusaders		

So rich is the extraordinary record of Byzantine survival over a millennium that we can find evidence in imperial statecraft and strategy for virtually any favored theme. It is necessary to remember that Byzantium survived the descent into chaos and the "fall" of the Western Roman Empire in the fifth century[48] and the growth of the successor Frankish warrior kingdoms. Byzantium also outlasted, indeed it ended, Persian imperialism; it halted or deflected the Arab conquests of the seventh and early eighth centuries. In particular, it survived the great Arab sieges of 674–678 and 717–718, with naval defeat of the besiegers critical in both cases. Byzantium's successful defense against Islam in the form of the Ummayyad Caliphate of Damascus led fairly directly to the supercession of that dynasty by the Abbasid Caliphate of Baghdad (founded in 762). In practice, that event amounted to the capture of Islam as a military force by all-but-reconstituted Persian Empire.[49] The Caliphs of Damascus had seen their political-military destiny as a Mediterranean power, while the Caliphs of Baghdad focused primarily on the heartland of the old Sassanian and Persian Empire on the Iranian Plateau and toward Central Asia. The Mediterranean world was on only the geostrategic fringe of their interests. As if the Persians and the Arabs had not provided challenge enough, Byzantium next had to cope with the growth of new Slavic powers in the Balkans and north of the Black Sea (particularly the Bulgars and the Russians), the irruption into the territorial heartland of the empire in Eastern Anatolia of the Seljuk Turks after 1071, and then the greed and ambition of Norman adventurers, as well as the religious hostility of Latin "crusaders" (including a half-century of Latin conquest and rule after the fall of Constantinople in 1204). From the late eleventh century, the commercial imperialism of the maritime states of Italy (preeminently Venice, Genoa, and Pisa) parasitically undermined the empire while also rendering essential services.[50] Internal weakness, the absence of external support, and Turkish gunpowder (though Western-manufactured artillery in many cases) wrought the final demise of Byzantium on May 28–30, 1453.

As the record of the Punic Wars demonstrates, it is not true as a generalization to maintain that Republican Rome and its imperial legatee commanded the sea by first conquering the land. However, it was the case that courtesy of total coastal control, the Mediterranean was entirely an inland sea for the Roman Empire. When Justinian I (527–565) embarked on his ambitious scheme to restore the territorial greatness of Rome, as a precondition for success he had to regain that security of command of maritime communications that his Italy-based predecessors had enjoyed for more than five hundred years. By the destruction of the land and sea power of the Vandals and the Ostrogoths, Justinian briefly restored Roman command throughout the Mediterranean and the Black Sea. That command endured until the close of the reign of Heraclius in 641 and played a vital role in saving Constantinople

123

itself in 617 and again in 626. It has been suggested, contentiously though plausibly, that

> what Justinian created and what was maintained by his successors down to the last years of Heraclius some eight decades later was essentially a naval empire. Justinian's empire was more like the empire of eighteenth and nineteenth century Britain than it was like the earlier Roman Empire from which it had sprung. Sea power held it together, and not the legions or network of roads upon which Augustus, Diocletian, and Constantine had depended.[52]

Sir Steven Runciman has good reason to label command of the sea "the most valuable asset" of the Byzantines.[52] Pre-eminently, Byzantium was a Mediterranean power. Justinian's maritime empire entailed defense commitments beyond its strength to sustain. In common with every other maritime power, for example, the Athenian Empire in the first phase of the Peloponnesian War— when it sought, unsuccessfully to add a major continental imperium (in Boeotia) to its maritime supremacy—the Byzantine Empire faced enduring strategic problems pertaining to the allocation of scarce defense resources between both the sea and the land and between different perils on land. Justinian pursued the third priority of Byzantine strategic policy at the expense of the first two priorities. In descending order or criticality for security, the empire had to protect its heartland in Asia Minor, its Balkan provinces, and it could bid to restore imperial sway over Sicily, Italy, and North Africa. The empire was rarely strong enough to perform well on two of those geostrategically disparate fronts, and it was never strong enough to pursue an ambitious forward strategy on all three. Even at the height of the Byzantine strategic revival in the 970s and soon after, the Macedonian dynasty of great warrior emperors wisely declined to attempt to restore the Mediterranean realm of old Rome. This is not to deny that these emperors overextended the power of the state in the form of the unwise weakening of potential buffer polities in Armenia and Bulgaria but at least that overextension was confined to two fronts.

Byzantium's improbable survival for a thousand years is a history of superior statecraft and strategy—of performance good enough, time and again, to avert potential disaster and even to extract the state from the jaws of looming catastrophe.[53] The first line of Byzantine security was not military power but a professional tradition in diplomacy and intelligence (statecraft, broadly) which sought to pit the enemies of the empire against each other. But Byzantium eventually made errors in domestic policy, in diplomacy, and in war from which genuine security recovery could not be effected.

The victories over the Arabs in the seventh and eighth centuries could not prevent the loss of Palestine, Syria, and North Africa, including the principal granary of the empire in Egypt, with the permanent threat implied thereby to maritime communications throughout the central and western Mediterranean. Unlike the Turkish threat of the eleventh century and after, the Arab menace to Byzantium was predominantly maritime—ironic given the absence of a maritime tradition among the desert dwellers. In the high century of Arab conquests, Constantinople was attacked three times: in 669, 674–678, and 717–718. Those were the only occasions when Arab sea-based armies reached the triple land walls of the city.[54] Fortunately for Byzantium and for the Latin West, geography and climate prescribed that the major trunk routes for maritime traffic in the Mediterranean by and large follow the northern littoral of that sea.[55] Thus, Christian sea power enjoyed a structural advantage over Muslim sea power (analogous to the advantage that position and prevailing weather patterns accorded British sea power vis-à-vis the Dutch in the seventeenth century). This structural, geographical advantage in the terms of seafaring enabled the crusader states of Palestine and Syria (Outremer) to be sustained by Italian sea power, notwithstanding repeated disasters on land. The crusader states of Outremer essentially were maritime enclaves on an Islamic continent.[56] Byzantine history demonstrated the complementary character of continental and maritime strength and weakness. The continental holdings of Byzantium in Asia Minor and the Balkans were essential for the military strength of the empire. They provided the tax and manpower base, as well as the food, for the defense of the whole system. Maritime strength alone could not protect the Danubian or Anatolian landward frontiers, to cite a theme common in the security problems of many maritime empires. However, the history of Byzantium from the close of its last period of sustained strategic preeminence in the first half of the eleventh century to its final demise as no more than a city-state that already had acknowledged Ottoman overlordship (in 1373) shows that the neglect of sea power precluded even the possibility of the kind of imperial recovery that had been effected in the eighth, ninth, and tenth centuries.

Byzantine sea power—an imperial fleet at Constantinople and provincial fleets based on the islands of the Aegean and particularly on the south coast of Asia Minor—derived from the wealth of the empire and worked strategically to support a land power that was fit to be helped. The gradual loss of most of the interior of Asia Minor in the decade after the defeat at Manzikert in 1071 marked a geostrategic shift that was to be permanent.[57] In the eighth and ninth centuries, Arab *razzias* (raids) had troubled the Anatolian uplands with great regularity. Indeed, "the character of these incursions was so well understood on the Arab side that in the ninth century it was an accepted rule that two raids were made each year, one from 10 May to 10 June when grass was abundant, and, after a month's rest for the horses, another from 10 July to 8 September, with sometimes a third in February and March."[58] Those raids were expressions of an Arab power that knew it could not *take and hold* Asia Minor beyond the barrier of the Taurus mountains and the Euphrates plateau. It had to be the character of the Byzantine state at this time, the weaknesses in Byzantine society, and the character of eventual assistance from the rest of Christian Europe which rendered the disaster at Manzikert so significant. After all, Byzantium had suffered great disasters before (for example, at Adrianople in 378, at the Yarmuk in 636, which meant the loss of Syria and Palestine, and Egypt also, and at the hands of Tsar Simeon of the Bulgars at Archialus and Catasyrtae in 917) and had even been reduced to the bounds of the capital city but had always bounced back. Unlike the Battle of Manzikert in 1071, where Byzantine military losses were minor, at the Battle of Archialus on August 20, 917, the entire Byzantine army was massacred. Following the defeat of a second "scratch" Byzantine force at Catasyrtae, only the walls of Constantinople stood between the victorious Bulgars and the complete ruin of the empire.[59] Defeat in a land battle—in fact in a battle wherein most of the imperial forces retreated in panic rather than fight—on the far eastern frontier of Asia Minor should not have been an event of epochal significance. Moreover, far from heralding an irresistible flood of Turkish invaders, the defeat triggered an enemy occupation of the empire's heartland in Asia Minor so slow that it took more than ten years to consolidate. By the end of the thirteenth century, Turkish control of the southern and western coastal regions of Asia Minor was to provide the geostrategic basis for first-class sea power, as well as the timber, previously lacking, for the construction of ships.

Eventually a mix of rapacious Latin Western interests (land-hungry Sicilian Normans, wealth-seeking maritime city-states, German competitors for the religious and political mantle of "Roman" authority), Slav empire builders, Islamic empire builders, and domestic enfeeblement was certain to terminate the Byzantine experience. Great empires do not fall for a single reason, but the loss of virtually all of Anatolia as a consequence of the defeat of Romanus IV at Manzikert in 1071 registered a territorial shrinkage of empire that could never be recovered on any lasting basis by the Byzantium of that period.

Complementary to the Turkish incursions of the late eleventh century was the pressure from the West. In order to hold what remained of his empire, Emperor Alexius Comnenus signed a treaty in 1082 (the "Golden Bull") granting special commercial privileges within his domain to the rising maritime power of Venice, a former vassal of Byzantium. In practice and henceforth, although the Comnenian dynasty sought to rebuild Byzantine naval power, the empire became dangerously and ultimately fatally dependent upon Venice for its maritime security and lost control of most its seaborne trade.[60] Byzantine recognition that it had given away the keys of the kingdom led to repeated endeavors throughout the twelfth century to balance the power of Venice with that of another maritime city-state, Genoa. A brutally handled revocation of Venetian trading privileges in 1171 had the practical consequence that Venice decided its traditional policy of buttressing the empire of Byzantium had served its time. True security for Venetian commerce in the eastern Mediterranean, so it was reasoned, could repose only in the actual takeover of the empire. The result was the destruction and half-century-long suppression of the empire in 1204 at the hands of the Fourth Crusade, whose Frankish participants were in debt to a Venice which had transported them to the city of Constantinople.

Norman, Venetian, and Seljuk and later Ottoman Turkish pressures, with much assistance from the Slav warrior kingdoms in the

127

Balkans, were the agents most obviously fatal to the prospects for recovery of the Byzantine Empire from the catastrophe of the late eleventh century. In a more narrowly military dimension, however, the failure of the later dynasties to provide a sound basis in sea power for naval strength (and this is to exclude the naval revival effected by the Comneni on the uncertain basis of the hiring of Italian mercenaries) rendered continental recovery impossible and ensured the final demise of the imperial city itself.[61] External pressure probably would have proved fatal eventually, regardless of the course of Byzantine statecraft and strategy. Nonetheless, the surrender of imperial control over its seaward security to others was the most certainly fatal of the errors in Byzantine policy. Constantinople was less fortunately situated as a base for sea power than was Venice or England, but the longevity in political independence of those two maritime states was by no means attributable simply to the benefits conferred by a favorable physical geography.

Unlike the strategic contexts of 626, 677, 717, and 941, there was no Byzantine navy to rout the besiegers in 1204 and 1453. The Byzantine Empire could survive for century after century only with a system of statecraft and strategy which made full *synergistic* use of land and sea power—the whole manipulated by a wise, subtle, and agile diplomacy, backed by a stable currency, a coherent doctrine of Christian empire, and a tolerably efficient machinery of state. Byzantium did not succeed the final fall of the Roman empire in the West by 977 years because of the leverage of her sea power alone or even very largely because of the leverage of that sea power. Nonetheless, the empire could not survive without a strong navy whose periodic neglect invariably led to dire, and eventually terminal, peril. It is true that the empire had long and geographically exposed land frontiers in the Balkans and in Eastern Anatolia and that she was of necessity a continental power. It is not true as a long view, however, to claim "that behind the Byzantines excessive indifference to maritime defense lay the correct belief that the empire was essentially a land power."[62]

In her very long final era of decline and fall from the mid-eleventh to the fifteenth centuries, Byzantium suffered primarily from the consequences of huge and irretrievable errors in continental statecraft. It was the very extent of the Byzantine continental resurgence in the tenth and early eleventh centuries that undermined

128

the future security of the state. Potential buffer-state neighbors (Bulgaria and Armenia) were destroyed, albeit for reasons that seemed sound at the time, and the process of protracted continental campaigning generated an all but feudal military aristocracy which came to dominate society and state at the expense of other interests. Particularly under Basil II, Byzantium reached for a scope of continental security which strategic geography would deny her for long. The combination of extraordinary wealth of all kinds—treasure, land, the spiritual wealth in the reliquaries gathered in Constantinople—and crossroads strategic geography between East and West and North and South was deadly for any aspirations for a peaceful life for the empire. There would always be a new foreign danger from the East, the West, the North, or perhaps from all three directions simultaneously. To survive, Byzantium required sustained statesmanship of the highest order and, when confronted with the ultimate danger to the very citadel of the empire in Constantinople, the services of a sea power able to maintain the great city's maritime connection with the outside world.

The strategic leverage of sea power is as obvious for the maritime republic of Venice as it is arguable for the substantially continental imperium of Byzantium. Although she flirted with large-scale continental acquisition in northern Italy in the fifteenth century, Venice was nothing as an independent strategic player if it were not for the leverage of her sea power. As an imperial state, Venice's career extended from her acquisition of the port of Tyre in 1124 to her political extinction by Napoleon in 1797. In maritime support of Byzantium against the Normans of Sicily and Italy and then of the newly minted crusader states of Palestine and Syria against the Muslims, Venice positioned herself for greatness in the twelfth century. The next century registered the first of two peaks of Venetian power as she transported the Fourth Crusade to Constantinople in 1203 and herself secured the most solid-seeming benefit from the rape of Byzantium. The end of the Latin Empire at Constantinople in 1261, which was so largely the creation of Venice, also meant the temporary eclipse of Venetian commercial fortunes in the favor of her arch-rival Genoa, which, naturally enough, helped sponsor the Byzantine restoration. The closing decades of the thirteenth and virtually all of the fourteenth century comprised a period of more or less acute peril for Venice.

129

Imperial Venice's second successful bid for great empire and great profit occurred in the first half of the fifteenth century. With her major maritime rivals and continental foes distracted by other challenges, Venice was able both to enlarge her insular holdings in the Aegean and to acquire a landward empire in Italy. But then Venice declined by identifiable stages from the 1460s and 1470s until the eighteenth century. The great and exhausting war of 1463–79 with an Ottoman Empire still flush with its final triumph over Byzantium in 1453 plainly marked the end of Venice and her maritime empire as a Mediterranean-wide power of the first rank. Based on the coastal assets of the now all but totally suborned Greek world, the Ottomans in the 1460s had added a mighty naval armament to their already preeminent land power.[63] Venice was outclassed. Similarly, the first two decades of the sixteenth century saw Venice squeezed out of her continental holdings in Italy; she ceased to be a great land power. In the seventeenth century the Dutch and later the English completed the commercial ruin of Venice's previous near monopoly of the spice trade with the East, and the Venetian Empire ceased to be a great trading state. Following her loss of Crete to the Turks in 1669, Venice was reduced to the status of being an Adriatic power, and in the eighteenth century she accepted a client relationship with Austria. This rise, lengthy decline, and fall of the Venetian Empire is all about the strategic leverage granted by sea power.[64]

Medieval Venice sought an overseas commercial imperium and was prepared to wage war to advance her mercantile interests, though she much preferred an agile diplomacy. As an offshore city-state with a population that could not be sustained in the face of recurrent outbreaks of the plague at numbers much in excess of 120,000 (and often the population fell below 100,000),[65] the power of Venice lay overwhelmingly in the wealth that flowed into the city as a result of its fluctuating fortunes as a principal conduit for trade between the Levant and Europe.

The Venetian experience began as a lagoon and marsh-protected refuge from the barbarian Lombard invaders of Italy in 568. Until the late tenth century, the commercial prosperity of the city was founded upon control of the riverine trade of the Pô valley and the shallow coastal waters of the Gulf of Venice at the head of the Adriatic. Over the course of the next century, Venice became increasingly important in East-West trade. Under great pressure in

130

the west and the east, the Byzantine Empire extended exclusive, though limited, commercial trading privileges to the city, a development that stimulated Venetian shipbuilding (and led to the founding of the Venetian shipbuilding arsenal in 1104). Until that time, Venetian trade concentrated heavily upon the carrying of European timber and slaves in return for Islamic specie.[66] With the arguable exception of its policy of continental imperialism in Italy in the fifteenth century, Venetian statecraft and strategy was admirably steady in the identification of goals and the prudent balancing of limited means with attainable ends.

> The Venetians sought sea power, not territorial possessions from which to draw tribute. Their wars were fought to effect political arrangements which would be disadvantageous to rival sea power, which would make Venice's established trades more secure in Levantine waters, and which would gain them trading privileges permitting commercial expansion into new areas.[67]

Writing of Venetian strategic relations with the ascendant Ottoman Turks of the mid-fifteenth century, Frederick C. Lane has observed that "basically the policy of Venice was to maintain control of the sea, to defend cities that could be protected from the sea, to pick up more when that was easy, and to retaliate for Turkish acts of aggression by seaborne raids."[68]

From an occasionally useful *demandeur* in its commercial and naval relations with Byzantium, after the Byzantine disasters of 1071 at Manzikert and Bari (whence the Byzantines were expelled by the Normans) Venice was the principal external prop for the empire. From the outset, Venice was a Byzantine foundation. It was established in the sixth century out of the mainland wreckage of an Eastern Roman power which at that time was centered upon Ravenna. Although the Byzantine Empire recognized the autonomy of Venice as early as 742, Venetio remained nominally a province of the empire.[69] The treaty and Golden Bull by which Byzantium licensed what amounted to a Venetian monopoly over the seaborne carrying trade of the empire (except in the Black Sea) was a critical accelerator of both Venetian sea power and Venetian interest in the internal politics of the empire. In order to protect its monopoly of trade through the Adriatic, the bedrock of Venetian commercial security, the city was more than content to make com-

131

mon cause with the empire against Norman adventurers from the south of Italy. By coastal control from southern Italy, from Albania, and from Dalmatia—an area Venetians regarded much as the English were to view the Low Countries—the Normans threatened to achieve the geostrategic potential for maritime blockade of the Strait of Otranto. The Byzantines were in no position to resist the Normans in the Adriatic and Greece. For Venice, to wage war against Norman imperialism was both a strategic necessity and a source of commercial advantage. The issue at stake included freedom of Venetian trade throughout the Adriatic, the arresting of Norman ambitions to secure territory from a sorely pressed Byzantium, and commercial benefit from a dependent empire. Venice turned later to the direct plunder and conquest (1204) of the Byzantine Empire only when it became apparent that no other course of action could restore Venice's erstwhile most privileged trading position within the Empire.

Venice acquired an "empire of naval bases" as the principal element among its spoils from the Latin conquest of Byzantium in 1204.[70] As with the British in the eighteenth century prior to the vast territorial gains of the Seven Years' War (1756–63), Venice was in search of empire for business reasons. It sought a maritime-defensible network of the trading posts and naval bases essential for the sustenance of galley traffic. There was room for strategic improvement, certainly, but the combination of insular and coastal-enclave colonial gain from the indebted Fourth Crusaders who seized the Byzantine Empire, effective control over the trade of the new Latin Empire at Constantinople, and complete domination of the Dalmatian coast of the Adriatic amounted to preeminence for Venice. In the early decades of the thirteenth century, Venice was *the* eastern Mediterranean maritime power.

Over the next two hundred years, Venice struggled to retain as much as she could of her gains of 1204 from the consequences of the collapse of the ramshackle Latin Empire in 1261 and in the face of the rise of Genoa to renewed strength as a trading and naval rival. Indeed, it was the alliance between the Greek Emperor Michael Paleologus (by the Treaty of Ninfeo, 1261) and Genoa which led to the interposing of Genoese naval power in the Aegean between a vengeful Venice and a Constantinople which might be retaken, absent the Genoese Navy. Genoa and Venice fought four maritime wars for commercial preponderance in the thirteenth and fourteenth centuries (1253–68, 1289–1311, 1343–54, and 1378–81). As in the Anglo-Dutch and Anglo-French wars, the maritime wars between Venice and Genoa were waged in both the home waters of the two city-states—respectively the Adriatic and the Tyrrhenian Seas—and throughout the length of the trade routes (to the Levant, through the Aegean to the Dardanelles, to the Crimea, and even to the mouth of the Don at Tana on the Sea of Azov.)

The greatest crisis in Venetian history occurred in its fourth war with Genoa (1378–81). Venice temporarily lost control of its home waters in the Adriatic and was nearly taken in the siege of 1379–80. Finally, somewhat after the fashion of the Athenians at Syracuse in 413 B.C., the besiegers become the besieged. The belated return to the home waters of the Gulf of Venice of a powerful Venetian raiding squadron broke the siege and compelled the surrender of the Genoese and Paduan besiegers. Venice survived because of the stability of its domestic political arrangements, the domestic instability and rivalries among its enemies, and the steadiness of its statecraft in pursuit of commercial and security goals. Indeed, she emerged from what could have been a definitively ruinous two-hundred-year-long competition with Genoa in such a sound condition that the next century, the fifteenth, witnessed the apogee of her commercial and military success.

But by the end of the fifteenth century, Venice had lost much of her overseas commercial security as a result of the appearance of Ottoman naval power on a very large scale, beginning in the 1460s. Nonetheless, whereas the Venice of 1400 was still emerging from a close brush with total disaster at the hands of Italian rivals, the Venice of 1500, though at war with an even more powerful Ottoman enemy, had eclipsed all of her Italian rivals on land and as commercial competitors overseas. The city-state waged war, albeit on balance unsuccessfully, against the Ottomans for sixteen years from 1463 to 1479 and again from 1499 to 1503. In fact, Venice waged eleven wars with the Turks over the course of three centuries. Venice and the Ottoman Turks were at war in 1416, 1425–30, 1444 (the Varna Crusade), 1453 (belated efforts to relieve Constantinople), 1463–79, 1499–1503, 1537–40, 1569–76, 1645–69, 1684–99, and 1714–18. The point cannot be overemphasized that Venice was in the business of business, not of glory. Prior to 1453, the city's much preferred stance vis-à-vis Byzantine-

Turkish conflict was that of a profitable neutrality. Venice enjoyed extensive trading privileges within the Ottoman Empire, but the Turks were approaching their most dynamic period of imperial expansion and threatened the security of Venetian trading entrepôts, bases, and clients on the Dalmatian and Albanian coasts, and indeed all around the Greek littoral. The Turks found strategically functional allies in Italy among states desirous of reducing Venetian power (particularly Milan, Naples, and Florence), while Venice found a continental ally in Iran to the East of the Ottoman Empire.

By its nature as a wealthy city-state with a small native population, Venice could reward clients, fund domestic instability among rivals, and rent a mercenary military instrument. But Venice lacked the resources necessary to sustain any role other than that of a maritime city-state of consequence. The new landward focus of Venetian statecraft in the century of recovery after the Fourth War with Genoa did not lack for a rationale. Venice required a secure continental hinterland to its seaborne imperium. Certainly it needed a more extensive territorial base if it were to compete with an effectively united Spain (the *Reconquista* was completed in 1492), with a France rid at last of an English problem on its soil, and with an Ottoman Empire which was still growing. Moreover, the only alternative to winning at the game of Italian balance-of-power politics might well be losing. Whether the extent and persistence of Venetian landward ventures in Italy are judged to have been an error, the fact remains that Venice was not at strategic liberty to make a choice between maritime and continental efforts. The city's commercial well-being and security were menaced on the one hand by the expansion of the Ottoman Empire toward the Adriatic and on the other by the actual or potential hegemonic aspirations of Italian rivals.

Fifteenth-century Venice confronted rich and complex opportunities—and problems for its grand strategy. Consideration of both military security and economic well-being tugged Venetian statecraft in opposite geographical directions. Venice was determined to sustain her overseas trading empire, but increased security and commercial advantage beckoned also from the Italian mainland. On balance, Italian ventures would seem to have been basically ill advised as a determined pursuit for a very small maritime power which lacked most of the assets needed to make a success of im-

134

perium on land.[71] The Turks could play Italian politics against Venice, just as the Persians had played Greek politics against Athens. Moreover, since Venice was obliged to give first priority to the defense of her overseas trading empire, an empire increasingly menaced by Turkish expansion by land *and sea,* it would always lack for a free hand to devote to empire building in Italy.

The relative decline of Venice in the sixteenth century bears some similarities to the later decline of the Dutch and of the British. Venice was a maritime state with too narrow and geostrategically too exposed a base of resources at home to compete with emerging much larger sea and land powers. Sea power had accomplished all that sea power could accomplish for a state as confined in its ability to expand its home base as was the maritime empire of Venice. The extent of the Venetian achievement, and the general quality of its sea-leaning statecraft, may best be gauged in recognition of the fact that the city maintained an unbroken independent existence from its lowly Byzantine beginnings in 568 until Napoleon saw fit to snuff it out in 1797.

Physical geography, climate, and technology will always shape critically the terms of tactical application of sea power, and those terms will vary dramatically from period to period and region to region. Nonetheless, what is remarkable is not so much the tactical continuities between galley warfare in the fifth century B.C. and in the sixteenth century A.D. but rather the patterns in strategy that endured. It is true that quintessentially continental polities tended to triumph over maritime polities in the closed waters of the Mediterranean of the galley era, but that surface fact all but conceals a deeper truth. Spartans, Romans, Arabs (unsuccessfully), and Ottoman Turks (with much Greek assistance), all distinctively continental in their strategic *mentalités,* were obliged to take to the sea to try to secure the strategic effectiveness needed for victory. The historical record of the Mediterranean world of ancient and medieval times does not demonstrate the superiority of land power over sea power. Rather, it shows that land power tended to be able, in that environment and at that time, to generate a strategically superior sea power.

135

CHAPTER 5

SEA POWER IN THE AGE OF SAIL

Trafalgar was the really decisive battle of the Napoleonic War.

H. W. Wilson, "The Command
of the Sea, 1803—15," in
Cambridge Modern History (1906)

Over the course of 250 years, from the beginning of England's long struggle with Habsburg Spain in the 1560s to the close of her even longer conflict with France in 1815, sea power was transformed as a strategic instrument. Sea power became public rather than private (which is to say privately owned for private profit), professional rather than amateur, permanent rather than occasional, and truly oceangoing rather than coastal. The naval and merchant services increasingly were distinguishable by the career commitment of people, as well as by the specialized and standardized design of ships. Thought and practice accumulated concerning the proper uses of naval power to generate strategic effect.

The story of the rise of English, and then—after the Act of Union with Scotland in 1707—British sea power from the 1560s to the 1810s will serve to explain the strategic meaning of the age of fighting sail. Britain as a case study brings out the themes that are important. British sea power, the Royal Navy, British foreign policy, grand strategy, overall military strategy, and maritime strategy, lend themselves to a unified treatment covering these 250 years. The centerpiece is the gradual emergence of a navy increasingly capable of yielding strategic utility in support of British policy. It was a notable evolution from logistically ill-supplied, disease-ridden, and short-range ships in the 1570s and 1580s to a

136

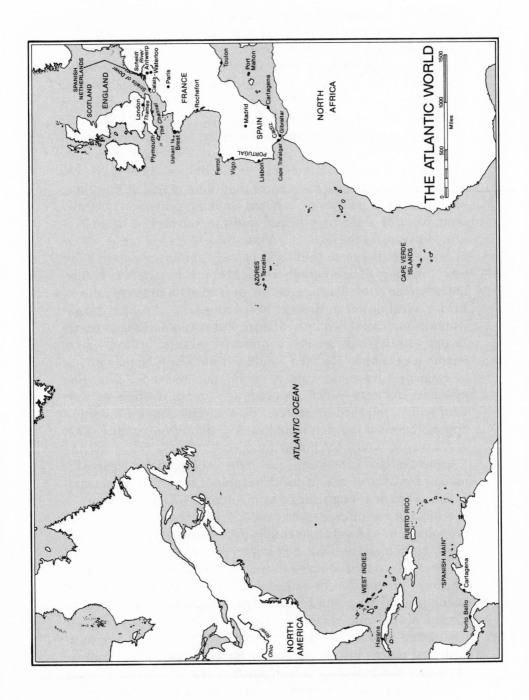

THE ATLANTIC WORLD

world-wide navy in the 1800s that enabled a British way of war to undermine and eventually defeat a great continental power. The long period from the 1560s to the 1810s is about the emergence of England as a great power and about the rise of navies as strategic instruments. Furthermore, this period saw the persistence of a geostrategic pattern of conflict that pitted maritime-led coalitions against continental powers and coalitions.

Tactical competence, strategic objectives, and policy functioned synergistically to spur advances on all fronts. For many years maritime theorists had had strategic ideas for the leverage of sea power which required a naval instrument that did not and, at that time, could not exist. However, forward thinking on the strategically desirable uses of the navy helped motivate the process of innovation to overcome the tactical limitations of ships and crews. Overall, countries began to think strategically about sea power as an asset for policy. The epigraph to this chapter characterizes boldly, indeed to the brink of exaggeration, the end-state strategic value of British naval power in this age of fighting sail. Of course, Napoleon was not cast down by Trafalgar. But that is never how navies "work" strategically against continental powers. Nelson's great victory on October 21, 1805, could not itself beat Napoleon, but in eminently traceable ways it set in train the more damaging dynamic elements which induced the French Empire to self-destruct by landward overextension. Trafalgar *enabled* Britain to apply a theory of war that would work in due, if long, course. That is the way in which sea power functions.

From the late 1560s until the early 1600s, England played a modest but critical role in the thwarting of overgreat continental power. That first long struggle to maintain a balance of power *in Europe*, not with Europe, the case of Spain, was followed by the geopolitically and geostrategically parallel struggles to frustrate royal, revolutionary, and then imperial France; by the repeated life-or-death contest to save Europe, and hence in due course Britain, from domination by imperial and then Nazi Germany; and finally by playing a key role in organizing, and then helping to sustain, the Atlantic Alliance of the Cold War era against the latest continental menace, the Soviet Union. Sea power was the most basic and potent British weapon in each of these mighty endeavors—after the power of British finance, that is. The sea power weapon usually was wielded in conjunction with other instruments, it was occasionally allowed to grow dull and blunt, and it was mishandled from time to time, but overall, the story of the growth of English, then British, then Anglo-American, then largely American, sea power is the story of how maritime alliances persistently thwart continental tyrants.

The opportunities and need for English sea power to play a critical role in frustrating the overmighty empire of the Habsburgs have to be understood in the context of the balance-of-power politics of the late sixteenth century. There is always a danger that a maritime focus will abstract the sea power dimension of a conflict and treat it out of its context and out of perspective in war as a whole. Important though the English role came to be in the European wars of the late sixteenth century, that role should not be exaggerated. The central power struggle of the period was not between the Imperial Spain of the Habsburgs and the small island (shared uncomfortably with an independent Scotland) that was distinctly nonimperial England; rather, was it between Spain and France.[1] The primary English interest in the Franco-Spanish contest was to ensure that *neither* side achieved continental preponderance. R. B. Wernham made the point well when he argued that "England could live, had been living, in a world of true Leviathans; she could not live where there was but one."[2]

Through most of the sixteenth century, English balance-of-power policy had been concerned most immediately to thwart real or anticipated threats from France. England's enemy in the reign of Henry VIII (1509–47) had been France, not Spain. The pattern of Anglo-French antagonism continued from the 1540s into the 1550s. Mary Tudor (1553–58) married Philip II of Spain and engaged England actively in the Habsburg column. For nearly the next forty years, as a result of no fewer than eight domestic wars of religion (1560–98), France generally was so disunited internally as to be incapable of protecting her own territory, let alone of making a bid for continental hegemony. From the perspective of England's Elizabeth I (1558–1603), Spain and France ideally would have been so evenly matched that England's modest alliance or benign neutral value would have been a diplomatic card of disproportionate political, and financial, worth. Unfortunately for England's freedom of action, and hence for the profitability of an agile foreign policy, however, French internal disarray was so severe in the 1560s, 1570s, and 1580s that the summit of practicable English ambition had to be the denial of definitive victory to Catholic, pro-Habsburg, elements in France. In the light of succeeding events, it is somewhat ironic that Madrid was fearful in 1560 that England had given over-much offense to Paris with the treaty of Edinburgh, which closed "the post gate of the North" (Scotland) against French influence.[3] Elizabeth's long reign was not ten years old before the traditional assumption of menace from France temporarily was laid to rest, as Spain waxed unprecedentedly strong as a military power in northern Europe. Still, notwithstanding the religious and commercial rivalries that fueled Anglo-Spanish hostility, Spain and England were natural allies against France. Imperial hubris was to oblige Spain to prosecute more war than was wise against England in the 1580s, just as greed and *realpolitik* led England to escalate hostilities. But geostrategically, the principal European foe of Spain and England had to be France.

England was both fortunate and unfortunate in having a strategically objective ally in the Dutch provinces of the Spanish Netherlands. Those provinces revolted against their politically arrogant, financially rapacious, and religiously intolerant Catholic Spanish masters in 1566–68, beginning what was to be nearly an eighty-year war. The commitment to suppress the Dutch revolt proved in the long run a ruinous distraction for the Habsburgs from their more vital endeavor to achieve Western European and Mediterranean dominance. It was fortunate for England that Spain was so heavily and inconclusively distracted from her geostrategically more significant French problems and opportunities. But England was unfortunate in that the revolt in the Spanish Netherlands attracted what unquestionably was the finest and best-commanded field army of the day, first under the Duke of Alba and after 1578 under the Duke of Parma. The Dutch revolt brought an excellent potential invasion force within close striking distance of an England whose land defenses were scarcely more than a joke compared with the highly professional soldiery of the Habsburgs and whose naval power had suffered a long eclipse since the close of Henry VIII's reign. Elizabeth's discomfort with the appearance of the best army of the age in the Spanish Netherlands prompted her decision in 1568 not to release four Spanish ships driven into English ports by Huguenot privateers—ships that carried an £85,000 Genoese loan to pay Alba's soldiers. When added to the

140

irritation and pain caused Madrid by English maritime commercial adventurers (Sir John Hawkins in particular, in the 1560s) in Spain's American colonial preserve[4] and the moral offense committed by England with the Protestant succession of Elizabeth, Elizabeth's seizure of the monies for Alba provided Philip II with powerful motives to define England as a strategic problem in need of resolution. The Protestant succession per se was not a mortal moral offense in Philip II eyes. Philip was not unfriendly to Elizabeth in the early years of her reign; indeed he was even interested in marriage. But one must not discount the distinctly Catholic, as apart from the pragmatic power-political, impulses behind Spanish policy. Nonetheless, Elizabeth's rival for the throne, her cousin Mary Queen of Scots, for many years was a protegée of Catholic France, not of Catholic Spain. Philip was not at all eager to face an Anglo-French coalition; hence, in part, his wooing of Elizabeth.

It is plausible to argue that although strategic circumstances, first in the Mediterranean and then in the Netherlands and again in the south, obliged Philip to defer attempted settlement of his English difficulties until the mid- to late 1580s, the decision to confront Elizabeth one day was latent policy from very early in his reign.[5] Religious duty, imperial dignity, geopolitical rationales—to neutralize the threat to the Habsburg maritime supply line to the Netherlands, and indeed to northern Europe in general—and fears for the financial stability of the empire all commanded Philip to deal firmly with the England of Elizabeth. England's value as an ally against France was not denied by this policy logic. A Catholic post-Elizabethan England could serve as a reliable instrument to contain France.

The Anglo-Spanish struggle in Elizabeth's reign had the aspect for Spain of a distraction within a distraction. To a noteworthy degree, Spanish policy motives certainly were personal and religious as well as imperial and geostrategic. The Spanish struggle for preponderance preeminently was with the Turks and the French, with the Dutch revolt playing an important role in Spanish policy and strategy toward France. Quite briefly in the 1580s and 1590s, England figured significantly as a player worthy of major Habsburg attention. The launching of the Great Armada in 1588, and the subsequent dispatch of armadas in 1596 and 1597 certainly dignified the English foe. Distraction within a distraction though England generally was, her flanking position to the Spanish Netherlands and her inaccessibility to Spanish soldiery rendered her an intractable strategic problem. Superpowers in any age function much on strategic credit. Their writ, that is, runs much more on the basis of their reputation for effective coercion than on the actual exercise of power. The Enterprise of England—the Great Armada—was launched in good part because the superpower of the day could not afford to be seen to be thwarted by a distinctly second-echelon state.[6] Habsburg imperial dignity required the chastisement of England in 1588, much as America's dignity in 1990–91 required the chastisement of Saddam Hussein's Iraq. England's hostility meant that Spain could not resupply her large forces in the Netherlands by sea. After 1568, virtually every effort to send reinforcements and cash (the lifeblood of an army) from Spain to the Netherlands by sea was a failure.[7]

Although the English were to prove second to none in their aptitude for piracy and privateering, they were relatively late starters in pursuing *guerre de course* against Spanish seaborne trade and supply. French Huguenots, operating out of the Biscay ports, waged profitable and righteous war against Spanish commerce for decades before John Hawkins and Francis Drake appeared on the scene in the 1560s. By the early 1570s there was a highly active three-way maritime threat to Spain at sea. Protestant privateers from the Netherlands, from the Huguenot coast of western France, and from England effectively closed the Channel to Spanish shipping.[8] By way of a general judgement, however, "it was the hostility of England which, above all else, made the Channel unsafe for Spanish shipping after 1568."[9] As a result, Spain had to depend upon the land lines of communication close to the inland frontiers of France, known generically as the Spanish Road. Worse yet, English privateering damaged the financial credit of Madrid with its Italian bankers by the typically exaggerated threat posed to the Spanish transatlantic treasure route. In the mid-1560s, in the wake of the increasingly damaging depredations of Huguenot corsairs, Spain reorganized her system of annual convoys from the (Spanish) Main, via Havana and the Azores, to Cadiz and Lisbon.

The mercenary regular soldiers of Spain would not fight if they were not paid.[10] Elizabeth helped finance the Dutch revolt, helped fund Huguenot opponents of the pro-Habsburg Catholic League in France, and eventually paid for a modest English contingent of

7,000 men to fight in the Netherlands (a policy made official on August 20, 1585, with the treaty of Nonsuch and understandably critical to Philip's decision to attempt an invasion of England).[11] In addition, Elizabeth sent forces to fight in Brittany in support of Henry of Navarre against the Catholic, and hence Spanish, cause and provided a persistent and enfeebling distraction for a Spain that for all her wealth and military power was strategically over-stretched.

England, let alone English sea power, was not by any means the largest factor in the eventual thwarting of Spanish ambitions for European hegemony. Spain under Philip II and his successors over-strained her limited resources in continental wars that she could not afford, even though the sea route to the Americas was rendered tolerably secure. In the early 1540s Spain began to convoy her bullion from the New World in an annual *Flota*.[12] As French and Dutch privateers were joined by English commercial adventurers in the 1560s and 1570s, Spain strengthened her convoy arrangements. Francis Drake's devastating raids upon Vigo in northwest Spain, the Cape Verde Islands, and the Caribbean in 1585 and Cadiz in 1587,[13] followed in 1588 by the failure of the Great Armada, promoted acute realization in Madrid that the maritime links of the empire were dangerously vulnerable. As a result, Spain built an oceangoing navy and massively fortified, or refortified, such Caribbean keys to her American empire and its wealth as Puerto Rico and Porto Bello.[14] In addition to her status as Europe's greatest land power, Spain in the 1580s and, particularly, the 1590s became Europe's greatest naval power. But in the 1580s it was England, not Spain, that enjoyed the strategic services of some approximation to a Royal Navy. By way of contrast, the 1590s have been called "the golden age of the Spanish Navy."[15] The 1580s had begun promisingly with the acquisition of Portugal and her blue-water ships in 1580 and with the Marquess of Santa Cruz's defeat of a French fleet at Terceira in the Azores in 1583, but their dismal conclusion pointed unarguably to the need for a much sharper Spanish maritime sword.

Popular English histories have tended to assume that the failure of the Enterprise of England in the summer of 1588 signaled English victory in the undeclared war. Nothing could be further from the truth. Filipe Fernandez-Armesto offers a valuable, if possibly somewhat over-exuberant, corrective to English mythology:

143

The problems of Spain in the 1590's arose not from depressed morale but from excited expectations. This was a decade in which the conquest of France was attempted and that of China projected; in which the defences of the monarchy were modernized from Manila to Milan; in which three more Armadas were assembled, and two launched, and in which the crown's efforts were supported by almost the entire monarchy, with the exception of the Netherlandish rebels and, briefly, some pockets of disaffection in Aragon.[16]

The Habsburg achievement truly was remarkable. After all, the *Reconquista*—the seven and a half centuries-long crusade to free all of Iberia from the Moors—had been concluded only in 1492, the year in which Columbus first crossed the Atlantic. The Spanish Empire of the final quarter of the sixteenth century was the rapid creation of dynastic accident, a large domestic tax base, American gold and silver, and the best army (that money could rent) in Europe. By way of sad contrast, English land forces performed well enough when protected by dikes and strong town walls, but they were not in the same league as the Spanish *tercios*. In the open field, had the Armada taken Plymouth, say, in 1588, or succeeded in escorting Parma's continental veterans to north Kent, the English soldiery would have stood about as much chance as did their successors in 1940 against the German Army.[17]

In the 1580s, England was a small and divided (remember Scotland) island with a low domestic tax base. The Royal Treasury could gather in only approximately £400,000 to £500,000 per annum. The last vestige of England's medieval European empire vanished in 1558 with the loss of Calais in the terminal year of Mary Tudor's reign. England lost the coast of Normandy and Picardy to a resurgent France in 1450 in the last phase of the Hundred Years' War, and Paris secured the Duchy of Brittany in 1491. This meant that a single great land power now occupied the southern coast of the Channel and, with the acquisition of Breton ports, held the weather gauge against English ports. It can be easy to forget that although Henry VIII constructed a fine navy, and some elements of an English naval policy can be traced back to the twelfth century, the fact remains that England in the sixteenth century was not the heir to a great seagoing tradition.[18] With the exception of Catalonia, the same point applies to Spain. Spain was a great land power which acquired, by stages in the 1580s and 1590s, an oceangoing navy good enough to deter and defend

144

against any challenges to the profitability of her American and Far Eastern empire as expressed in the Carrera de Indias. But the burden of those defenses was cumulatively ruinous when added to the cost of the eighty-year war with the Dutch and the reckless pursuit of the Counter-Reformation in Germany.[19]

One might speculate that although Anglo-Spanish hostility was inevitable, perhaps a major armed struggle was not.[20] No truck should be held with that view. The strategic geography of north-western Europe, in the context of Habsburg sovereignty over a heavily Protestant and commercially prosperous Low Countries, set the stage for the conflict which ensued. The fuel for the Anglo-Spanish conflict included an insecure-looking Protestant succession in England, an arguably greatly overextended, vulnerable looking, treasure-laden Spanish maritime empire, and greedy and ambitious English seagoing merchant-adventurers (and land-bound financial backers). As if those factors were not sufficient, one must add to the brew a largely self-absorbed France and the novel and sudden appearance of Spanish military power on a large scale on the coast of Flanders. By way of a capstone is the fact of a Habsburg emperor supremely confident that he enjoyed divine blessing for his enterprises in Christian statecraft as well as the potent consideration of imperial dignity and reputation. Once the pieces were in place, as they largely were as early as the 1560s, this struggle was anything but accidental or avoidable.

Nothwithstanding the unarguable evidence of repeated Spanish support for inept Catholic plots to topple her,[21] Elizabeth believed, perhaps until the year prior to the Great Armada's sailing, that Philip could be deterred by what a later era would call coercive diplomacy. In a monumental policy miscalculation, Elizabeth in 1585 purposely raised the stakes in the undeclared contest by signing a formal treaty with the Netherlanders in revolt against Habsburg rule. She sent modest financial assistance and an expeditionary force to hold key fortress towns on the Scheldt below Antwerp. She sent also an imperiously regal leader, her favorite, the Earl of Leicester, to rule the lands then in revolt against Spain. Lest her determination to oppose the expansion of Habsburg dominion be misunderstood, Elizabeth also unleashed Francis Drake to ravage the coasts of Spain and the Spanish empire overseas. By these blatantly belligerent acts, Elizabeth intended to encourage second thoughts in Madrid about the wisdom of its policy of

145

undermining her position and indeed the Protestant succession in England. Philip, however, was incited rather than deterred by the sharply warlike turn in English policy in 1585, and he concluded that the reconquest of the Netherlands could never be consummated so long as England was ruled by Elizabeth. His principal general in Flanders, his nephew the brilliant duke of Parma, disagreed. Parma was always of the opinion that, absent strategic surprise, the invasion of England should follow, not precede, the complete subjugation of the Netherlands. By 1586–87, however, notwithstanding awesome setbacks—including Drake's punishing preemptive beard-singeing raid on Cadiz in 1587, which delayed the Enterprise for a year—the Armada had become an imperial political necessity. Since Philip's intention to invade England had been leaked in Rome in the early 1580s, the prestige of the Habsburg Empire was committed inalienably to the great adventure of an invasion. That adventure required continentalist Spain to chance her arm in the teeth of England's instrument of excellence, her armed sea power. That instrument was not truly excellent in absolute terms or by comparison with its successors a century and two centuries later. But to contest Spanish freedom of action to transport and escort an army to invade England, English sea power was very much the cutting edge of Elizabeth's power to resist. At the time as well as long since, however, the question of whether Elizabeth made proper use of her maritime strength has excited debate.

Some historians and naval theorists, while applauding the strategic uses to which Elizabeth's England applied her sea power, have alleged that that power was not applied systematically and effectively. Those scholars, captured by the naval ideas embodied in the practices and exploits of Edward Vernon, Hawke, Jervis, and Nelson in the eighteenth century, have had difficulty understanding that England did not enjoy the services of a Nelsonian fighting instrument at sea in the 1580s and 1590s. Sir Herbert Richmond, for example, complained that Elizabeth's continental subsidies and continental land force commitment cost "about £800,000," while the cost of ten years of military operations in Ireland "ran close to £ 3½ millions." He proceeded to argue that "for a fraction of these sums a navy might have been equipped and maintained which would not merely have checked an army's advance in Picardy and caused anx-

146

iety in Madrid for treasure ships, but would have brought the whole structure of Spain tumbling about the King's ears. With a base in the Azores and a strong fleet in constant cruising there, no Flotas could have expected to pass unmolested."[22]

There have been two, and just possibly three, waves of interpretation of the strategic utility of sea warfare in the Elizabethan period. In the first wave of modern commentary, Martin Oppenheim and Julian Corbett advanced the view that in sea power Elizabeth enjoyed the potential services of an instrument of strategy that could have wrought ruin upon overextended Spain. Those authors heaped praise upon the blue-water vision of Hawkins and Drake for an offensive maritime strategy and a "silver blockade" at the Azores; they condemned the smaller and more continental aspirations of Elizabeth and advanced the general proposition that English sea power in the late sixteenth century could and should have been an instrument of decision in war. Corbett argued that

> unfortunately for Drake, in the Elizabethan age the principles of naval warfare were as little understood as its limitations. He could convince the Government of neither the one nor the other.[23]

Oppenheim was even more forthright in his fault finding:

> Study of the forty-five years of glorious naval history on which her [Elizabeth's] renown is mainly based, leaves the impression that more might and should have been done with the Navy. . . . Under conditions more favorable to ascendancy at sea than have ever existed for England, before or since, the successes of the Navy itself, as distinguished from the expansion of the commercial marine, were, although relatively great, limited by the hesitation with which the service was pecuniarily starved, and the settled doctrine underlying her maritime essays that an expedition should be of a character to return a profit on the outlay.[24]

The doyen of a second, massively revisionist, wave of interpretation has been R. B. Wernham, whose work sharply corrected the overly maritime view of his predecessors.[25] Wernham has argued persuasively that the premier policy concern of Elizabethan England had to be the alleviation of balance-of-power perils across the Channel. Rather more contentiously, Wernham and those who have followed him have argued that if England lost the conflict for

147

balanced power in northwest Europe, her distinctly modest fighting power at sea would not suffice to protect the realm. In short, a continentalist school of thought has taken over scholarship on Elizabethan policy and strategy.

Small signs of discontent with second-wave, overly continentalist interpretation have been discernible,[26] but the issue is one of emphasis only. There is no question of a return in fashion to the kind of combined-arms enthusiasm which had Corbett lament that

> the idea of following up the victorious Armada campaign by the capture of Lisbon and the liberation of Portugal was as obvious as it was sound. The navy had laid the way open, and all that was required to deal Spain a mortal blow was a small compact military force properly equipped and organized.[27]

Apart from the nontrivial objection that Elizabeth sought only to frustrate Spain's grander designs, not deal her a "mortal blow," in 1588–89, England enjoyed the services neither of Wellington's peninsular veterans nor of the great Duke himself. It is a safe prediction that against the Spanish regular army of the late 1580s, an English expedition seriously committed to the conquest of Portugal would have ended in a bloody rout. Whatever the many limitations of England's sea power in this period, that power was an exemplar of military prowess in comparison with her land forces.

Maritime war with Spain was at least as much a private as a public enterprise under Elizabeth. The great Western squadron—later the Channel, Home, or Grand Fleet—that was the pivot upon which the Royal Navy blockaded French sea power in the eighteenth and early nineteenth centuries bore scant relation to the squadrons of ships that Elizabeth either herself could afford to send to sea or could persuade investors to fund as a commercial proposition. Whether or not Elizabeth understood the concept of command of the sea scarcely signifies. She lacked the means to make a strategic reality of such a concept. England was fortunate that maritime-dependent Spain had less grasp of the essentials of maritime warfare in 1588 than she did herself. It is important to remember just how great a power Spain was in the sixteenth and early seventeenth centuries. By way of illustration, the principal reason that French and British colonial endeavors in the Americas were pursued so far from the tropics, was precisely because of a well-founded fear of Spain.[28]

Policy and strategy devolve ultimately upon the ability of tactical and logistic units and organizations to perform. From the early 1570s until the close of this struggle with the Treaty of London in 1604, England enjoyed marked advantages in ship design for employment in northern and Atlantic waters, in the availability of skilled seamen, in ships' ordinance of most kinds, and in naval administration. These critical material, human, and administrative advantages mounted through the 1570s and 1580s and diminished in relative terms only after 1588 as Spain emulated English marine architecture with the construction of tolerable facsimiles of England's race-built galleons. The race-built ship, first constructed in 1570, was long relative to her beam (on a length-to-beam ratio of approximately three-to-one), eschewed the traditional high fore and aft "castles," lay relatively low in the water, and was designed to provide a reasonably stable gun platform in choppy seas. The new class of English ships was developed to express a new notion of sea fighting; a stand-off gunnery duel and not an infantry combat at sea. In the immediate aftermath of the Great Armada, Philip funded the construction of twelve 1,000-ton galleons along English race-built lines. Imitation is the sincerest form of flattery.

English sea power *might*, with more luck than obtained, have wrought definitive preemptive damage upon the Armada of 1588 on the coasts of Spain and Portugal (far beyond that achieved at Cadiz by Francis Drake in 1587). Also, in 1588 England's sea power *might* have followed up promptly on the Armada's protracted catastrophe at sea in order to wreck such of the fleet as regained Spanish ports. In addition, English sea power *might* have forestalled Philip's rebuilding of Spanish naval power, had Drake and Sir John Norris obeyed orders in their great raid upon Portugal in 1589. Finally, England *might* have instituted an effective maritime blockade of the annual treasure *Flota* from the Spanish main (as was attempted, for example, in the forlorn hopes of 1591 off the Azores and 1595 in the West Indies), which might have crippled Spanish land power by financial atrophy. However, although the critics of blue-water thinking have gone too far in discounting what sea power did and could achieve, the practical limitations of Elizabeth's maritime instrument were daunting. Moreover, those limitations embraced all aspects of their subject:

149

material, human, financial, administrative, geographical, and even conceptual. But the proper measure of strategic achievement is the quality of policy result compared with the quality of outcome required. In other words, the question was not, "Was the strategy a thing of beauty?" but rather "Was it good enough?" In its wartime impact in the 1580s and 1590s, English sea power did well enough to contribute noticeably, perhaps critically, to the frustration of Spain's imperial ambitions. The very dispatch in 1588 of the Great and "Invincible" Armada, the Enterprise of England, as well as the organization of three subsequent such ventures, is persuasive evidence of the depth of annoyance and intensity of strategic pain that England's maritime harassment and continental commitment was causing the Spanish Empire.

The strategic achievement of Elizabeth's England is difficult to exaggerate and was vitally maritime in executive agency. Elizabeth's multifaceted opposition to Imperial Spain contributed critically to Spain's inability to consolidate her position in the Netherlands and in France. Viewed strategically, the Great Armada of 1588 and its successors comprised an enormously wasteful diversion of scarce Spanish wealth, material, manpower, and attention, from her primary drive for continental supremacy. At the level of grand strategy, in aid of a crystal-clear policy of maintaining a balance of power in Europe, Elizabeth performed wonders in the field of what the Pentagon in the late 1980s would call "competitive strategies." By modest financial subsidy and troop commitment, Elizabeth helped vitally to keep anti-Spanish fighting fronts alive in the Netherlands and in France. Meanwhile, the menace that English sea power posed to the maritime dimension to Spanish wealth and security compelled a level and extent of imperial defensive provision which, although successful in the 1590s and generally for long thereafter, sharply limited Spain's ability to take and sustain the offensive in Europe.[29]

When considering how well or poorly England fared in her struggle with Spain and whether she used her sea power properly, it is essential to remember the character of the war she sought to wage. England could not, and had good reason not to seek to, effect the downfall of the Spanish Empire. Any such result must only produce, by default, a greater French menace in the future. Rather, Elizabeth endeavored to keep the coast of Europe facing southern England in divided hands. Somebody had to protect the

Low Countries from French ambitions, and that somebody preferably would be distant Spain. A powerful Spain could not be as great a menace to England as would a powerful and united France, if only for the most fundamental reasons of strategic geography. France was nearer, and her recently gained ports in Brittany enjoyed the weather gauge for a Channel which typically enjoyed a westerly air flow.

It may be an exaggeration to claim, admittedly with hindsight, that "looking back, most observers—even Spaniards—saw the failure of the Armada as the point at which the decline of Spain as an imperial power began."[30] Nonetheless, that failure was a blow to Spain's reputation and an encouragement to her many foes. Although Elizabeth's shift in policy to open hostility in 1585 triggered more war than she had anticipated, her sensibly limited objectives were all met in due course. England indeed shaped the course and outcome of the long struggle, particularly through her maritime assets. All of the essential state players were kept in the game of international politics, or sustained so that they could revive, with the result that a tolerable peace could be concluded in 1604 soon after the accession of James I, albeit to the chagrin of some of the more predatory of the financiers and shipboard leaders of the maritime war. England had done all that reasonably she could aspire to do to discomfort and frustrate, but not ruin, the Spanish Empire. In the process, English sea power saw great material, human, and even strategy improvement over the course of three decades.

Continentalist theorizing is sound as a corrective to romantic navalism, but for the Elizabethan period as for later eras, fallacies must be guarded against. England's sea power in the 1580s and 1590s was a weak reed as a strategic instrument—certainly by comparison with the Royal Navy of the 1750s and 1760s. But that weak reed was a solid oak tree in comparison with England's contemporary military prowess on land. In countering impracticable blue-water ideas, it is appropriate to cite the logistic inadequacies of Tudor sea power. It is also appropriate, however, to cite the awesome reputation in Spanish eyes enjoyed by English fighting ships and sailors. The gentlemen-volunteers of the Earl of Leicester in the Low Countries occasioned annoyance but not the dread raised by fear of the appearance of Drake.

There has been a long-running controversy over the feasibility of the Invincible Armada of 1588. Rather like the Battle of Britain in 1940 and the German campaign in Russia in 1941, the Armada is all too easy to present as a forlorn hope. Hindsight can have the effect of putting blinkers on historians. By way of contrast, a strategist looking backward is impressed with the achievements of Spain in 1587–88 in the prosecution of the undeclared war with England. The Invincible Armada could have gone down in the history books as "Philip II's masterpiece."[31] Not too much good fortune would have been required for Medina Sidonia and the Duke of Parma to have solved their land power–sea power junction problem for a great descent upon the Thames estuary. Some recovery of order in the Armada after the fireship attack in Calais Roads and a subsequent shift in the wind would have sufficed to hold the Armada available to escort Parma's troop barges, assuming that Calais had been occupied as the port of departure. These and similar points can be presented to the limits of the imagination. The point is that the Armada was by no means bound to fail. The belief that failure was inevitable is one of the more recent of the Armada myths in history books. One may judge that Philip II missed a "window of opportunity," an "international situation in 1571 uniquely favorable to an invasion of England,"[32] but historians are more adept at spotting those strategic moments than were the historical players. Whether opportunities to achieve a favorable decision were missed by fallible political leaders, what can be said overall about the leverage granted English policy by the country's sea power?

English sea power, public and private, denied Spain the ability to apply her theoretically unmatchable land power with sufficient effectiveness in the Netherlands. In a very real sense, English sea power sustained life in the Dutch revolt. That sea power, flanking Spain's maritime line of communication to the Netherlands, critically helped shape the general course and character *and eventual outcome* of the Dutch revolt against Spanish rule. That achievement was massively distracting for an overstretched Spain with ever more severe problems of creditworthiness. Moreover, English sea power ensured that Elizabeth could intervene militarily in the Netherlands and northern France virtually at will, finances permitting and when there was an allied army active in the field. In other words, an enforceable freedom to use the sea meant that English communications with the Continent were entirely reliable.

In the last resort, that freedom to use the sea rests upon a willingness and ability to conduct a fleet battle to affirm some recognizable facsimile of command. Behind the secure communications lay a readiness to meet any maritime challenge in broadside-to-broadside battle. All sea-dependent policies and grand strategies, in all periods, ultimately must lean upon preparedness to wage contemporary variants of that battle.

With the admixture of luck, much of it merited, English sea power was sufficient to deny Philip a direct option against England. He always believed that he had the choice of invasion; after all, he did assemble four Armadas and dispatch three of them. The weatherliness of England's race-built ships in the hands of professional seamen, the handiness of England's shipboard ordnance (four-wheel gun trucks designed for in-board reloading), and the frequently appalling climatic conditions in the Narrow Seas all conspired to frustrate Philip's nominal invasion option. In sum, given the general self-sufficiency of the late Tudor economy and the availability of Hanseatic alternatives to Antwerp as continental entrepôts for English woolen cloth, Philip II's Habsburg Empire was critically short of leverage against England (particularly after Elizabeth's execution of Mary Queen of Scots in 1587).

English sea power contributed usefully, if imprecisely, to the periodic bankruptcy of Spain, as well as more certainly to the perpetual shakiness of Habsburg credit. For the reverse of the coin, the depredations of English sea power contributed modestly, but still usefully, to the financing of an Elizabethan grand strategy which was ever on the brink of fiscal impracticality. Nonetheless, it was Philip's Spain which was obliged to declare bankruptcy, not Elizabeth's England. Finally, whether in semipiratical or Royal Naval guise, the sea power of late Tudor England yielded a prestige, indeed a geostrategic and political consequence, in the affairs of Europe unobtainable from any other source. Gravely flawed though Elizabeth's naval cutlass certainly was as a strategic instrument, England had no other lever as powerful with which to help shape her security environment in this period.

Eight and a half decades on from the close of Anglo-Spanish hostilities with the Treaty of London of 1604, the pattern of late-medieval antagonism between England and France reappeared. For geographical reasons, if for no other, France was a more formidable foe to maritime England than Spain could ever be. From the time of Louis XIV to that of Napoleon I, France posed the threat inherent in overmighty continental power which had driven Elizabeth to oppose Philip II's Spain. And the French menace lay scarcely more than twenty miles distant across the Strait of Dover, a fact which rendered the possibility of invasion a shadow over-hanging British defense provision and shaping British strategy. The primary national instrument of that strategy was the Navy.

Between 1688 and 1815, a 127-year period, Britain and France waged seven major conflicts and were at war, though not always formally so, for no fewer than 62 years. Furthermore, minor war-fare was either an ever-present or ever-imminent reality, both on land in North America between the British and French colonies and their Indian allies and on and from sea in the West Indies. The great wars of this extensive period were the Nine Years' War, 1688–97; the War of Spanish Succession, 1701–13; the War of Austrian Succession, 1740–48; the Seven Years' War, 1756–63; the American Revolutionary War, French phase, 1778–83; the French Revolutionary Wars, 1793–1802; and the Napoleonic Wars, 1803–14, 1815. The degree to which the Anglo-French struggle from the accession of William III in the Glorious Revo-lution of 1688 to the demise of Napoleon in 1815 warrants unified treatment is worth debating, but not very seriously. One could take exception to the omnibus term, "The Second Hundred Years' War."[33] The seven wars had some distinctive causes.

Different kinds of wars yield different terms of military engage-ment and hence distinctive conditions for the strategic utility of sea power. History-based strategic theory must follow Clausewitz closely, albeit with a noteworthy *caveat*:

> The first, the supreme, the most far-reaching act of judgment that the statesman and commander have to make is to establish by that test the kind of war on which they are embarking; neither mistaking it for, nor trying to turn it into something that is alien to its nature. This is the first of all strategic questions and the most comprehen-sive.[34]

A *caveat* is needed to signify that wars do not have an inherent "nature." The nature of a war is a matter to be settled by skill in statecraft and grand strategy. When continental and maritime

154

states face off for war, each will seek to shape the course and conduct of events such that the nature of the ensuing war is structured to the home team's net advantage.

It can be argued that the Nine Years' and Spanish Succession wars, as well as the wars of the French Revolution and Empire, were all "fought to prevent French hegemony over Europe, and to curb the power of the French state."[35] By way of contrast, allegedly, the War of Austrian Succession, the Seven Years' War, and the War for American Independence (1775-83) were all maritime in character and commercial and colonial in motivation. This division is not without merit, but on balance it confuses and threatens to conceal more than it clarifies and reveals. Virtually regardless of the relative strength of shifting policy motives among belligerents in war after war, the grand and military-strategic interplay of continental and maritime options runs like a silver thread throughout this era. It is true, for example, that the political nation in Britain insisted upon war with Spain in 1739 (Jenkins' Ear) for the crassest of commercial motives. But it is no less true that within a year, the conflict had slid into a heavily continental mold as a Prussian menace to the integrity of the Austrian Empire threatened to remove the land-power balancer to France effectively from the stage for a while.

Similarly, the Great War for Empire, the first world war that was the Seven Years' War, did indeed begin in the Ohio valley and undoubtedly was about who would exploit the rich potential of North America. Unfortunately for simplicity in analysis, however, influential Frenchmen and Britons regarded victory in America as the strategic high road to superior stature in Europe. Moreover, the outcome to that war, although nowhere near as draconian in its terms as Pitt demanded, was believed throughout Europe to have upset the maritime balance of power in Britain's favor. There is reason to be careful lest significant differences among conflicts over the course of a century should lead to injudicious generalization. But there is also better reason not to be fearful of a holistic approach to Anglo-French conflicts from 1688–1815.

England's Royal Navy experienced mixed fortunes in the period between the termination of the Anglo-Spanish conflict in 1604 and the ignition of the Anglo-French struggle in 1688–89 by the ouster from London of the Stuart dynasty and their Catholic succession. It is true that the Navy of Oliver Cromwell's

Commonwealth had humbled the Dutch in 1652–54, enforced the Navigation Act of 1651, which expressed and legalized mercantilist theories of wealth accumulation, and had been a formidable instrument of state policy. Statesmen could conceive of a Western Design in 1654 intended, at least in the ambitions of Cromwell, the Lord Protector, "to overrun the entire Spanish empire in the Americas."[36] Nonetheless, as Samuel Pepys revealed in his diary, the Royal Navy in the seventeenth century was distinctly flawed as an instrument of state. Indeed, it was the flaws in the administration of the state that critically helped flaw that naval instrument. The later Stuarts lacked the influence with an ever more suspicious Parliament to secure adequate funding for the Navy, and the political and religious turmoil of the period was made duly manifest in the fleet. For a more extreme analogical case, the French Navy was unable to recover in the early 1800s from the depredations of the Revolution in the 1790s, and the former Soviet Navy in the 1990s is barely an operational shadow of its former self.[37]

The Royal Navy at the beginning of the eighteenth century was improved out of all recognition from its predecessor of a century earlier. It would be a serious error, however, to view it as anything other than the product of its period. Ideas about sea power need to be anchored in contemporary realities. The eighteenth-century navy, though a tool of state, also was a tool for the private profit of officers, even men, and contractors. Certainly prior to the American war and even to some degree thereafter, pervasive realities of the Navy included rotting ships (with unsheathed bottoms), sick men, inflexible tactics, and very limited smashing power in gunnery against solidly constructed enemy ships. If ships and men cannot perform tactically because teredo worms have eaten away ship timber and scurvy has decimated the crew, policy and strategy rapidly become irrelevant or worse. In the space of less than a hundred years (the 1700–99 period), notwithstanding the fundamental technological stability of the era of fighting sail, Britain acquired an all-weather, year-round, global military instrument in its Royal Navy. Particular notice is required of three key innovations: copper sheathing, mandated for all naval vessels in 1778; the required distribution of lemon juice so that scurvy was defeated by the mid-1790s; and the metallurgical advances of the Industrial Revolution, which enabled the Carron Ironworks in

156

Scotland to produce in 1779 the thin-walled, short barreled, and relatively lightweight ship-smashing carronade.[38]

The material and geostrategic aspects of the Anglo-French struggle, important though they were, should not overwhelm recognition of the critical significance of political culture. That culture had major impacts upon the strategic utility of sea power in the Anglo-French wars. Above all else, the spirit of the age educated statesmen, generals, and admirals to be moderate in their goals and methods.[39] As a guide to statecraft the balance of power, that "cloudy and indefinite concept,"[40] called for military strategies to exert leverage for advantage, not for the overthrow of the enemy. When policies of overthrow were attempted, as by Pitt the Elder after 1760 in the Seven Years' War, the society of states labeled it an aberration and an illegitimate quest after "immoderate greatness," to quote that quintessentially eighteenth-century historian, Edward Gibbon. That same European society which approved the order, tidiness, and control of brute forces of nature implicit in the vague concept of the balance of power understandably favored a similar approach to naval warfare. The formal enshrinement of the line of battle for a century as *the* combat formation in admirals' fighting instructions made every kind of tactical sense, given the material limitations of the ships, the gunpowder, and the problems of tactical control in battle of the period.[41] But it was the case also that the orderly line of battle, as contrasted with the mob activity, or melees, of some of the battles of the Anglo-Dutch wars, was exactly what educated men in the Age of Reason would prefer, almost regardless of tactical considerations.

The systematic corruption and venality that pervaded most aspects of public life was a product of the political culture of the period. As late as 1802–4, Lord St. Vincent, the First Sea Lord, launched a massive and comprehensive campaign to root out corruption in the naval dockyards and by private contractors. This laudable, if belated, endeavor was rendered less laudable in that it coincided with the most desperate period of the wars with France, following the brief time of the miscalled Peace of Amiens. To adapt the familiar saying, there is a great deal of ruin in a navy. The security of the state requires that its sea power be strategically useful. Ideally, in its naval dimension, that sea power would be honestly administered and the wonder of its age for efficiency. In practice, states are obliged to settle for military instruments good enough to do what policy and strategy command, because a search for the best navy can breed a perilous intolerance of a navy which is literally good enough. The leading historian of the administration of the Royal Navy in the eighteenth century has offered the following ironic and sobering reflections:

> Venality and neglect were so extensive in the eighteenth-century navy that an administrative historian, if he did not know in advance that the British navy was by far the strongest and most consistently victorious navy of the period, could easily end with a catalogue of reasons for British naval collapse. In fact, *one historian who investigated the British navy in the early eighteenth century was so appalled by what she found that she concluded the empire must have been won by trade, for it could not have been won by the navy.*[42]

The major naval powers of the eighteenth century were refining a fighting instrument that had been fashioned and at least partially professionalized in the previous century. There were important technical developments in this period. The innovations late in the century of coppering ship's bottoms and the development of the short-range, heavy caliber carronade were significant. Scarcely less important were the improvements in the health and general fitness of crews achieved by advances in the science of diet and nutrition.[43] Nonetheless, there was an effective unity in the military tools of conflict among all of the wars of this long period. The same holds for war on land, which helps explain why Clausewitz chose not to single out technology for explicit treatment in *On War*.

In order to resist the unhistorical perils that flow from hindsight, it is instructive to notice the radical differences in geostrategic challenges posed the Royal Navy in the eighteenth century compared with the twentieth. From 1900 to 1950 the Royal Navy successively anticipated future combat against a Franco-Russian alliance, then an Imperial Germany expected to challenge for battle-fleet command of the North Sea (and hence for surface command of the world's oceans), next a Nazi Germany wedded of near-term necessity to a commerce-raiding doctrine, and finally against a Soviet Union whose maritime ambitions were obscure. That fifty-year span witnessed what would have been judged a breakneck pace of geostrategical and technological change by any standards, let alone that of the eighteenth century.

By way of contrast to its twentieth-century experience, the British Royal Navy in the eighteenth and early nineteenth centuries faced a continuity in identity of chief enemy, and therefore in geostrategic context, in operational, tactical, and administrative problems and in technical possibilities also. These continuities allowed the accumulation of relevant experience for the solution of France-focused problems in the conduct of war. Countries that fight each other seven times for 62 out of 127 years can scarcely help but become expert anticipators of the style of war favored by the traditional enemy. John Creswell penetrated to the heart of the matter:

> One can understand the advantages enjoyed by the great seamen of the end of the eighteenth century. There were giants in those days, not necessarily because they were more favored at birth than the men of our generation, but *because many of them had experience of two or even three wars and each man was carrying on a living tradition from the generation before him*: carrying it on, too, in a century which saw little material change in naval warfare, when the experience of the past had more direct application to the future than may be the case in our own day.[44]

It was unfortunate for the Royal Navy that the tactical training it had acquired so painfully at the hands of the Dutch from the 1650s to the early 1670s was to prove for strategic reasons to be generally inappropriate to the new enemy, France.[45] In the seventeenth century the Royal Navy adopted a tactical system of combat suitable for the waging of decisive fleet battle with a Dutch enemy who could not afford to concede command of the high seas to England. The Dutch lived by the profit of their seaborne commerce; they had no practicable choice other than to stand and fight for freedom of passage of their heavily convoyed trade or lose by default. As always, tactics had to flow from strategy. The Fighting Instructions first issued in 1653 by General George Monk reflected the experience of the previous seventy-five years,[46] the English tactical style in sea warfare (which was for a stand-off artillery duel), and the reaction of the general and his fellow soldiers-at-sea, Generals Robert Blake and Richard Deane, to the disorderly and undisciplined melees of 1652 and 1653, their first experiences of battle afloat.[47] The keystone of the Fighting Instructions was the order to deploy for battle in line-ahead formation. The instructions changed only in detail over the course of the next century from campaign to campaign and from admiral to admiral.

Preservation of the line was intended to vest and maintain real tactical control amid the smoke and confusion of combat solely in the hands of the admiral in command. As a closely related secondary matter, the line of battle was intended to concentrate firepower, insofar as firepower could be concentrated by ships confined to broadside firing (with no more than 25 percent deviation in arc of fire possible, fore and aft of the beam). By the beginning of the War of Spanish Succession at the latest, "the Permanent Fighting Instructions became the only possible tactical code. They ceased to be 'Collected Wisdom'—even 'Short cuts to experience.' They became—*the Law*. And the Line was the graven image set up by the Law—the parallel, conterminous, inviolable Line."[48] The consequences of the allegedly holy writ of the line were that "a British fleet did not once inflict a whole-hearted defeat upon any enemy in a stand-up fight between the battle of Barfleur in 1692 and that of the Saints in 1782. Ninety years!"[49]

Probably critics have exaggerated the contribution of British fleet tactics to the indecisiveness of major naval combat in the eighteenth century. The fact is that stoutly built ships of that period were exceedingly hard to sink. Gunnery was not accurate, the ships were anything but tactically agile, and tactical command—which is to say, signaling—was primitive.

Contrasting naval strategies and the superior sailing qualities of French and Spanish naval vessels contributed to the British tactical problem in bringing the enemy to a decisive fleet engagement. The generally moderate spirit of the age also was a factor for restraint, reducing the likelihood of a battle of annihilation. Postreligious and prenationalist Europe was rarely marred by political or military urges to annihilate a foe. Just as high policy and strategy did not seek an enemy's overthrow, so admirals and generals typically were content to win, as one might say, on points. For example, much has been made by historians of the victory achieved by Admiral George Rodney at the Saintes in 1782. The literature abounds with close variants on the judgment that "this battle introduces a new phase in naval warfare."[50] In fact, however, Rodney with thirty-six ships was content with a victory which yielded only five French losses out of a fleet numbering thirty. The

160

Saintes did witness the first use of the carronade in a fleet action, and Rodney accidentally (actually he had little choice, given the variable light winds and disorder in the French line) broke the enemy's line. But Nelson would not have been satisfied with a tally of five out of thirty. The Saintes was a distinctly eighteenth-century battle fought in the time-honored manner by gentlemanly eighteenth-century admirals (although Sir Samuel Hood, Rodney's second-in-command, believed that a more punishing victory would have been achievable with more determination in the pursuit).[51]

The French, and later the Germans—unlike the Dutch—lacked immediate strategic need to hazard their fleet by a roll of the dice in naval battle. Whereas an uncommanded sea could mean ruin for the Dutch, for the French it was an expensive nuisance, a distraction, and only in long-term perspective a principal source of their grand-strategic undoing. A continental state aspiring to hegemony on land has many policy options for attempting to cope with a hostile power on its maritime flank. Typically, though with leading exceptions in 1690 and 1779, France was so expensively engaged in continental enterprises that her naval power was too weak to offer battle with a reasonable prospect of success.

It could be argued that France, and then Germany, as great continental powers, did not need to challenge Britain for command of the sea in its classic sense. The concept of a "luxury" fleet unnecessary for national security, as Winston Churchill termed Germany's High Seas Fleet in 1912, expressed this error. It is almost as fallacious as would be the claim that Britain and the United States, as great sea powers, have had "luxury" armies. The preponderantly European and landward ambitions of the continental powers allegedly found their appropriate strategic complement in naval doctrines of sea denial. France, Germany, and later the Soviet Union strictly did not need to exercise command of the sea in a positive sense; they could succeed on land in the absence of secure sea lines of communication. But time and again success on land was only a temporary success with operational art; it was not victory in war as a whole. Continental failure at sea enabled the maritime foe to shape a lengthy conflict for the unraveling of continental empire. The wartime importance of maritime communications to a sea power foe has to be the measure of its importance to the continental state or coalition. The naval strategies of the two sides are likely to differ, since they will express both the effort that each is able to commit to the maritime environment and the different strategic purpose behind the effort (command for sea control versus sea denial). In the period of focus here, though prior to Nelson, French tactics probably were better adapted for the support of French strategy than were British tactics in support of British strategy.[52]

The important question, though, is whether French naval strategy was the correct one—that is, whether it could accomplish the purposes set for it by national policy, given the immensity of the difficulties posed by the workings of British sea power. French naval strategy was oriented around the ideas of a fleet in being, commerce raiding, and direct support for land operations. Through its protracted strategic operation as an enabling agent, British sea power indirectly was a war-winning instrument. British naval strategy did not require the defeat of the enemy's navy in fleet-scale battle, only its neutralization. But given its fundamentally positive maritime mission, to allow British commerce and military power to use the seas, the Royal Navy was obliged to be willing to fight fleet actions. An ethos of battle avoidance of the kind characteristic of French, and later German, naval behavior would have been totally incompatible with British strategy. Whether French naval strategy was well served by French tactics, the record of Anglo-French conflict in the age of sail demonstrates that France lacked the naval means to make a success of its chosen strategy. Moreover, the naval means which were lacking were not confined to numbers of ships.

The French Navy, particularly in the Napoleonic Wars, often was short on seamanship, on discipline generally, on efficiency in serving the guns while under fire, and on leadership by example on the part of the officers. These typical failings were multiplied many times by the ill effects of the early years of the Revolution. Amateur enthusiasm and ideological fervor have some value as a substitute for skill in an army, but they have no such value for a navy. The French fleet which was beaten tactically on the Glorious First of June 1794 was a mere shadow of the one which the British Royal Navy had met in the American War only a little over a decade earlier. Overall, the French Navy was strong on the finer points of ship design, administration (particularly manning), and tactical theory. French deficiencies lay in numbers of ships—unless allied with Spain or other states with noteworthy fleets (e.g., the

Dutch or the Danes)—ship handling, access to naval stores in wartime, resolution in battle, the influence of national strategic geography on fleet deployment, and practical strategy. The last point refers to the fact that if strategy asks more of the tactical instrument—the fighting fleet—than that instrument can provide, it is a wrong strategy. Napoleon's grand design in 1805 for the concentration of the French fleets and squadrons for the evasion or destruction in detail of the Royal Navy illustrates the folly to which policy may succumb when it ignores its basic strategic problem of insufficient means for the ambitious goals selected.[53]

Intended to facilitate central command and control in battle, the Royal Navy's admiral's Fighting Instructions had the effect of minimizing the prospect of inflicting annihilating defeat upon an uncooperative enemy. But they had the strong if negative virtue of reducing the risk that one's own fleet would suffer defeat in detail. (It was for precisely this reason that Jellicoe's Grand Fleet deployed for battle in line ahead at Jutland on May 31, 1916.) Married to what sometimes was an effective system of naval blockade of the principal French fleet bases at Brest and Toulon (as well as Rochefort, plus Ferrol, Cadiz, and Cartagena in Spain), the weight of British sea power repeatedly provided the conditions that enabled France's continental ambitions to be thwarted. Maintenance of the blockade came to rest upon a well-developed system of flexible concentration of force off Ushant, in Torbay, at Port Mahon, or at Gibraltar—depending on political and geostrategic circumstances (the scope of commitments, the sizes of the respective fleets, and the character of contemporary British naval leadership), and the weather.

The point is that France, and later Germany, was unable to be sufficiently superior to her continental enemies for long enough so as to be able to construct a naval power capable of removing Britain from the struggle. The contribution of British sea power writ large to the weight and agility of British grand strategy frequently was critical to the landward frustration of French ambitions.

The possibility of swift decision in land campaigns increased geometrically with the political conditions created by the French Revolution. When those conditions were exploited by a military genius, armies again became instruments of rapid victory. The

163

enhanced effectiveness of French land power, however, inevitably proved to be a wasting asset. The new nationalism of France inexorably triggered countervailing nationalism elsewhere, particularly in Germany. The eighteenth-century armies of the First, Second, and Third Coalitions that France swept away so decisively were superseded by forces substantially remodeled for modern times (with the notable exception of the British Army). Napoleon and his marshals trained their enemies in the hard school of defeat in the field. The period 1688–1815 illustrates clearly a strategic fact that the twentieth century has confirmed, albeit to the surprise of many theorists: the increase in the strength of potentially hegemonic continental powers has been more than offset by the increase in the strength of continental-size opponents. In the twentieth century the aspiring European hegemon has been obliged to cope with the offsetting power in the rising economic, and hence potentially military, weight of extra-European continental-size states. Necessarily, command of maritime access to and from those states has been critical to the balance of power in Europe and Asia.

There was method and purpose in British and French grand strategies and patterns in strategic behavior. Allowing for a historically average level of skill and ineptitude in both countries, nevertheless political culture and calculations of dynastic and state interest shaped policy, policy tended to drive strategy, and strategy molded tactical choices. Notwithstanding the strong elements of unity in this hundred years–plus era of recurring Anglo-French war, it is the very richness of the grand-strategic and military-strategic records of the belligerents and their sundry and shifting alliances which invites discovery of doctrines or systems in statecraft. There is some evidence for every major school of thought, clustered as they are around blue-water versus continental or balance-of-power theories of British policy and strategy. The latter view, now long in the ascendant, might more accurately be termed the mixed continental-maritime school,[54] though with a fairly consistent tilt toward continentalism.

Each of these seven wars was different, but virtually the same elements structured them all. Britain's strategic dilemma was how to deter or wage war effectively in the absence of a large army;[55] the French strategic dilemma was how to deter or wage war effectively in the absence of a navy capable of challenging for command of the sea. Neither nation could afford to build and maintain

164

first-class fighting instruments by land and sea. Both countries made occasional grand-strategic and military-strategic errors, but by and large each performed adaptively as it had to. Each did what it could to find the leverage sufficient to achieve the generally modest goals of high policy. There were some constants through these wars, but they did not drive the detail of strategy and operations in any mechanistic fashion. For example, Britain was permanently sensitive to the issue of which state controlled the Low Countries in general and the mouth of the Scheldt, with the ports of Flushing and Antwerp, in particular. The strategic utility of the Low Countries to a foe of Britain, however, depended critically on the offshore context—the balance of naval power. The Spaniards, the French, and the Germans successively overran the coast of Flanders, but that continental fact, worrisome to London though it was, did not guarantee the feasibility of invasion. The enemy in Flanders always had to seek a solution to the problems posed by the Channel Fleet of the Royal Navy. By their close blockades of Brest, Toulon, Rochefort, and the other naval bases of French (and Spanish) sea power, St. Vincent, Nelson, and William Cornwallis, negated the value to France of control of the Scheldt.

Two persisting linked causes explain the near constant of France's faring badly in the eighteenth century in the contest for maritime commercial wealth and colonies. First, France's continental situation obliged her to give strategic pride of place to the negation of landward perils, as well as tempted her to imprudent bids for continental empire. Second, repeated continental distraction condemned France to failure in sea-dependent enterprises. If, as Corbett argued, "command of the sea . . . means nothing but the control of maritime communications," it has to follow that the inability to secure and use that command must lead inexorably to the failure of *overseas* designs, both military and commercial. The common technology, common geography, common short-list of major state players (with Brandenburg Prussia emerging as a great power in the 1740s and 1750s, as Britain and Russia had done in the 1690s and 1710s), and common political and strategic cultures (until the 1790s) necessarily yielded a series of wars which were all variations upon a central sea power–land power theme. When an author observes that "it will always remain a matter of controversy whether it was the navy that failed Napoleon or Napoleon who failed the navy,"[56] it is instructive to note that the conundrum makes equal sense if Louis XIV's name is substituted for Napoleon's. There were enduring reasons that the navy of royalist, republican and later imperial France time after time disappointed its political masters.

Until the 1790s, at least, Britain and France neither sought nor plausibly could achieve the military overthrow of the other. Indeed the savagery of the notion would have been in contradiction to the dominant spirit of the age. Napoleon and Nelson sought annihilation, but they were heralds of a new era. State or dynastic policy goals fluctuated in detail, but generally, on the British side, they may be summarized as consolidation of the Protestant succession and of the broad terms of the Glorious Revolution—the alliance with France from 1716–31 usefully precluded practical help from that quarter for the Stuart cause—and the accumulation of wealth (Britain was not much in the glory business in this period). In addition, the frustration of French ambitions for dominance in Europe and empire overseas and, particularly from 1715 to 1760 (the reigns of George I and II), protection of the monarch's personal patrimony as Elector of Hanover were important.[57] These were not immoderate goals. However, some of the practice of wealth accumulation, the abrogation of most neutral shipping rights in wartime, and the cynical use and abuse of continental allies generated foreign envy. In fact, Britain was no more perfidious an ally and paymaster than were other states, while her frequently ruthless treatment of neutral shipping was as grand-strategically necessary as it was certainly high-handed.

Prior to the declaration of ideological warfare upon the *anciens régimes* of Europe in 1792, French policy aims through most of the eighteenth century, except the first decade, were much of a piece, though in continental context, with those of Britain. France's great ministers of state in this long period—Cardinal Fleury, the Duke de Choiseul and the Count de Vergennes—were not precursors of Napoleon in style or ambition.

Assessed overall, just how, and how well, did Britain's sea power serve the goals of policy from 1688 to the final downfall of Napoleon in 1815?

Through blockade or combat—and blockade was the threat of combat—the battle fleet of the Royal Navy typically secured a maritime command sufficient for British overseas trade to prosper, even in the face of a *guerre de course*. That British maritime preponderance caused French and French-allied trade virtually to cease and for most of the colonial basis of enemy trade to be seized at source for British exploitation. It would be an exaggeration to claim that the Royal Navy in wartime was self-financing—the record of the national debt belies such a notion—but still there is some truth in it. War invariably meant high taxation, unique risks to maritime trade, and an expansion of the national debt (which quadrupled between 1793 and 1815). But there is no doubt that commercial interests could profit from maritime war, that the national economic profit and loss account in war was distinctly mixed, and that Britain was far better able to finance war in the eighteenth century than was France. Expectation and realization of profit did not always match, of course. Nonetheless, the prospect of maritime-colonial war tended to be popular among some major commercial interests in Britain, and London repeatedly demonstrated that its purse was much longer than was that of Paris. Warfare in the eighteenth century was not always a paying proposition. John Brewer has observed that "every war [in the eighteenth century] raised the profile of public debt: each conflict produced a pattern of sharp and ever taller escarpments punctuated by the declining plateaux of peace."[58] Certainly he was correct, but British society could afford that debt.

Overall, the Navy provided the general strategic conditions of security for Britain, the protection of her centers of gravity, so that she could continue a war and subsidize and support continental allies. It was by the seizure of the enemy's profitable colonies, as well as by the taking of his ships, that the merchants of Britain accumulated wealth and could fund the national debt. "Filching sugar islands" in the West Indies was sound statecraft.[59]

The taxability of the British maritime-commercial, agricultural, and increasingly industrial economy by the "fiscal-military" state,[60] and hence Britain's creditworthiness, rested heavily in wartime on the ability of the Navy to safeguard overseas and coastal trade. In war after war the financial health of British governments was critical for the subsidization of variably motivated continental allies. One must not oversimplify. The 1690s saw what amounted to the beginning of a revolution in the administration of public finance in Britain,[61] and the pursuit of scientific agriculture in the following century meant a radical improvement in the profitability and hence taxability of land. Also, the second half of the eighteenth century witnessed the beginning of the Industrial Revolution in Britain, a development that was to augment dramatically the basis of wealth upon which British governments could draw in order to finance the wars with Revolutionary and Napoleonic France. The French trade embargoes against Britain in the 1800s were doomed to defeat by the unique attractiveness of British manufactures to all societies in this period.

Eighteenth-century Britain's decisive advantage in her serial contest with France lay in the realm of finance and public administration of that finance. Certainly geography and military strategy played a role, but the business of war had to be handled well enough for armies to be supplied and paid and for ships to be manned and maintained in commission. The British Army could be effective despite the modest scale of its typical continental commitment because British finance kept relatively large allied forces in the field. British wealth rented foreign soldiers in order to provide fighting fronts on land for the distraction of France from major maritime endeavors, as well as for the protection of the royal patrimony of Hanover. Occasionally, as in 1813–15, for example, the function of allied land power in London's eyes, with or without a noticeable British land contribution, was not so much to distract France from the sea as rather to effect her military overthrow. The British contribution to significant campaigns in this period varied from 10 percent at Minden (1759), through 17 percent at Blenheim (1704), 30 percent at Waterloo (1815) (the same percentage as the British contribution to the Western Front in 1918), to 36 percent at Dettingen (1743). Because the Royal Navy safeguarded and increased the wealth that often enabled London to keep continental coalitions in the field, Britain could pursue a continental dimension to its military strategy with only a modest commitment of British soldiers.

France was distracted from concentrating her formidable national, and allied and client states', resources upon war at sea by the continental alliances that Britain's sea-dependent economy helped critically to fund. British statemen were sensible to fear the menace of a united and hostile continent, but one should not rush to judgment over the true quality of peril that such an eventuality would produce. There was an actual case of an isolated Britain's effectively taking on the whole world—moreover, in a context of

168

major extra-European continental commitment, as well as of maritime war. The example is of the period 1778–83. Britain's expeditionary forces in the American colonies did not enjoy the blessings of an Atlantic maritime sanctuary. Although Britain lost the continental war, most emphatically she did not lose the maritime conflict. Also, it is one thing for a European continental empire to have the total assets of all kinds necessary to build a fleet of unmatchable proportions; it is quite another for that continental power to be able to produce a good fighting fleet out of mere ships or to be able to effect strategically useful concentrations of force. Virtually regardless of the nominal tally of vessels, ships and squadrons scattered around the ports of Europe do not necessarily comprise a mighty navy.

On the rare occasions when the Royal Navy lost command of the Narrow Seas, the result could have been defeat in war. It was as true for Britain in the eighteenth century as it is for the United States today that a continental commitment to Eurasia—indeed the conduct of any military expedition overseas—requires that the seas be tolerably commanded or that a working control be secured. In the words of a classic text,

> But a great land campaign based on the sea—a campaign analogous to the British struggle to maintain its hold upon the revolted American Colonies, or to the Crimean War, or to the Japanese invasions of Manchuria—is obviously impossible without naval preponderance. And naval preponderance can only be assured by defeating the hostile seagoing fleets, or else by shutting them up in their fortified harbours and destroying them if they venture to emerge.[62]

The Royal Navy was the critical enabling agent for Sir John Moore and then the Duke of Wellington's Peninsular campaigns, which cost Napoleon an average of 40,000 men a year for the better part of seven years, as well as a great deal of that awe and respect so vital to the economical governance of an often shaky empire.[63] Similarly, superior sea power was the shield behind the protection of which amphibious expeditions were able to seize the lion's share of the French and French-allied colonial empires.

A Britain preponderant at sea could not be overthrown militarily or so harassed by economic pressures as to be obliged to accede to a very disadvantageous peace. But it was always possible for

France to be so successful on land that she could free herself of major landward distraction and construct a fleet that might over-match the Royal Navy. From the sixteenth to the twentieth centuries, this theoretical danger motivated British leaders generally to abjure the superficial attractions of a purely maritime strategy (plus some home defense).

The security of the home islands provided by the Royal Navy's robust command of the country's coastal waters enabled Britain to protract conflicts in the face of military disasters on land to the coalitions that she variably led and helped finance. Command at sea bought time for the continental enemy to commit ultimately fatal errors of policy and grand strategy and for friendly forces to learn the trade of modern war on land. This was the true significance of Nelson's annihilating victory over the Combined Fleet of France and Spain at Cape Trafalgar on October 21, 1805. Trafalgar was the decisive battle of the Napoleonic War; it set the strategic conditions which maximized the prospects for the self-destruction of Napoleon's landlocked empire.

It is an axiom that that which is tactically impossible cannot be strategically sound and renders theoretically interesting strategy strictly moot. To be successful in her wars with Britain or in the wars in which the defeat of Britain was a precondition for lasting continental success, France needed to dispute maritime command. France did not need to secure substantially unhindered passage for her own trade or overseas military ventures, but she did need to dispute command at sea so vigorously that British trade and overseas military enterprises would be paralyzed. At the very least French naval power needed to achieve sea denial.

It may have been sensible for France to eschew determined bids to secure positive military command, as contrasted with sea denial. But the alternatives pursued—of menace posed by fleets in being, the *guerre de course*, and ever more elaborate invasion designs—amounted repeatedly in practice to a futile strategy of evasion, a fact Jean Colbert (1619–83), Louis XIV's great Minister of Marine, for one, certainly understood. It was true that French opinion tended to be impressed with "the futility of a major success" at sea.[64] But this bafflement in the face of success, in 1690 as again in 1779, betrayed an enduring French inability to understand sea warfare, as well as "the function of the fleet in war."[65] The French preference for sea denial was shown time and again to lack a sufficiently potent tactical instrument to be effective as a strategy against Britain. "Having committed themselves to the commercial war [the *guerre de course*], the French were confronted with the fact that naval supremacy was in the last resort essential to it," wrote two historians about a persisting dilemma.[66] Given the constraints on the likely durability of the authority of French conquests on land and the demonstrated utility of British sea power for the discomfiture of France's landward dominion, France either had to deny Britain command at sea or eventually lose in war. There was no practicable middle course.

The long period of development and maturing of English, then British, sea power in the age of fighting sail revealed patterns in statecraft and strategy which united the policy of Elizabeth with that of Pitt the Elder and the Younger. It would be unduly Mahanian, as well as historically inaccurate, to repeat the old saw that "the last word lay with sea power."[67] In fact the last word in the great war between Britain and the French Empire lay with the distinctly polyglot land power of the allies near the village of Waterloo in southern Belgium. It is rarely possible for sea power strategically to have the last word. Instead, superior sea power shapes the course of a conflict so that there is little doubt as to whose land power shall have the last word.

Impressive achievements should be claimed for the ramshackle sea power of late Tudor England, although those achievements pale in absolute comparison with the strategic utility of sea power to Britain in her long struggle with France. In the latter case, British manufactures (cheap trade goods) purchased slaves in West Africa for the working of plantations in the West Indies and the southern colonies of North America, which in turn sent sugar and other tropical products to Britain as the entrepôt. By analogy, the grand-strategic story of the long Anglo-French struggle also is one of interconnections. British sea power was not independently decisive in the wars with France; unfavorable outcomes averted and favorable outcomes achieved were the products of the whole conduct of war. Sea power could shape, or significantly help shape, the general course and character of war after war, but that shaping was enabled by what for the period was Europe's most advanced system of public finance and administration and was shared by national, allied, and mercenary land power. Nonetheless, sea

171

power was both the principal military instrument of the most consistent state-adversary of French policy and grand strategy from 1688 to 1815, and it was the principal reason that Britain rose to and retained the status of a great power. It is all very well to note that a superior system of public finance comprised Britain's most important advantage over France. But French armies and navies, commerce and colonies, were not overcome directly by tax collectors, clerks, and financiers, no matter how capable they may have been.

The sea power of Elizabeth's England denied Spain the ability to win on land and enabled England to intervene with land power on the Continent when finances permitted and an ally was in the field. That sea power also denied Spain the ability to strike effectively at England's center of gravity at home by invasion and contributed to the actual bankruptcy of Spain and a loss of international banking confidence in Madrid's creditworthiness. Finally, England's sea power was the source of great prestige and respect. Each of these claims apply, though much more so, to England's long struggle with France. The frustration of Habsburg imperial ambitions was very much a team effort among Spain's host of foes; so also was the repeated thwarting of French policy and grand strategy a team enterprise among sea power, land power, the power of money, and different countries.

To describe British sea power as a critical enabling agent both overstates and understates the case. It is an overstatement in that tax money and public loans—the sinews of war—and armies also were enabling agents. It is an understatement in that unlike tax money and armies, sea power contributed positively to the conditions favorable for its own strategic utility. The triangular trade connections among the British Isles, West Africa, and the Americas were enabled by naval strength. Similarly, the rich Levantine and East Indian trades were enabled to flourish by the distant protection afforded by the Royal Navy's blockading squadrons off French and Spanish naval bases.[68] Of geostrategic and commercial necessity, the navy was Britain's military instrument of excellence. Without a superior fighting navy, Britain in the eighteenth century would not have been a great power, would not have been able to enforce her domestic dynastic, religious, and political preferences, and would have lacked the capital from maritime-colonial commerce and some of the markets to launch her industrial takeoff.

172

British sea power preserved the country's political independence, was vital for augmentation of the country's wealth, and was essential for the country to play any role as an independent actor in European security affairs. Of course, there was much more to Britain than just the first navy in Europe.

Britain benefited from new departures in scientific agriculture, in a general stability in public finance, and in the industrial application of new technologies. Many of the relatively positive attributes of eighteenth-century Britain (relative to conditions abroad) flowed from conditions of domestic political stability. Those conditions were not the natural gift of the blessings of geostrategic insularity. The sea is only a powerful "moat defensive" if it has a potent naval guardian.

Of the seven Anglo-French contests considered here, three may be counted as draws (1688–97, 1740–48, and 1778–83), one as a semi-loss (1793–1802), and three as wins (1701–13, 1756–63, 1803–15). Sea power alone did not fail to avert losses, force draws, and secure wins, but it was the principal enabling instrument of British grand strategy in all of those conflicts.

CHAPTER 6

SEA POWER IN THE FIRST WORLD WAR

Although the war was won as the direct consequence of an un-exampled series of land battles, it was profoundly true that this result was attained only through the conduct of the war at sea.

C. R. M. F. Cruttwell, *The Role of British Strategy in the Great War* (1936)

The century that separates the Napoleonic Wars from the First World War registered epochal shifts in military-naval technology (steam, guns, armor, oil), and conflicts of abiding interest—pre-eminently the miscalled Crimean War of 1854–56, the American Civil War of 1861–65, the wars of German unification culminating in the struggle with France in 1870–71, and the Russo-Japanese War of 1904–1905. A host of lesser conflicts—for example, the U.S. war with Mexico (1846-48), the Sino-Japanese War (1894–95), and the Boer War (1899–1902), to cite but a very few—also stud this century. None of these conflicts, however, add anything critically important to my argument. Notwithstanding the relative modernity of the nineteenth century conflicts just cited, and the scope and scale of the technological advances achieved, none of them approaches in grand-strategic and military-strategic richness the ancient and medieval cases, for example, treated in Chapter 4. It is with particular regret that I pass over the Crimean and American Civil Wars, both of which are rich sources for confirmatory insight into land-power–sea-power relations, but the argument for interposing them between discussion of the Napoleonic and First World Wars is attractive rather than compelling.

174

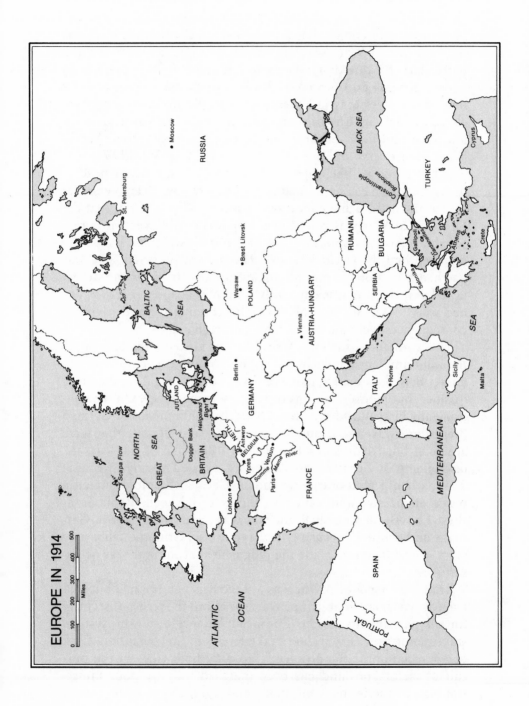

EUROPE IN 1914

*   *   *

No other major conflict has attracted so much controversy as has the First World War. Scholars continue to debate its causes and particularly the question of German war guilt.[1] Indeed, opinion on why a general European war broke out in early August 1914 remains as diverse as judgments on why the Roman Empire declined and fell. By way of sharp contrast to the consensus of opinion, then and now, on both the Napoleonic and Second World Wars, controversy still rages on whether the First World War was worth waging. If "the object in war is to attain a better peace," many people have been unable to identify the 1919 Versailles settlement with such a condition.[2] Given, *with hindsight*, that the First World War was round one of a two-round event, it is reasonable to speculate that the need for round two could have been removed had the Great War of 1914–18 not occurred. The war has had a bad press from all angles of view. It is commonly believed that the war was eminently preventable and hence was unnecessary, that it was abominably conducted, and that its consequences were almost entirely unfortunate.

The truth about the First World War is virtually the obverse of the still-dominant scholarly and popular opinion. The war was not an accidental or inadvertent event waged for trivial reasons in a manner that mocked notions of military competence. On the contrary, the First World War was *about* the containment of German power and was waged on all sides for reasons of state that were anything but frivolous or trivial. The true stake of the war, the disciplining of German ambition, was revealed starkly in March 1918, when a temporarily ascendant German Empire dictated a peace of massive annexation to the new Bolshevik Republic at Brest-Litovsk. In a nutshell, the war was about the power of Germany and hence the security of everyone else. Grim though it may seem, it is difficult to evade the judgment that the war was necessary.

That the First World War was a tragedy is not at issue; but that tragedy was unavoidable. The war was about the terms of security for all participants in the European balance-of-power system, stakes comprising survival or vital interests by any definition. Lack of appreciation of the problems faced by both sides in the pursuit of victory on land has been matched fully by poor understanding of the terms, conditions, and significance of the war at

176

sea. So tentative has been the overall grasp of the shape and course of the war that the strategic impact of sea power, as well as the operational and tactical handling of fleets and armies, remain today almost as live a set of topics for debate as they were in the 1920s.

Admiral Sir John Jellicoe, as Commander-in-Chief of the Royal Navy's Grand Fleet from August 1914 until November 1916, in effect guarded the ability of the Allies to wage and eventually win a world war. The Grand Fleet stood between Germany and the ability to make the conflict a strictly continental war. Had Germany's High Seas Fleet been able to isolate the continental campaigning grounds from overseas intervention, the Central Powers (Germany, Austria-Hungary, Bulgaria, and Turkey) certainly would have triumphed. Whereas almost four years of land combat were required before the unmistakable promise of a military decision could be discerned and whereas the campaign to defeat the U-boats occupied more than twelve months from spring 1917 to spring 1918, in theory it was possible for the balance of surface naval power to be drastically upset in a matter of hours or even minutes. For the sea-dependent Allies, the issue in such a potential upset was nothing less than the outcome of the war. The coalition of Britain, France, Russia, Italy, and eventually the United States could not win the First World War at sea, but they could lose it there—and in the course of a single afternoon. Aside from the high drama of its' being the first full-scale clash of Dreadnought-era battle fleets, not to mention its' being also the first fleet engagement worthy of significant note for the Royal Navy since Trafalgar in *1805*, the Battle of Jutland on May 31, 1916, was about Britain's, and hence the Allied, ability to continue to wage war.

The British public in 1914–16 expected Jellicoe to perform with "the Nelson touch": why else would he have been hand-picked by Admiral "Jackie" Fisher for so important a command? What Jellicoe did, and failed to do, in the fading light of the last day of May 1916 continues to stimulate controversy. Jutland can stand for the mythology of the whole war in microcosm. It was an accidental clash (on the German side) which allegedly was thoroughly unnecessary for a British Royal Navy which, again allegedly, only stood to lose by the grand hazard of a fleet battle. Moreover, British leadership and overall German leadership—the High Seas Fleet commander, Vice-Admiral Reinhard Scheer, but not the bat-

177

tle cruiser commander, Vice-Admiral Franz Hipper—have been criticized brutally for supposed errors in fleet handling.

Jellicoe has been variously criticized: for his crucial signal issued at 1815 hours on May 31, 1916, to deploy into single line his twenty-eight modern (Dreadnought and super-Dreadnought) battleships on the port-wing column of the fleet with a course of southeast by east—that is, away from the approaching High Seas Fleet (with its sixteen modern battleships and six pre-Dreadnoughts); for his scarcely less crucial decision at 1922 hours to turn his battle line away from an unfolding mass destroyer attack; for his subsequent refusal to pursue the retreating Germans into the mist and smoke—and, as he feared, into a hastily laid minefield; and for his lack of aggressive handling of the fleet in the critical hours of darkness when Scheer escaped through the Grand Fleet's rear to Horn's Reef—to cite only the more prominent issues.[3] The most important fact is that Jellicoe did well enough for his Grand Fleet to drive the Germans back into port. By escaping destruction, Jellicoe and his fleet ensured that the strategically bested High Seas Fleet would continue to be neutralized as a potentially war-winning element. The verdict at Jutland meant that British sea power would enable the Allies ultimately to win the war on land. A more heroic and politically satisfying outcome to the battle would have been very welcome in the Allied camp, but the superficially indecisive outcome actually was good enough.

Sea power does not have strategic effect as an independent tool of war. Unlike the Entente Allies, who increasingly were dependent upon maritime lines of communication, the Central Powers could not be defeated at sea. The importance of maritime command for the Allies grew as Britain and later the United States played larger and larger roles sustaining the protracted continental war. The Central Powers could be defeated on land in critical part because they failed to find a maritime strategy which could deny the exercise of command at sea to the Allies.

In 1930, Basil Liddell-Hart wrote as follows:

> That [British Royal] Navy was to win no Trafalgar, but it was to do more than any other factor towards winning the war for the Allies. For the Navy was the instrument of the blockade, and as the fog of war disperses in the clearer light of these postwar years that block-

ade is seen to assume larger and larger proportions, to be more and more clearly *the decisive agency* in the struggle.[4]

The decisive agency? What of the French, Russian, British, and American armies? The Royal Navy functioned for decisive effect in the First World War in the same strategic manner that it had in the wars with France over a century earlier. Its ability to keep Britain in the war indefinitely, to provide Britain and her allies with secure access to the world beyond peninsular Europe, as well as to all except the most heavily defended of littorals in Europe (and to deny the same to the enemy), meant that the Central Powers were unlikely to win the war. It would not only be difficult to assess the relative wartime impact of sea power; it would be trivial and even absurd to make the attempt. The argument over which instrument or instruments of grand strategy were the more truly decisive in the defeat of the Central Powers was fueled in Britain in the 1920s and 1930s by the desire to make a case for a return to what allegedly had been the traditional British way in warfare; subsidizing continental clients, establishing supremacy at sea by the defeat in battle or blockade of the enemy's navy and merchant marine, exploiting maritime command for the control of seaborne trade, conducting occasional land campaigns in, as well as raids upon, coastal regions (Portugal, Catalonia, the mouth of the Scheldt, and so forth), and providing a continental commitment for direct support of European allies.

Liddell-Hart and others judged British strategy in the First World War to have been fundamentally in error. By implication at least, the critics suggested that a more maritime orientation to Britain's war effort would have been vastly preferable to the course that had in fact been followed.[5] With benefit of hindsight, they were determined to persuade anyone who needed persuading that never again should Britain commit a mass continental-scale army to the principal theater of a war. They argued that Britain should not have permitted her war effort to be commanded so thoroughly by the strategy of France—that is, in allowing herself to be dragged into waging the wrong kind of war (for Britain). In addition, they argued that Britain, once committed to continental warfare *à outrance*, should have waged it more competently. Since then it has been open season on "the donkeys," as Britain's military leaders of the 1914–18 era have been labeled.[6] It has, however, been unfashionable since World War II to challenge the basic continental thrust of British policy, grand strategy, and strategy in the First World War.

Britain's dilemma in both world wars was that offshore sea power could not afford to be indifferent to a continental imbalance of power. The Channel, the Atlantic, or the Pacific cannot provide absolute security. The prerogatives of command at sea have been enjoyed in modern times by Britain because continental enemies either were insufficiently well endowed to fund an effective challenge at sea or insufficiently strategically motivated to make the attempt. The task of British statecraft was to try to ensure that if and when a continental power was motivated to challenge Britain at sea, it would be so heavily preoccupied with more immediately pressing tasks on land that it would lack a sufficiency of naval means.

It is important to understand how prewar and early wartime strategic policies, and the expectations upon which those policies were founded, shaped events after 1914–15. Although in retrospect it is reasonable to criticize the government of Germany, and indeed of Britain, for failing to coordinate its plans for land and sea warfare, criticism needs to be tempered by empathy for the dominant belief of the time. Neither country had plans for sea warfare; and Britain lacked both a plan of its own for land warfare as well as up-to-date knowledge of the plans of its probable continental allies.[7] None of the political and military leaders anticipated waging a very long war, though the autocratic, secretive, and very unbureaucratic Lord Kitchener, Britain's Minister of War for 1914–16, was lonely in his expectation of at least a three-year conflict. If the great war of the future was to be decided in scarcely more than a single short campaign on land by the mobilized mass of conscript armies, it was difficult to see how navies narrowly, or sea power broadly, could deliver significant strategic value. In the early years of this century, the dominant scenario for the next great war was an anticipated replay of the Franco-Prussian War of 1870–71. The principal complication was that in 1914 Germany did not confront an enemy who was diplomatically isolated. Since the late 1870s, Germany had made and remade its war plans with the potential problems of a two-front conflict uppermost in the minds of the Great General Staff. Field Marshal Helmuth von Moltke (the Elder) had predicted in 1890 that the next war would last for seven years.[8]

180

Prior to early August 1914 it was not certain that Britain would be a belligerent in a continental war, although, in retrospect, the British decision for war on August 4, 1914, appears inevitable.[9] The record of Britain's continental commitment is quite inexorable. The Committee of Imperial Defence agreed in June 1909 that "an Expeditionary Force of four infantry divisions and one cavalry division should be sent to reinforce the left flank of the French Army, landing at French ports and being ready for action by the twentieth day after mobilization."[10] (In practice, Britain declared war at midnight August 4, 1914, and the BEF first met the German Army in combat at Mons in Belgium on August 23.) In 1911, the Royal Navy similarly came to assume that Britain would intervene to assist France in the event of an attack by Germany. Nonetheless, at the time of the Agadir crisis which brought the Entente and Central Powers to the brink of war in 1911, a majority of the British Cabinet believed that Britain could elect to wage a fairly strictly blue-water mode of warfare on behalf of France. That same body behaved at the beginning of August 1914 as if it enjoyed discretion in policy between war and neutrality.

The British contribution to a land war was intended only as a limited commitment, albeit a commitment of major proportions for the small regular Army of Britain. It is ironic that, contrary to all reasonable predictions, the history of August–November 1914 assigned the BEF a critical role just as Colonel Charles Callwell and the General Staff had hoped would be the case. As early as 1905 the General Staff concluded that

> an efficient army of 120,000 troops might have just the same effect of preventing important German successes on the Franco-German frontier and of leading up to the situation that Germany, crushed at sea, also felt herself impotent on land. That would almost certainly bring about a speedy and, from the British point of view, satisfactory peace.[11]

This was an ambitious, highly speculative theory of decisive intervention at the critical place *and time* by a British Expeditionary Force.

The BEF in August 1914 comprised four infantry divisions and one large cavalry division: a force that could be augmented hastily by the addition of two infantry divisions and perhaps by a modest contribution from the Indian Army. By an extremity of effort, after massive redeployments, the regular British Army could field eleven infantry and three cavalry divisions. The fourteen divisions of the distinctly part-time home-defense-oriented Territorial Army could not be ready to take the field for many months. These numbers need to be considered in the context of the following orders of battle for August 1914: France, seventy divisions—1,071,000 men; Germany (on the Western Front), ninety-two divisions—1,485,000 men. Unless Sir John French's five divisions (for a total of 110,000 men) happened to be either at the right place at the right time or very readily transportable to the same, British land power could not do other than make a respectable *effort de sang* in the clash of million-man armies.

The widespread expectation of a short land war meant that sea power could hardly be expected to have any impact upon the course of the war.[12] Even had the Germans been certain that the BEF would be dispatched with alacrity to France, why would they judge it important to place any significant fraction of the hugely outnumbered High Seas Fleet at risk in the southern part of the North Sea or in the Channel in order to deter or interdict its passage? The High Seas Fleet needed to be husbanded in its fortified coastal bastion behind Heligoland. Its wartime missions were to exploit any imprudent far-forward deployment by units of the Royal Navy and to function as a fleet in being. As a fleet in being the German Navy should encourage Britain to be compliant toward the political settlement that Germany would impose after its expected six-week-long unraveling of French military power and its subsequent battering of unsupported Russians in the East. The defensive mission of the fleet in being, however, generally was not anticipated prior to the outbreak of war, because "by 1914 the German navy was still anticipating a naval battle which would take place under circumstances favourable to it."[13] The German Navy chose to believe that after the spirit, though not always the practice, of Drake, Hawke, and Nelson, the contemporary Royal Navy would make "the enemy's coast our frontier."[14] German naval officers neglected to recognize that Nelson was not a rigid believer in the close blockade and that the justly celebrated "Nelson touch" perennially was the product of a very fine professional calculation of risks.

The willingness of the British Cabinet in 1914 to permit its soldiers, as well as French soldiers, to determine how the country would wage war was a surrender of responsibility quite contrary to typical British practice from the Armada to Waterloo. In effect, Herbert Asquith's government made no attempt worthy of note to influence where and to what ends Britain would wage the war to which it had narrowly and reluctantly committed itself. That would change, but the abdication of responsibility in 1914 by the civilians was quite remarkable. Gordon Craig has observed that this abdication of responsibility for the direction of strategy in war

> was a curious attitude for a British statesman [Asquith] to take, for Great Britain was a sea power and, at war against predominantly land powers, it had strategical options, the choice between which could not, or should not, be made by the military alone.[15]

With the blessings of hindsight, it is clear that the British government should have considered and reconsidered its strategic choices with respect to Britain's interests and comparative advantages, but at the time it had few practical choices. At least until late in 1916, the British government thought it was informed by its expert military advisers that victory was achievable sooner rather than later.[16] Though sometimes profitable for Britain in the eighteen century, the conduct of protracted, let alone militarily indecisive, war had rarely been the strategy of choice. Behaving adaptively, Britain typically elected to wage protracted war rather than settle for an unsatisfactory peace in the near term. Britain had not usually sought or required a clear military decision over France—her defeat, let alone her overthrow. Rather Britain had chosen to wage more war, for longer, than France could afford, in the context of a generally favorable balance of territorial gains and losses in Europe and overseas.

Because Britain came to wage continental warfare on a continental scale in 1916–1918 and endorsed a punitive peace settlement, it can be easy to forget that the policy, strategy, and political mood of late summer 1914 in London was far from guided by some notion of total war. As in the War of Spanish Succession, Britain wanted the current disturber of the balance of power humbled, not destroyed. In 1914 Britain chose to fight to reduce the power of Germany, to contain the ambitions of her own current allies of convenience in the Treaty of London (September 5, 1914), and—perhaps above all else—to protect the empire. In 1914 there was no notion in London that the BEF eventually would have to function as the cutting edge of the coalition on land. Britain had not gained and augmented her great-power status by bleeding profusely in long continental wars.

Protracted conflict always was the strategy of necessity against a continental enemy whose landward resources were too great to be overthrown or attrited to the point of terminal political discouragement in a single campaign. It follows that the modest continental commitment of the BEF in August 1914 was entirely sound in the best tradition of British balance-of-power statecraft. It could be catastrophic for British security were Germany to achieve a Napoleonic-style hegemony over the continent; Tirpitz's High Seas Fleet flagged all too plainly that the new Germany sought self-expression through overseas empire;[17] France and Russia appeared to be very capable as allies; and France provided a fighting front readily accessible to the British Army. Moreover, British leaders had good reason to believe, or hope, that a land commitment to the defense of France, whether or not it should prove militarily critical, would secure a measure of political influence in Allied councils that maritime endeavor alone could not achieve. Although British leaders were properly impressed by Germany's military reputation, they were also respectful of the French military revival.[18] The political ambiguity surrounding the commitment of the BEF to the French Army's left wing played a small but possibly important role in encouraging French Marshal Joffre to adopt in 1913 the extreme variant of the operational offensive which came to be the ill-fated and appalling Plan XVII.[19]

There was no pressing reason for London to reconsider the basic strategic direction of the war if a favorable decision would be achieved on land, overwhelmingly at the expense of French and Russian blood, in a matter of weeks in the late summer and fall of 1914. But expectations of imminent victory were shattered by the French defeat in the Battle of the Frontiers (August) and by the subsequent successful German stands on the Aisne (September) and in Flanders (October–November), while France anticipated executing victorious offenses in Champagne in 1915. Furthermore, the hitching of British military effort to the French wagon in 1914 resulted effectively in the (temporary) battlefield loss of the BEF as an offensive instrument. By November 30, 1914, the 110,000-

strong BEF of August had suffered 86,237 casualties. In the words of the British official history, "The old British Army was gone past recall, leaving but a remnant to carry on the training of the New Armies."[20]

In the fall of 1914, at the Marne, on the Aisne, and in front of Ypres, maritime Britain was not prudently at liberty "to take as much and as little of the war" as it might have preferred. The BEF's extraordinary fighting value had proved critical for the avoidance of Allied defeat. Britain might have waged the war differently in 1915 as newly formed and trained divisions slowly were readied, but France was in the saddle for the direction of Allied strategy in the West. In 1915 it seemed plausible to believe that victory on land in France was possible that year, while British civilian leaders lacked the information, the understanding, the courage, and really the incentive to insist upon strategic schemes contrary to those demanded by Marshal Joseph Joffre, the "victor of the Marne" and the savior of France. The German occupation of the sacred soil of France, not to mention the obligation to the memory of the "old contemptibles" who died at First Ypres, as well as plain logistic expediency, served effectively to preclude Britain from seriously considering any strategic alternative to allotting the Western Front first draw upon her mobilizable military resources.

The year 1915 probably should be regarded as the year of lost Allied opportunities. From May until September, the Germans and Austrians were massively preoccupied with their great campaign in Poland; the Western Allies enjoyed an average seven-to-four manpower advantage in France and Belgium; Italy declared war on Austria on May 23 and on June 23 launched the first of what were to be twelve battles of the Isonzo; Serbia was undefeated, thereby providing a potentially active front for exploitation in the Balkans; Turkey was isolated by Serbia's successful self-defense and by the continuing neutrality of Bulgaria and Rumania; Russia was very much in the war (and was the principal object of German-Austrian attention in 1915); and the Royal Navy, as anticipated, was supreme at sea. The strategic context appeared to be distinctly favorable for the Allies. Their land power was growing, as Britain mobilized, trained, and began to arm an unprecedented mass (though still volunteer) army, their credit was still healthy for the economic sustenance of the conflict, and the enemy's war plan had failed and he was about to attempt in the East what he had failed narrowly to achieve in the West in 1914. If ever there was a second chance for London to attempt to secure that grip on war strategy which it had failed to secure in August of 1914, it was in 1915.

By the late summer of 1915 the strategic opportunity, if such it was, had passed. By August 19 from the War Office Kitchener reluctantly advised Douglas Haig (then commanding the First Army of the BEF) to "act with all our energy and do our utmost to help the French, even though, by so doing, we suffered very heavy casualties indeed."[21] It seems probable that Kitchener had hoped to be able to withhold most of his undertrained, under-equipped, and poorly led New Army divisions from large-scale commitment to battle until perhaps 1917.[22] Kitchener, the old blue-water imperialist, intended that Britain's much mistrusted continental Allies should bleed as profusely as might be necessary in their blunting of Germany's army, leaving the BEF to secure victory relatively cheaply in 1917, much as was to be the role of the American Expeditionary Forces (AEF) in 1918.

> The New Armies were intended to win the peace for Britain, after the French and Russians had all but won the war. But the *sine qua non* of this policy was that the British could not afford to commit the great bulk of their armies to a costly continental land war until early 1917.[23]

Kitchener's quintessentially British scheme was undone by a combination of factors. There was an unexpectedly early appearance of war weariness on the part of the French and Russians, one or both of whom, it was feared in London, might opt for a negotiated peace rather than continue to fight Britain's battles for her. Also, Kitchener's own secretive and inarticulate style of leadership meant that very few people comprehended his "cunning plan," if such it was. And most British military leaders tended to believe that their forces could accomplish important objectives soon, and they sought a more glorious role for themselves and for their troops.

A sea power in wartime often has to choose between continental and maritime campaign options. For example, during the invasion scare of 1759, Pitt the Elder was much criticized for reinforcing British garrisons in America, dispatching new expeditions thither, and generally reducing the weight of British military power afloat and ashore at home.[24] A country of roughly 8 million people, at war with a France with its 20 million, lacked the ready manpower to conduct simultaneously large amphibious expeditions of colonial conquest and continental campaigns on a major scale. In addition, German Allies had to be financed, and a healthy superiority was needed in naval strength over all plausible and continental maritime threats. To assert that war has to be perceived in its entirety, that sea power and land power are complementary, and that victory is achieved by the exercise of combined arms is not to suggest that choices of military direction and application can be eschewed.

A classic instance of the refusal to choose was the British endeavor in 1915 to conduct offensive operations both on the Western Front and from the sea against the Turkish Empire at Gallipoli. The first British landings on the Gallipoli peninsula were effected on April 25, 1915, three days into the Second Battle of Ypres. Gallipoli may or may not have been a forlorn hope, but it was a maritime stroke condemned to failure by the gross inadequacy of the military means available and the deficiencies in military method revealed.[25] The dominant problem was that Britain was insufficiently in command of the strategy which directed her growing military power. The unofficial, but not unauthorized, military staff conversations between the British and French armies, initiated in 1906, resulted in 1914 in the BEF's being committed as a wholly Paris-controlled subsidiary in the French scheme of war. In 1914 there was no unified war plan designed to direct all of Britain's military strength for the conduct of war on land and at sea according to a British perspective. General Sir Frederick Maurice, who was in a position to know, advised that prior to the outbreak of war in August 1914, "no attempt was made to correlate the political, naval, and military objects," and commented that "this was indeed impossible because the military plan had been concluded before the consideration of policy was begun."[26] (Indeed, he was in a position to know, for during the war he was both Director of Military Operations at the General Headquarters of the BEF, and then Director of Military Operations at the War Office in London.) British strategy in the First World War never succeeded in escaping its preemptive capture by the principal continental ally. The focus of that ally, understandably, was almost wholly upon its national need to expel the German invader from its sacred home territory.

The German Army had to be denied victory, perhaps roundly defeated, in the field. But the terms and circumstances of British participation in the war could hardly have been less propitious for statesmen and military leaders in London to pose searching questions about the conduct of operations.[27] *After* the British government had declared war on Germany at midnight on August 4, 1914, it called a Council of War on the afternoon of August 5. In the words of John Terraine, the purpose was

> to decide what to do. In other words, in spite of all the labours of the Committee on Imperial Defence, in spite of Agadir [crisis in 1911], in spite of the War Book [detailed mobilization plans], in spite of the fact that the only military strength of the nation was already on the move for France in accordance with a prearranged plan, the British Government had not grasped what the nature of its commitment was, and *neither had its chief professional advisers.*[28]

One must bear in mind the global domain of Britain's interests, the commanding strength of the Royal Navy, and the weight of Britain's industrial and financial power in 1914. In that context it is amazing, and perhaps even ironic, that Britain entered the most severe test of war in its history to date not merely unprepared in strategic thought for its effective conduct but chained to the unpredictable immediate needs of a continental ally whose plans were unknown in detail by British soldiers, let alone politicians. Terraine has written:

> The haplessness and the misfortunes of so much British (and allied) strategy in after years can only be fully understood if this is held in mind. The truth of the matter is that the binding force of this commitment [to fight with, and for all intents and purposes as a part of, the French Army] only now became apparent, and when the distinguished gathering delved into it, they found that the only area of initiative left to the United Kingdom was the decision whether the Expeditionary Force should concentrate at Maubeuge or Amiens.[29]

The choice of Maubeuge proved nearly catastrophic, because it was very far forward in face of a German invasion of unknown scope, pace, and direction; the BEF and the German right wing blundered into each other at Mons on August 23. It is debatable just how much choice the British government really had in 1914. But Asquith's tame and ignorant acquiescence in an immediate continental commitment was light years removed from the quality of direction of Britain's national military strategy as demonstrated, for example, by William Pitt the Elder in the Seven Years' War.[30] (It might be fairer to compare Asquith with Pitt the Younger's less-than-inspired higher direction of long periods of the wars with Revolutionary and Napoleonic France.) There was no unified vision in 1914 of how war should be conducted, or even for what ends, beyond the liberation of Belgian and French territory.[31] Nothwithstanding his weaknesses of character as a war leader, even Pitt the Younger at least saw continental and maritime war within a common framework of potential effort.

Adding the slide toward full-scale continental commitment in 1915 to the sad tale of absent leadership in August 1914, make the terms of reference for the British war effort of 1914–18 all too apparent. British grand strategy was heavily adaptive in this period,[32] but it was adaptive to circumstances dominated by the choices of performance of other powers. In 1940 Britain was driven to the waging of blue-water, peripheral warfare by France's definitive failure. In 1915–16, by way of contrast, Britain was locked into an unprecedented continental commitment because of a mixture of fears of failure by coalition partners and hopes for near-term military success. In both historical cases, Britain, the dominant sea power, found her grand-strategic choices massively constrained by the ill consequences of her having only a small army at the beginning of hostilities.[3] To note that fact is not necessarily a criticism. Insular democracies, even effectively insular super states, generally do not maintain continental-scale armies in peacetime.

Britain had barely fifteen months in which she might have decided on a radically different geostrategic allocation of her burgeoning land forces. To risk erring on the generous side, Britain had between the close of the First Battle of Ypres on November 24, 1914, and the opening of Erich von Falkenhayn's great offensive against the French Army at Verdun on February 21, 1916, in which to reconsider her course in strategy. But the dominant political fact of the matter was that Paris had a lien on the higher direction of the British war effort. The most appropriate comment has been provided by C. R. M. F. Cruttwell. That scholar-participant remains the most persuasive of the British historians of the Great War. In 1936 he wrote that

> the master idea of French soldiers, which reflected the passionate longing of public opinion, was to drive the enemy as quickly as possible out of the national territory. *Starting from the true premise that the war on land could be lost only in France, the Higher Command proceeded to the conclusion, which at least in 1915 was unsound, that the war could be won only in France.* As it was certainly necessary in the interest of Russia for the Western Allies to attack somewhere in strength in 1915, they had to attack in France, as they had renounced any great effort elsewhere. The British Army was reduced to the role of an autonomous auxiliary of France, attacking when and where the French Higher Command thought useful to help a larger French effort.[34]

Gross deficiencies in military method and material precluded success in France in 1915. Furthermore, the voracious demands of that front, married malignly to poor military method, denied practicality to the great expedition to open the Dardanelles.

In 1915 it seemed politically necessary for the British government to bow to the demand of its senior partner that the unfinished business of 1914—defeat of the German Army then occupying French soil—be completed expeditiously. But after the German assault on Verdun in late February 1916, there could be no question of Britain's making her major land effort anywhere other than in France. Indeed the Inter-Allied Military Conference at Chantilly on December 6–8, 1915, had agreed that 1916 should be the year of "coordinated offensives" in the "principal theaters," with Britain accepting that her major effort should be in France.[35] The Allies expected to be able to defeat the Central Powers in 1916. In part this was an expectation driven by suspicion of necessity—an anxiety that the great efforts planned for 1916, in addition to those already expended, could not be sustained into 1917. This anxiety was to prove well founded, as subsequent events in Russia and even France were to demonstrate.

From the opening of the great battle of attrition at Verdun, designed by the German High Command to enforce an intolerable bloodletting upon a French Army already gravely weakened by its own abortive offensives in 1914–15, until the end of the war, the BEF literally was indispensable for the defense of France. The freedom of global maneuver that the Royal Navy's (surface) command at sea provided for Britain's sea-projectible land power, was vitiated by the necessity to concentrate and attack, and persist in attacking, in France in 1916 and 1917, lest the continental war be lost. The Commander-in-Chief of the BEF, Sir John French, and his successor, Sir Douglas Haig, persistently were hindered and frustrated by the constraints on their discretion in operational command by the exigencies of the French military situation. This was coalition warfare indeed. Nevertheless, these generals were enthusiastic supporters of the proposition that the war had to be won in France and Belgium. Over the course of the war as a whole, French's views on geostrategic priorities were nowhere near as steady as were those of Haig. This was hardly surprising since French was relieved of his command of the BEF on December 15, 1915, in the wake of his obvious mishandling of the attack at Loos.[36]

By the spring of 1917, it had become clear that Britain would have to provide and wield her own continental sword if victory were to be achieved. This followed from the experience of the protracted campaigns of Verdun (February 21–December 18, 1916) and the Somme (July 1–November 13, 1916), and even more plainly following the defeat of General Robert Nivelle's offensive (April 16–20, 1917), the subsequent mutinies in the French Army, and the turmoil of revolution in Russia in 1917. The commitment to play the leading role in a great land war in Europe was, and remains, a unique episode in the history of British statecraft and strategy.

The high hopes entertained by the Allies for 1916 were not fulfilled. In the spring of 1917 the French Army, though still massively in the field and probably reliable in defense, was shaken in morale, exhausted by losses, and for an indefinite period of time incapable of assuming responsibility for a major offensive. In addition, the Russian Army had bled itself white in extended and repeated demonstrations of fidelity to its Western Allies.[37] That army now was a spent force, wracked with political disaffection and war weariness and hobbled by ammunition and other material shortages. Meanwhile the Italian Army had battered itself terribly and abortively in ten battles of the Isonzo to date. Allied rejoicing at the American declaration of war on April 6, 1917, was appropriate with respect to the implications for war finance, but knowledge that the U.S. Army was perhaps two years distant from being able to provide much genuine relief in the land war in France restrained Allied enthusiasm.

The time factor dominated grand-strategic and military-strategic choices on both sides in the war. Sea power came to play so important a role in the defeat of the Central Powers because the war was of long duration. That long duration—to close the circle of interactions and blur cause and effect—was in part enforced by sea power. Dominant sea power played a large role in creating the strategic context wherein it could exert maximum enabling influence upon the course and outcome of the conflict. Notwithstanding the prescient insights of Lord Kitchener, significant military opinion in Britain and France expected victory to be achieved, successively, in 1914, 1915, and 1916. Inevitably, the military methods adopted in those years were geared to a moving short-war timetable and had a major negative impact upon military effectiveness in the unexpected "out" years. When all but supreme efforts fail, and fail repeatedly, the military instrument that remains is certain to have been severely bruised in the attempts.

The course and outcome of the war is much clearer to today's observers than it was to the hopeful yet baffled leaders of 1914–18. In 1915 and 1916 it was believed that victory would be possible "this year," *if only* last year's errors could be corrected. For 1915 that meant more men and, particularly, more material. For 1916 it meant that "Great Britain, France, Italy, and Russia will deliver simultaneous attacks with their maximum forces as soon as they are ready to do so and circumstances seem favorable."[38] As France faltered and Russia disengaged in 1917, Britain stepped up to assume the principal burden of land fighting in the West (in 1917 and 1918), and the United States mobilized, trained, equipped, and deployed so as to become an important factor by the summer and fall of 1918 and potentially a decisive one in 1919. The Allies' race to succeed while their strength and will yet endured thus was won because of the massive accretions of British land power after 1915 and American financial, manpower, and material strength after the spring of 1917.

The time factor in war was even more pitiless in its meaning for Germany than it was for the Allies. Germany's failures on land and at sea caused her leaders to make a succession of time-driven

192

choices, really of gambles against the clock, which ultimately proved fatal. For example, the new military leadership of Germany decided in 1916 upon a program of total industrial mobilization for war, called the Hindenburg Program. The program was so punishing in its effects upon German society that it required the country's armed forces to win in 1918 before the civilian economy ground to a halt. In addition, the German decision of January 9, 1917, to initiate the third bout of unrestricted U-boat warfare rested upon an indifference to the certainty of U.S. entry into the war. That indifference could be justified only by confidence that victory would be secured in a matter of months. In fact, the strategic and tactical failure of the U-boat campaign drove the German High Command to the desperate and unrepeatable great offensive of spring and early summer 1918. From the overly taut schedule of the modified Schlieffen Plan in 1914, to the race against the clock of American deployments and German domestic (and rank-and-file military and naval) disaffection in 1918, the time factor, or belief about the meaning of that factor, shaped German no less than Allied grand and military strategies.

On May 31, 1916, in what from the German point of view was the unexpected and undesired encounter Battle of Jutland, Jellicoe's first duty was not to lose. Similarly, the overriding task of the Royal Navy in 1917 and 1918 was to prevent the Germans' winning at sea through submarine commerce raiding the victory that their Army had failed to secure on land. Understanding of the war on land is essential if the strategic influence of sea power is to be comprehended properly. As always in conflicts between land powers and sea powers, the wars on land and at sea from 1914 to 1918 were intimately related. Both sides went to war anticipating that the struggle would be brief, if climactic. Neither coalition had developed anything remotely resembling a national or coalition military strategy embracing cooperative, or even complementary, action by land and sea forces. In that context, German bids for victory and their meaning for the influence of sea power on the course and outcome of the war can be identified.

FIRST BID: A much modified Schlieffen Plan was executed in August–September 1914 for the purpose of producing victory over France (with or without the active assistance of a BEF) within forty-two days. With France eliminated from the war, Russia subsequently could be battered into acquiescing in a disadvantageous peace settlement. The Baltic would be a German lake, the Black Sea would be closed to the Royal Navy by Turkey at the Dardanelles and the Bosporus, and Italy would remain neutral. In short, Britain might command the Narrow Seas and lay maritime siege to a German-reorganized peninsular Europe but would have difficultly prosecuting the war in the absence of continental allies.

Controversy still attends the question of whether the younger Moltke's changes in Schlieffen's great plan truly were critical to the failure of August–September 1914.[39] The plan that Schlieffen bequeathed to his successor in January 1906 called for ninety infantry divisions overall: ten of them serving as a covering force in East Prussia and eighty to be deployed against France. Of the eighty allocated to the West, ten were to stand on the defensive in Alsace-Lorraine and seventy (in five armies) were to execute a gigantic right wheel through the Maastricht "appendix" of Holland, through Belgium, and then through northern France. As modified and implemented by the younger Moltke in 1914, the plan employed eighty-seven divisions: nine allocated to East Prussia and seventy-eight to the West. Of that seventy-eight, twenty were committed to what should have been the "anvil" defensive role in Alsace-Lorraine, with fifty-eight allotted to the five armies of the right wing. Although Moltke nominally weakened the force ratio of the all-important right wing as compared with the left wing (two armies) from seven-to-one to less than three-to-one, it would be unwise to make too much of that fact. In practice, Moltke saved the Army the necessity of defeating Dutch troops, and he detached only two corps for the observation and investment of the Belgian Army in Antwerp (as contrasted with the five corps that Schlieffen had intended). The logistic dimension of the plan was always tenuous. It is probable that Moltke's modifications—the thinning out of the right wing and the shortening of its line of march—were of sufficient logistic benefit as to offset substantially their negative strategic and tactical aspects.[40] Apart from the unresolved issue of whether the plan was a logistic impossibility is the pertinent question of whether the German armies on the far right wing, which were to lunge very deep into France, could be commanded in mobile warfare in any meaningful sense.[41]

In practice, the German right wing itself was threatened with envelopment and then, as it reacted to that danger, to penetration by the BEF through the gap that opened up between the First and Second Armies. By September 5–6 at the latest, the German attempt to win the war in the West in a single very short campaign had failed. It is intriguing to speculate whether a German advance even farther than the Marne might have produced a literally decisive defeat for their arms.

SECOND BID: With the failure of the Schlieffen Plan by the close of the first week of September 1914, Germany attempted to pull victory from the jaws of stalemate by outflanking the allied armies in Flanders. Thanks principally to the Belgian Army, which escaped from its investment in Antwerp, the BEF, which was extracted *en bloc* from the Ainse and inserted around Ypres, and the Royal Navy, which helped vitally to break up the German assault along the coast against the retreating Belgians, this second and increasingly desperate bid had failed by late November.

THIRD BID: Against his better judgment, General Erich von Falkenhayn, Moltke's successor as Army Chief of Staff, turned in 1915 from renewing the offensive in France and Belgium to the seemingly more tractable mission of ruining, if not routing, the Russian Army. At least this mission seemed more tractable to Paul von Hindenburg and Erich Ludendorff and other "Easterners" at that time. Unexpectedly, Germany had inflicted great damage upon the Russians in the battles of 1914 with minimal forces. That undeniable fact argued strongly for finishing the job promptly. There were other considerations. Germany's Austrian ally was in a desperate plight, and Russian armies in the enormous Polish salient posed a continuing threat to the Prussian heartland of Germany in the East. In addition, the difficulty demonstrated in 1914 of achieving success on a strategic scale in the West, as well as the need to relieve pressure on Turkey in Eastern Anatolia and the strong desirability of discouraging Rumania from entering the war on the side of the Allies, all suggested great merit in a big push on the Eastern Front.[42]

As an all-too familiar element in coalition war making, Germany was compelled to act strongly in the East in 1915 in order to arrest and reverse an unfolding disaster that threatened the Austro-Hungarian Army in the empire's border province of Galicia. The Germans succeeded in imposing massive manpower losses upon the

Russians (who suffered 2 million casualties in 1915—1 million of them as prisoners) and secured vast territorial gain. In particular, the Polish salient from which Russian armies menaced the whole of Eastern Germany, including Berlin, was eliminated. But as Falkenhayn had predicted, the enterprise was overly ambitious. Its price was the ability to take the offensive against the BEF before it became a formidable ally. Although the Western Allies may have squandered golden geostrategic opportunities in 1915, the Germans lost a year. They could ill afford to lose this time against a coalition which commanded the sea and could, as a consequence, draw upon the world beyond Europe for sustenance. In both world wars, as in the Great War between Britain and Napoleonic France, a long war means an economic war, and an economic war is structured by, and favors, the sea power which grants global access.

FOURTH BID: At Verdun in 1916 Falkenhayn endeavored to inflict such damage upon the French Army that its will to continue the struggle would be destroyed. It was expected that, as a consequence, Paris would be amenable to a German-dictated peace settlement. The Battle of Verdun, which cost the French Army some 542,000 casualties, was waged against the background of the catastrophically expensive French military failures of 1914 and 1915. As in 1915 in the East, the Germans again miscalculated, although they did achieve the attrition of French soldiery intended. But battles of attrition necessarily are two-way contests, and Germany could less afford the 434,000 casualties of Verdun than could the Allies the more than half-million suffered by France. Moreover, while the German Army was battering France at Verdun, the British Army launched and sustained its long anticipated first major offensive, on the Somme. In desperation at the strategic failures of 1916, Paris and even London were moved to endorse for early 1917 the glittering, but counterfeit, promise of General Nivelle to win the war "at a stroke" with a breakthrough in twenty-four hours. A *masse de manoeuvre* of twenty-seven divisions literally was to roll up the German line.[43]

In 1916 the Germans had miscalculated the powers of resistance of the French Army in a protracted defensive battle. Also, the German Army of that year was subject to both unduly rigid direction from the top and was notably predictable and inflexible in its tactics in both offense and defense. The German Army would change under Hindenburg and Ludendorff, but at Verdun and then on the Somme, that Army fought itself into a condition of severe military crisis by late 1916. Michael Howard's sweeping judgment that "until the end of 1917 the German armies had been consistently victorious"[44] can only be labeled wrong. The Marne and First Ypres in 1914, and Verdun and the Somme in 1916, were none of them German victories on any plausible assay. A consistently victorious army would not have effected first a defensive, then an offensive, revolution in its tactics in late 1916–early 1918, and neither would so successful a land force have needed to endorse on January 9, 1917, the Navy's extravagant promises of victory via submarine *guerre de course*.

The BEF in 1916, by then a million-man army, was not outstanding in tactics and operational art. But after its disastrous experience on July 1, it was more than good enough to take most of the pressure off the French (Falkenhayn halted German offensives in the Verdun battle on July 11), inflict casualties that Germany could not afford (particularly among the regular noncommissioned officer corps, the backbone of the German Army), and provide hope to France that at long last a large fraction of the burden of the war on land could be shifted reliably to an ally.[45]

FIFTH BID: Early in 1917, Germany turned belatedly and in desperation to its Navy to achieve the favorable decision which thus far had been sought in vain. To date Germany had failed in the West (in 1914) and achieved nothing obvious of lasting value in the East (in 1915). She had suffered an intolerable stalemate, amounting to a defeat, in the attritional battles of Verdun and on the Somme (in 1916) and been compelled to reorganize her defensive tactics and system of fortification along much of the Western Front, with the so-called Hindenburg Line (in the winter of 1916–17). Bereft of attractive options for the use of the High Seas Fleet, the Navy promised in the course of a five-month submarine campaign to defeat a Britain which had become the mainstay of the enemy coalition. By unrestricted warfare against the seaborne trade of the Allies, Germany aspired to sink 600,000 tons of Allied or Allied-serving shipping per month and drive a critical fraction of neutral shipping out of the profitable business of supplying the Allied War economies. It was calculated that such a sustained level of loss would require Britain to sue for peace by August 1, 1917.

Primarily because of the belated introduction of the convoy system on May 10, the U-boat campaign narrowly failed in its strategic object in the summer of 1917. Convoying, the most basic tactic for the protection of shipping in the days of sail, was believed by the Royal Navy over 1914–early 1917 to be impracticable for an age of steam. The Admiralty was convinced that Britain's maritime trade was too numerous to be defended usefully in convoys, that the administrative burdens would be intolerable, and that convoys would present wonderful fat targets.[46] The fact was that convoys had the effect of apparently emptying the ocean of targets. Convoys do present a dense target array, but in the immensity of the ocean, convoys, even large ones, occupy insignificant space. In short, the U-boats found far fewer targets in convoys than they did as isolated vessels. The Royal Navy was appallingly ill equipped to wage war against the U-boats in 1917, but the U-boats were desperately bereft of operational intelligence that they could use on convoy departures and routing. Bearing in mind the German Navy's objective to sink 600,000 tons a month, it is sobering to realize that the tonnage actually sunk was as follows: February (1917)—464,599; March—507,001; April—834,569; May—549,987; and June—631,895.[47]

SIXTH BID: Recognizing in the fall of 1917 the failure of the maritime counterblockade of Britain, which included the attempt to close the North Atlantic to the transfer of American soldiers and war material, Ludendorff determined to try what John Terraine has called "the gambler's fling" of a last great offensive on the Western Front.[48] In his memoirs Ludendorff wrote:

> Owing to the break-down of Russia the military situation was more favourable to us at New Year, 1918, than one could ever have expected. As in 1914 [in the West] and 1915 [in the East], we could think of deciding the war by an attack on land. Numerically we had never been so strong in comparison with our enemies.[49]

He transferred forty-two divisions to France from the victorious and now effectively concluded front in the East, and he impressively retrained and reequipped elite "storm battalions" of bachelor *Stosstruppen* for assault by infiltration in blitzkrieg-style infantry warfare.[50] He also encouraged the perfection of the new

198

artillery tactics first employed at the siege of Riga in September 1917.[51] As it evolved, the First World War on land above all else was an artillery war.

With sixty-two divisions in the assault, the first phase of the German Spring Offensive of 1918 was unleashed on March 21, 1918, against the weakest sector of the BEF's front in France.[52] Despite large initial territorial gains, the Offensive failed to achieve strategic success. Moreover, the cost of tactical success was a rate of loss among elite troops so heavy as to prove ultimately fatal in face of a numerically and materially much stronger enemy coalition. In 1918 Germany lacked the military strength in depth to achieve a favorable strategic decision by a series of tactical victories. Neither side in the West had the cross-battlefield mobility needed promptly to transform tactical into strategic victory. The initial showy tactical achievements of the March 21 Offensive were as alarming to the Allies as was Hitler's Ardennes Offensive of December 16, 1944, but for similar reasons, both were forlorn hopes. In the summer and fall of 1918 the Western Allies had the strength in manpower and material, married to a generally competent military method, to be able to win the war mile by mile. With the partial exception of the Allies' near-capture of the German forces in Normandy in the late summer of 1944, the record of both world wars demonstrated that the German Army could not be beaten in the field by maneuver warfare. Hard fighting, attritional combat, is always needed to beat the best-quality army of the period.

The strategic failure of the 1918 Spring Offensive proved decisive in Germany's defeat because it marked the ultimate failure of the Central Powers' theories of victory. The Offensive was all the more devastating to German military and civilian morale because of the extravagant hopes invested in it. The more immediate elements in the chain of strategic logic that produced the ruinous Spring Offensive were: the unrestricted U-boat campaign begun on February 1, 1917, which inevitably drew the United States into the war, as Berlin had expected; the necessity to attempt some war-winning stroke on land before the U.S. Army could arrive in France in overwhelmingly numbers—the U-boat campaign narrowly but definitively having failed in 1917–early 1918; the apparent availability of an instrument for swift victory—in the form of close to 1 million men rendered surplus to the needs of the Eastern Front by the Russian collapse in 1917, and new ideas and some new instruments for offensive success at the level of tactics; and frank recognition by the High Command that Germany lacked the strength to fight on indefinitely beyond 1918.

With the exception of the unrestricted U-boat campaign of 1917–18, the German Navy played no role of great significance in its country's war effort. Strategically this was curious, because the High Seas Fleet had everything to gain for Germany. Theoretically, in the span of a few hours of successful combat, it might have achieved victory in a fleet action and thereby have compelled Britain to sue for peace. If the battle line of the High Seas Fleet had been sunk in such an action, the strategic consequences for the Central Powers would, at worst, have been only modestly negative. Of course, this was not the way the strategic cost-benefit analysis was calculated in Berlin. For nearly four years, Germany anticipated winning the war with her traditional military instrument of excellence, the Army. Given the increasingly unfavorable naval odds, it is understandable why the High Seas Fleet was not offered up for near-certain destruction in the North Sea. Over 1914–16, when Germany expected to win the war on land, the High Seas Fleet was deemed operationally valuable as a fleet in being—for example, denying the Royal Navy the ability to attempt a close blockade of the U-boat bases. In addition, it was anticipated that the fleet could be important both for the terms at a peace conference and as the foundation for a long-term bid to construct an unarguably superior navy.

When explaining the reasons for his involuntary resignation as First Lord of the Admiralty over the issue of the forcing of the Dardanelles, Winston Churchill said in 1915 that

> the old wars were decided by their episodes rather than by their tendencies. In this war the tendencies are far more important than the episodes. Without winning any sensational victories we may win this war.[53]

As these words suggest, the impact of sea power for the Allies has to be assessed in the broadest of strategic terms in relation to the conduct of the war as a whole. Command of the sea, albeit a command threatened or disputed first by the High Seas Fleet and then by the U-boats, was a precondition for British, and later American, participation in a protracted war. Without British and American belligerency, Germany would have triumphed. Indeed, it was anxiety over the implicit German threat to her maritime supremacy which most surely propelled Britain into the ranks of the anti-German coalition. Britain and the United States could not wage continental war if they could not move men, war materiel, and other goods more or less at will by sea. More fundamental still, Britain could not wage war at all if her seaborne trade was held in port for fear of assault.

The character and direction of Imperial German statecraft in the early years of the century had rendered Anglo-German conflict inevitable. Britain was correct in fighting with France and Russia and, in British perspective, the abominably expensive victory of 1918 was worth its cost, *given the practicable alternatives*. That last point is not to deny that a compromise peace in 1916 or 1917, while American influence over Allied high policy was still trivial, would have served Britain better than did the peace of victory achieved in 1918. Britain could have coexisted in peace indefinitely with a Bismarckian Germany but not with the anti-British naval construction program of Wilheminian Germany and her vague aspirations for grandiose *Weltpolitik*.[54] With respect to military performance on land, none of the armies of 1914–18 had effective means for the flexible command of operations once troops were committed to the attack or counterattack, and none had the services of a mobile arm for the operational exploitation of tactical success. The generals of the period may be criticized for pursuing strategic missions with a fatally flawed tactical instrument, but it is unlikely that any other generation of generals and staff officers would have performed any better *in a similar technical context*.

Germany was defeated on land in 1918 by a global coalition of states whose ultimately overwhelming concentration of fighting power on the Western Front was the direct result of the mobilization of economies oceans apart and highly interdependent in their production of war materiel. Writing of the post-Jutland period, Cruttwell observed that

the Navy in fact had become and remained the gigantic and indispensable instrument for pumping the blood of commerce into the

arteries of the entente, and for the slow strangulation of its enemies.[55]

In addition, the economic blockade of the Central Powers ultimately proved fatal to their cause, *in the context of a protracted and very hard-fought land war*. The blockade had to be
considered in conjunction with the enemy's beleaguerment on
land, with reference to the full panoply of economic warfare and
in the light of the evaporation of popular expectations of victory.
Prior to 1914, economic blockade was not thought to play a significant role in the conduct of major war since no government
expected the next great conflict to last for years and engage the
full economic resources of the belligerents. The extent of Germany's economic dependence upon seaborne trade for raw materials, particularly for fertilizers and concentrated feedstuffs for
agriculture, was grossly underappreciated. That dependence
could become a truly debilitating strategic vulnerability only if
the war was a long one and entailed a massive diversion of labor
and material from the civilian economy to the immediate war
effort. Also it was important that the German Army should not
compensate by economic acquisition through conquest on land
for the loss of sources of overseas supply. Most critical of all for
Germany's prospects in a long war was the attitude of Britain. If
Britain was an enemy and if she applied "The Rule of War of
1756," which denied the principle of "free ships, free goods,"
then Germany truly would be landlocked in the economics of
war.[56] The strategic power of the blockade was as much of a
surprise to the Allies as it was to Germany.

Fatal though the blockade proved to be in a long war, its execution—in the context of other measures of economic warfare—
was fraught with difficulties for Britain. A practical problem for
the Royal Navy over 1914–16, for example, was the attitude to
adopt toward American goods probably bound for Germany via
Dutch ports and carried on American or Dutch (or other neutral—
Norwegian, Danish, Swedish, and so on) ships. Holland was neutral in the First World War. In his memoirs, Sir Edward Grey
(British Foreign Secretary from the outbreak of war until December 11, 1916) makes it plain that London calculated U.S. goodwill
as being of greater value than the blockade of Germany. He wrote
that the

blockade of Germany was essential to the victory of the Allies, but the ill-will of the United States meant their certain defeat. After Paris had been saved by the battle of the Marne, the Allies could do no more than hold their own against Germany; sometimes they did not even do that. Germany and Austria were self-supporting in the huge supply of munitions. The Allies soon became dependent for an adequate supply on the United States. If we quarrelled with the United States we could not get that supply. It was better therefore to carry on the war without blockade, if need be, than to incur a break with the United States about contraband and thereby deprive the Allies of the resources necessary to carry on the war at all or with any chance of success. *The object of diplomacy, therefore, was to secure the maximum of blockade that could be enforced without a rupture with the United States.*[57]

Overall, in the context of bitter military disappointments on land and at sea, the economic blockade was critical for the defeat of Germany in 1918. The British official history of *Seaborne Trade* in the First World War is explicit in its conclusions on the inter-dependence of German military failure in the field and a growing economic debility that both sapped the public willingness to en-dure longer, as well as reduced the weight of German military power:

The motive for endurance was gone. Much might have been en-dured for the chance of a victory which would bring in its train a renewal of the supplies so urgently needed for the restoration of Germany's economic life; but a people debilitated by hunger, cold, and disease [the total number of German civilian deaths from 1915 to 1918 exceeded by 760,000 mortality expectations based on pre-war statistics], disillusioned, distrustful of their rulers, and without hope, were in no mood to rally for a desperate defence against overwhelming odds.[58]

Maritime command allowed the Allies to commit their armies wherever the opportunity appeared to beckon on the periphery of the landlocked fortress of the Central Powers. The only exceptions were in the proximity of strong shore defenses, through coastal waters commanded by the Central Powers, or to regions where the enemy could counter-concentrate rapidly by land. The British and American concentration of force in France and Belgium was entirely dependent on the security of sea lines of communication. The expeditionary warfare waged on a major scale at the Dardanelles, from Salonika, in Palestine, and in Mesopotamia similarly was a tangible expression of sea-based land power. The British failure to make better offensive use of her maritime command reflected in part the French dominance over Allied strategic policymaking. In 1916 and 1917, as France tired, Russia dropped out, and the United States had yet to appear in the field with a battle-ready mass army, the time had passed in which Britain might have been able to pursue any strategy other than that of the application of heavy pressure on the Western Front.

Notwithstanding a legion of contemporary and subsequent critics, the Gallipoli adventure of 1915 might have succeeded and gone down in the history books as Churchill's masterpiece. The grand-strategic possibilities at Gallipoli were inviting indeed, particularly when the geography of the war allowed very few opportunities for the direct, offensive use of sea power against the Central Powers' continental bastion. The strategic possibilities of success at Gallipoli pertained to the fact that the expedition was launched in 1915.

When the expedition was considered, the fact that the war was at an early stage meant that victory at Gallipoli and Constantinople could have been exploited by major allies who, though badly bloodied, were still far from exhausted. The problem with the strategic inspiration for the expedition in early 1915 was that Britain's tactical fighting instrument was incapable of performing the tasks assigned to it, unless fortune chose to bless the enterprise. One of the best judgments on Gallipoli may be located in a historian's conclusion on the venture to the Scheldt, the Walcheren expedition, in 1809:

> The concept of this expedition was not entirely wrong but it was based on scanty information and confused aims and was led by the wrong general.[59]

Gallipoli provides a classic example of how the tactical and strategic levels of war can fail to cohere. The prospects for a true strategic success were compromised fatally at the political and grand-strategic levels by the prior British promise (November 12, 1914) to deliver Constantinople to Russia, an embarrassing fact

204

which probably precluded a pro-Allied coup in the Turkish capital.[60] The British government formally accepted the Russian demand for postwar control of Constantinople on March 12, 1915. At the tactical level of war, British Imperial forces lacked the military competence to overcome the other disadvantages besetting the enterprise. Success was improbable but not impossible. Inspired tactical leadership on the beaches, drive from the expedition's commander offshore, better-trained forces, or even just luck might have turned a semidisaster into a triumph. Nonetheless, so many were the military errors committed and so thoroughly ignored were the lessons of the history of combined operations that the expedition did not deserve to succeed.

States do what they can with what they have. So long as she held Gibraltar—and after 1882, Egypt and the Suez Canal also—Britain's Navy could not be cut off in the Mediterranean (unlike the Baltic). Confined though the Mediterranean may be and constraining though the prevailing winds were in the age of sail, still those waters provided opportunities as a maritime theater for the potentially profitable use of superior sea power. It is scarcely surprising that a Britain with few attractive continental options in war after war should seek to accomplish whatever there was to accomplish in a theater where her fighting arm of excellence could be deployed to potentially disproportionately powerful effect.

Britain certainly mishandled the Gallipoli campaign from the outset. She diverted scarce resources to large campaigns of imprecise purpose in Palestine (beyond the defense of the Suez Canal) and Mesopotamia (beyond the defense of Basra and the Persian oil fields) and permitted France to insist upon a very large (as many as 600,000 men in 1917) and inactive expedition-garrison around Salonika in Thrace. Those facts say a great deal about the quality of Allied strategic imagination in 1914–18 but relatively little about what might have been achieved by Allied armies based on a commanded sea. One may argue as to whether the Gallipoli campaign was soundly conceived, though there can be no dispute with the verdict of history concerning its faulty execution. More interesting than the multiple "what ifs" of Gallipoli[61] is the speculation that a full-throttle Western expedition into the Balkans in 1915 might have achieved far-reaching results. In that year Germany and Austria were heavily preoccupied with Russia, German military resources in France and Belgium were virtually nontransferrable elsewhere, Serbia was flush with its success over Austria in 1914, Italy was eager to grab some of the spoils of victory—and, as events demonstrated, was prepared to pay heavily to secure them—and Turkey was isolated and menaced from all geostrategic directions.

The unity of war and the interconnectedness of the strategic options for its conduct are classically illustrated by the scope of the failure of German strategy in the First World War. Germany bid for continental hegemony to overthrow her enemies with a single battle-campaign in the West and then in the East and failed in September 1914. That failure condemned the Central Powers to the conduct of a protracted war. Protracted conflict was not the long suit of a Central Europe besieged by the resources of what amounted virtually to the rest of the world due to the mobilization value of maritime dominance. The continental hostage-taking strategy so familiar from the Anglo-French struggle served to incite the Western Allies to fight on, not to work as a lever for favorable peace terms. At the same time, the strategy of maritime ambush was pursued fitfully and with little courage. Commerce raiding by submarines was attempted in a serious way in three campaigns (1915, 1916, 1917–18), but the lack of numbers of U-boats, of suitable geography for their basing, and of operational intelligence on convoy routing condemned this most promising of strategy options to failure.

Most interesting are the ways in which the continental and the maritime dimensions of the war reinforced each other. The contrast in the course of this war with the events of 1939–45 is especially enlightening. Over 1914–18 Imperial Germany was never sufficiently liberated from immediate and desperately pressing continental concerns as to be able to do other than improvise a tenuous strategy for the direct defeat of Britain. To balance the argument, however, it is necessary to recognize that over 1914–18, unlike 1939–45, Germany did have an all but first-class, short-range surface navy, which ought to have yielded much more strategic value than proved to be the case.

Tactics and their partner, technology, have meaning for strategy and high policy and often are driven by strategic considerations. With varying success, states try to invest in military technologies that will provide weapons with characteristics most suitable for the protection or advancement of distinctive national interests. For example, Britain's coal-, then oil-, fueled Navy was relatively uninterested in long endurance in its ships because of the availability of sovereign bases around the world. The U.S. Navy, in contrast, traditionally required an endurance in its ships and later developed a fleet train for at-sea replenishment, suitable for a country lacking sovereign bases in abundance overseas. For a future case, the United States will perfect an antiballistic missile technology to provide the missile defense, complementary to the air defense, essential if she is to the play the role of superpower guardian of menaced allies and friends or executive agent for collective security. The tactical demands upon forces are driven by the foreign policy choices that command them.

Given the grip which the clash of battle fleets at Jutland long has exercised upon armchair Jellicoes and Scheers and given the potential for significance of that clash, it is fitting to offer some brief observations on the contest between the Grand and High Seas Fleets. Britain had no strategic choice other than to do whatever was most prudent to ensure that she enjoyed working command of the sea lines of communication to France and to the world beyond Europe. If Britain lacked such command, she could not participate in a European war. The first and overriding mission of the Royal Navy was to safeguard those sea lines, not to sink the High Seas Fleet. Long experience of maritime war had taught that an enemy's ability to dispute command at sea could be thwarted either by his defeat in battle or by the neutralization of his naval power through blockade. The former option was preferable, if not always practicable. Victorious battle disposed of the threat to surface command in a definitive manner and liberated naval assets for the direct protection of trade as well as for offensive purposes. But the Royal Navy did not have a tradition of accepting grossly imprudent risks. British sailors had much experience of frustration, though of continuing strategic effectiveness, in the face of inferior enemy fleets which declined to put to sea to be sunk.

Throughout the course of the First World War, the Grand Fleet and the High Seas Fleet were both obliged to resort to stratagems for intended ambush. The High Seas Fleet sought to entrap a portion of the Grand Fleet or to oblige it to run over a hasty minefield or a U-boat picket line, while the Grand Fleet endeav-

207

ored to entice the High Seas Fleet to battle (at least until January 1918). The disparity in their strengths precluded agreement on mutually acceptable terms for fleet engagement. Neither side needed to accept battle on unfavorable terms. On January 2, 1918, the Commander in Chief of the Grand Fleet, Admiral Sir David Beatty, told a naval conference in London that because of the diversion of fleet assets to trade protection duties, "the correct strategy of the Grand Fleet is no longer to endeavor to bring the enemy to action at any cost, but rather to contain him in his bases until the general situation becomes more favorable."[62]

Anchored as it was across northern Europe's access routes to oceanic commerce and military transportation, the British Grand Fleet could win its strategic victory with tactical inactivity. As a fleet in being in the Jade estuary, parading in the Heligoland Bight, or even carefully venturing into the southern North Sea, the High Seas Fleet could not dispute British maritime command. To dispute that command intelligently, it had to prod the Royal Navy into making mistakes so as to level the odds. Fortunately for the Allied cause, Admiral Sir John Jellicoe understood as well as could be both the strengths and the weaknesses of the instrument that he wielded. Jellicoe's un-Nelsonian conduct at Jutland—particularly the deployment into line away from the enemy and the turn away from the torpedo attack at 1922 hours—was the logical consequence of both the strategic context and his net assessment of the fighting power of his fleet under varying circumstances. On balance, the combat superiority of the Grand Fleet lay in the number of its modern capital ships, the weight of its massed firepower, and the skill in centralized fleet handling of its leader. In 1916, at least, the Grand Fleet was modestly disadvantaged in fire control for its big guns, shell penetration, night fighting, and the ability of some of its ships to sustain battle damage.[63]

Germany's position as world leader in the production of optical instruments found deadly expression in range finders for the guns of her fleet. German instruments and tactics made for an accuracy in the opening salvos of an engagement that the Royal Navy of 1914–16 could not match. But the Royal Navy had a superior centralized fire-control system which, in the course of a lengthy gun duel, more than offset the German advantage in optics. To be maximally effective, the German range finders required that their operators not have their personal performance degraded by strain, tiredness, or poor visibility. Overall, modern German capital ships emphasized protection for a certain tonnage, whereas their British counterparts were designed to favor weight of gunpower. In addition, the superiority of German metallurgy translated into superior penetrating power from lower caliber (a saving of weight), and German willingness to invest in very large dry docks permitted a width of beam in capital ships—important for protective options—which the Royal Navy could not emulate. The truly critical weakness in the British battle cruisers was the neglect of flash protection for the hoists between the gun turrets and the magazines. This weakness had been common to the British and the German navies, but the Germans had the benefit of a highly educational scare in this respect at the Battle of the Dogger Bank (January 24, 1915) and had corrected the problem. German shell design and manufacture unquestionably was superior to the British in the early years of the war, and the ability of German capital ships—battleships and battle cruisers—to take punishment again was ahead of the British, though not to a dramatic degree.

When the High Seas Fleet was surprised at Jutland, Jellicoe was obliged for strategic reasons to be more concerned not to lose the battle than he was to win it. Furthermore, he was obliged to conduct the battle in such a way that the particular strengths of his fleet—its numbers and weight of gunpower—were not fatally offset by unfavorable tactical circumstances. His interpretation of the balance between potential gain and risk led him to deploy his battle line as a single relatively easily commanded force (deployed in a column five and two-thirds miles long for battle) and to avoid needless risk taking in the face of concentrated destroyer attack (i.e., turn away to outrun, rather than turn toward to "comb," the torpedoes). He prohibited individual initiative, or tactical opportunism, on the part of subordinate commanders, who might as a consequence permit the fleet to be defeated in detail, and he avoided the potential chaos of night fighting.

Jellicoe's problems and responsibilities were great and his strategic and tactical skills admirable. Nonetheless, there are grounds for wondering whether he tried sufficiently hard to solve the tactical conundrum of how *prudently* to maintain an effective grip upon an enemy who wished to flee. Commenting upon a letter that Jellicoe wrote to the Admiralty on October 30, 1914, in which he laid out his intentions in some detail, Barnett observed, "It is a significant thing that among the eighteen paragraphs of this letter, there is not one that discussed how to grip the enemy so that he might be annihilated."[64]

With the exceptions of the British Admiralty's Chief of the War Staff, Vice-Admiral Sir Henry Oliver, and Grand Admiral Alfred von Tirpitz for Germany, all of the principal naval figures on both sides of the North Sea merit far more sympathy and praise than they do opprobrium for their handling of the battle-fleet dilemmas that came so close to a decision in the dim light of early evening on May 31, 1916. Jellicoe's fleet handling at Jutland was close to a faultless performance. Notwithstanding the cumulatively serious materiel problems with the Grand Fleet, appalling lapses in accurate provision of operational intelligence from the Admiralty's Operations Staff and from the Battlecruiser Fleet, Jellicoe twice achieved the tactical triumph of crossing Scheer's T and compelled him to execute no fewer than three emergency battle (complete) turn-aways. Had the Admiralty passed promptly and fully to Jellicoe the decoded signals intelligence made available to it, the prospects were that the High Seas Fleet—cast in the Franco-Spanish role—would have faced its Trafalgar early on the morning of June 1.

Well enough as the Grand Fleet performed on May 31, 1916, under Jellicoe and later under Beatty, that fleet moved energetically in 1916–17 to correct the deficiencies revealed by Jutland. The Grand Fleet of 1917–18 was a wholly more formidable instrument than it had been early in 1916. The history of the High Seas Fleet from Jutland until its surrender at Scapa Flow attests to its agreement with that judgment. Without forgetting that Jutland was a clash of battle fleets that Scheer had not sought, the meaning of the fact that the U-boats became the instrument of choice to dispute maritime command is self-evident. Jutland was a defensive strategic victory for the Royal Navy albeit not the victory that it anticipated or much welcomed.

In British perspective it is all too easy to misunderstand the role of sea power in the First World War. The shock of continental warfare and the tactically inconclusive outcome of Jutland thrust land combat to the center stage of public attention. In some important respects, the architecture of the war more closely approximated the protracted struggles with the France of Louis XIV than anything since. Notwithstanding its post-1939 title as the First World War, the war was overwhelmingly a European struggle waged in Europe for very European motives. In retrospect, there would seem to have been a twofold misreading of the strategic influence of sea power upon the course and outcome of this war. First, there was a contemporary and near-contemporary tendency to be dismissive of sea power. This attitude flowed principally from the wholly unexpected and unprecedented fact of ever greater British absorption into a protracted land war; from the absence of unmistakable naval victories to offset the preoccupation with the bloody continental conflict; and from public belief that the Navy was not performing very well (witness the escape of the High Seas Fleet at Jutland, that fleet's ability seemingly to bombard English east coast towns at will, and the 1917 crisis caused by the U-boats).

Second, by the late 1920s and early 1930s, the initial tendency to undervalue what the Royal Navy was doing, or recently had done, for the Allied cause had been fairly comprehensively overtaken by the reverse error. As former Prime Minister Herbert Asquith proclaimed extravagantly and far ahead of fashionable belief, on December 9, 1918: "With all deference to our soldiers this war had been won by sea power."[65] The economic blockade of Germany enforced by the Navy allegedly was *the* critical lever for Allied victory. Postwar Britain repudiated a continental strategy which came with a price tag of a million British Empire dead. British opinion leaders found in the theory and practice of economic warfare, the blockade, a respectable claimed alternative to "the slaughter on the Western Front" and suchlike deeply pejorative characterizations of modern land warfare.

The First World War was a ghastly national and industrial-age variant on a familiar pattern of great coalition wars. The pattern was not recognized widely in Britain because the British were not used to bearing a principal burden of actual land combat themselves, and they had been educated to a tradition of victory in fleet battles. A people reared on all but mythic folk memories of Trafalgar, the Nile, Cape St. Vincent, and the rest, battles whose meaning even for the course of the French wars was not well understood, were not likely to understand the strategic value of a Grand Fleet generally at anchor in Scapa Flow.

CHAPTER 7

FROM WAR TO WAR
Sea Power and the Crisis of 1940

The master of western and central Europe, he [Hitler in summer 1940] confronted a weakened but intransigent foe in the west, and a suspicious, demanding continental colossus in the east. His one European ally [Italy] was of uncertain strength, and the only friendly maritime power was on the other side of the globe. His military resources comprised a peerless army, which, for the moment, had no place to go; a powerful and eager air force which was however, of unproven value for independent strategic employment; and virtually no navy.

Telford Taylor, *The Breaking Wave: World War II in the Summer of 1940* (1967)

If the British experience of war in 1914–18 was reminiscent of Marlborough's campaigns and grand-strategic designs in the first decade of the eighteenth century, the experience of war in 1939–45 had more in common with the struggles with Revolutionary and Napoleonic France. In the Second World War, as from 1793 to 1815, British land power repeatedly was expelled from the Continent (Norway, France, Greece), peripheral (blue-water) warfare was waged *faute de mieux*, old allies fell and new ones had to be cemented into a working coalition, and sea power was employed to set the enemy up for his necessarily continental demise.

The parallels are extensive. The Royal Navy abandoned the Mediterranean in 1796, a step considered seriously on occasions in 1940 and 1941. The French Republic and Empire sent, or attempted to send, expeditions to Ireland (in 1796 and no fewer

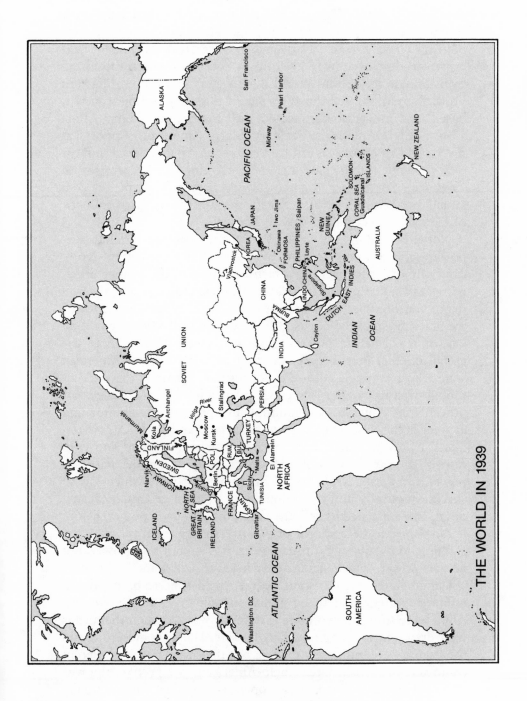

THE WORLD IN 1939

than three times in 1798), as well as to invade England itself (most seriously in 1805), ventures contemplated by Hitler in 1940. Napoleon's *Grande Armée* was ruined in Russia in 1812, and his next army was destroyed in 1813–14 by a Fourth Coalition subsidized by Britain. In the Second World War, it was the war on the Eastern Front that so blunted the *Wehrmacht* that Anglo-American sea-based land power could succeed with the Second Front in June 1944.[1] Anglo-American, but particularly American, support for the Soviet war effort was critical in its effect. That material support was vital not for the slowing, then stopping, of the invasion in 1941 (the Soviet armed forces achieved that fundamental goal largely by their own effort), but for the subsequent great rollback of German power all the way to Berlin.

Notwithstanding the general robustness of the familiar sea-power–land power paradigm, World War II was shaped significantly by two effectively new factors central to the further development of my argument. First, the strategic utility of sea power in major war becomes more and more an Anglo-*American* story. For the first time since the 1690s, Britain was obliged to wage coalition war at sea. The sea power which sustained and structured the global conflict increasingly was that of a continental American state whose strategic culture is not insular-maritime.[2] Second, although victory is not achieved independently by strategic air power, that power is a ubiquitous and necessary facilitator and enabler of the conduct of operations on land and at sea. Air power, like sea power, has strategic meaning for war on land and with respect to war as a whole. However, also in parallel with sea power, air power is a classical instrument of war, which has to succeed tactically and operationally in its own geographical medium, albeit assisted by friendly land power and sea power, before it can aspire to be a source of positive strategic utility.[3] Also, as can be said by analogy for sea power, it is superior air power, not just air power, which significantly helps to win wars.

United States, even to some degree Anglo-American, grand and military strategy had to be global in domain. But the Western Allies were to wage two quite distinctive wars, though the means were drawn from a single basket of assets. The wars in Europe and the Pacific were intimately related, but they were of very different character. In British, later Anglo-American, perspective, the war against Germany was a siege operation against an essentially continental bastion. In American perspective, the war against Japan was a siege operation against an essentially maritime bastion. Common to both sieges was the decisive significance of the transoceanic projection of American power. Both sieges were sea dependent for their conduct by the Allies, and both were fueled massively, effectively totally in the Pacific case, by the continental-size base of American sea power.

World War II comprised three principal conflicts, with significant connections among them: the Anglo-American war against Germany (and Italy), the Russo-German conflict on the Eastern Front, and the (substantially) American war against Japan. There were, of course, some important complications to this elementary tripartite picture: the Anglo-French phase of the conflict from September 1939 until June 1940, the period of isolated British belligerency from June 1940 to June 1941, and the six-month period of Anglo-Russian alliance prior to Pearl Harbor. Also significant was the military and domestic political pull of the Pacific war upon limited U.S. resources, notwithstanding the cardinal agreed principle of "Germany First," and the interdependence of Russian resistance on land and Western Allied sea-based military activity. Furthermore, the promise and the actual strategic utility of the Allied strategic bombing offensive against Germany can muddy the waters of simple explanation.

The Western Allies, really the United States, were obliged by unfolding circumstances to plan on a global basis the conduct of two major wars. Fortunately, the Axis powers were more co-belligerents than allies. Germany and Japan differed radically in their geostrategic ambitions and never attempted, even in a very pale imitation of the joint planning by the western members of the enemy's Grand Alliance, to concert their grand and military strategies.[4] Nonetheless, the progress of the wars in Europe and the Pacific necessarily had major implications for each other. With a finite pool of shipping available at any one time, attack transports and landing craft assigned to Admiral Chester Nimitz in the Pacific could not be employed in the same campaigning season in the Mediterranean or the English Channel.

The early course of World War II was shaped significant by the events of what was called "the long weekend,"[5] the interwar decades. In its turn, behavior on that long weekend was driven by the memories and alleged lessons of the Great War of 1914–18. The victims of that war approached the challenges of an all but unthinkable round two very much in the shadow of recognition of the costs of that victory.

Even when due allowance is made for the different sizes in population in different periods, the extraordinary character of the First World War for Britain is readily apparent.

BRITISH BATTLE DEATHS IN THREE WARS[6]

WARS	BATTLE DEATHS	POPULATION (in millions)
Napoleonic	100,000 (approx.)	20 (1815)[a]
First World War	744,702[b]	45 (1911)
Second World War	397,762[c]	46.5 (1930)

[a] 14–15 million in 1793.

[b] United Kingdom dead and missing: British Empire total was 947,023.

[c] United Kingdom total.

Official historian C. Ernest Fayle observed of 1914–18 that

> it was no new thing that Great Britain should keep the seas, should finance and supply her Allies, and should furnish a contingent in the field. That she should bear the main brunt of the war at sea and of the economic and industrial effort, *while providing and equipping an army on the continental scale, was altogether without precedent.*[7]

By way of contrast to the size of the strictly British force commanded by Wellington at Waterloo, 24,000 men, Field-Marshal Haig in November 1918 commanded a BEF totaling 1,794,000 men organized in fifty-nine divisions. Whereas Haig's British armies engaged ninety-nine German divisions in the victorious "hundred days" campaign in fall 1918, General Bernard Montgomery met only four German divisions at Alamein, the Allies encountered twenty-two German divisions in 1943–45 in Italy, and Field Marshal Gerd von Rundstedt attacked in the Ardennes in December 1944 with twenty divisions. The unwanted, unexpected, and subsequently deeply regretted experience with a preponderantly continental strategy from 1916 to 1918 had a profound impact upon London's approach to both continental commitment in the late 1930s and the conduct of the Second World War. John Gooch has written aptly that "Britain was a European power for the duration of the war [1914–18] and for no longer."[8]

In the winter of 1938–39, in the immediate aftermath of Hitler's demolition of the Munich Agreement, Britain began belatedly and overoptimistically to construct a coalition intended to deter further German aggression. London sought to organize her continental sword in the form of a Germany-bracketing (two-front) coalition among countries in Western and Eastern Europe. It had been made plain to British politicians that in the absence of a tangible British continental commitment, France might just elect to bandwagon with a Germany successful thus far in her expansionist course.[9] On February 6, 1939, London formally reversed her previous policy denying a continental commitment and promised Paris that a field force initially of six divisions would be dispatched promptly to France in the event of war. The decision was prompted by false rumors of German designs upon Holland.

The British intention in 1939 was to defeat Germany with much the same grand strategy that had proved successful in 1914–18 but with a critically important caveat that this time British land power, though present as a noticeable contribution on the Continent to stiffen the French, would not be permitted to grow to the scale of that achieved in the Great War.[10] In a resolute spirit of "never again," the British Army would not assume the Allied cutting-edge role that was so bloodily implemented from mid-1916 to November 1918. The French, however, were no less determined that next time they would not bear the scale of burden in continental warfare that had been their lot over 1914–18.[11]

It was unclear in 1939 just how much hard fighting would be required to secure the defeat of Germany. The British government was confident that the Western Front on the French border was a fortress the Germans could not carry by assault and therefore anticipated that no near-term military decision on land was likely in the West. This prognosis should permit Britain's tradition of maritime siege and pressure, augmented by the novel instrument of air power, eventually to transform the material balance of forces greatly to the Anglo-French advantage. Ironically, on February 20, 1939, the British Chiefs of Staff drafted "European Appreciation, 1939–40," which was to stand the test of events remarkably well in outline, if with some significant changes in detail.[12]

Notwithstanding its reasonable assumption of the permanent existence of a continental Western Front, as in the Great War, the Chiefs of Staff's 1939 Appreciation was distinctly maritime in inspiration as a theory of success in war. Above all else, the Appreciation was structured around the concern to manage time competitively. The argument was that time would work to the *long-run* advantage of the maritime alliance of the West. David French's thought that "convinced that they [the British Chiefs of Staff] could not win a short war, they had no option other than to plan to win a long one," has merit, but it points to less than the whole truth.[13] Despite dire warnings from the Treasury over Britain's inability to pay for a long war or even for a protracted period of rearmament, the Chiefs of Staff seem genuinely to have believed that Germany and Italy must lose anything other than a short war. In retrospect, they were right. Britain did manage time to her grand-strategic advantage. Germany and her ally-satellites eventually were drowned in a sea of mobilized material. Of course, in this war, the role of the 1914–18 Western Front was assumed by the post-June 1941 Eastern Front, and France was replaced as the principal ally by two super-scale states which in key respects were neutral in 1939–40.

A mix of historical accidents and enduring geostrategic principles in action produced a structure to the war against Germany which was broadly as envisaged by the British Chiefs of Staff in February 1939. A short-term prescience in 1939 would have predicted for Britain an unhappy combination of bankruptcy and all but inexorable growth of the field force from blood token toward continental-size mass army. Time, viewed financially, would scarcely have worked for the Anglo-French Allies—unless, that is, one believed that Germany would succumb politically precipitously to economic blockade. However, the political and military events of 1938–40 preempted and radically transformed the previously dire German economic situation.[14] Albeit with the unfortunate fact of their own financial vulnerability as an unresolved problem in 1939–40, the Allies were correct in identifying the German economy as a prime and fundamental source of weakness in a long war.

It was probably just as well that Britain's burgeoning mass army was obliged to share a live theater of operations with the main forces of the *Wehrmacht* for scarcely more than three weeks in

May–June 1940.[15] When next the British Army in *its* main force met the Germans on a Western Front, in June 1944, most of the German Army was busy elsewhere. Of course, this could not be foreseen or planned for in 1939, but always granted the happy escape from short-war defeat in 1940, there is little doubt that the structure of the war against Germany approximated British preferences and interests, given the poor set of choices available following the failure of deterrence in 1939 and the continental defeat of the following year. But, why was British sea-based power obliged to lay siege yet again to Germany? What was done, or left undone, in the 1920s and 1930s which led to the desperate circumstances of the early years of World War II?

Britons in the mid-1930s dared not expect that if and when a new war came, the British Empire would be allied with a great land power which would divert the lion's share of German military strength toward Eastern Europe, and a great sea power which would relieve Britain of impossible burdens in the Pacific as well as Europe. Britain's geostrategic position was critical for her maritime ascendancy, and indeed for her national and imperial security. As succeeding generations of Spanish, Dutch, French, and German strategists discovered to their chagrin, Britain enjoyed the grand-strategic benefits which flowed from the possession of a superior fleet and breakwater position *vis-à-vis* continental Europe. But in the late nineteenth and early twentieth centuries, political modernization and economic development in distant climes torpedoed this fortunate condition for Britain and her suddenly potentially embarrassingly global empire. A far-flung empire could be a source of net grand-strategic strength, provided there was no severe tension between its far-flung needs for protection and the security of the British homeland. If all substantial maritime threats to Britain emanated from continental Europe, then the traditional methods of naval concentration in home waters, close or distant blockade of European ports, and the encouragement of landward menace to the continental naval threat should answer the policy challenge.

Unfortunately for Britain, the great expansion of her imperial responsibilities coincided with the dramatic transformation for the worse of her global security condition. The emergence in the first decade of this century of navies potentially of the top class in

North America and in East Asia comprehensively unraveled the feasibility of a unilateral British imperial strategy. Britain could concentrate a fleet to discipline the Japanese, or could more than match the growing—but still modest—U.S. Navy, or could over-awe the evident naval threat from Imperial Germany in the North Sea. But Britain in the early 1900s could not do all three simultaneously.

The solution to the dilemmas of overstretch in British imperial grand strategy lay in the judicious use of diplomacy, indeed of appeasement.[16] A steady policy of friendly accommodation toward the United States and of actual alliance with Japan (in 1902) allowed Britain to restructure the Navy and concentrate her battle fleet in home waters to meet the emerging German menace. Britain's principal foes of the previous century, France and Russia, were removed from, or at least demoted upon, the enemies' list by limited agreements on colonial issues in 1904 and 1907. Thus it was that although the Royal Navy was to be severely tested in 1914–18, Britain's geostrategic condition in 1914, broadly considered, was as favorable as could have been asked. No matter what surprises the realities of war would bring, at least in principle Britain and her empire faced the possibilities of combat from a sound grand-strategic and naval basis. That was not so in the mid-1930s.

Genuine strategic dilemmas drove British policy in the 1930s. Too many people subsequently condemned reflexively a British policy of appeasement which was initiated symbolically with the signing of the Anglo-German Naval Agreement on June 18, 1935. The roots of appeasement may be located in the 1921–22 Washington Conference on naval arms limitation and security problems in the Pacific. At American insistence—really as a condition for improved Anglo-American relations and for agreement on naval arms limitation—Britain was obliged not to renew her treaty with Japan in December 1921. On balance, the exchange of regional protection in the Far East for accommodation with the United States was a good bargain as well as being inevitable,[17] in the sense that the British government welcomed the economical opportunity to surrender its naval supremacy gracefully to a condition of leg-islated parity with the United States rather than face the prospect of having the United States achieve naval supremacy by dint of competitive effort. (With hindsight it is apparent that Washington was scarcely in a better political condition to persist with a naval race than was London, but that is another story.) The military and naval advisers to the British government in the mid-1930s did not have the luxury of the responsibility-free long view available to historians. From the advisers' perspective, Britain had exchanged a Japanese alliance for nothing worth mentioning. Britain had not acquired the United States as an ally to substitute for Japan in the Pacific. In fact, the abrupt jettisoning in 1921 of the long-standing alliance, as well as the superficially inequitable terms of the Washington system of naval arms limitation (the five-five-*three* ratio in capital-ship tonnage allowed, respectively, the United States, Britain, and Japan) contributed actively to a Japanese anti-Western resentment, which was to explode in due course (with a beginning already registered in Manchuria in 1931).

Britain's traditional grand strategy of a heavily maritime focus and variable measure of continental commitment could not work in the nightmarish strategic context which seemed imminent by the mid-1930s. In its Third Report of November 21, 1935, the Defence Requirements Sub-Committee said that it was

a cardinal requirement of our national and imperial security that our foreign policy should be so conducted as to avoid the possible development of a situation in which we might be confronted simultaneously with the hostility, open or veiled, of Japan in the Far East, Germany in the West, and any Power on the main line of communication between the two.[18]

In the 1930s the British government confronted the possibility, even the probability, of a war it could not win. Even if France was a reliable ally and if Anglo-French strategy was well coordinated, still the British Empire could not be defended simultaneously in Europe, the Mediterranean/Middle East, and the Far East. Maritime empire is a source of strength only when the relevant seas are commanded either by that empire, by allies, or by friendly neutrals. The British Empire of the interwar period was indefensible if threats arose in both Europe and the Far East and if the United States was not an ally. The now-traditional reasons for finding grave fault with Britain's would-be appeasers in the 1935–38 period have substantial merit, but there is no evading the fact that British policymakers and defense planners, absent successful ap-

221

peasement or additional powerful allies, had too many commitments to defend with too few assets. The Admiralty was at least as
enthusiastic for appeasement as was the Treasury. Also, although
Germany was thoroughly unready for war in 1938, that is not
what British leaders were told at the time by their experts.[19]

Britain never had to face the triple-Axis threat either alone or
only with a Russian land power ally. Plainly, as London had recognized since the turn of the century, there could be no strictly
national British military solution to simultaneous strategic challenges in Europe and maritime or continental (India) Asia. The sea
power problems and solutions of the 1930s and the subsequent
war years have to be viewed more widely in the contexts of land
power and air power and more widely still of grand strategy and
choices in high policy. But in 1940–41 it would be the Royal Navy
and the Royal Air Force which would have to buy the time for the
international context for policy and grand strategy to evolve in
Britain's favor. Historians today know that the U.S. Lend-Lease
Act of March 11, 1941, ensured the financing of Britain's war
effort. They know also that the Soviet Union would break the back
of the German Army, that the United States would thrash Japan
and provide the military muscle of all kinds necessary to help the
Russians beat Germany on land, that the Italian fleet would prove
desperately short of fighting power, and so on. None of this was
known to the responsible officials in London in the late 1930s or
1940, for whom the long-term possibilities of grand-strategic success were overshadowed by the near-term danger of military catastrophe.

German political, if not military, collapse was vaguely predicted
as the probable long-term consequence of the frustration generated by unbreakable beleaguerment by land, sea, and air and of an
increasing domestic privation in Germany caused by economic
blockade.[20] In addition, propaganda delivered from the air by
leaflet and on the airwaves was expected to lower German public
morale. Eventually, it was anticipated, some military pressure on
the ground would have to be applied. For understandable reasons
of casualty aversion, the British government hoped in 1939–40
that it could either deter or defeat Germany through promise or
application of a truncated version of the grand strategy that had
worked in 1914–18. Unfortunately, British grand strategy in the
late 1930s elected to ignore the close interweaving of continental

and maritime strategies that had produced victory twenty years earlier. Britain selected for emphasis those lessons that were most expedient. Anglo-French war planning finessed the issue of whether victory could be secured without the defeat of the German Army in the field.

On land, though not at sea, World War Two in the West in Europe began as the so-called Phony War. Of course, war had not been phony in Poland, the ostensible detonator of the Allied declarations of belligerency. Once that unfortunate country had been erased, however, there was no action on land through the winter of 1939–40, except in the North, where Stalin was seeking a strategic buffer zone at Finland's expense.

The spring and early summer of 1940 saw the radical transformation of the strategic context as Germany invaded Denmark and Norway on April 9 and the Low Countries and France on May 10. The Norwegian venture was preemptive on Hitler's part. He anticipated British intervention in Norway and sought to ensure by his bold forestalling move the security of transit in winter for the vital supply of Swedish iron ore to Narvik, and thence through Norwegian coastal waters to Germany. Hitler's invasion of Norway was geostrategically sensible. Given his long-term aggressive designs against the Soviet Union and the fact of British belligerency, it made sense to occupy the country which flanked the shortest of the practicable sea routes between them.[21] Furthermore, naval and air bases in Norway brought German naval power 500 miles closer to the North Atlantic.[22]

There was both strategic discomfort and comfort for Britain in any net assessment of its vastly incompetent Norwegian adventure in counterintervention. The discomfort was all too obvious. The first blooding of the British armed forces in war on land indicated plainly deficiencies in quality of training for cooperation among the services and among the arms within a service (the Army, in particular), as well as in the equipment and the lack of military skill. The potential benefits to Germany of having outflanked the North Sea maritime blockade were clear to all, but those benefits could be assessed only in regard to the prospective whole course and direction of the war. The strategic utility of Germany's success in Norway must depend upon the war that followed and Berlin's ability to exploit that success with sea power.

223

Notwithstanding the long-term geostrategic value of Norway to Germany, it is just possible that Hitler's victory in Norway may have cost him the war. (This possibility could not have been apparent in Berlin in April or through much of May 1940, but it is an obligation upon statesmanship to look ahead.) When Hitler invaded Denmark and Norway and hazarded his very immature navy, he, of all people, knew that his gamble for victory against the Allies in the West was imminent. His strategic sin over Norway was the willingness to place at grave risk his near-term irreplaceable, already grossly inferior, surface fleet, in the service of a military operation which, even if successful, could be of great benefit only in a long war with Britain. But on April 9, 1940, Hitler was not planning to wage a long war with Britain. He was a sufficiently well self-instructed student of modern history to understand that continental powers have not fared well in protracted conflicts with an insular sea power. In common with the other political leaders of the period, Hitler was alert to what he believed to be the lessons of 1914–18. He was more than a little respectful of the damage that Britain's maritime blockade had inflicted in those years, just as he was genuinely admiring of the worldwide British Empire. In the mid- and late 1930s, Hitler's Germany sought first to secure a broad agreement with Britain on spheres of influence. Hitler would concede, at least *pro tem*, Britain's extra-European preeminence, in return for British acquiescence in a German continental hegemony. Among the many explanations of Hitler's statecraft from 1938 through the summer of 1941 which contain more than a grain of truth is the proposition that, educated by the grim experience of 1916–18, he sought to render his Third Reich a truly blockade-proof *Festung Europa*. With the Soviet Alliance of August 1939 and victory in the North and West in April–June 1940, Hitler succeeded in unraveling the not-implausible 1939 British economic theory of victory in a long war.

The price of victory in Norway was the temporary near-obliteration of the German surface navy as a military factor in the summer of 1940. As Churchill wrote in his memoirs:

From all this wreckage and confusion [the Norwegian campaign] there emerged one fact of major importance potentially affecting the future of the war. In their desperate grapple with the British Navy the Germans ruined their own . . . [Churchill proceeds to list

224

the allied naval losses, which were serious but tolerable]. On the other hand, at the end of June 1940, a momentous date, the effective German Fleet consisted of no more than one 8-inch-gun cruiser, two light cruisers, and four destroyers. Although many of their damaged ships, like ours, could be repaired, the German Navy was no factor in the supreme issue of the invasion of Britain.[24]

A Nazi German government with a short-war strategy, determined not to repeat the errors of Napoleonic France and Imperial Germany, sacrificed its already inadequate naval strength for a secondary objective as it was about to launch the campaign of decision against a Western Alliance whose center of strategic gravity was offshore. Perhaps as strategically fatal for Germany as the loss of ships in the Norwegian campaign was the negative impression that the relatively poor combat performance of Grand Admiral's Raeder's surface vessels made on the mind of the Führer. An invasion of Britain would never have been ordered lightly by a land-confident but sea-ignorant and fearful Hitler. Nonetheless, his propensity to boldness in a short-haul maritime enterprise in the summer of 1940 might have increased noticeably had the German Navy performed over Norway more aggressively and effectively.

The Norwegian invasion was an exceedingly, perhaps imprudently, aggressive strategic operation. The *Kriegsmarine* launched a complex invasion over an uncommanded sea. At the ship, squadron, and even fleet levels, German sea power off Norway, as off the River Plate as recently as December 17, 1939, with the "pocket battleship" *Graf Spee*, and throughout World War I, was never imbued with that determination to close with, and destroy, the enemy which was the tradition in Britain's Royal Navy. As with the French in a previous era, the Germans either lacked a superiority in force or they had ulterior objectives in mind, in support of which the hazards of battle would be an arguably needless complication. Such inglorious prudence did not resonate well with Hitler, an Austrian land animal. There was always some tension between Hitler's political-symbolic view of the value of large surface vessels, a view which disinclined him to risk them, and his admiration for combat prowess.

Success in Norway, as later in France and Belgium, reinforced Hitler's swelling sense of infallibility in statecraft and conviction of historic mission. For many of the same reasons that great amphibious enterprises tend to exhaust the military imagination of their planners with the securing of a beachhead, so great enterprises in continental conquest have a way of running out of capital in strategic imagination when they reach the water's edge. Conclusion of the victorious continental campaign in the West in May–June 1940 left Hitler acutely short of a dominant strategic idea.

Absent a favorable political deal with London, Germany had to think seriously about naval matters. In strategic terms, Hitler's Navy was anything but a luxury fleet, and it would be needed desperately in the summer of 1940 if a successful campaign on land were to be exploited promptly to secure a victorious outcome to the war as a whole. Germany could afford to expend her naval power to cover an invasion of Britain but not on a Norwegian campaign that would have strategic significance only for a protracted war, which better German leadership would have precluded.

The pivotal year of the conflict for the relationship between sea power and land power in the war for Europe was 1940. The Allies' defeat on land in May–June, and the surrender of France on June 21 mandated that Britain revert to the conduct of peripheral maritime strategy in the exercise of the purportedly British way in warfare. On the basis of an imperfect historical precedent, Hitler might be excused the belief that Britain would choose to acquiesce in the verdict of the continental battlefield and come to terms. Notwithstanding the novelty of the military reach over land granted by air power, Britain's war-waging choices in late June 1940 were more than casually reminiscent of a previous era. In 1801, following the collapse of the Second Coalition against France, Britain was quite unable to conduct continental warfare.

Not without a bitter domestic political debate on the issue, a Britain supreme at sea but shut out on land in Europe was prepared to make peace with Napoleon Bonaparte in 1801. In the Treaty of Amiens of 1802, Britain signed on for a peace settlement heavily weighted in France's favor. Britain had waged war for nine years, to no obvious advantage. In the summer of 1940, inevitably there was a peace party in London, indeed in the Cabinet Churchill inherited[25]. Unfortunately for Germany, though, unlike the strategically analogous case of 1801–2, a peace policy was not politically viable in Britain in 1940 once it became apparent that the

British Army would escape from France, that Hitler was not bent upon immediate invasion, and all the while Churchill could tell plausible lies to his colleagues about the good prospects for the United States's coming to Britain's rescue very soon. The demonization of Hitler and his Nazi regime in the mind of the British public and in the conviction of most British politicians had advanced too rapidly since the rape of Czechoslovakia in March 1939 to render formal acquiescence in Hitler's continental hegemony a legitimate option for policy.

Churchill, personally, probably was determined *under all circumstances* to prevent a negotiated peace in 1940. Both Churchill and the British opinion that he helped shape in 1940 were irrevocably committed to the position that Hitler could not be trusted to abide by any agreement which he would subsequently be motivated to break.

The military disaster in northern France and Belgium which led to the evacuation of the BEF from Dunkirk (as well as later from other French ports on the Channel and the Bay of Biscay) at the cost of all its heavy equipment was not viewed in Britain as an unmitigated setback. The Dunkirk evacuation and subsequent total collapse of France at least had settled for a long while to come the four-centuries-long issue of how Britain should allocate her resources for war as between maritime-peripheral and continental enterprises. The latter were precluded by the verdict of events. Moreover, no matter how advisable it had been to balance power on the Continent, British opinion was never enthusiastic over the roles of paymaster and blood donor. This insular sentiment was expressed faithfully in a private letter written by King George VI to his mother: "Personally I feel happier now that we have no allies to be polite to and pamper."[26]

Although Britain's latest venture in the conduct of balance-of-power war with continental allies had been defeated, the surrender of France provided the comforting certainty that there would be no repeat of the terrible 1914–18 experience. Neither Britain nor France intended in 1939–40 knowingly to undertake campaigns that might carry a casualty tag in the millions. But many people in Britain feared, and many in France hoped, that the thirteen-division-strong (or weak) BEF of spring 1940 eventually would grow through inertia or force of circumstances to a scale of continental commitment comparable with that achieved in 1917–18 and be committed to the role of cutting edge for the alliance performed in those years.

British policy after Dunkirk and the fall of France was to hang on and hope for something to turn up. That "something" would have to take the form of a new major ally or allies, most plausibly the United States but possibly the Soviet Union (then Hitler's non-belligerent ally). Britain could not come to grips with German strength on land after June 1940, for there was no active fighting front in Europe manned by a worthy ally. When Britain lost France as an ally, she lost an ally with ninety-four divisions. The Royal Navy and the RAF were Britain's instruments of excellence for the execution of military policy. British sea power in 1940–41, strongly augmented in its traditional anti-invasion mission by an air force which had learned its trade in half a year of war (by September 1940), provided the country with the time in which to train its land power to a *moderately* competitive professional standard. Far more significant, the Royal Navy and the RAF denied Hitler a near-term victory and thus the short-war option. They could not win the war for Britain; only Hitler's misdirected statecraft and bungled operational designs could accomplish that. Near-term victory denial set Germany up for eventual defeat. Hitler could no more settle down to consolidate his ill-gotten gains of 1940–41 than Napoleon could be satisfied with the geostrategic settlement of the Peace of Amiens.

Such is the fractured geopolitical organization of the Eurasian landmass, even in the age of the railroad and the internal combustion engine, that hegemony-intending land power, unlike commanding sea power, generates would-be countervailing land power. In failing to bring the struggle with Britain to a decision in 1940, Hitler's victorious and expanding continental imperium turned away from what hindsight reveals to have been its only short-war prospect. In the early summer of 1940, a hastily improvised German invasion of Britain would have stood a reasonable chance of succeeding. Given the stakes, Hitler should have tolerated almost any level of military loss in return for the elimination of Britain as an active enemy. Those stakes included the freeing of Germany's western and southern flanks from harassment from the sea and the air and the liberty to wage a one-front war against a politically and strategically isolated Soviet Russia with undivided attention and resources (beyond policing functions in the West).

228

Admittedly, in the early summer of 1940, the prospect of effective American intervention via a British base in Europe lay somewhere between dim and remote. Nonetheless, statesman Hitler understood very well what had happened in 1917–18.

Britain was probably fortunate in the survivable disasters on land that she suffered in 1940–42. At Dunkirk she only lost the heavy equipment of her army; she could have lost the army itself and possibly the war, as a direct consequence. All of the disasters of 1940–42—Norway, France, North Africa, Greece, Crete, and then Malaya and Singapore—were survivable and instructive passages of arms. Britain's precipitately created mass army of 1940–42 was not ready for war; it lacked almost everything necessary for success in the field, including leadership, skill in the coordination of arms, and effective equipment (particularly armor and antitank artillery). The U.S. Army was to learn painfully, if profitably, in Tunisia, Sicily, and Italy that the undoubted British casualty shyness rested upon a well-founded respect for German fighting power. The overtrained but generally battle-inexperienced Allied divisions which landed in Normandy in June 1944 needed every ounce of advantage that unhindered support from the sea and the air could give them. Those advantages were needed even against a German enemy long past its combat peak, massively preoccupied in the East, somewhat distracted in Italy and the Balkans, and inflexibly commanded by remote control by Hitler.

CHAPTER 8

SEA POWER IN THE SECOND WORLD WAR

For the Western Allies, therefore, seapower remained as ever the midwife of victory on land.

> Correlli Barnett, *Engage the Enemy More Closely: The Royal Navy in the Second World War* (1991)

At its core, World War II was round two of a balance-of-power war waged to control the burgeoning strength of Germany. But it was also another struggle between a power dominant on land and a coalition dominant at sea, with air power adjuncts to both. In the most elemental of terms, the European focus of World War II was a gigantic siege operation by sea-led power against Nazi Germany's landlocked continental fortress. The fact that the *Wehrmacht* was ruined primarily in its huge adventure in the continental East does not weaken the force of this interpretation. Allied sea power could not win the war in Europe—though it could and did win the war in the Pacific—but it tied together a maritime coalition and enabled the war to be won on land and from the air

The sequence of events, the military-technological context, and the tactical and operational details of 1940–41 were unique to that period, but the structure of strategical competition between sea power and land power was a replay of the long British struggle with Revolutionary and Napoleonic France. Although the worst year of the war for the Allies was 1942 (the rough equivalent of 1797), it was evident in Britain as early as spring 1941, before the execution of Barbarossa, that the near-term danger of invasion had passed.[1] Nonetheless, the war could be lost on the shipping lanes[2] or might eventually be lost should Hitler not be distracted on land and as a consequence be at liberty to amass overwhelming strength in the air and build a truly powerful navy. But a year after Dunkirk, Britain materially had recovered from her early disasters and was sufficiently well armed as to be invasion-proof.

The course and outcome of the German invasion of Russia on June 22, 1941, and of U.S. entry into the war in Europe were the consequences of Hitler's failure at the water's edge on the Channel in summer 1940. Although Hitler had deep-seated geopolitical and ideological motives for the invasion of Russia, his geostrategic purposes prominently included a determination to defeat British sea-based and maritime-inaccessible power, as it were by continental proxy on land.[3] The conquest of Russia arguably was feasible for Germany in 1941–42 but probably not in the context of a two-front struggle. Always a chancy enterprise because of the restricted strategic reach of the *Wehrmacht*, the plunge into Russia had to succeed rapidly in one or, at most, two campaigning seasons. In the absence of victory in the East in 1941–42, British, and then Anglo-American, maritime power would be certain to use the passage of time to assemble a concentrated weight of sea-based military assets that could not be resisted reliably by the forces Germany could spare from the Eastern Front for the garrisoning of *Festung Europa*. Moreover, as Napoleonic France, Imperial Germany and even Nazi Germany in 1939 had understood, the conduct of a two (plus)-front land war against materially superior enemies more often than not proceeds synergistically to ultimate disaster. In theory, the geostrategic problem was manageable by efficient employment of the interior lines of land communication granted by modern roads (noticeable for their absence in the East) and by the railroad (after the 1840s and 1850s). But in practice the arithmetic of material inferiority thus far has led repeatedly to the defeat of continental power.

The fundamental German strategic problem in World War II was how to secure a death grip upon an offshore sea power. Hitler's failure to invade Britain in 1940 proved to be an irredeemable error. That failure did not mandate an abortive invasion of Russia, nor did it launch the Japanese gamble for a secure expanded imperium which brought the United States into the conflict. But the

231

stalemate at the Channel set in motion the complex elements which by interaction were to produce an unbeatable anti-German Grand Alliance. Hitler should have understood Britain's foreign policy tradition of balancing continental power with continental power organized, subsidized, and modestly supported by direct military means from the security of her domestic Navy-protected bastion. He should not have been misled by Britain's policy of appeasement.

It is important to identify the basic architecture of Germany's defeat. Germany crossed a threshold in British anxiety and public determination with her brutal demolition of the Munich settlement on March 15, 1939, and thenceforth confronted a British-organized coalition of states embracing Eastern and Western Europe. Albeit very half-heartedly, Britain also attempted to engage the Soviet Union in her new antihegemonic Grand Alliance, a venture doomed to failure by Polish objections. Germany ran wild on land for more than two years, including substantial breathing spaces between the Polish and French campaigns and the French campaign and the invasion of Russia. In both cases the breathing spaces were not welcome to Hitler. He was concerned lest the momentum of conquest be lost by a German people prematurely convinced that the struggle was concluded.[4]

The third year of territorial expansion, 1941–42, produced a high-water mark on the Volga and in the foothills of the Caucasus, but the great twin-headed drive in the South in 1942 no longer was at the expense of a defeated foe. Germany won all that could be won on land in the West and then all that her short-reach military instrument could win in the East. Unwilling to risk the humiliation of possible failure in an invasion of Britain in 1940, Hitler also declined to concentrate his military assets for a land-based assault upon the British lifeline of empire through the Mediterranean, against Gibraltar and Malta.[5] Instead, he elected to place his faith on the ability of his army, with the air power adjunct, to defeat the Soviet Union in a campaign of five months' duration (originally planned for May–October 1941), and perhaps on the ability of Admiral Raeder's *Kriegsmarine* to succeed with surface and subsurface *guerre de course*. The qualification of *perhaps* is important; Hitler never showed a level of interest in the war at sea commensurate with the proposition that he was determined to

232

seek a decision in that environment against Britain. Nonetheless, on May 23, 1939, he had envisaged a long war with Britain. At that time he speculated:

> If Holland and Belgium are successfully occupied, and if France is also defeated, the fundamental conditions for a successful war against England will have been secured. England can then be block-aded from Western France by the Air Force; the Navy with its U-boats can extend the range of the blockade. England will not be able to fight on the Continent. . . . Time will not be on England's side. Germany will not bleed to death on land. Such strategy has been shown to be necessary by World War I.[6]

His reasoning was valid. But Hitler chose neither to gamble on an improvised invasion in the summer of 1940 nor to concentrate Germany's newly massively augmented resources for the conduct of peripheral warfare against Britain and her empire. Instead, he succumbed to the temptation to seek a speedy and, he believed, more reliable resolution of his strategic problems by the use of tried-and-true land power against the Soviet Union. Following Napoleon's example when he abandoned his invasion camp at Boulogne in August 1805 to turn upon the Austrians, Hitler—with the generally enthusiastic endorsement of the High Command—sought the continental route to empire. It is paradoxical, as Telford Taylor has argued,

> that in order to shatter British hopes of Russian aid, they [those hopes] would first have to be fulfilled. To *defeat* Russia might perhaps have the desired effect on Britain. But to *attack* Russia would bring about the very state of affairs for which the British hoped—a war between the Nazi and the Communist colossi that would divert the main weight of the Wehrmacht to the east, lift the threat of invasion, and relieve Axis pressure in the Mediterranean.[7]

It has long been open season on Hitler's misconduct of the war, but given the nature of the man, the character of his regime, and the contemporary best-guess estimates of the risks and opportunities open to him, the decision to seek comprehensive continental victory in 1941 or 1941–42 was by no means wildly imprudent. Indeed, in the winter of 1940–41 the continental path to empire looked to be the only feasible one. Hitler knew that in the medium term he might face a powerful Anglo-American maritime alliance, a possibility which argued for the urgent resolution of Germany's only serious source of continental insecurity, the Soviet Union to her rear. If, as Hitler had excellent reason to believe, his *Wehrmacht* could collapse the rotten edifice of Stalin's Soviet Union in a single campaigning season, then truly he should be master of an impregnable continental imperium.

Hitler was thwarted, though perhaps only narrowly, by a number of factors. He paid a price he could not afford in time (one month, May–June 1941) and scarce Luftwaffe assets to rescue his Italian ally from catastrophe in the Balkans and the Mediterranean. He was the victim of appalling intelligence blunders on the depth of Soviet military power and of a reckless disregard by his professional military advisers for predictable logistical difficulties in Russia. In addition, he and his generals displayed a lack of consistency in operational grip in the execution of Barbarossa. Finally, via the agency of Japanese incompetence in grand strategy, the arguably gratuitous addition of the United States to the Reich's formal enemies' list with Hitler's impulsive declaration of war on December 11, 1941, was the step from which there could be no recovery.

John Keegan is plausible when he writes that "in the final enumeration of Hitler's mistakes in waging the Second World War, his decision to contest the issue with the power of the American economy may well come to stand first."[8] That formulation is true with respect to the full course of the war. In December 1941, however, Hitler did not enjoy the benefit of an end-to-end understanding of the conflict as a whole. The American economy for war was indeed an awesome engine for the generation of brute military power, but that engine would have faced monumental strategic and operational difficulties had Germany succeeded in closing down the war on the Eastern Front in 1942. The comprehensive strategic value of the U.S. economy in 1942–45 was very dependent on the geostrategic context it largely inherited in 1942. Hitler and his generals were responsible for those geostrategic terms of U.S. belligerency which enabled the American economy to play its decisive role. Britain was still very much in the war and available as a forward base, and the Soviet Union was absorbing most of Germany's mobilizable military energy. Germany's leaders were not so much responsible for British or U.S. belligerency:

234

Given the basic character of the Nazi polity such belligerency was inevitable. But Germany's failure to take Britain out of the war in 1940 enabled the United States to translate her great war potential into concentrated military power deployed forward to menace and attack *Festung Europa*. Germany's subsequent failure to defeat Russia enabled the United States and Britain eventually to assault that fortress successfully.

Germany's inability to win in the East in 1941 or 1942 meant that Hitler's sins of statecraft and strategy must produce eventual defeat. The combat skills of the German Army would protract the conflict, but no amount of operational or tactical artistry could deny ultimate victory to the grossly superior military weight of the Grand Alliance. The Alliance was able to win by brute force, though there is a tendency to exaggerate German military prowess and understate Allied military skill.[9] It is easy to forget that the German Army was an old-fashioned force massively dependent on railroads and animal power for its logistic sustenance. As the war proceeded, particularly after 1942, mobility (operational and even some tactical choices) diminished more and more as a result of the loss of air cover for the Army, the attrition suffered in motor transport, and lack of fuel.

In order to win the war after 1942, Germany needed to succeed in one or more ways. First, Germany required the thorough breakup of the Grand Alliance, thereby freeing her hands to concentrate her diminished military power on either the maritime/air foes to the West and South or the continental enemy to the East. Second, Germany needed to achieve a military stalemate in the East or the West at a modest cost in forces required, again thereby permitting concentration for possible vicitory against one or the other enemy. In the East this option would have entailed voluntary surrender of conquered territory on a heroic scale for the shortening of the front and the dramatic easing of logistic difficulties. In the West, there would have been a need for the U-boat campaign to succeed in paralyzing Anglo-American ability to project sea-based power. Third, Germany might have won the race to become the world's first atomic power. Finally, Germany might have been able to capitalize opportunistically on a truly major, and in effect irredeemable, Allied strategic mistake (for example, a premature invasion of France in 1942 or 1943).

It is tempting to argue that a more intelligent naval policy might have purchased Hitler sufficient time to stand some chance of saving the country from total defeat. Such a policy would have been geared not to produce a strategically more effective version of Imperial Germany's balanced High Seas Fleet by 1946–48 but rather a force of U-boats (and long-range maritime strike-reconnaissance aircraft) able to dispute the Western Allies' use of the sea. The principal problem with this "might have been" is that it is deeply unhistorical. The actual, historical Adolf Hitler and Nazi Germany chose to be slow with naval rearmament because prior to the spring of 1938 it was hoped that a far-reaching bargain could be struck with Britain. It may have been madness for Germany to rearm only slowly for sea warfare, but there was contemporary method in that madness. Furthermore, prior to the late fall of 1940, Hitler did not expect to be obliged to wage open-ended trade tonnage war against Britain (notwithstanding his occasional flashes of inspiration, as in the May 23, 1939, remarks quoted already). Even after the winter of 1940–41, Hitler's less than ruthlessly resolute approach to the war at sea needs to be considered in the light of the continental theory of victory he had chosen. Also, the lead-time for combat-ready naval power is long indeed. In the early years of the war, for example, twenty-one months was the average time from the ordering of a U-boat to its operational readiness. It may not be wise for a land-minded statesman who plans to achieve definitive continental success in a five-month campaign to be unexcited about the strategic utility of protracted war at sea, but it is understandable.

Probably Germany would have won, or at least enforced a compromise outcome, against her formal active enemies' list of June–December 1941 (the Anglo-Russian Alliance, with American Lend-Lease assistance). But the entry of the United States into the conflict meant that Germany had to win in the East in 1942 or certainly lose the war. Again, that judgment assumes the absence of a heroic scale of error on the Allied part. One might say that in 1943–44 the war was the Allies' to lose (whereas in 1940–42, it had been Hitler's to win). Of Japan's widening of the war, Hitler is reported to have exclaimed: "For the first time we have on our side a first-rate military power."[10] Hitler hoped that Japan would preoccupy the United States for a year or so—long enough for him to settle accounts with the Soviet Union and present the Anglo-American alliance with the challenge of an impregnable Eurasian fortress.

*   *   *

Anglo-American sea power was the critical enabling agent for the long-projected, decisive continental campaign that would destroy the Third Reich. It took American political leaders and some military planners a long time to appreciate that the sea-based continental campaign could not be launched until the U-boats were defeated in the Atlantic, specialized assault shipping was amply available, the German Army was blunted in the East, and the Luftwaffe was incapable of intervening effectively against the invasion fleet and the beachhead. The Normandy invasion would have been a catastrophe had it been attempted in 1943. Had the Germans contested an Allied beachhead in Normandy with a healthy fraction of the first-line ground combat power that they frittered away at Kursk in July of that year, together with the assistance of a Luftwaffe yet to be defeated, the result would have been the replication on a grand scale of the debacle of the Dieppe raid of August 13, 1942. The Allies' shortage of assault shipping of all kinds would have restricted severely both the scale of the initial amphibious assault and then the rate of buildup on shore.[11] The unavailability in 1943 of the artificial harbors (Mulberries) constructed in 1944 in lieu of immediate access to a deep-water port alone would have been a logistic show-stopper.[12] It is true that the Reich's Atlantic wall was in poor condition in 1943, but so was the Allies' ability to effect forcible entry. The balance of advantage in that year decidedly lay with the German defenders. Failure literally at the water's edge with the large raid on Dieppe was a minor, if very instructive, embarrassment. The failure of Overlord would have had dire strategic consequences.

Historian C. R. M. F. Cruttwell claimed that Britain traditionally was able to determine the "general course and character" of continental wars.[13] In World War II this ability rested on the freedom of military action conferred *after September 1940* by the high level of security of Britain's home territory from risk of capture or devastation. On the offensive side of the coin of maritime command, British ability to shape the course of a war rested on the liberty in direction of sea-based power projection conferred by a superior navy. Sea power is inherently mobile. Its flexibility, however, is the product not of its technical-tactical character but rather of its specific operational and strategic relationship to a particular enemy. Sea powers find security in superior naval power. Whether the Western Allies employed their command at sea to the best possible offensive purpose against the overextended German continental fortress is an interesting but academic question. Obviously, from the testimony of the outcome of the war, that command was employed well enough. Save relatively briefly in 1942 on the convoy routes to northern Russia and from Gibraltar and Alexandria to Malta, the Allies never lost a sufficiency in maritime command as to imperil any necessary military task. For the Allies, sea power was the engine of strategic possibilities.

Simply by remaining in the war after the continental disaster of 1940, Britain provided the necessary, though not sufficient, political and geostrategic framework for the United States to transit slowly to formal belligerency. Britain could remain in the war because her naval power and land-based air power deterred invasion. That naval power sufficed to keep the sea lanes open, albeit perhaps narrowly at times. In repetition of a pattern from previous times of peril, freedom of wartime communication was both the necessary and sufficient condition for Britain's continued belligerency. The American buildup in Britain for the forcible Allied reentry onto the Continent required all the preponderance at sea which had been secured by British endurance, Anglo-American tactical and technological skills, and American shipyards.

Germany was defeated by the Grand Alliance as a whole and by all the instruments of grand strategy. That point can be asserted even though the linkage between Anglo-American and Soviet strategies was tenuous.[14] Neither the Soviet Union, nor Britain and America, could have defeated Nazi Germany on their own without the massive distraction provided by the other. In the politically and morally important terms of human and economic cost, there is no question but that the Soviet Union paid by far the highest price among the great Allies for victory. Furthermore, except for the wild-card factor of atomic fission, it is unarguable that the definitive military overthrow of Hitler's Germany could be accomplished only through the executive agency of Soviet land power. The challenge is not to pick a winner among the Allies or among land, sea, and air power but rather to understand the complementary interactions among allies, different theaters of war, and the several military instruments. No less a proponent of maritime power than Julian Corbett advised as follows:

Now, as Nelson lamented, where great empires are concerned, wars cannot be concluded upon the sea. Such wars cannot be made by fleets alone. But just as land operations demand the co-operation and just co-ordination of horse, foot, and artillery, and as sea operations demand the co-operation and just co-ordination of battleships, cruisers and flotillas, so are great wars conducted by the ordered combination of naval, military, and diplomatic force.[15]

As a simple matter of geography, the Grand Alliance was a maritime alliance that could lend direct support among its members only by sea. Similarly, Anglo-American land power could be projected ashore for combat only if the sea was sufficiently commanded—below, on, and above the surface. In its defensive mission of defeating the German strategy of sea denial, Anglo-American naval power was a necessary precondition for the conduct of the war. Germany and Japan's failure to deny working command of the sea to their enemies meant that the full human and economic potential of the Grand Alliance could be mobilized and then deployed with the flexibility that only maritime supremacy allows. The Axis powers, with 1938 populations totaling 193,380,000 as contrasted with their enemies' 359,940,000, controlled only 17 percent of world manufacturing capacity; their enemies controlled directly more than 60 percent.[16] Anglo-American command at sea meant that these gross numbers and percentages could be translated into logistical sinews for a strategy for victory.

Next, without denying the critical role of the RAF over July–September 1940, the Royal Navy kept Britain in the war in the 1940–41 period and thereby helped critically to set up Germany for the commitment of those errors in grand and military strategy, as well as in operations, which ultimately resulted in her defeat. British sea power set the stage for the plot of the play to be a Teutonic tragedy. British sea power also set the stage for American entry into the conflict, as well as for her subsequent effectiveness in the transoceanic conduct of war. In addition to sustaining Britain's independence and belligerent status in the most basic of ways, sea power was employed to advertise the fact that Britain remained a competitive participant in a war which, for a twelve-month period, lacked a major fighting front in Europe. The mobility and flexibility of British sea power enticed Churchill into some military follies in 1940–41, but there was a pressing need for American observers to understand that Britain was anything but resigned to a stalemate peace, let alone to defeat.

British, later Allied, sea power was able to function positively in its prosecution of the maritime (and aerial) siege of *Festung Europa* precisely because it enjoyed an eventually ample command. For the Anglo-American Allies, the approaches to Hitler's continental domain were all maritime. It was only by sea, except for a trivial scale of delivery by air, that Britain and the United States themselves could project power or provide material assistance to the land war in the East. The invasion of occupied France on June 6, 1944, rates as the most impressive demonstration of offensive sea power in history. Prior to formal U.S. entry into the European war on December 11, 1941, the Battle of the Atlantic, strategically viewed, was a defensive campaign waged to keep the British war effort in business. But after that date, the Battle of the Atlantic was very much a strategically offensive enterprise, waged for the superordinate purpose of bringing the war to Germany at home on the ground (as well as in the air).[17]

Considered overall, sea power was the principal enabling agent for global policy and strategy. Allied shipping of all kinds enabled the physical fact of oceanic continuity to work against the geostrategically fractured Axis powers. Sea power is applied by ships, and thanks to the scale and efficiency of U.S. shipbuilding, the Allies eventually had sufficient of them to wage two different kinds of war half a world apart. As George Baer has argued, a U.S. wartime shipbuilding program which produced 5,777 freighters and tankers was "the *sine qua non* of victory."[18]

In addition, Allied sea power in World War II—as in World War I—as a general rule denied Germany whatever benefit, economic and military, she might have derived from the positive use of the sea. With the exception only of the Norwegian invasion of April 1940 and the modest scale of adventure of the *Afrika Korps* in 1941–42, German military strategy was obliged to be continental. Germany's strategic culture was of course distinctly land shaped and focused; nonetheless, her all but total absence of capability for positive maritime ventures yielded great advantages to a sea-dependent enemy coalition. The maritime foe was accorded virtually untrammeled scope for exercise of the initiative. This is not to deny that the imprudent conduct of peripheral warfare by inferior sea power simply produces hostage-victims for the maritime coalition (e.g., Hitler's unwise decision to pump additional forces into Tunisia in late 1942). Furthermore, from the time of the Allies' landings in Sicily (Husky, July 9–10, 1943) and Hitler's stalled offensive at Kursk until the end of the war, the distraction of German military power to provide cover against the Western Allies' threat from the sea was on such a scale as to preclude even the possibility of stalemate in the East. Hitler could not be certain where or in what strength amphibious blows would fall. The numbers tell the basic story, even when allowance is made for the widely differing strengths of units.

As of June 6, 1944, Germany had 154 divisions of all types deployed on the Eastern Front and 128 divisions of all types deployed elsewhere abroad (excluding 10 divisions in Finland).[19] Some modest fraction of those 128 divisions were engaged in occupation garrison duties (in the West) or counterguerrilla operations (in the Balkans). But the scale and location of that deployment and the pinning of so great a fraction of Germany's scarce military resources away from the land war in the East is attributable directly to the Allied threat from the sea. Late in 1943 Hitler was fearful of whither the Allies would proceed next, following on from the solid gains they had made so painfully in Italy. He anticipated an invasion of the Balkans, he was anxious lest Norway be invaded, and he had to deploy forces in France, Belgium, and Holland capable of defeating the expected Second Front. The quality of the Western threat from the sea was attested to in Hitler's Directive No. 51, issued on November 3, 1943. He wrote:

> For the last two and one half years the bitter and costly struggle against Bolshevism has made the utmost demands upon the bulk of our military resources and energies. This commitment was in keeping with the seriousness of the danger, and the over-all situation. The situation has since changed. *The threat from the East remains, but an even greater danger looms in the West: the Anglo-American landing!* In the East, the vastness of the space will, as a last resort, permit a loss of territory even on a major scale, without suffering a mortal blow to Germany's chance for survival.
>
> Not so in the West! If the enemy here succeeds in penetrating our defenses on a wide front, consequences of staggering proportions will follow within a short time. All signs point to an offensive against the Western Front of Europe no later than Spring [1944], and perhaps earlier.

241

For that reason, I can no longer justify the further weakening of the West in favor of other theaters of war.[20]

Since undifferentiated division numbers can mislead, it is worth noting that on June 6, 1944, the most potent instrument in the German Army, the *Panzer* division, was deployed on the order of twenty-five on the Eastern Front and twenty-one elsewhere (eleven in France and the Low Countries, seven in Italy, one in Denmark, and one in the Balkans). With respect to military manpower, an authoritative contemporary German source cites the facts that in the fall of 1943, Germany deployed 2,800,000 soldiers in Russia and 2,440,000 in the West outside the homeland.[21] This is the critical strategic arithmetic of two-fronted war.

Yet another element in the story of the contribution of Allied sea power to victory is the fact that Western maritime supply of the Soviet war effort was on such a scale and of such a scope and importance of range of items as to warrant description as essential. The supply routes were to the Arctic ports of Murmansk and Archangel, via the Indian Ocean through Persia, and across the Pacific to Vladivostok in freighters under the Soviet flag. The heroic story of "the Kola run," with the severe convoy battles of 1942 (and particularly the disaster of Arctic convoy PQ 17, June 27–July 11, when, fearing that the German super-battleship *Tirpitz* was loose, the Admiralty in London ordered the convoy to scatter, and 23 of 37 merchant ships were sunk) is well known. Less well known is the sheer magnitude of the Anglo-American material support by sea of the Soviet war effort, or the fact that while the perilous run to Soviet Arctic ports delivered 25.2 percent of the aid that was sent from 1941 to 1945, 47.1 percent (classified as "nonmilitary," given Japanese connivance at this sustenance of her ally's enemy) was transported undisputed across the Pacific, and 23.8 percent was delivered from the South through Persia.[22]

A careful chronicler of the Western maritime supply effort has noted that

at the end of the war the equipment holding of the Soviet Armed Forces amounted to 665,000 motor vehicles. Of these, 427,000 had been provided mainly from United States sources during the war years; contemporary evidence indicates that over fifty percent of all vehicles in Red Army service were of American origin. These trucks, together with the thousands of locomotives and railway flats, gave to the Red Army the strategic and tactical mobility required to destroy the German forces. At Teheran [November 28–30, 1943] Stalin had attributed the Soviet success to the ability to move the High Command Reserve, which he put at no higher than sixty divisions, from theater to theater in turn. This mobility could not have been achieved without this United States material aid.[23]

The motorization of the Soviet Army was critically important in the face of a German Army that dramatically demotorized from 1942 onward.[24] The significant shift in mobility in favor of the Red Army helped greatly to offset the German advantage in tactical skills. Those skills could be denied the opportunity to be most effective when their practitioners were denied the power of rapid movement and were simply swamped by the flood of enemy men and machines. The scope of American assistance extended far beyond trucks and jeeps (and tanks [10,000—10 percent of Soviet tank production in wartime] and aircraft [18,700—12 percent of Soviet wartime production]):

> In addition [to provision of petroleum products of a kind not available in the Soviet Union—blending agents and high-octane fuels] numbers of complete oil refineries, tyre factories, electric generator stations, machine tools, explosives and raw materials of all types formed part of this aid. A very large proportion of the food for the Soviet Armed Forces (estimated at 1 lb. a day of concentrated ration for six million men over the whole duration of the war) came from United States and Canadian sources and much of the Red Army's clothing and footwear came from America and Britain.[25]

Finally, of geostrategic necessity the American contribution to the great Combined Bomber Offensive that pounded Germany from 1943 until 1945 used British territory as though it were an anchored aircraft carrier. The Allied sea power which sustained Britain in the war and protected and seized real estate in the Mediterranean was the vital precondition for the conduct of the bomber offensive. Whatever its deficiencies in material and method through much of the war, that offensive incontrovertibly had a major indirect impact upon the war on land in the East (and eventually the West). The sheer scale of Russian geography denied the Luftwaffe the kind of command in the air and battlefield impact it had enjoyed in the short campaigns in Poland, the West, and the Balkans in 1939–40. Nevertheless, German air power did fulfill critically positive support roles for the Army through the time of the last great ground offensive in the East in July 1943 at Kursk. By the late summer and fall of 1943, however, British and American offensive air power posed so severe a threat to the Reich that the Luftwaffe was massively redeployed for air defense duties at home.[26]

In 1944 more than 65 percent of the Luftwaffe was deployed at home and elsewhere in the West. The redeployment was intended to combat the Anglo-American strategic bomber threat and, to a lesser degree, to be ready to support the Army in a counteroffensive against the anticipated Allied Second Front. In mid-1941 the ratio in Luftwaffe deployment between East and West had been sixty-to-forty. Führer Directive 51 stated that

> the offensive and defensive effectiveness of Luftwaffe units in the West and in Denmark will be increased to meet the changed situation. . . .
>
> The Luftwaffe ground organization in southern Norway, Denmark, north-western Germany and the West will be expanded and supplied in a way that will—by the most far-reaching decentralization of own forces—deny targets to the enemy bombers, and split the enemy's offensive effort in case of large-scale operations.

Sea power enabled Britain to remain in the war and hence collect the United States as an ally, steps essential for the eventual frustration of Hitler's landward grand designs, and it was the critical agent for the functioning of a maritime alliance which pivoted geostrategically on Britain. Moreover, by the threat that it posed to *Festung Europa* from Norway to the Aegean, Allied sea power denied Hitler the ability to win or even to force a tolerable stalemate on land in the East, and it provided direct military and economic assistance of kinds and on a scale to Russia such that it probably made the difference between victory and defeat on land in the East. Also, Allied sea power protected and sustained the forward British and (later) Mediterranean bases which gave U.S. strategic air power the reach that it needed to strike at the German war economy. To repeat, Anglo-American sea power was the engine of strategic possibilities. It did not guarantee victory, but it made victory possible.

The Grand Alliance comprised great-power partners who were the heirs to very different strategic cultures. Superiority at sea and in the air were necessary conditions for the Anglo-American nexus of the Grand Alliance to work militarily: they were not, however, sufficient conditions. Knitting the parts together were the politics of wartime partnership.

The separate national experiences in the First World War were important for the strategic policies pursued in the Second. The long debate in World War II between Britain and the United States over strategy for the defeat of Nazi Germany makes sense with reference to the respectively extensive, and minimal, experience of Britain and the United States in the waging of continental warfare in the First World War and to their differences in strategic culture.

The Anglo-American debate of 1942–43 focused on the purpose and timing of a cross-Channel invasion. The naive self-confidence and enthusiasm with which Lord Kitchener's (all-volunteer) New Army divisions, and British society behind them, approached The "Big Push" in 1916 on the Somme was more than somewhat akin to the dominant U.S. view in 1942–43 of how the war against Hitler's Germany should be conducted. As with the British in 1916, the Americans in 1942–43 were confident that an *early*, massive, direct assault upon the main strength of the enemy would produce victory. The U.S. Army had to learn, as had the British already, just how professional an enemy the German soldier could be. Also it had to learn that "massive" and "early" were contradictory qualities.

The United States is a maritime power with a continental-size home base. In her national experience, military tradition, strategic culture, and way of war, however, the United States in World War II was not a maritime power after the British model. Indeed, until 1889–90 the American way in naval warfare was distinctly continentalist. Coastal defense and *guerre de course* were the American preferences. For the first century and more of her existence, the United States either could not afford or did not need a battle fleet. Military and logistic feasibility educates and helps shape preferences in strategy. The British tradition in grand strategy was a tradition forged by the experience of a country short in manpower, strong in finance (after the 1690s), dependent for its economic stability upon the security of seaborne commerce, and blessed by geography with a home territory so situated that statecraft and naval performance of only average competence could deny practicable invasion options to continental enemies. Moreover, within living memory of 1939–45, Britain had waged more continental warfare than her political and strategic culture was habituated by historical experience to deem acceptable.

Anglo-American disagreements over the strategic direction of the war against Germany,[27] which may appear to have been a clash between continental and maritime approaches, had several fueling elements. To a degree not fully appreciated in Britain either then or since, the pull of the war in the Pacific set important limits to the time that the United States could devote to major preoccupation with the war in Europe. In terms of domestic politics, the United States was fighting in World War II because of Pearl Harbor (and the Bataan death march), not because of the long-term threat to U.S. national security that would be posed by Axis domination of Eurasia.

The United States in 1941–42 had no historical experience of a kind that would encourage her to be extremely respectful of the military power of European or Asian enemies. With regard to both Germany and Japan, the U.S. government in 1941–42 underrated the fighting power of the enemy and overrated American ability to develop as much military power of all kinds as would be needed to achieve their utter ruin. The only American experience of European continental warfare prior to World War II had been in 1918 against a small fraction of a German Army, which, though still erratically formidable in defense, was very much a blunted sword. In that war, 1919 was to have been the American year. The scale of the U.S. economic mobilization for war over 1942–45, was unprecedented in the history of war, but it was not possible for the United States simultaneously to have American industry function as the arsenal of democracy, to construct and man the world's largest Navy and Air Force, to have close to half a million men in a six-division Marine Corps, and to develop an Army of 215 divisions (to be achieved by June 1944). As envisaged on December 6, 1941, Major Albert C. Wedemeyer's Victory Program anticipated that the United States would require an army with an order of battle in excess of 200 divisions as a precondition for offensive campaigning. In fact, the U.S. Army was to activate only 91 divisions in the course of the war, of which 16 were armored (no fewer than 61 armored divisions had been projected).[28] This is not to criticize Wedemeyer's strategic reasoning, only his judgment as to practicability. If, as he assumed, the Western Allies were obliged to assault Hitler's Europe in the absence of an active Russo-German front in the East, then a 200-plus division U.S. Army certainly would have been needed.

The United States regarded British aversion to an early (e.g., fall of 1942, then 1943) cross-Channel attack not as a masterly contemporary variant of Britain's allegedly traditional maritime-peripheral strategy but rather, at best, as a bid for the promotion of distinctively British imperial interests. (Less charitable explanations pointed to a British inclination to be casualty shy. The shadow of the Somme and Passchendaele persisted over World War II.) In addition, the Mediterranean had a magnetic attraction for London which it signally lacked for Washington. Any rare, history-minded American defense planner could track the role of operations in the Mediterranean in British statecraft and strategy from the sventeenth century—and the acquisition of Gibraltar in 1704 during the War of the Spanish Succession—through the Seven Years' War, the wars against Revolutionary and Napoleonic France, the Crimea, and the "Eastern" options pursued half-heartedly in 1914–18 (e.g., Gallipoli, Salonika). With hindsight, Americans can be grateful that Churchill and the British Chiefs of Staff generally prevailed in the higher direction of Allied strategy in 1942 and 1943. There would have been a major risk that a cross-Channel attack in those years would have produced a disaster on such a scale that Hitler subsequently could have regrouped his military assets for a more concentrated defense in the East. Kent Roberts Greenfield, the general editor of the official history of *The U.S. Army in World War II*, has advised that

> the strategy in Europe which the Americans followed, step by step, as events unfolded, and which they found it wise to follow, was much closer to that which the British proposed at the ARCADIA Conference in December, 1941, and which the Americans had then accepted, than it was to the deviation from that strategy which the Americans proposed in the Spring of 1942, and for which for more than a year they vociferously contended.[29]

247

Churchill's motives in pressing his shifting and opportunistic Mediterranean preferences inevitably were mixed as well as variable in their respective weight over time. Certainly he was nervous lest an invasion of France be launched before the *Wehrmacht* was far enough advanced in its decline. He was determined to do all he could to minimize the amount of hard fighting that British soldiers would have to perform (and the casualities that would have to be taken). British official historian Michael Howard has written tellingly:

> As for the British, they did not conceal their reluctance to repeat the experiences of Passchendaele and the Somme. Their army did not have the size, and perhaps did not have the *morale*, to stand heavy casualties. Training in small-scale operations, it had difficulty in adjusting itself to the necessity for large-scale land power, and attaining the requisite standard of expertise.[30]

Churchill saw that the Mediterranean was the only theater of war in Europe wherein Britain could sustain a preponderant voice on strategy and operations. Overall British authority in the Grand Alliance, relative to American, declined rapidly through 1943 and early 1944 as an inexorable result of the unmatchable scale of the U.S. military effort. Furthermore, Churchill was concerned lest the collapse of the German imperium in the Balkans should redound strictly to the political and strategic advantage of the Soviet Union. There has been a great deal of *ex post facto* rationalization about the weight of this motive for British strategic preferences. On balance, it would seem that in 1942–43 London was less interested in forestalling any postwar preoponderance of Soviet influence in the Balkans than it was in maximizing endeavor in a "British" theater of war, almost as an end in and of itself.

For once after the classic manner of a maritime power, the United States was exceedingly anxious to wield the Soviet Army as her continental sword against Imperial Japan. Although both Britain and the United States did everything reasonable to ensure that Stalin did not seek a separate peace with Hitler, the United States uniquely was determined to have Soviet land power assail the land power of Japan, a power heavily concentrated in China, particularly in its Kwantung Army in Manchuria. In the absence of Soviet continental assistance, the United States anticipated suffering heavy casualties in an invasion of Japan's home islands.[31] The Soviet Union would not break her neutrality treaty with Japan until Germany was defeated. It is easy to appreciate the strength of the U.S. interest in not crossing Stalin in Europe and in striving for the earliest feasible military overthrow of Germany. Whatever the arguable strategic merits of Churchill's schemes for peripheral warfare against the German southern perimeter in Europe, those merits were inconsequential in the face of the pull of the Pacific upon U.S. grand strategy.

The pull of the Pacific constrained U.S., and hence Anglo-American, choice among the strategic alternatives that might have been pursued in the European theater. Only the strategy which offered rapid but reliable military results, defined strictly with reference to the military overthrow of Germany (and not to such "ulterior objects" as securing a favorable balance of power and influence in postwar Europe), was acceptable to a President who understand that the war his country really wanted to wage was the one against Japan. Nazi Germany affronted American values and posed in its expansion what could become an intolerable geostrategic danger to North America. But Germany never engaged America's sense of affronted honor, not to mention America's racial antipathies, to anything approximating the degree of the country which had long been ravaging China and had attacked so treacherously on December 7, 1941.

The pull of the Pacific was a powerful factor that disinclined the White House, and the U.S. Chiefs of Staff to an even greater measure, from reviewing very seriously any strategic alternative for victory in Europe other than a concentrated cross-Channel thrust to the heart of Germany. However, this is an example of redundant causation. Even without any Pacific complication for U.S. strategic policy, it is unlikely in the extreme that U.S. political and military leaders would have signed on for some contemporary British variant of the peripheral maritime strategy upon which Pitt the Elder had agreed with Frederick the Great in their grand design for the conduct of the Seven Years' War.[32]

The United States had no tradition in the conduct of maritime warfare after the system of Pitt the Elder, as extolled and exaggerated in the 1900s by Julian Corbett and in the 1930s by Liddell-Hart. The American way of war was different from the British way of war. It was hardly surprising that large-scale di-

249

rect participation in continental warfare was not the British preference in strategy. Prior to the twentieth century it was not even
feasible. Britain typically maintained a numerically weak and often unprofessional army, while its navy was the greatest in the
world. By way of some distinction, for the United States the
moralistic, as contrasted with the pragmatic, public fuel for its
war making mandated speed in the conduct of war, just as it
mandated a war aim of military overthrow rather than of compromise settlement. For Americans, war has been viewed as so
great an evil, and its foreign instigators by definition as so ma-
levolent, that the adoption of a strategic direct approach is all
but foreordained by national political and strategic culture. A
massive attack upon the German homeland was the direct approach; it was the American way.

As a country newly mature in her material preponderance in
mobilization potential, if not ready military power, it was close to
un-Amercian to promote the idea of waging war on anything other
than the most massive scale against the main strength of the enemy. U.S. military leaders in World War II viewed British arguments for Mediterranean campaigning much as the "Westerners"
on the British General Staff in World War I had viewed the peripheral schemes of Churchill and Lloyd George. The idea of ex-
pending American lives for any objective other than the most
expeditious rout of the enemy was culturally alien.

These points do not detract from the argument that the U.S.
government waged the war in Europe under a time pressure imposed by the global struggle to which American arms, uniquely,
were committed. But they do suggest that American traditions,
and a material strength on a scale developed from a continental-
size national base of resources, would have driven Washington to
the same strategic policy preferences as those which the Pacific pull
happened to encourage. Two quotations highlight the same central
point about the American way of war in Europe. The first quota-
tion is American in authorship, the second is British.

From the beginning the [Americans] thought in terms of taking on
the main German armies and beating them. To launch a major
cross-Channel attack on a definite target date represented to them
the best hope of ending the war quickly and with the fewest casualties.[33]

250

The Americans saw their initial strategic decisions as being very straightforward. One simply looked at a map of the world, picked the most direct routes to the heart of Germany and Japan, and then drew up plans to dispatch as many troops as possible, as soon as possible, along these routes.[34]

Victory in the Pacific so obviously was the more or less direct outcome of the weight and quality of U.S. sea power in all its forms that its exploration does not offer a challenge at all comparable to that posed by the difficulty of explaining just how, and in broad measure how much, Anglo-American sea power contributed to the defeat of landlocked Nazi Germany. Whereas Nazi Germany waged war very much according to centralized political direction and generally more than adequately at the level of operational art, but with a near-void in strategy, Imperial Japan waged a supremely strategic war, with a near void in clear political calculation and only minimal competence in operational art. This negative judgment on Japanese operational competence may seem harsh given the brilliance of the Malayan, East Indies, and (first) Burmese campaigns. However, the quality of the British opposition in Malaya and Burma was so low that the course and outcomes of those campaigns were unduly flattering to Japanese military skills.

By tradition and preponderant direction of ambition, Imperial Japan was a great land power. The principal role of the Imperial Japanese Navy was to cooperate in the designs of the Army. Japan went to war in the Pacific in 1941 seeking a defensible oceanic flank for the seizure and exploitation of the raw materials of South East Asia—raw materials essential for the conclusion of the war in China launched on July 7, 1937. The goal was not to acquire an extensive maritime imperium.

In retrospect, Japan's ambitions toward China probably rendered war inevitable with the United States,[35] just as Tirpitz's naval program was critical for Anglo-German conflict in the 1900s. The partial analogy invites further development. Schlieffen's insistence upon the invasion of Belgium (and Holland), to secure space for the enveloping movement of the right wing as it maneuvered in pursuit of the great *Kesselschlacht* (cauldron battle of encirclement), virtually guaranteed that Britain would make an immediate decision to fight and hence raised severe risks for Germany of a long war. By analogy, the Japanese strikes at Pearl Harbor and the Philippines were a political blunder of the first order, because—whatever their limited military merit—they guaranteed that Japanese strategy would not succeed. Japan aspired to wage only a limited maritime war for the defensive purpose of securing an island-anchored oceanic perimeter behind which the continental campaign in China could be won.

Japan harbored no illusions that she could defeat the United States in total war. The Japanese theory of victory lay in the hope that the United States would elect to acquiesce in most of the empire's territorial gains rather than pay the heavy price necessary for transoceanic reconquest. Japan hoped that a United States focused on the German peril in Europe and the Atlantic, and not overly appreciative of the merit in the European colonial empires in Asia, would make the strategic judgment that the ends in view were not worth the probable cost to secure them. This theory of victory looks absurd in retrospect, and particularly in a restrospect that includes the exposed American nerve-ends of Pearl Harbor and Bataan. Viewed historically, however, and allowing the non-necessity of the Pearl Harbor attack, Japanese reasoning begins to appear unduly adventurous rather than absurd or irrational.

Japan was motivated to move when she did by the malign synergistic effect of a sharply deteriorating oil supply, a plainly predictable naval inferiority in the western Pacific that would unfold by the mid-1940s, and the preoccupation of the Soviet Union with her struggle for survival in the face of the German attack.[36] Until August 1941 Japanese leaders kept their options open with respect to an advance to the north or the south. By August, however, Japanese military intelligence had concluded that the Soviet Union would not be defeated that year,[37] while the future oil situation had just deteriorated catastrophically. Unbeknown to President Roosevelt, anti-Japanese hawks in his administration had used his absence from Washington to attend the Placentia Bay conference with Churchill to translate a July 24 decision to freeze all Japanese assets as meaning a total embargo on oil exports.[38] This was not what Roosevelt had intended; he had realized how provocative a total embargo would be. Nonetheless, he could not signal weakness by reversing the policy course just set in his absence. The complete U.S. oil embargo settled whatever remained to be settled in Tokyo with respect to argument over an attack upon Russia versus expansion to the south toward the oil fields, and tin and rubber, of South East Asia.

It is ironic that just as the total U.S. oil embargo evaded veto by an absent U.S. chief executive, so the Japanese decision to open their campaign with an attack upon the U.S. Pacific Fleet at Pearl Harbor was a decision made at the highest level of the Navy *and kept secret from the rest of the government*. The Imperial Navy apparently believed that "there was no necessity to talk of the attack on Pearl Harbor, it was only a naval operation and did not involve strategy but tactics."[39] Thus the Japanese government at the highest level never considered the probable incompatibility between its aspiration to wage a successful limited war which would be concluded with a negotiated peace and a surprise attack on the U.S. Navy.

With regard to the leverage of sea power and the strategic advantage conveyed by a superior navy, the maritime war in the Pacific provides some points of enduring interest.

The basic reality shaping the strategic context was that the depth and breadth of the U.S. economy enabled construction of a maritime instrument of a scale and quality which rendered it a near-perfect expression of the American way of war. Eventual material abundance (after mid-1943) and a superior willingness and ability to adapt made tactically feasible the U.S. Navy's strategic preference for a great concentrated thrust across the Central Pacific—on the model of the old War Plan Orange, the U.S. scenario for the conduct of war with Japan, which had evolved *since 1907*.[40] These advantages also facilitated Douglas MacArthur's fairly agile clamber up the north coast of New Guinea toward the Philippines. If ever there has been a historic demonstration of the meaning of industrial muscle for high policy and strategy, it was provided in June 1944, when, nine days and half a world apart, Anglo-American-Canadian forces landed in Normandy and U.S. forces landed on Saipan in the Marianas. Both huge amphibious enterprises relied fundamentally on the principle of mass, on brute force. Deception, resting upon the inherent flexibility of sea power, was important in both cases, though particularly in the invasion of France. In the last resort, however, although deception is a valuable aid, it cannot be relied upon as the key to victory. Cunning plans have their place, but against the German and Japanese armed forces, there could be no substitute for the ability to concentrate for, and sustain, hard fighting.

"Germany First" supposedly was canon law for Allied strategy, but with the American conteroffensive in the Solomons beginning at Guadalcanal as early as August 7, 1942, it was evident that a large measure of "both/and" would be the rule. The U.S. war economy was able to succor the Russian land war in the East, equip its own and much of the Anglo-Canadian army(ies) as well, construct two-plus ocean sea power in all its forms, build two-theater strategic and tactical air forces, and develop the atomic bomb. Material abundance enabled the United States to secure the surrender of Japan only three months after the demise of the Third Reich. In all theaters of war America's economic strength permitted Allied forces to pursue multiple, sometimes redundant, paths to victory. (By way of caveat, there was an important shortfall at the tip of the spear on land. The U.S. Army was not abundantly supplied with first-class infantry.)

The center of military gravity for Japan was not, as Japan believed, with her armies on the mainland of Asia; rather, given the kind of war she chose to wage, it was on the maritime approaches to the home islands through the Central Pacific. The Japanese strategy of extended perimeter defense on the oceanic flank was unsound in principle and desperately impracticable in the face of a sea-air power as strong as the United States. It was the ill-founded Japanese hope that land-based air power, operating from widely separated fortress islands, would inflict a prohibitive level of attrition upon U.S. sea power. The Japanese concept of perimeter defense was sunk by the soundness of the familiar formula that sea power is the product of geographical position and of size and quality of fleet. Unfortunately for the Imperial Japanese Navy, it was denied the time to fortify intended island fortresses to the degree anticipated. The U.S. Navy defeated distance with its mobile fleet train, and the sheer quantity of U.S. combat power meant that such bastions on the perimeter as were not bypassed were isolated from support and overwhelmed in detail.

In the context of the U.S. ship and aircraft building surge of 1942–44, Japanese combat losses at Midway, during the six-months' maritime campaign for Guadalcanal, and to U.S. submarine activity, meant that she lost the strategic and operational initiative relatively early in the war. The U.S. way of war in the

Pacific preponderantly was a series of amphibious operations selected to secure island air bases for the prosecution of strategic air bombardment of the Japanese home islands. The U.S. Navy began its break-in with the initiation of the Central Pacific drive at Tarawa in the Gilberts in November 1943. The seizure, or threatened seizure, of key island fortresses all but obliged the Japanese Navy to sail into harm's way and give battle. The great naval-air battles of the Philippine Sea and Leyte Gulf were both set up by the U.S. amphibious threat to Japanese positions on land. In common with the Luftwaffe in the same period, Japanese naval-air power in 1943–44 demonstrated that the combat efficacy of a numerically inferior force declines under pressure at an accelerating rate. No matter how heroically or even efficiently the Japanese could perform at the tactical level of war in 1944 and 1945, they were already defeated operationally and strategically.

U.S. sea power defeated a Japan that launched the wrong war in the wrong fashion. Japan was beaten by the fast carriers, the fleet train, the amphibious assault forces, the submarines (which eventually acquired torpedoes that worked), and the long-range bombers flying from the island bases seized by assault from the sea. The Pacific was a maritime theater of war and, unlike the case of the war for Europe, Japan was brought down by U.S. sea power. This self-evident fact renders the Pacific War a conflict of relatively modest interest for this book. The argument here is concerned with the hard cases of land power and sea power, not the strategically easier ones of sea power and sea power. Also, it could be inappropriate to apply insights or conclusions from the overwhelmingly maritime Pacific War to more general problems of the strategic utility of sea power.

U.S. sea power won a maritime command over an expanding area of the southwest, central, and western Pacific Ocean, which enabled all subsequent military ventures to proceed and succeed. Sea power was, or projected, the force that defeated Japan. It seized the island bases from which the B-29s could batter Japan at home; in the form largely of submarines, it massacred Japan's nonconvoyed or, after November 1943, poorly convoyed, merchant shipping. Finally, the quantity and quality of U.S. sea power permitted a flexibility in operational style which kept the Japanese permanently wrong-footed. Moreover, by late 1943, the sheer scale of the U.S. military effort in the Pacific was such that tactical and operational errors could be tolerated.

255

The United States persisted into 1945 in underestimating the strategic input of her sea-air power upon the Japanese ability to conduct the war effectively. It is apparent that Japanese military assets always were grossly maldeployed as well as frequently badly mishandled operationally. For example, in the crucial protracted Solomons' campaign of 1942–43, Tokyo seemed determined to repeat the characteristic British errors of 1915 at Gallipoli: the repeated commitment of too little too late and the reinforcement of failure. The Japanese Army was sensibly distrustful of Russian intentions; briefly in 1941–42 it hoped to take prompt advantage of the expected collapse of Russia under German attack and exact revenge for the humiliation suffered at Khalkin Gol in 1939. But the dramatic worsening of Japan's oil supply story and the unexpectedly resolute quality of Russian resistance to German invasion settled the policy argument in August 1941 in favor of expansion to the south. The continental orientation of the Japanese Army is attested by the fact that of its fifty-one divisions available in late 1941, only eleven were allowed to the southward sea-based venture in expansion. Thirteen divisions were held in Manchuria to observe the Russians, while twenty-three were garrisoning, or fighting in, China. The remaining five divisions were deployed at home, on Formosa, in Korea, and in Indochina.

The United States persisted unreasonably over-long in believing that the defeat of Japan required the continental distraction of her large forces on the Asian mainland. Doggedly, Washington anticipated that suitably equipped Nationalist Chinese armies would conduct effective campaigns of continental diversion. U.S. determination to secure Moscow's delivery on the promise of a great land offensive against the much vaunted and feared Kwantung Army in Manchuria endured almost to the end of the war. To be fair, one must recognize that the United States government did not know until July 16, 1945, that the atomic bomb would work, while the strategic air offensive was seen to be effective only in the spring and summer of 1945. The quality of Japanese military performance in defense of Iwo Jima (February 19–March 24, 1945) and Okinawa (April 1–June 22, 1945) boded ill for the effort required to conquer the Japanese home islands, and the tightness of the maritime-air blockade of Japan against the return of military units from the mainland might leave something to be desired.

Even when due allowance is made for the perils to empathetic historical judgment which flow from hindsight, Washington still would seem to have been remarkably obtuse in the persistence of its misunderstanding of the war in the Pacific. By the close of 1944, and certainly by the late spring of 1945, it should have been glaringly obvious that Japanese land power, deployed on the mainland of Asia or on the home islands, was not relevant to the outcome of the war. At least, that would be true if the United States conducted the war intelligently. By the success of her sea-air power, the United States in 1945 had no need to fight, or bribe others to fight, the bulk of the Japanese Army on the Asian mainland. In 1945, notwithstanding the exceptionally bloody campaigns for Iwo Jima and Okinawa, the United States was performing in a strategically admirable manner—a manner permitted by brute-force material superiority, committing her strength at sea and in the air against Japanese weakness. The contingent decision to invade Japan was unwise and thoroughly strategically unsound in the conditions of mid- to late 1945.

Contrary to prewar plans and expectations, the U.S. government found itself obliged by the disastrous events of early 1942 to assume responsibility for the defense of Australia and New Zealand and, necessarily, of the sea lines of communication to that region (for which there was no prepared logistic infrastructue), and of the islands in the path of the Japanese advance southward. Prewar planning—the succeeding variants of War Plan Orange—had focused upon a great thrust across the central Pacific toward the Philippines. The United States could have elected to concentrate on the Army's geographically natural axis of potential advance from New Guinea to the Philippines and then perhaps to the coast of China and to Formosa. Alternatively, the U.S. Navy's no less natural preference for an advance across the wholly oceanic approach to the Philippines or the Ryukus could have been chosen. In practice, both axes of advance were pursued because the U.S. government could not resolve its interservice command problems. The southwest Pacific campaign in good part was the product of politics and strategic opportunism. Official creation of the Douglas MacArthur legend to provide some political offset at home for the discomfort of the Dunkirk-that-was-not at Bataan all but guaranteed that the hero-general evacuated from Corregidor would be the focus of a major new military effort. War is often a matter of necessity and expediency. By accident of history the U.S.

Commander-in-Chief in the Philippines was propelled by events unexpectedly to Australia. Simultaneously, the tide of Japanese advance reached the Coral Sea and the Solomons, all the while the U.S. Navy was nowhere near ready to exploit its June 1942 victory at Midway with a central Pacific drive.

Some scholars have criticized the ambivalence of U.S. strategy in the Pacific war.[41] They have noted the dispersion of effort between Admiral Chester Nimitz in the central Pacific and MacArthur in the southwest Pacific and have argued that the American victory was a triumph of logistics and not of strategy. That criticism is well founded in the sense that Washington failed to resolve a strategy dilemma but not with regard to the consequences of its inability to decide. In practice, the twin axes of advance confused the increasingly inferior Japanese defense effort more seriously than they detracted from a desirable concentration of effort on the American side. Nonetheless, the endorsement of two axes of advance did produce potentially dangerous scarcities of assets at what mght have been negatively decisive points, particularly for MacArthur. Japanese incompetence in operational art helped to make a virtue of U.S. ambiguity over strategy. Japan so disposed her forces that in battle after battle she had inferior military power at the decisive point.

The greatest surprise of World War II was the absence of major surprise (except for the atom bomb) as well as the failure of historical events to validate some long-predicted transformations in the terms of war. Turn-of-the-century Mahanian exaggeration of the strategic value of sea power had come to be well balanced by rival claims for a new preeminence for great continental power and, in the 1920s and 1930s, for "victory through air power." World War II demolished these strategic propositions. The war showed how sea power derived from a continental scale of resources could be more powerful than ever. The war showed also how sea power could co-opt and merge with air power.

The details of the outbreak and course of World War II necessarily were historically unique. The patterns which appeared in the wars in Europe and the Pacific, however, were anything but unique. The principal difference between the two theaters of war was that the conflict with landlocked Germany could be concluded only by continental action, just as her progressive weakening had to be achieved largely by combat on land, while the war with Japan could be waged and concluded directly by superior sea power. The contrast is that while sea power enabled the Grand Alliance to win the war in Europe, the war in the Pacific actually was won by U.S. sea power. The struggle against Nazi Germany, with the exception of the critical period of June 1940–June 1941, was a thoroughly coalition war.[42] The details of this war were *sui generis*, but the strategic problems and opportunities were more complex variants upon familiar historical experience. Air power in its several forms provided the leading complicating layer to historically familiar patterns of activity.

Sometimes the point is made that World War I stands out in the grim record of the folly of statecraft as a conflict ruled by the brute arithmetic of industrial-age mass society. Unfortunately for the cogency of that view, the great coalition wars waged against France from 1792 until 1815 and against the Axis powers in World War II also were both protracted episodes in the exercise of muscle as the basis for strategic and operational dexterity. No single element shaped the course and determined the outcome of World War II. The closest one can approach plausibly to a monocausal explanation is to cite the sheer size of the U.S.—and more broadly the Allied—economy and, narrowly, the quantity of shipping of all kinds provided by that economy. Other things being tolerably equal, numbers deliver victory. Average statecraft, strategy, and operational and tactical skills can be blended to achieve success reliably when they function in the fault-tolerant environment provided by friendly superior mass.

The great coalition wars waged to bring down Napoleonic France and Imperial, then Nazi, Germany, showed a pattern of quantity parenting quality. As a general rule, large but still inferior navies, armies, and air forces deteriorate rapidly in their fighting power as heavy attrition generates a sharply progressive decline in combat ability. A seriously overstretched or overmatched military instrument—Napoleon's Army and Navy, the Kaiser's Navy, Hitler's Luftwaffe and Army, for example—tends to deteriorate at a rate disproportionate to combat loss, both as heavy casualties cannot be replaced and as an ever more disadvantaged military plight yields the benefits of the initiative to the enemy.[43]

As early as the fall of 1943 it was evident that both Germany and Japan had commmitted the twin errors of waging the wrong wars in the wrong ways. The Japanese cause was compromised from the outset, doomed by the extraordinary and gratuitous folly of the Pearl Harbor attack. That attack was as politically fatal as it proved operationally damaging to its perpetrators. The destruction or temporary incapacitation of the entire U.S. battleship fleet in the Pacific mandated what proved to be a timely reversal of traditional roles between large fleet carriers and battleships. Admiral Isoruku Yamamoto thus enforced a wise restructuring of the U.S. Navy and its battle tactics and, by his failure to sink the carriers on December 7, 1941, generated the need for the baited trap that was to be the disastrous battle of Midway.

Some poor policy and strategic choices can be redeemed by operational brilliance. For example, Hitler's failure to resolve his British difficulties in 1940–41 by diplomacy, invasion, aerial bombardment, *guerre de course*, or peripheral operations in the Mediterranean still might have been redeemed by a swift continental victory over Russia. If better directed in 1941, the *Wehrmacht* might have negated by maneuver and hard fighting in the East some of the strategic disadvantage accruing from failure, or incomplete success, in the West. Continental statecraft and strategy persistently has failed in modern times in the conduct of war. Hitler's weaknesses and errors were hardly original. When moral issues are admitted to the discussion, the familiar limitations of a continentalist mind-set assume even more fatal a character. The barbaric nature of the Nazi regime and the frightfulness of its occupation policies, amplified the geostrategically distinctive difficulties typically triggered by land power on the rampage. The racial exclusivity of Nazi ideology denied it any value as a tool of imperium over non-Aryan peoples.[44]

In both the German and Japanese cases, it was the failure to fashion an answer to Allied, but especially U.S., sea power which proved most damaging. At root the problem for the Axis was the war-making potential of the Allied, and particularly the American, economies. To a degree, Germany and Japan understood this. Both devised short-war schemes intended to evade the problems of the mobilization potential of possible enemy coalitions. But by her failure to complete victories in the West in 1940 and the East in 1941–42, Germany effectively ensured that Allied sea power would be allowed the time to project unmatchable military capability. Germany's short-war failures in 1940–42 amounted to delivery of a party invitation to U.S. sea projectible power—an invitation duly accepted and exploited. Some "might have beens" of history provide intriguing topics for speculation. Certainly there are policy and strategy courses for Germany and Japan that ought to have yielded outcomes superior to those achieved. Indeed it would have been difficult for any German or Japanese policy and strategy choices to have produced outcomes worse than those actually secured. Such speculation aside, the record of Axis political, strategic, and operational failure is plain enough, as is the central enabling role of Allied sea power in their separate defeats.

Some major themes provided a rich yield of insight for help in understanding the leverage of sea power in World War II. National, political, and strategic culture contributed hugely to policy and strategy error. Political leaders often did not understand how policy choices for peace or war were framed and considered abroad. In the military realm, racial and political stereotyping encouraged the British and the Americans to discount Japanese combat prowess,[45] just as Germans could not believe that the purportedly inferior Slavs of Russia would be able to resist Teutonic onslaught. Ethnocentric error was pervasive.

As a major theme, geography requires no more than terse recognition, given the obviously all-embracing character of its influence. From the German seizure of U-boat bases on the Biscay coast of France, to the meaning of the German occupation of Norway for the feasibility of Britain running convoys to Russian Arctic ports in Winter, to the logistic meaning of oceanic and continental distances, physical geography is the stage for war. That geography, with its oceanic continuity and the relative efficiency and flexibility in the maritime transportation of large and heavy goods, made Allied sea power the great enabler of strategic grand designs.

With regard to technological change and it implications, World War II reveals that a very large war by coalitions in three geophysical environments over a long period of time is not shaped, and certainly its outcome is not determined, by superior weaponry. The patterns of statecraft and strategy in the major wars of modern times have not been stamped by trends in military technology. By contrast, the tactics and operations of World War II naturally were shaped by technological factors. But the Allies did not defeat the Axis powers in any very important sense because they procured better weapons. Indeed in some cases the Allies did not procure better weapons. The technological competence of the belligerents was sufficiently equal when viewed overall that other factors were dominant (particularly economic strength for sheer numbers, the total assets of the coalition, skills in grand and military strategy, and general societal adaptiveness). The war for Europe demonstrated clearly that although victory required a team effort by combined arms, sea power was as critically significant an enabling agent as ever it had been in the other great conflicts of modern history. Sea power was not independently decisive in the defeat of Germany, but then neither was "strategic" air power, the U.S. economy, or the Russian Army.

CHAPTER 9

THE COLD WAR

Sea Power in the
Nuclear Age

NATO is a maritime alliance, held together by the broad highway of the North Atlantic and, to a lesser extent, by the Mediterranean, the Channel, and the Baltic. Its wartime survival as
an alliance, *requires*, then that it achieve and maintain command of those vital seas.

Norman Friedman, *The U.S.*
Maritime Strategy (1988)

The twentieth century has seen the leverage of sea power challenged by the rise of great industrialized continental states, the
invention and development of the airplane, and most recently the
coming of nuclear weapons. Experience has shown, however, that
reports of the strategic demise or even obsolescence of sea power
have been greatly exaggerated. Sea power in this century has co-
opted or otherwise neutralized every takeover challenge that has
appeared. The judgment that the Allied victories in World Wars I
and II were enabled by a superior sea power applied with equal
veracity to the U.N.'s war with Iraq in 1991. Nonetheless, it is
more obvious to people in the 1990s than it was in the Cold War
decades that the strategic leverage of sea power has not reached a
dead end. Today, following the formal demise of the U.S.S.R., it
would be close to absurd to suggest that the nuclear age has radically demoted the strategic utility of sea power, but matters were
not always quite that self-evident. A prospectively massively nuclear World War III cast a discouragingly giant shadow over the
strategic utility of sea power—or did it?

263

Bernard Brodie is reported to have reacted to the news of Hiroshima by claiming "that everything that he had written thus far on strategy had been rendered obsolete."[1] More than four and a half decades on from that poignant moment, such a judgment by the author of *Sea Power in the Machine Age* and *A Layman's Guide to Naval Strategy*[2] can be logged as a plausible fallacy, or at most a half-truth. Major war among super and great, which today has to mean nuclear, powers could never be the same again. Henceforth, any war or even crisis between those powers would be a nuclear war or a nuclear crisis, whether or not nuclear weapons actually were employed. In the absence of historical experience, however, all theories about the probable course and outcome of nuclear war need to be treated with great caution. No matter how distinguished and thoughtful the theorist, this is a realm of speculative theory. It is prudent to worry about, and plan against, what could be an automatic escalation process from small-scale to very large-scale nuclear warfare. But there are rational military uses for nuclear weapons in every environment of possible conflict—land, sea, air, and space. Moreover, both sides to a conflict would have the strongest conceivable motive, self-preservation, to employ nuclear weapons very carefully, if at all.

Alfred Thayer Mahan believed that his strategic precepts were valid for all time:

> The principles which should direct great naval combinations have been applicable to all ages, and are deducible from history; but the power to carry them out with little regard to the weather is a recent gain.[3]

Whether the nuclear revolution has rendered all, or most, of prenuclear strategic history misleading at best, and dangerously irrelevant at worst, and whether nuclear weapons have changed the nature, character, and purposes of war are vital questions. An orgy of mutual mass destruction, with the cost of combat vastly disproportionate to potential political gains, would bear little relationship to the idea that war is an instrument of policy. If any major war inevitably must see the employment of nuclear weapons and if any nuclear war must proceed inexorably to the destruction of the combatant societies, then war indeed would have changed its nature from that familiar prior to 1945. The character of war

264

would be that of a more or less rapidly unfolding holocaust, and no policy could be served by its conduct.

Prior to 1945 it was orthodox to affirm that contemporary, like historical, war could solve political problems which were beyond resolution by other means. Dire predictions of economic, social, and political collapse were issued by a few who believed that machine-age mass warfare would prove intolerable for complex, economically interdependent modern societies, but such nay-saying did not attract a large following. War was an acceptable instrument of policy, deemed capable of improving external security and even of quieting some domestic political problems. Of course, war aims and results were not in balance for the countries that lost, while even countries that won frequently discovered that theirs had been Pyrrhic victories. The two world wars of this century discouraged the peoples of Europe from believing that war either was just another policy instrument or was a socially bracing, glorious, and even potentially profitable phenomenon, to cite beliefs that were fashionable prior to 1914. For most of Western Europe at least, the great divide in attitudes toward the nature, purposes and utility of war, occurred in 1916–17 (Verdun, the Somme, and Passchendaele) rather than in 1945. There was next-to-no popular enthusiasm for war in 1939, unlike 1914, even in Germany. American political culture is deeply averse to war, as the Western Allies can attest from their experiences in 1914–17 and 1939–41. In both world wars it was only outrages against American life and property that tipped the policy scales for war.

The direct answer to the question of whether nuclear weapons have changed the nature, character, and purposes of war, therefore, is a prudent "yes" with regard to a great war between super or great powers. But it is precisely that prudent "yes" which drove the superpowers in the Cold War to attempt to fireproof their strategies, campaign designs, and military postures against both the necessity for resort to nuclear use and the perils of a mindless gallop to Armageddon should nuclear weapons nonetheless be used. The presence of nuclear weapons in the hands of an enemy, an enemy's close ally, or an enemy's friend of convenience must cast a shadow over all plans of campaign. While granting the possibility of nuclear holocaust, the apparent fact remains that states have found a variety of ways to negate the potentially paralyzing power of that shadow. Mutual deterrence is only the most obvious of the means and methods applied for practical nuclear weapon negation.[4] Nuclear weapons, like sea power, are not an abstraction; the influence of those weapons must always be specific to time, place, issues, and adversaries. Nuclear weapons are not the problem; rather, the problem is who owns them. As the 1990s advance, old answers to nuclear problems couched heavily in terms of yesteryear's East-West relations require change or augmentation for application to nuclear-armed regional powers whose policymakers express strategic cultures alien to reliable manipulation by the traditional American theory of deterrence.

The issue is whether nuclear weapons have changed the strategic meaning of geography and altered fundamentally the value of allies. If nuclear weapons were to be employed massively at the outset of a war, then the contexts of physical and political geography that so heavily influence strategy and operational designs for armies, navies and air forces would be of scant significance. Regardless of the measure of an enemy's malevolence or policy desperation, however, the era of secure second strike capabilities means that a nuclear Schlieffen Plan must be self-defeating. This is not to deny that self-defeating policies can be selected and that even if nuclear use were militarily senseless in a would-be disarming attack between super states, still it could deliver an old-fashioned military victory in war between regional powers. A large body of opinion holds that the use of nuclear weapons would not produce positive campaign results in any circumstances. This judgment is applied to both the land and the sea, separately and in combination.

The strategic geography of the East-West standoff of the Cold War had to give historians a pervasive sense of *déjà vu*. A maritime alliance denied a continental land power domination of Europe and Asia. That land power confronted strategic problems of awesome dimensions on at least two widely separated fronts (Europe and China). Moscow's ability in war to trouble the maritime alliance beyond the Eurasian landmass, or to outflank the operations of that alliance on that landmass could have been thwarted by the Eurasian rimland strategic geography on which the Western Alliance could anchor distant sea-air blockade.

History never repeats itself exactly, but the analysis of maritime choke points does not differ in its strategic essentials whether one

266

is considering the Hellespont and the Bosporus in ancient times, Gibraltar and the Strait of Dover in the age of fighting sail, or the la Perouse and Tsushima Straits in the 1980s. The geography, and particularly the maritime choke points, of interest now embraces much of the globe, but that fact is not the product of nuclear weapons. After 1945 the continental enemy was both a European and an Asian power in its contiguous metropolitan territory. In World War II the Axis powers were a coalition in name only; there was no coordination of strategy between Tokyo and Berlin. The German invasion of the Soviet Union was as much of a surprise to Japan as Japan's attack on the U.S. Pacific Fleet at Pearl Harbor was a surprise to Germany. The United States had to exercise judgment in the allocaiton of its resources between the Atlantic-Mediterranean and the Pacific theaters, and within those theaters, but it was fighting two geostrategically distinctive, indeed isolated, enemies in distinctive wars. For much of the post-1945 period, the allies of the superpowers played only modest strategic roles. Nuclear weapons were some part of the reason for that condition, but the larger part stemmed from the historically unusual degree of preponderance enjoyed by the aptly labeled "superpowers." In 1945 the United States was more of a super state even than Great Britain had been in 1815, though some parallels could be drawn between the two.

Given its requirement for maritime command and air superiority as conditions for the successful conduct of military operations anywhere on land around the Eurasian periphery, it is unlikely that the United States, alone, also could generate a quantity of land fighting power suitable for the defeat of the ground forces of a superpower foe in European or Asian theaters of operations. As in World Wars I and II, continental campaigning in a future great war would have to be a coalition undertaking. In the 1950s, the scale of U.S. strategic nuclear advantage was such that the new weaponry appeared to have rendered all but irrelevant the traditional factors of time, distance, terrain, weather, and allied military contributions.[5] If the strategic nuclear forces had been unleashed upon the Soviet homeland in response to an invasion of Central Europe, the war—if that would be the correct expression—effectively would have been concluded in one or two days.

The dawning of mutual deterrence and, from the mid-1960s, the balanced modernization of the Soviet armed forces undermined

267

any confidence there might once have been that nuclear weapons had transformed or transcended the strategic meaning of geography. Furthermore, it was not the case that friends or allies were reduced prospectively to the status of irrelevant onlookers to a central strategic-nuclear battle of decision. Rational strategies and tactics for nuclear employment can be devised, but the military disadvantages that could follow their use render more likely than not the prospect that any future major war would more closely resemble World War II than the galloping holocaust of popular fiction (or probable fact circa 1960). At least that was the tentative conclusion reached, virtually in parallel, by important segments of American (but not NATO-European) and Soviet strategic opinion by the mid-1980s.[6]

The nuclear and nuclear-associated facts of weaponry and the (erstwhile) degree of joint superpower preponderance among states have been historically extraordinary. But although an ICBM can be said to have diminished the importance of distance by its ability to cross an ocean in less than half an hour, that ICBM is not a practical instrument of war. The strategic problem is the ICBM in the hands of the enemy. Practical or not as engines of war, nuclear weapons have been indispensable as tools of deterrence. Far from being sidelined by the sheer rapidity with which distance can be conquered, the spatial relationships of geography actually have organized, even driven, the terms and outcome of nuclear policy debate and strategy in the Western Alliance. The geopolitics of the Cold War meant that the U.S. superpower prudently was obliged to extend nuclear protection over allies and friends an ocean away from its homeland.[7] The making of credible nuclear threats on behalf of others required "war-fighting" prowess in nuclear forces. Geography may not be king, but it is regent because the king (nuclear weapons) cannot be allowed to rule.

The maritime alliance of the West won the Cold War without having to wage a direct hot war, but what sense is there in the notion that nuclear weapons revolutionized grand or military strategy? For grand strategy, choices among policy instruments for the support of national interests, nuclear weapons make an important difference at both ends of the process of armed conflict. With respect to the initiation of war, the threshold of offense or indignity or the scale of anticipated gain for the *casus belli* has been raised significantly. This expresses the principle of proportionality. Rational statesmen do not roll the dice for decision by combat if the risks are high and the possible gains are low. The benefits of success in contemporary major war between nuclear-armed states are arguable (what would be the victor's inheritance?), but the scale of possible liability to damage is not. The nuclear danger has rendered statesmen and societies unusually reluctant to attempt to solve their problems by war.

With reference to the trailing edge of war, both sides would conduct military operations with a view to dampen enemy incentives to wage (nuclear) war *à outrance*. A strategy of military overthrow may be suitable at the operational level of war for theater campaigning, but such an ambitious intention obviously risks the enemy's using every weapon in its arsenal to attempt to evade such an outcome. Had Nazi Germany and Imperial Japan been nuclear armed, the January 1943 Casablanca formula of unconditional surrender would have been most unwise.

To date, nuclear-armed states have behaved in their security relations with great, and perhaps historically unprecedented, caution. The facts of nuclear armament should restrict the scope of ambition of war aims and war plans. There are, however, many partial precedents in prenuclear historical experience. Great trading states, while frequently finding war ultimately to be profitable, scarcely less frequently discerned the specter of economic ruin in the disturbance of war. The nuclear age injunction against cornering a desperate enemy is particularly important, but hardly novel, advice for statecraft, strategy, or even tactics. The nuclear facts of the late twentieth century obviously shaped much of U.S. and Soviet statecraft and strategy during the decades of Cold War. Those facts may be said to have had a truly revolutionary impact upon strategy in that they effected a potentially massive disequilibrium between available military means and particular ends.[8] However, if nuclear weapons encourage a caution in the conduct of military operations, as a consequence they are likely to encourage the protraction of hostilities. The longer hostilities last, the more likely it is that the side dominant at sea will be able to shape a conflict to its overall advantage.

Virtually all of the common wisdom on nuclear questions in the United States pertains to, and draws upon, Cold War phenomena with the former Soviet Union. But the meaning of nuclear weapons for deterrence and defense with respect to superpower conflict need not be identical to their meaning for regional crises and wars. The terms of regional conflict, and for superpower intervention in such conflict, are changing with the proliferation of high-technology weaponry. Similarly, the geostrategic terms of great-power relations are altering as a post–Cold War Europe shakes down. With regard to the structure of the problems of statecraft and strategy, there are no compelling reasons to disdain prenuclear history. Indeed, the very possibility of nuclear devastation on a scale that would render political war aims of trivial significance should serve to police conflict against escalation that would utterly disconnect means from ends. Political, technological, and tactical details can alter dramatically in a period only of decades. Nonetheless, the relationship between sea power and land power, modified by the conditions of the day, has retained an enduring integrity over time which allows the scholar and the policymaker to seek enlightenment for the present and future from the past.

All that has been argued so far is that nuclear weapons have provided a land power or continental coalition with the physical means to thwart an enemy's sea-based strategy. A continental coalition, anticipating defeat in a long war organized and conducted by a maritime foe with some land power allies, could shoot for a military decision with nuclear weapons in the space of an afternoon. That, admittedly, is a radical prospect, which truly represents a historical discontinuity of almost breathtaking proportions. Before rushing to pronounce the demise of maritime leverage, however, some offsetting considerations command attention.

The danger of rapid nuclear escalation, while menacing the strategic utility of sea power, also attests to that utility. Why would a great continental power choose to throw the nuclear dice against a maritime-oriented enemy? The answer has to be that it has despaired of success in what otherwise would be a long war. To be fair, it could be a maritime coalition which elects to throw the nuclear dice should it slip into a condition of intolerable disadvantage on land. Throughout the Cold War, the proximity of NATO-Europe to Soviet armies drove the United States and her allies to adopt a nuclear-dependent strategy for deterrence. The politics of NATO understandably obliged the Alliance to adopt a nuclear strategy in 1954, much modified in 1967, which sought to give the appearance of a rough equivalence of risk as among the geostrategically very differently placed members. The ability of effectively insular sea power to endure disasters suffered by its continental allies, yet still return to win in a protracted war, is not an idea that has ever been popular with those allies. Unsurprisingly, the U.S. NATO allies always preferred that there should be a short fuse connecting a battlefield in Central Europe with U.S. strategic nuclear forces in North America and at sea.[9]

The subject here is a war that was—the Cold War—and a war that was not—an East-West/Soviet-American World War III. By winning the former, the Western world has precluded any necessity for waging and attempting to survive the latter. It is tempting to dismiss a hypothetical World War III as a peril now passed with the demise of the Soviet Union. That would be a mistake. It is true that throughout the remainder of this century another Great War, a World War III, will be exceedingly unlikely to occur. Currently there is no superpower class of challenger to the survival or vital interests of the United States. But, history suggests that a new menace to the balance of power in Europe and Asia will arise, and the traditional pattern of maritime-continental conflict is too marked to be dismissed without evidence as conveniently *passé*.

Nuclear weapons did not provide all-purpose answers to U.S., NATO, or Soviet strategic problems. Indeed, for most of the first postwar decade, the bilateral facts of atomic scarcity obliged both superpowers to plan to refight World War II, only with the benefit of some atomic assistance for strategic bombing (the first Soviet atomic test was in 1949). This decade saw the development of an offensively cast maritime strategy by the U.S. Navy, designed to exert strategic leverage against a great continental enemy. That mission was a novel challenge to a Navy trained and recently victorious in blue-water warfare against insular Japan.[10] The geopolitical and geostrategic architecture of the new Western Alliance (NATO, 1949) was classical indeed.[11] Offshore powers, the United States and Britain, would lead and help finance a mixed maritime-continental coalition for the purpose of denying European hegemony to a great land power. The offshore powers themselves would make an open-ended continental commitment, while the greater of the two, the United States, also would provide the theater commander for the Alliance (the Supreme Allied Commander Europe, or SACEur).

271

The 1950s and 1960s witnessed first the all-but-total takeover of NATO's strategy by nuclear threats (for deterrence) and then the ebbing of extreme nuclear dependency as the Soviet antagonist acquired strategically offsetting capabilities. The dual problems with nuclear weapons were that they were too powerful to be very credible in prospective use and that they were acquired by the foe.

By the mid-1960s formally, though perhaps five years earlier in reality, U.S. and NATO strategy had retreated from a seemingly one-dimensional nuclear menace. The trend toward a prospective flexibility in military response amounted to an attempt to manage uncertainty in Soviet minds over the likelihood of nuclear employment by NATO. The U.S. strategic problem was to convince the Soviet Union that should their armies invade NATO-Europe, they would risk setting in train a process of nuclear escalation which might lead to a bilateral holocaust. From nuclear response on day 1 of a conventional attack in Europe, the intention in the mid- to late 1950s, NATO believed in the 1960s and 1970s that nuclear use would be credible only in the context of a large, ongoing nonnuclear conflict. In addition, just as NATO-Europeans did not wish to be expendable in a protracted nonnuclear war, by the 1960s Americans had become unwilling to endorse a strategy which would guarantee prompt nuclear escalation to their homeland. NATO-Europe wanted to maximize the prospect of Soviet leaders' believing that a war which began in West-Central Europe would not long remain there. It was argued in Europe, reasonably enough, that strategic doctrines which amounted to a limited liability for the superpowers were bad for deterrence. But Americans were determined to press the Alliance to a military condition wherein a war which began in Europe just might remain there. Washington favored a strategic context wherein decisions on nuclear use could be made later rather than earlier.

The U.S. Navy contributed significantly to the strategic nuclear forces, first by the nuclear delivery possible from aircraft carriers and then, after 1960, via the fleet of SSBNs. The questions of most interest here, however, are how Western sea power exerted strategic leverage which contributed to eventual victory in the Cold War and speculatively how, and to what effect, that sea power might have functioned had the Cold War turned hot.

Once NATO decided that there should be a period of strictly conventional resistance to a Soviet invasion of Europe—the so-called pause prior to nuclear use—then the security of the sea lines of communication (SLOC) across the North Atlantic became truly critical for the integrity of the Alliance's strategy. NATO could promise credibly to sustain an all-conventional defense of Western Europe for a matter of weeks, and perhaps months, only if it could use the sea more or less at will. In the 1980s, as in the 1940s, heavy and bulky cargo had to be moved by sea. In 1947 an American naval theorist noted correctly that "only when the bulk of the freight now carried by merchant ships is airborne can the term 'air power' be used in a sense that compares to 'sea power.' "[12] Desert Shield/Storm in 1990-91 showed that the movement of the equipment, supplies, and fuel for heavy expeditionary forces remains overwhelmingly dependent upon sea transport. If NATO's sea power could not sustain a fighting front in Europe, a grim and perhaps intolerable burden of nuclear escalation would have descended upon the United States. While NATO could lose in a nuclear holocaust, it could lose the European air-land war either on land *or by defeat at sea* on its western flank.

In the 1970s and 1980s it was common wisdom in the West to believe that in time of war the Soviet Union would commit its navy primarily to defensive missions. Those missions included protection of the SSBN force, particularly as the ever greater range of sea-launched ballistic missiles (SLBMs) permitted operational deployment in coastal bastions, and seaward defense of the approaches to especially sensitive portions of Soviet territory. This rather comforting belief encouraged the matching opinion that NATO's wartime shipping probably would confront only a modest scale of difficulty early in a war in performance of the European reinforcement and resupply role. Exactly how the Soviet Navy would have been instructed to wage World War III must forever remain a matter for speculation, but there is no denying that style in war at sea, as well as the likelihood and character of nuclear use, would have been influenced critically, perhaps driven, by the unfolding of events on land. In NATO's perspective, the North Atlantic SLOC could have strategic meaning only if there was a continental bridgehead holding across the ocean.[13] In Soviet perspective, major setbacks in a continental campaign against NATO in Europe might well have served to license truly desperate measures to choke the enemy at sea. But measures taken by the Soviet Union to attempt to strangle NATO's SLOC would have needed to

273

work with a swiftness of strategic effect quite uncharacteristic of the leverage generated by, or against, sea power.

From the mid-1970s until the close of the Cold War, there was a noticeable shift in U.S. naval thinking about the leverage which sea power might exert in pursuit of victory in war.[14] On the one hand there was a reconsideration of how best the SLOCs vital to the West could be secured in time of conflict. Geography, technology, and tactical conditions permitting, superior navies always have preferred to achieve what today is called sea control—the ability to ensure the reasonably secure passage of friendly ships, and denial of same to the foe—by an offensive strategy. First-class navies cannot help but be attracted to securing a more or less general and lasting maritime command by means of obliging the enemy's navy early on to fight a decisive fleet engagement. The trouble has been that the superior navies of the twentieth century, indeed of the early nineteenth also, typically have lacked the ability to compel second-class navies to come out from fortified ports or coastal waters and give hopeless battle. In two key respects in the 1980s, courtesy of superior submarine technologies and human tactical skills, as well as of excellent fleet air defenses, the U.S. Navy and the navies of its NATO allies returned to basics concerning securing the seas and exploiting that security for leverage in war as a whole.

First, it was announced that, insofar as conditions would permit, Western navies would seek to win a future Battle of the Atlantic *at source*, by taking the sea war to the Soviet enemy in his home waters and in his coastal regions ashore. NATO shipping would be protected not so much passively by a naval barrier between Greenland, Iceland, the Faeroes, and Britain—a barrier intended to repel Soviet surface, subsurface, or aerial attempts at penetration to the shipping lanes—but rather by a naval-air war waged in the far North. Also, and as a vital contributor to SLOC defense, U.S. and some British naval power would seek to protect NATO's northern flank in Norway by controlling the Norwegian Sea and generally pressing upon the Soviet SSBN force and against Soviet naval surface and air assets in the heavily foritified region of the Kola Peninsula. (This offensively cast grand design was at the level of a strategic concept of operations. The U.S. Navy would have proceeded with all due prudence about the business of hazarding its irreplaceable attack carriers in narrow waters close to the shores of a first-class enemy.)

274

Second, the proposition that a Soviet Navy fighting for its life close to home could not menace NATO's SLOC in the North Atlantic was embedded in a more expansive offensive concept of maritime strategy altogether. The U.S. maritime strategy of the 1980s was a conceptual design which drew upon the centuries of historical experience of first-class sea powers with "the function of the fleet in war." No one can say how the United States, or NATO as a whole, actually would have waged war at sea. But it was apparent that by the early 1980s that a major and long-overdue effort was underway in the U.S. Navy to attempt to maximize the strategic leverage that superior sea power should accord the Alliance.

The U.S. Navy was not just thinking about how best it could see to the safe transport of critical war supplies across a potentially vulnerable North Atlantic (as if it were the maritime equivalent of a railroad system). Much more extensively it was asking what it could contribute positively to the course and outcome of a war. Overall, the leading official naval theorists and planners in the West reasoned that if NATO's nuclear attack submarines (SSNs) could threaten and attrit Soviet SSBNs early in a war and if sea-based power could be projected against Soviet coastal assets as well as assets close inland, then useful leverage could be exerted. The landlocked Soviet foe would find his extraordinarily lengthy continental perimeter menaced from the seaward approaches in different regions and would be obliged to divert scarce military power (particular air units) to far-flung flank protection. Also, as the hypothetical campaign against the SSBN fleet might have proceeded, so the balance of strategic nuclear power would be shifted forcibly against Moscow but not in a very escalatory manner (i.e., submarine sinkings at sea).

In addition to establishing a robust sea control by a seizure of maritime command through naval battle in the sea approaches to Soviet territory in the North Atlantic and North Pacific, Western sea power would perform its classic missions of allowing time and the resources of a sea-accessible global geography to work for strategic advantage. In short, Western sea power in a World War III *in which nuclear weapons were not used extensively* should have enabled its political owners to succeed in a more or less protracted struggle against a wholly continental enemy. Scarcely less persuasive is the proposition that that prospect of eventual

275

defeat in a sea-shaped long war, in the context of no good short-war strategies, should have enhanced deterrence.

Of course, the argument is all speculation. The political nerve of East or West might have cracked; the war could have been either brief and nuclear or brief and concluded to the advantage of one side. What matters here is recognition that in its closing years in the 1980s, the Cold War saw serious defense planning by both sides for truly lengthy major conflict. The dominant scenario for the U.S. maritime strategy was a world war which would be non-nuclear (or virtually so), global, and protracted in time. The various distinctive and offsetting strengths and weaknesses of the two great coalitions, in a context of thoroughgoing mutual nuclear dread, rendered the concept of a long world war far from ridiculous. Such a war would have been a conflict wherein sea power, yet again, could have functioned as a vital *enabling* agent for Western victory.

The possibility of a great war between the United States and the Soviet Union was erased in 1991 with the formal and practical demise of the latter. It does not follow, however, that major armed conflict between coalitions with a continental and a maritime character has been banished, or even necessarily banished for very long. Also, although the most dramatic and important strategic setting for the leverage of sea power since 1945 pertained to the world war that did not occur, the United States was able to wage the wars that she did only because of the sea power at her disposal. Unless she can control the sea for the free movement of friendly shipping, the United States is unable to wage war beyond southern Canada or northern Mexico. Questions of politics and strategy quite aside, the wars in Korea, Vietnam, and the Persian Gulf were logistically possible for the United States only because she could enforce the right to use the sea without effective hindrance. For reasons of comparative transportation economics, the United States cannot function as a world power unless she is a great sea power. Without the ability to use the seas, which comprise 70 percent of the earth's surface, American military power simply cannot be projected where it might be needed across the oceans. Much can be done with air and space power, but either for a persisting distant presence that is politically nonprovocative (it is offshore and by definition sovereign based) or for the movement of material in bulk, there is no substitute for sea power. Moreover, there is no substitute for superior sea power. The strategic advantages conferred by inferior navies have been shown to be less than glittering.

Sea power has been the midwife of victory, the—or at least *a*—great enabling factor in war after war through the centuries. Indeed, except for the decade from the mid-1950s to the mid-1960s, even in the relations of East and West in a heavily nuclear age, the performance of sea power potentially has been vital to the working of strategy. The American understanding of NATO's strategic concept of flexible response required success against any prompt Soviet efforts to choke the transatlantic SLOC. The details vary and matter, but protection of the North Atlantic convoy routes was debated in the 1970s and 1980s in terms reminiscent of 1941, 1917, 1801, and even 1701.[15] Strategy-thwarting, even history-ending, nuclear use was always possible in a Soviet-American World War III, but the arguments for mutual restraint became more and more widely appreciated as the Cold War matured and then waned.

The idea that the continental and landlocked Soviet Union could reap massively asymmetrical benefit from the use of nuclear weapons at sea, since she would seek only to deny the use of the sea to NATO not to use the sea herself, did not withstand close scrutiny.[16] Commonsense, not to mention U.S. policy, denied the probability of nuclear war confined to one geophysical environment. A NATO uniquely at risk to the strategic consequences of nuclear war at sea probably would have responded in the environment where Soviet power had most to lose: on land. By the 1980s, when the United States reoriented its doctrines for both air/land and sea warfare in a more offensive direction and when Soviet leaders were endorsing the notion of large-scale nonnuclear conflicts, the continuities in the history of the strategic leverage of sea power became clearer than had been the case for decades. That long history of the leverage of sea power also is a long history of the relative influence and interdependence of sea power and land power.

CHAPTER 10

LEVERAGE FOR VICTORY

Sea power did not win the war [World War II] itself; it enabled the war to be won.

Herbert Richmond, *Statesmen and Sea Power* (1946)

In modern times, sea power has enabled wars to be won. In ancient and medieval times, dominant land power generated the sea power that enabled wars to be won. The twentieth century has witnessed the strategic condition wherein air power, in support of sea and land power, has become a critical enabler of victory. More recently, nuclear deterrence, when appropriate, has functioned to enable conventional forces to be effective as threat and in action. For the final complication, today and for the future space power has become vital to sea power,[1] as it has to land power and air power also. War is a team enterprise. No matter how fashions in doctrine and military organization have evolved, the historical reality has been one of joint, if frequently ill-combined—land-sea or sea-land—effort in the quest for strategic advantage. Great sea powers have required a land power dimension to their strategy, and great land powers typically have discovered that without a strong navy or naval allies, everything that they thought they had secured on land could be menaced by unreachable foes offshore with the time to make mischief.

The leverage of sea power writ large, and the strategic advantage conferred more narrowly by a superior navy, are relative to other forms of military power. Each form has a distinctive strategic utility. There are tasks that a first-class navy is good at performing, just as there are tasks that it performs either badly or not at all. In recognition of the practical necessity for a combined-arms

278

approach to war, as well as for more parochial reasons of service advantage, it is stunningly noticeable just how inclusive and expansive a great navy can become. The U.S. Navy, for the leading example, in addition to its surface and subsurface combat and support ships (and boats), also accommodates a small army in the Marine Corps, and a medium-sized air force on its carriers and on naval air stations, and it operates the largest element in the strategic nuclear forces in the form of the nuclear-powered ballistic missile submarine (SSBN) fleet. As if that were not comprehensive enough, the U.S. Navy is claiming that sea power must include space power, and, in fact, it is the largest user among the services of space systems.

For reasons of geopolitics, the major wars of the Western world in modern times typically have been conflicts characterized by large geostrategic asymmetries between the principal antagonists. Even in the rare cases when war at sea has been of equal strategic salience to both sides, the more maritime-oriented state inevitably has had a great deal more to lose than has the continental foe. A case in point is the Anglo-French War of 1778–83. The unusual superficial symmetry of this war, the substantially maritime character of the struggle, was the product of the facts that Britain was tied down in a continental war an ocean away from its home base of strength, while France had assembled a united continental European front.

Wars between maritime and continental states or coalitions cannot usefully be dissected for precise determination of the relative importance of sea power or land power. A military literature which solemnly discusses the less-than-riveting issue of whether sea power, land power, air power, or economic warfare was or was not truly decisive in a particular war trivializes its subject. Any number of factors can be argued to have been decisive, in the sense that victory would not have been gained in their absence. For example, although the German Army had to be beaten in the field in World War II because the political structure of the conflict precluded a compromise peace, if unaided strategically by the Anglo-American siege of Hitler's *Festung Europa* Soviet land power almost certainly could not have beaten the Germans. That Anglo-American siege necessarily was maritime in character, though it was a siege, and then a forcible irruption on land, utterly dependent on command of the air. What then truly was decisive or most decisive? The question is absurd.

279

After the defeat of Austria at Marengo and Hohenlinden in 1800 and again after the defeat of Russia at Friedland in 1807, France decisively, indeed repeatedly, won the war on land. Hitler was in a similar favorable condition by mid-June 1940. In the British case in war after war, she won whatever there was to win at or from the sea. Enemy and enemy-leaning neutral fleets were either sunk or contained by blockade, while enemy commerce was sunk, captured, and driven from the high seas. But to achieve success in war as a whole, the center of gravity of the foe has to be assailed convincingly. Neither sea power nor land power can be considered separately as instruments of decision in war, even with reference to a maritime-organized continental challenge to land power or a continental-based maritime challenge to sea power. Virtually by definition a great continental power can be overthrown only on land, and a great maritime power can be overthrown only at sea. But the land power that could write *finis* to a French or German Empire, or the sea power that might have terminated the maritime empires of Venice or Britain, was, or would have been, power exerted in one environment that derived its strength primarily from the other—with the *caveat* that sea power cannot be independent of material strength ashore.

Venice declined in its relative standing in the sixteenth century not because sea power generally was in decline—quite the reverse was true—but rather because a small city-state with an insecure landward frontier could not compete with the sea power of an ascendant Spain or Ottoman Turkey. Furthermore, the age of transoceanic discovery shifted trade patterns away from the Mediterranean. Similarly, Britain's decline as a great power in the twentieth century was a measure not of any general decline in the diplomatic or wartime military value of sea power but rather of Britain's relative material standing vis-à-vis other countries.[2]

Many generalizations about the importance of sea power transpire to be misleading half-truths, or truths from only one strategic perspective. It is essential to specify whether a particular claim about the significance of sea power—for example, its effect on the duration of a war—pertains to maritime effort by or against a continental state or coalition. The influence of success by a continental power on land or on the sea, and of similar success by a maritime power, requires careful treatment. For example, the influence of land power upon sea campaigns is at least in part strategic in nature. The course and outcome of combat on land will determine the geostrategic terms of reference of conflict at sea, as well as the balance of resources that a continental power is at liberty to devote to maritime campaigns. Also, a sea power lives or dies by its maritime communications but obviously not literally at sea. Defeat at sea, or even a condition of severely contested command, will have a much shorter audit trail to comprehensive national defeat for a sea power than is the case for a land power beaten afloat, but the effect may still be indirect. Actual military defeat—the loss of command through a naval disaster—will lead a sea power to anticipate conquest by invasion or perhaps a maritime blockade which would cause an intolerable depression of economic activity.

Preponderant continental power can function strategically for the intended ultimate humbling of offshore sea power. Because land power can achieve decision on and against the national territory of its enemies in a way that sea power cannot, it does not follow that it is less strategic in character than is sea power. When confronted with the barrier of an uncommanded sea, land power ceases to be an instrument of military decision. One argument is that modern history has shown the inability of preponderant continental powers to fashion potent enough maritime (or air) instruments for the defeat of offshore sea powers. Another, more convincing, is that no land power has been sufficiently preponderant on land as to have the surplus resources necessary for the conduct of successful war against great-power enemies offshore.

Sea power, land power, and air power are partners rather than foes. Each needs the others if success in war is to be achieved. And they are always specific to country, strategic context, and tactical feasibility. Sea power always is about the performance of particular missions in particular places with an actual quantity and quality of force and ancillary services, in face of a particular enemy. General analyses that purport to track comparatively the relations of net advantage as among sea power, land power, and air power may have some limited utility—for example, with reference to the evolving basics of transportation economics assessed in the currency of comparative ton-mile costs—but they can easily lead the unwary astray. In tending toward the isolation of sea power from its dependence on a particular territorial base of resources, discussion of maritime-continental strategic interaction fundamentally may fail to understand the structure of its subject. For example, the debate in the 1980s over the U.S. maritime strategy was plagued with strategic-theoretical generalities which often obscured the fact that the sea power of the Western Alliance united, and was a partial expression of, truly gigantic landward economic resources.

Nothwithstanding the vast differences of detail as among ancient, medieval and modern times, there has been a sufficient continuity in the leverage of sea power for statecraft and strategy as to lend itself to presentation as unified conclusions. Moreover, these conclusions speak as clearly to the present and the future as they do to the past.

Two general truths obtain with respect to the significance of maritime prowess for the outcomes of wars between sea powers and land powers. *First, a continental power can win a war by securing military command at sea, by achieving sea denial, or even just by disputing command at sea very vigorously.* Occasionally, traditionally continental powers have proved capable of developing or renting a quality and quantity of naval power sufficient to render the further prosecution of war impracticable for a sea power foe. Unlike land powers, sea powers can lose wars as a more or less direct consequence of defeat or damage suffered at sea. For example, courtesy of rentable maritime allies and Persian gold, Sparta discovered that the only strategy likely to bring down an already much weakened Athens was blockade of the Athenian grain supply at the choke point of the Dardanelles. For another case, in the First Punic War, the Roman Republic was sufficiently robust in public spirit, and well endowed with continental resources that it could build and rebuild a fleet such that the maritime empire of Carthage was at a greater disadvantage in the seaward dimension of the struggle in Sicily than it was on land. In modern times, neither France nor Germany succeeded in sustaining a naval challenge to Britain to the point where Britain was obliged to sign a peace of humiliation, let alone actual surrender. The Treaty of Amiens of 1802 most closely approximated such a settlement, but it was more the product of unassailable French land power than of near-term naval danger to Britain. But in the early years of the wars against Louis XIV, during the war with France occasioned by the American War of Independence, in the

282

First World War, and again in the Second World War, Britain's war effort was severely at risk to the naval power of a continental enemy.

Second, for a sea power or a maritime-dependent coalition, command at sea provides the strategic conditions indispensable for success in war. The British official historian of the land war in Western Europe in the fall of 1914 makes this point most eloquently and persuasively:

> Whilst the British Expeditionary Force was playing its part in bringing to a standstill and then rolling back to the Aisne the great German onrush, the British Empire was slowly making the first movements to assemble those troops and acquire those material means that it was obvious would be indispensable if the war was to be brought to a successful conclusion. The German plan, long evolved and well tested at war games and staff tours, which was to have decided the campaign in the West in six weeks, had failed; *and Britain, behind her advanced guard of professional soldiers and her fleets, had leisure to organize her resources.* Already had fear entered into the hearts of the rulers of Germany that, in their haste to dominate Europe and the world, they had struck against a real World-Power; and that this Power, centuries established, tenacious of purpose, and never yet brought to her knees, stood between them and victory. It was for Britain to ensure that this fear should never cease to grow and should finally become a certainty. *Time, much time, was requisite to collect and organize the strength of the Empire; but which the enemy could not afford to disregard and which those fighting for Britain never forgot*—even when from the Allies' point of view the situation seemed most hopeless [in the last week of August and the first week of September, 1914].[3]

British sea power in 1914–18, Anglo-American sea power in 1939–45, and NATO's sea power in the Cold War brought the resources of virtually the whole maritime-accessible world to bear upon a continental struggle in Europe. Furthermore, as Napoleon and then Hitler discovered, an uncommanded sea places strict geographical and hence military, economic, and political limits upon what can be achieved by victorious land power. When triumphant armies reach the water's edge, they reach the limit of their military competence. The question, then, is whether continental victory can work as an enabler for success at sea. For the

283

land power, that success need take the form only of sea denial, since the critical strategic necessity is to prevent the maritime enemy from using the sea for self-sustenance by overseas supply or for power projection against the shore.

The discussion of land power and sea power subsumes the air power most appropriate to each. World War II demonstrated conclusively, while every war since has driven the principle home further, that lasting success on the ground and at sea requires success in the air. Overall judgments on the leverage of sea power and the strategic advantage conferred by superior naval strength incorporate recognition of the roles and significance of air power, when relevant historically.

Superior sea power enables a maritime-dependent state or coalition to protract a conflict in time in pursuit of victory. For reasons of geopolitics, economic geography, and the political instability of empires, protracted conflict tends strongly, if painfully, to favor the prospects both of insular power and of continental power that has extraordinary depth. There is a centuries-long pattern of democratic, or relatively democratic, commercial-minded sea powers choosing to neglect their defenses in peacetime, riding out some military setbacks at the outset of a war, and then, with the benefit of sea control, organizing and mobilizing a materially overwhelming coalition for the overthrow or profound discouragement of an aspiring continental hegemon. In similar ways, the Dutch Republic, Britain, and the United States have all been able to rely on their own or another state's naval power to keep their homelands secure for a period of mobilization. In the late seventeenth and early eighteenth centuries, the Dutch were rendered insular to an important degree by the barrier fortresses of the Spanish (later Austrian) Netherlands and by their ability to breach their dikes at will.[4] The Channel under the working control of the Royal Navy allowed Britain to survive the disasters on land in the wars against the French Revolution and Empire, provided a totally secure flank for Anglo-French land power in 1914–18, and denied Hitler the short-war victory, or peace negotiated under severe duress, that he believed he had earned in the summer of 1940.

Given the generally tolerable congruency of its vital interests with those of Britain, save briefly late in the Napoleonic period, Britain's maritime-dependent antihegemonic policies served the United States almost as well as they did Britain itself. In earlier periods, in the face of disasters on land, the effective insularity conferred upon the citadel of the Byzantine Empire by the un-breachable Great Wall of Theodosius (until the coming of heavy siege artillery using gunpowder) that protected Constantinople on its landward side, or the long walls to Piraeus that rendered inland Athens militarily an island, enabled the sea power of Byzantium and of Athens to keep the state alive and to protract conflicts in hope of a change in strategic fortune.

It is not inevitable that time must work in favor of a dominant sea power in conflict with a dominant land power, but the structure of security politics in continental Eurasia and the increasing economic significance of the world beyond that dual continent makes it more likely than not that that will continue to be so. Although today it can be threatened with bombardment from the air, the world beyond the reach of armies in Eurasia can be approached only by sea.

Next, superior sea power provides a large measure of control over the geostrategic terms of engagement in war. Among the examples worth citing are the great Athenian expedition to Sicily in 415–413 B.C., Republican Rome's ability in the Second Punic War to regulate the scale and scope of war in Spain for the purpose of discouraging Carthage from reinforcing Hannibal in south-central Italy, and the English fine-tuning in the sixteenth century of the wars of attrition against Spain on the Continent that were waged in the Netherlands and in Brittany. Further cases include the "Spanish ulcer" that Britain sustained with its protracted (1808–14) Peninsular commitment, the Anglo-French extended raid to the Crimea (and the Baltic) in 1854–55,[5] Gallipoli and Salonika in the First World War, and virtually the entire Anglo-American geostrategic direction of the Second World War in Europe and the Pacific.

There is another side to this story. An enemy superior on land is certain to be able to seize continental prizes which a maritime coalition would very much like to be able to defend and will need to recapture or otherwise recover. Also, goegraphically eccentric axes of peripheral attack may be forced upon a sea power by the strength of enemy land power. From 1940 until 1945 the Western allies were enabled by their supremacy at sea to choose to prosecute war in North Africa, and then in Sicily and on the Italian mainland. But they were fighting in the Mediterranean because they lacked the strength to fight in the main theater of operations: in France, the Low Countries, and beyond to Germany itself.

The continuity of the oceans means that maritime command confers a global mobility and agility with which shore-bound or even air-transportable land power cannot compete. As Halford Mackinder and others predicted around the turn of the century,[6] the coming of the railroad (and subsequently the internal combustion engine) and more generally the maturing of continental-scale industrial economies provided a strategic and tactical mobility for military forces on land that previously they had most noticeably lacked. The inability of the leaders of Britain's Royal Navy in the years leading up to 1914 to persuade anyone of note outside its ranks of the military practicality of conducting useful raids on the German coast was evidence of the plausibility of the contemporary German view that such a threat had been long overtaken by developments in the logistics of land power.[7] Prior to that new-found political, industrial and military organization of the continents which Mackinder discerned as working to the great disadvantage of sea power, Britain reliably could wage peripheral land warfare at a logistical advantage over continental enemies. This was the case in both the Peninsula and the Crimea. The potential offensive value of superior sea power was demonstrated in the First World War at Gallipoli and Salonika. The hallmark of that offensive value lies in the mobility and flexibility with which sea-based force can be concentrated for surprise application. The actual benefit of the offensive use of the mobility of sea-based land power was shown on a heroic scale by the Western-Allied conduct of the Second World War in all theaters. Abstract notions pertaining to the contemporary tactical relationship between sea and land mobility were demonstrated from 1942 until 1945 to be thoroughly misleading guides to the realm of the militarily practicable. The invasions of North Africa, Sicily, Italy (including the instructive near-disaster of Salerno and the fiasco of Anzio), and France are not in any useful sense to be thought of as representational confrontations between land-based and sea-based power. Rather, the beaches of French North Africa, Sicily, Italy, and France witnessed the engagement in all dimensions of Allied and Axis military power in particular places at particular times.

The mobility of sea power translates as an inherent agility that maritime command can exploit to achieve surprise. By their nature, naval forces are maneuver forces. Surprise at and from the sea is facilitated by the fact that naval forces are not canalized in their axes of threat as land forces are by natural and man-made obstacles. Furthermore, the typically tenuous nature of the contact maintained between hostile naval forces at sea enhances the feasibility of surprise. It is traditional to talk of sea *lanes, highways, routes,* and *lines* of communications, but these territorial and geometric notions invite misunderstanding as to just how difficult it can be to locate ships precisely in the vast expanse of the oceans. In the summer of 1798 Nelson could only guess whither Admiral François Brueys' fleet was bound—with reference to the frustrating chase in the dark that eventually was concluded with the Battle of the Nile, after Nelson had pursued several false trails. For a further Nelsonian example, consider the Trafalgar campaign that was terminated so conclusively on October 21, 1805. The campaign opened in March with Villeneuve's evading the Royal Navy's blockade of Toulon and baffling Nelson as to his destination and purpose—the eastern Mediterranean or the Atlantic? And if the Atlantic—the West Indies or Brest and the Channel?

After the fashion of the German situation in the West in 1943–44, "fortress land power" may be certain that the sea-commanding enemy is coming and can estimate the risks and benefits of each plausible axis of attack. But as the Allies demonstrated even with regard to the execution of the largest amphibious assault in history to that date (Overlord, June 6, 1944), the natural mobility of sea power facilitates deception for operational surprise. Deception and surprise are not uniquely characteristic of the potential of sea power, but strategic and tactical surprise tend to be easier to accomplish at and from the sea than they are on land because of the multiplicity of routes that ships, but not armies, can take. Surprise is both more feasible at sea than on land, and its tactical, and possibly strategic, benefits can be far more devastating. The fleet caught at a disadvantage typically will not have fortified places into which it can retire promptly and safely. Moreover, the small number of major combat units (compared with land warfare) in war at sea means that a handful of salvoes could overturn a particular naval balance.

Time and again superior sea power has worked strategically to knit together geographically widely separated countries for the conduct of war as a coalition enterprise. Most critical of all for

287

eventual victory has been the role of sea power in tying together the war efforts of maritime and continental states acting in concert. Oceans can connect or divide, depending upon who commands them. The wartime impact of British, then Anglo-American, sea power from 1939 to 1945 was not a matter strictly of the fighting and mercantile maritime assets of those countries, or, more broadly, of the abstract value of sea power. Instead, the subject is the naval and mercantile assets generated by the specific national economies and security communities they expressed and connected. Anglo-American sea power, with its air power adjunct, brought an armed *world* to bear against Hitler's overmatched European fortress.

In modern times command of the sea has enabled the leading sea power to wage war of such a character on the sea and by land that the continental enemy has either retired exhausted from the contest or has been overthrown militarily. Moreover, the offshore sea power repeatedly has been able to organize, finance (and even equip), and support directly on land continental states connected by maritime strength to the seaward world controlled by superior naval power. Hegemonic land power has brought on its own arrest or destruction by the continental opposition that it cannot help but arouse.

There have been cases of continental states' acquiring navies that wrested command of the sea from more natural sea powers, though not in modern times. Even if a continental naval power seeks only the negative object of denial of sea control to its maritime enemy, however, achievement of that limited object truly could be decisive. Spain, France, and Germany successively and repeatedly failed to solve the maritime problems in war making which Britain imposed upon them. They might have succeeded. In principle, though not to date in practice, pursuit of the *guerre de course* was a sound strategy for a second-class navy. Britain's battle-fleet command and the sheer volume and distribution of value of its seaborne commerce in very many hulls defeated France in the "tonnage wars" of the antitrade campaigns of the late seventeenth, eighteenth, and early nineteenth centuries. But British experience twice in the twentieth century must suggest to the prudent that commerce raiding has the potential to defeat a sea power. Whether the oceans connect an overall overmatching war machine, or whether they divide "islands" of war-making resources

288

which cannot project their power, is a function of the ability of a maritime coalition to keep the seas secure.

The leverage of sea power works in a multifaceted *enabling* capacity. Naval strength, no matter how dominant, is rarely able by its own unaided action to exert decisive pressure upon an enemy. That is not a criticism. It is simply a fact to recognize that sea power, land power, and air power have unique and complementary capabilities. Superior sea power exerts leverage by its ability to enlist time as a critical ally and by its invaluable capacity to shape the geostrategic terms of engagement in war. By landlocking the foe, superior sea power can isolate, divert, and distract while using its inherent mobility to express a strategic and operational agility to achieve a useful measure of surprise. The landlocking of a typically impatient continental enemy encourages him to throw the dice in ever more ambitious continental adventures. A continental power frustrated strategically at the low-tide line will turn to try to maximize whatever gain his armies can secure on land. That was the strategic history of the fall of Napoleonic France and of Germany twice.

Dominant, if often challenged, sea power repeatedly has exerted the decisive economic leverage in war of a materially very superior coalition of states. British, or Anglo-American, sea power connected the entire world of friendly as well as unfriendly shorelines. The former comprised a maritime network of economic strength; the latter were potential targets for the projection of military power from the sea.

The future value to statecraft and strategy of the ability to use or deny use of the seas is predictable with high confidence. The connecting and isolating value to strategy of superior sea power is a persisting fact of physical and political geography. Humankind lives on politically organized territories which more often than not are imperfectly bonded by ground or air transportation. The slowness of sea passage relative to land, air, or missile conveyance is as unarguable as it remains inescapable but close to irrelevant for still critical purposes.

There are no trends extant—technological, economic, political, or military—which suggest an imminent diminution in the strategic leverage of sea power. The potency of air power certainly has improved dramatically, as witness its leading role in the Gulf War of 1991. The dominant navy of this age, however, the navy of the United States, has integrated air (breathing) power in its carriers and in it acquisition of conventionally armed cruise missiles. Furthermore, the U.S. Navy is well launched on the process of accommodating the force-multiplying benefits of space systems. On balance, far from threatening the strategic obsolescence of otherwise superior naval power, air and space power has made some navies unprecedentedly potent in relative terms.

Wherever and however one looks, high leverage for sea power in the future seems a certainty. On the political front, the demise of one of the superpowers eliminates for a while the most nominally persuasive of threats to the strategic utility of sea power: the peril of a war so brief and destructive that sea power's enabling action would be short-circuited. It is true that nuclear threats to the leverage of sea power are becoming regional or local rather than global in character, but it is also true that first-class sea power by the mid-1990s should provide convincing antimissile, as well as antiaircraft, defenses. The U.S. Navy is shifting its principal focus from sea control to power projection against the shore and from the deep ocean to shallow water. In the absence of a plausible enemy with a first-class sea power, American maritime strategists talk of operational maneuver from a sea whose control is unlikely to be in dispute for many years to come.

The predictable continuities in physical geography, in comparative transportation economics as among geographical environments, and in the political proclivities for conflict all argue for the enduring strategic leverage of sea power. If the coming of the railroad, internal combustion engine, air, missile, nuclear, and space eras could not demote the strategic value of sea power significantly, it is difficult to see what could emerge to do so over the next several decades.

NOTES

CHAPTER 1: THE NATURE AND USES OF SEA POWER

1. Martin Wight, *Power Politics* (New York: Holmes and Meier, 1978), p. 68.

2. Christopher Lloyd, *The Capture of Quebec* (New York: Macmillan, 1959), pp. 25–26.

3. See Herbert Richmond, *Statesmen and Sea Power* (Oxford: Clarendon Press, 1946), p. ix.

4. C. E. Callwell, *The Effect of Maritime Command on Land Campaigns Since Waterloo* (Edinburgh: William Blackwood and Sons, 1897), p. 29.

5. Alfred Thayer Mahan, *The Influence of Sea Power upon History, 1660–1783* (Boston: Little, Brown, 1918; first pub. 1890), p. 25.

6. As in Julian S. Corbett, *Some Principles of Maritime Strategy* (Annapolis, Md.: Naval Institute Press, 1988; first pub. 1911), p. 94.

7. Mahan, *Influence of Sea Power upon History, 1660–1783*, pp. 28–29ff.

8. See Halford J. Mackinder, *Democratic Ideals and Reality* (New York: W. W. Norton, 1962; first pub. 1942), which contains the 1919 title work, and "The Geographical Pivot of History" (1904) and "The Round World and the Winning of the Peace" (1943); and W. H. Parker, *Mackinder: Geography as an Aid to Statecraft* (Oxford: Clarendon Press, 1982).

9. An excellent sprightly essay is Barry S. Strauss and Josiah Ober, *The Anatomy of Error: Ancient Military Disasters and Their Lessons for Modern Strategists* (New York: St. Martin's Press, 1990), ch. 2. The best ancient and modern sources are, respectively, Thucydides, *The Peloponnesian War*, trans. Rex Warner (London: Cassell, 1962), and Donald Kagan's four-volume history of the war, the last of which is *The Fall of the Athenian Empire* (Ithaca, N.Y.: Cornell University Press, 1987). D. M. Lewin et al., ed. *The Cambridge Ancient History*, vol. 5: *The Fifth Century B.C.*, 2d. ed. (Cambridge: Cambridge University Press, 1992), also is important.

10. See F. E. Adcock, *The Greek and Macedonian Art of War* (Berkeley: University of California Press, 1957), p. 72. Martin Blumenson, "Of Landpowers and Seapowers," in George E. Thibault, ed., *The Art and Practice of Military Strategy* (Washington, D.C.: National Defense Uni-

versity, 1984), pp. 36–41, provides more general application of this argument.

11. Corbett, *Some Principles of Maritime Strategy*, p. 94.

12. S. W. Roskill, *History of the Second World War, The War at Sea, 1939–1945*, vol. 1: *The Defensive* (London: HMSO, 1954), p. 3.

13. See Admiral James D. Watkins, "The Maritime Strategy," in Watkins et al., *The Maritime Strategy*, U.S. Naval Institute *Proceedings, Supplement* (January 1986), pp. 11–13.

14. Quoted in John Terraine, *The Road to Passchendaele: The Flanders Offensive of 1917: A Study in Inevitability* (London: Leo Cooper, 1977), p. 72.

15. The background to the Royal Navy's rejection of convoy from August 1914 to April 1917 is ably presented in Bryan Ranft, "The Protection of British Seaborne Trade and the Development of Systematic Planning for War, 1860–1906," in Ranft, ed., *Technical Change and British Naval Policy, 1860–1939* (London: Hodder and Stoughton, 1977), pp. 1–22. The best study is Arthur J. Marder, *From the Dreadnought to Scapa Flow, The Royal Navy in the Fisher Era, 1904–1919*, vol. 4: *1917: Year of Crisis* (London: Oxford University Press, 1969). For the British experience in the age of sail, see Patrick Crowhurst, *The Defence of British Trade, 1689–1815* (Folkestone [U.K.]: William Dawson and Sons, 1977), esp. ch. 2.

16. The charge of "extraordinary amateurishness" is leveled persuasively in Peter Padfield, *Dönitz: The Last Führer: Portrait of a Nazi War Leader* (New York: Harper & Row, 1984), p. 229.

17. See Jeremy Black, *Natural and Necessary Enemies: Anglo-French Relations in the Eighteenth Century* (London: Gerald Duckworth, 1986), pp. 116–17; and J. S. Bromley, *Corsairs and Navies, 1660–1760* (London: Hambledon Press, 1987), ch. 5.

18. See John B. Hattendorf, "The Evolution of the Maritime Strategy, 1977–1987," *Naval War College Review* 41, no. 3 (Summer 1988): 7–28.

19. See Julian S. Corbett, *The Campaign of Trafalgar* (London: Longmans, Green, 1910).

20. J. Holland Rose, *The Indecisiveness of Modern War and Other Essays* (Port Washington, N.Y.: Kennikat Press, 1968; first pub. 1927), pp. 98–124. Of some interest is the French view in René Daveluy, *The Genius of Naval Warfare, I: Strategy* (Annapolis, Md.: U.S. Naval Institute, 1910; first pub. 1905), pp. 274–82.

21. Paul S. Dull, *A Battle History of the Imperial Japanese Navy (1941–1945)* (Annapolis, Md.: Naval Institute Press, 1978), p. 331.

22. See William Ledyard Rodgers, *Greek and Roman Naval Warfare: A*

Study of Strategy, Tactics, and Ship Design from Salamis (480 B.C.) to Actium (31 B.C.) (Annapolis, Md.: Naval Institute Press, 1983; first pub. 1937), pp. 279–91; and Brian Caven, *The Punic Wars* (London: Weidenfeld and Nicolson, 1980), pp. 32–35.

23. See Thucydides, *Peloponnesian War*, Bk. 7, esp. p. 478; and Donald Kagan, *The Peace of Nicias and the Sicilian Expedition* (Ithaca, N.Y.: Cornell University Press, 1981), chs. 13–14.

24. Corbett, *Some Principles of Maritime Strategy*, p. 167.

25. Carl von Clausewitz, *On War*, trans. Michael Howard and Peter Paret (Princeton, N.J.: Princeton University Press, 1976; first pub. 1832), p. 359. Emphasis in original.

26. Barbara Tuchman, *The Guns of August* (New York: Macmillan, 1962), p. 7.

27. Winston S. Churchill, *The World Crisis, 1911–1918* (London: Odham's Press, 1938), 2:1015.

28. On the alleged perils of such an approach, see Barry R. Posen, "Inadvertent Nuclear War? Escalation and NATO's Northern Flank," *International Security* 7, no. 2 (Fall 1982): 28–54; Desmond Ball, "Nuclear War at Sea," *International Security* 10, no. 3 (Winter 1985/86): 3–31; and Jack Beatty, "In Harm's Way, " *Atlantic* (May 1987): 37–46, 48–49, 52–53.

29. Quoted in Alfred Thayer Mahan, *The Influence of Sea Power upon the French Revolution and Empire, 1793–1812* (Boston: Little, Brown, 1898; first pub. 1892), 2:186.

30. Quoted in Julian S. Corbett, *Fighting Instructions, 1530–1816* (London: Navy Records Society, 1905), pp. 313–14, 318.

31. James D. Watkins, "Space Control Is Sea Control" (Remarks at the inauguration of Naval Space Command, Dahlgren, Virginia, October 1, 1983).

32. See Ronald Lewin, *Ultra Goes to War* (New York: McGraw-Hill, 1978), pp. 230–32.

33. See Christopher Allmand, *The Hundred Years War: England and France at War c. 1300–c. 1450* (Cambridge: Cambridge University Press, 1988), pp. 82–90.

34. Mahan, *Influence of Sea Power upon the French Revolution and Empire, 1793–1812*, 2:184.

CHAPTER 2:   THE PRACTICE OF SEA POWER

1. Good brief summaries are Herbert W. Richmond, *The Invasion of Britain: An Account of Plans, Attempts and Counter-measures from 1586–*

1918 (London: Methuen, 1941); Frank McLynn, *Invasion: From the Armada to Hitler, 1588–1945* (London: Routledge and Kegan Paul, 1987).

2. Cyril Falls, Introduction to Kent Roberts Greenfield, ed., *Command Decisions* (London: Methuen, 1960; first pub. 1959), p. xiv.

3. Michael Howard, *The Causes of Wars and Other Essays* (London: Unwin Paperbacks, 1984; first pub. 1983), p. 200. Cyril Falls was an official historian of World War I, Michael Howard of World War II.

4. See G. C. Peden, *British Rearmament and the Treasury, 1932–1939* (Edinburgh: Scottish Academic Press, 1979).

5. John Brewer, *The Sinews of Power: War, Money and the English State, 1688–1783* (New York: Alfred A. Knopf, 1989), p. xvii and passim.

6. Ibid., p. xvi.

7. See D. B. Quinn and A. N. Ryan, *England's Sea Empire, 1550–1642* (London: George Allen and Unwin, 1983), pp. 104–5.

8. On British plans for the blockade of Germany, see W. N. Medlicott, *History of the Second World War, The Economic Blockade* (London: HMSO, 1952), 1:Introduction; and N. H. Gibbs, *History of the Second World War, Grand Strategy,* vol. 1: *Rearmament Policy* (London: HMSO, 1976), pp. 677–79. On the Royal Navy and the beginning of the maritime blockade, see S. W. Roskill, *History of the Second World War, The War at Sea,* vol. 1: *The Defensive* (London: HMSO, 1954), pp. 43–45; but see Alan S. Milward, *War, Economy, and Society, 1939–1945* (London: Penguin, 1987; first pub. 1977), p. 307, on the enforcement of the blockade without the use of ships. An important analysis of the supply difficulties of the German defense economy in the late 1930s is Williamson Murray, *The Change in the European Balance of Power, 1938–1939: The Path to Ruin* (Princeton, N.J.: Princeton University Press, 1984), ch. 1. On the importance of the Soviet Union for the economic sustenance of Nazi Germany, see Esmonde M. Robertson, "German Mobilization Preparations and the Treaties Between Germany and the Soviet Union of August and September 1939," in Robert Boyce and Robertson, eds., *Paths to War: New Essays on the Origins of the Second World War* (Basingstoke [U.K.]: Macmillan Education, 1989), pp. 330–66.

9. See Cajus Bekker (pseud.), *Hitler's Naval War* (New York: Zebra Books, 1985; first pub. 1971), pp. 23–24.

10. Wolfgang Wegener, *The Naval Strategy of the World War* (Annapolis, Md.: Naval Institute Press, 1989; first pub. 1929).

11. See Arthur J. Marder, *From the Dardanelles to Oran: Studies in the Royal Navy in War and Peace, 1915–1940* (London: Oxford University Press, 1974), pp. 48–49, and *Old Friends, New Enemies: The Royal*

Navy and the Imperial Japanese Navy, Strategic Illusions, 1936–1941 (Oxford: Clarendon Press, 1981), chs. 1–2.

12. See Paul Kennedy, *The Realities Behind Diplomacy: Background Influences on British External Policy, 1865–1980* (London: Fontana, 1981), pp. 182–83, for a view skeptical of the influence of the blockade. H. P. Willmott, *Sea Warfare: Weapons, Tactics and Strategy* (Chichester [U.K.]: Antony Bird Publications, 1981), pp. 34–35, provides a contrasting view.

13. Murray, *Change in the European Balance of Power*, ch. 1. But see Robertson, "German Mobilization Preparations."

14. ASDIC/sonar: Allied Submarine Detection Investigation Committee/ sound navigation ranging.

15. See John Terraine, *Business in Great Waters: The U-Boat Wars, 1916– 1945* (London: Leo Cooper, 1989), p. 205.

16. See Johannes Hasebroak, *Trade and Politics in Ancient Greece* (Chicago: Ares Publishers, 1978), pp. 130–46.

17. See Robert A. Doughty and Harold E. Raugh, Jr., "Embargoes in Historical Perspective," *Parameters* 21, no. 1 (Spring 1991): 21–30.

18. For example, Julian S. Corbett, *Some Principles of Maritime Strategy* (Annapolis, Md.: Naval Institute Press, 1988; first pub. 1911), pp. 63– 67. An excellent later exposition is B. H. Liddell Hart, "Marines and Strategy," *Marine Corps Gazette* 64, no. 1 (January 1980): 23–31. This classic article was first published in July 1960.

19. Corbett, *Some Principles of Maritime Strategy*, p. 66.

20. I have borrowed these terms from P. H. Colomb, *Naval Warfare: Its Ruling Principles and Practice Historically Treated* (London: W. H. Allen, 1891), pp. 216–17.

21. See the discussion in Eliot A. Cohen, *Commandos and Politicians: Elite Military Units in Modern Democracies* (Cambridge, Mass.: Center for International Affairs, Harvard University, 1978).

22. Quoted in Corbett, *Some Principles of Maritime Strategy*, p. 69.

23. The Walcheren expedition of 1809 was a coastal raid on a grand scale. The best recent study is Gordon C. Bond, *The Grand Expedition: The British Invasion of Holland in 1809* (Athens, Ga.: University of Georgia Press, 1979).

24. See H. P. Willmott *The Barrier and the Javelin: Japanese and Allied Pacific Strategies, February to June 1942* (Annapolis, Md.: Naval Institute Press, 1983), pp. 118–19, idem, *Empires in the Balance: Japanese and Allied Pacific Strategies to April 1942* (Annapolis, Md.: Naval Institute Press, 1982), pp. 447–50; and Dan van der Vat, *The Pacific*

Campaign, World War II: The U.S.-Japanese Naval War, 1941–1945 (New York: Simon and Schuster, 1991), pp. 162, 172, 177–78.

25. See Colin S. Gray, ed., *Special Operations: What Succeeds and Why? Lessons of Experience* (Fairfax, Va.: National Institute for Public Policy, May 1992.)

26. Lord Anson, quoted in Geoffrey Marcus, *Quiberon Bay: The Campaign in Home Waters, 1759* (London: Hollis and Carter, 1960), p. 10.

27. Paul Kennedy, *The Rise and Fall of British Naval Mastery* (New York: Charles Scribner's Sons, 1976), p. 129. Michael Duffy's important study, *Soldiers, Sugar and Seapower: The British expeditions to the West Indies and the War against Revolutionary France* (Oxford: Clarendon Press, 1987), helps correct the overly negative view traditionally taken by historians of Pitt the Younger's West Indian strategy.

28. J. Holland Rose, *The Indecisiveness of Modern War and Other Essays* (Port Washington, N.Y.: Kennikat Press, 1968; first pub. 1927), p. 120.

29. J. H. Parry, *Trade and Dominion: The European Overseas Empires in the Eighteenth Century* (New York: Praeger, 1971), pp. 130–31.

30. See Jeremy Black, *Natural and Necessary Enemies: Anglo-French Relations in the Eighteenth Century* (London: Gerald Duckworth, 1986).

31. A good brief treatment is Hew Strachan, *European Armies and the Conduct of War* (London: George Allen and Unwin, 1983), ch. 4. For thorough analyses, see David Chandler, *The Campaigns of Napoleon* (London: Weidenfeld and Nicolson, 1967); Gunther E. Rothenberg, *The Art of Warfare in the Age of Napoleon* (Bloomington: Indiana University Press, 1980; first pub. 1978); Geoffrey Best, *War and Society in Revolutionary Europe, 1770–1870* (London: Fontana, 1982), pt. II; and Russell F. Weigley, *The Age of Battles: The Quest for Decisive Warfare from Breitenfeld to Waterloo* (Bloomington: Indiana University Press, 1991).

32. David French, *The British Way in Warfare, 1688–2000* (London: Unwin Hyman, 1990), p. 228.

33. See Herbert W. Richmond, *Imperial Defence and Capture at Sea in War* (London: Hutchinson, 1932), Pt. 2.

34. Gerald S. Graham, *Tides of Empire: Discursions on the Expansion of Britain Overseas* (Montreal: McGill–Queen's University Press, 1972), p. 37.

35. See Daniel A. Baugh, "Why Did Britain Lose Command of the Sea During the War for America?" in Jeremy Black and Philip Woodfine, eds., *The British Navy and the Use of Naval Power in the Eighteenth Century* (Leicester [U.K.]: Leicester University Press, 1988), p. 160.

36. For an important fraction of the British experience, see John M. Sherwig,

Guineas and Gunpowder: British Foreign Aid in the Wars with France, 1793–1815 (Cambridge, Mass.: Harvard University Press, 1969).

37. See Corbett, *Some Principle of Maritime Strategy*, ch. 3; and B. H. Liddell Hart, *The British Way in Warfare* (London: Faber and Faber, 1932), ch. 1.

CHAPTER 3: THE PRACTICE OF LAND POWER

1. See John Keegan, *The Second World War* (London: Hutchinson, 1989), p. 54.

2. The seriousness of Hitler's intention to invade Britain in the period July–September 1940 is endorsed in J. R. M. Butler, *History of the Second World War, Grand Strategy*, vol. 2: *September 1939–June 1941* (London: HMSO, 1957), pp. 290–94; and Norman Rich, *Hitler's War Aims: I, Ideology, the Nazi State, and the Course of Expansion* (New York: W. W. Norton, 1973), p. 160.

3. Herbert Rosinski, *The Development of Naval Thought* (Newport, R. I.: Naval War College Press, 1977), p. 71.

4. Paul Kennedy, *The Rise of the Anglo-German Antagonism, 1860–1914* (London: George Allen and Unwin, 1982; first pub. 1980), p. 422. Emphasis in original.

5. Quoted in Cajus Bekker (pseud.), *Hitler's Naval War* (New York: Zebra Books, 1985; first pub. 1971), pp. 23–24. Emphasis in original.

6. See J. Holland Rose, *Man and the Sea: Stages in Maritime and Human Progress* (Cambridge: W. Heffer and Sons, 1935), p. 229; and G. J. Marcus, *The Age of Nelson: The Royal Navy, 1793–1815* (New York: Viking, 1971), p. 427.

7. See Gerhard Ritter, *The Schlieffen Plan: Critique of a Myth* (London: Oswald Wolff, 1958; first pub. 1956), pp. 71, 72.

8. Quoted in Bekker, *Hitler's Naval War*, p. 22.

9. See David Chandler, *The Campaigns of Napoleon* (London: Weidenfeld and Nicolson, 1967), p. 740.

10. Alfred Thayer Mahan, *The Influence of Sea Power upon the French Revolution and Empire, 1793–1812* (Boston: Little, Brown, 1989; first pub. 1892), 2: chs. 15–16; Julian S. Corbett, *Some Principles of Maritime Strategy* (Annapolis, Md.: Naval Institute Press, 1988; first pub. 1911), pp. 233–61; J. Holland Rose, *The Indecisiveness of Modern War and Other Essays* (Port Washington, N.Y.: Kennikat Press, 1968; first pub. 1927), pp. 49–67; Arthur J. Marder, *The Anatomy of British Sea Power: A History of British Naval Policy in the Pre-Dreadnought Era, 1880–1905* (Hamden, Conn.: Archon Books, 1964; first pub. 1940), chs. 5, 18; Herbert W. Richmond, *The Invasion of Britain: An Account*

of Plans, Attempts and Counter-measures from 1586 to 1918 (London: Methuen, 1941); Richard Glover, *Britain at Bay: Defence against Bonaparte, 1803–14* (New York: Barnes and Noble, 1973); Philip Warner, *Invasion Road* (London: Cassell, 1980); John Gooch, *The Prospect of War: Studies in British Defence Policy, 1847–1942* (London: Frank Cass, 1981), pp. 1–34; and Frank McLynn, *Invasion: From the Armada to Hitler, 1588–1945* (London: Routledge and Kegan Paul, 1987).

11. Public anxieties periodically were fueled by alarmist novels such as the superb adventure story written by Robert Erskine Childers, *The Riddle of the Sands: A Record of Secret Service* (London: Collins, 1953; first pub. 1903).

12. Corbett, *Some Principles of Maritime Strategy*, p. 241.

13. Ibid., p. 239.

14. See McLynn, *Invasion*.

15. See the discussion of the successful quasi-invasion of 1688 which ousted the francophile James II from the throne in Arthur Bryant, *Samuel Pepys: The Saviour of the Navy* (London: Panther 1985; first pub. 1938), ch. 12.

16. See Rose, *Indecisiveness of Modern War*, pp. 119–21.

17. Ibid., p. 121.

18. Jehuda L. Wallach, "The Sea Lion That Did Not Roar: Operation *Sea Lion* and Its Limitations," in John B. Hattendorf and Malcolm H. Murfett, eds., *The Limitations of Military Power: Essays Presented to Professor Norman H. Gibbs on His Eightieth Birthday* (Basingstoke [U.K.]: Macmillan, 1990), p. 199.

19. Friedrich-Karl von Plehwe, "Operation Sealion 1940," *RUSI Journal* 118, no. 1 (March 1973): 52.

20. Quoted in Rose, *Indecisiveness of Modern War*, p. 114.

21. Quoted in Glover, *Britain at Bay*, pp. 157–58. Keith's reply was dated October 21, 1803.

22. See Julian S. Corbett, *The Campaign of Trafalgar* (London: Longmans, Green, 1910), pp. 246–54, on the problems of Vice-Admiral William Cornwallis, Commander-in-Chief of the Channel Fleet.

23. See Glover, *Britain at Bay*.

24. Quoted in Arthur J. Marder, *From the Dreadnought to Scapa Flow, The Royal Navy in the Fisher Era, 1904–1919*, vol. 1: *The Road to War, 1904–1914* (London: Oxford University Press, 1961), p. 356. Emphasis in original.

25. The best modern treatment is Geoffrey Parker, *The Dutch Revolt* (London: Penguin, 1979; first pub. 1977).

26. For example, John J. Mearsheimer, "A Strategic Misstep: The Maritime Strategy and Deterrence in Europe," *International Security* 11, no. 2 (Fall 1986): 30–31.

27. Paul Kennedy, *The Rise and Fall of the Great Powers: Economic Change and Military Conflict from 1500 to 2000* (New York: Random House, 1987), p. 53.

28. Caspar W. Weinberger, "Our Vital Presence in Europe," *Washington Times,* January 27, 1987, p. 1-D.

29. See Rosinski, *Development of Naval Thought,* pp. 78–81; Marder, *Dreadnought to Scapa Flow,* 1:367–77.

30. On the Battle of the Heligoland Bight (August 28, 1914), which showed how slim the difference could be between a small tactical victory, a major tactical victory, and a tragedy with strategic significance, see Julian S. Corbett, *History of the Great War, Naval Operations* (London: Longmans, Green, 1920), 1: ch. 7; Geoffrey Bennett, *Naval Battles of the First World War* (London: B. T. Batsford, 1968), ch. 7; and James Goldrick, *The King's Ships Were at Sea: The War in the North Sea, August 1914–February 1915* (Annapolis, Md.: Naval Institute Press, 1984), ch. 5.

31. Marder, *Dreadnought to Scapa Flow,* 1:377.

32. Quoted in Corbett, *Campaign of Trafalgar,* pp. 248–69.

33. Wolfgang Wegener, *The Naval Strategy of the World War* (Annapolis, Md.: Naval Institute Press, 1989; first pub. 1929); and Rosinski, *Development of Naval Thought,* pp. 33–34, 63–68. Also of interest is Theodore Ropp, "Continental Doctrines of Sea Power," in Edward Mead Earle, ed., *Makers of Modern Strategy: Military Thought from Machiavelli to Hitler* (Princeton, N.J.: Princeton University Press, 1941), pp. 446–56.

34. John Terraine, *Business in Great Waters: The U-Boat Wars, 1916–1945* (London: Leo Cooper, 1989), p. 444.

35. G. J. Marcus, *A Naval History of England: I, The Formative Centuries* (Boston: Little, Brown, 1961), p. 241. Also see Gerald S. Graham, *Tides of Empire: Discursions on the Expansion of Britain Overseas* (Montreal: McGill-Queen's University Press, 1972), p. 27.

36. Paul Kennedy, *The Rise and Fall of British Naval Mastery* (New York: Charles Scribner's Sons, 1976), p. 131. J. Holland Rose advises that in the period 1793–1803, the "average yearly numbers of ships clearing from the port of London was 11,673, a number which jumps to 15,211 for the period 1803–1813." *Man and the Sea,* p. 230. Following the

Peace of Amiens, British merchant shipping losses were as follows: 1803—222; 1804—387; 1805—507; 1806—519; 1807—559; 1808—409; 1809—571; 1810—619; 1811—470; 1812—475; 1813—371; 1814—145. Statistics in H. W. Wilson, "The Command of the Sea, 1803–15," in A. W. Ward, G. W. Prothero, and Stanley Leathes, eds., *The Cambridge Modern History*, vol. 9: *Napoleon* (New York: Macmillan, 1934; first pub. 1906), p. 242; and Marcus, *Age of Nelson*, pp. 382, 404.

37. J. R. Jones, *Britain and the World, 1649–1815* (London: Fontana, 1980), p. 143.

38. See F. H. Hinsley et al., *History of the Second World War, British Intelligence in the Second World War*, vol. 2: *Its Influence on Strategy and Operations* (London: HMSO, 1981), pp. 747–52, appendix 19, "The Breaking of the U-Boat Enigma (Shark)."

39. Ibid., p. 569. Also see Terraine, *Business in Great Waters*, p. 545.

40. Bekker, *Hitler's Naval War*, p. xiii.

41. Winston S. Churchill, *The Second World War*, vol. 5: *Closing the Ring* (London: Guild Publishing, 1985; first pub. 1952), p. 6.

42. Terraine, *Business in Great Waters*, p. 610.

43. See Clark G. Reynolds, "The Continental Strategy of Imperial Japan," U.S. Naval Institute *Proceedings* 109, no. 8 (August 1983): 65–71; D. Clayton James, "American and Japanese Strategies in the Pacific War," in Peter Paret, ed., *Makers of Modern Strategy: From Machiavelli to the Nuclear Age* (Princeton, N.J.: Princeton University Press, 1986), particularly pp. 706–7; and Michael A. Barnhart, *Japan Prepares for Total War: The Search for Economic Security, 1919–1941* (Ithaca, N.Y.: Cornell University Press, 1987).

44. See H. P. Willmott: *Empires in the Balance: Japanese and Allied Pacific Strategies to April 1942* (Annapolis, Md.: Naval Institute Press, 1982), p. 88, and *Sea Warfare: Weapons, Tactics and Strategy* (Chichester [U.K.]: Antony Bird Publications, 1981), p. 67.

45. Eli F. Heckscher, *The Continental System: An Economic Interpretation* (Gloucester, Mass.: Peter Smith, 1964; first pub. 1922), remains essential. In addition, see J. Holland Rose: *Napoleonic Studies* (London: George Bell and Sons, 1906; first pub. 1904), pp. 166–203, 204–21, and "The Continental System, 1809–14," in Ward, Prothero, and Leathes, eds., *Cambridge Modern History*, 9:361–89. Marcus, *Age of Nelson*, pp. 295–30, is also useful.

46. Rose, *Napoleonic Studies*, p. 197.

47. See David Gates, *The Spanish Ulcer: A History of the Peninsular War* (New York: W. W. Norton, 1986), pp. 5–6.

CHAPTER 4:   THE AGE OF GALLEY WARFARE: SEA POWER IN THE
MEDITERRANEAN

1. The alleged limitations of, or errors in, Alfred Thayer Mahan's theory of
   sea power vis-à-vis the ancient, medieval, and early-modern Mediterra-
   nean are emphasized in John Francis Guilmartin, Jr., *Gunpowder and
   Galleys: Changing Technology and Mediterranean Warfare at Sea in the
   Sixteenth Century* (Cambridge: Cambridge University Press, 1974), and
   Chester G. Starr, *The Influence of Sea Power on Ancient History* (New
   York: Oxford University Press, 1989). Andrew C. Hess, *The Forgotten
   Frontier: A History of the Sixteenth-Century Ibero-African Frontier*
   (Chicago: University of Chicago Press, 1978), and John G. Prior, *Ge-
   ography, Technology and War; Studies in the Maritime History of the
   Mediterranean, 649–1571* (Cambridge: Cambridge University Press,
   1988), also are highly relevant.

2. See Prior, *Geography, Technology and War,* chs. 1–3.

3. For the thesis that a political-cultural necessity for legitimation by con-
   quest helped drive Persian statecraft, see Barry S. Strauss and Josiah
   Ober, *The Anatomy of Error: Ancient Military Disasters and Their
   Lessons for Modern Strategists* (New York: St. Martin's Press, 1990),
   pp. 21–22. For essential background (in addition to Herodotus, *The
   Persian Wars,* trans. George Rawlinson [New York: Modern Library,
   1942]), see G. Buchanan Gray, "The Foundation and Extension of the
   Persian Empire," in J. B. Bury, S. A. Cook, and F. E. Adcock, eds., *The
   Cambridge Ancient History,* vol. 4. *The Persian Empire and the West*
   (Cambridge: Cambridge University Press, 1964; first pub. 1926), pp.
   1–25.

4. On Persian statecraft, see Adda B. Bozeman, *Politics and Culture in
   International History* (Princeton, N.J.: Princeton University Press,
   1960), pp. 68–70.

5. See William Ledyard Rodgers, *Greek and Roman Naval Warfare: A
   Study of Strategy, Tactics, and Ship Design from Salamis (480 B.C.) to
   Actium (31 B.C.)* (Annapolis, Md.: Naval Institute Press, 1983; first pub.
   1937), ch. 3; and J. J. Morrison and J. F. Coates, *The Athenian Trireme:
   The History and Reconstruction of an Ancient Greek Warship* (Cam-
   bridge: Cambridge University Press, 1986), ch. 3.

6. Strauss and Ober, *Anatomy of Error,* p. 36.

7. On the history of the Peloponnesian War, see Thucydides, *The Peloponnesian War,* trans. Rex Warner (London: Cassell, 1962); Bernard W.
   Henderson, *The Great War between Athens and Sparta: A Companion
   to the Military History of Thucydides* (London: Macmillan, 1927);
   G. E. M. de Ste. Croix, *The Origins of the Peloponnesian War* (London:
   Gerald Duckworth, 1972); Donald Kagan's monumental four-volume
   treatment, *The Outbreak of the Peloponnesian War* (Ithaca, N.Y.: Cor-

nell University Press, 1969), *The Archidamian War* (1974), *The Peace of Nicias and the Sicilian Expedition* (1981), and *The Fall of the Athenian Empire* (1987), as well as his superb biography of Pericles, *Pericles of Athens and the Birth of Democracy: The Triumph of Vision in Leadership* (New York: Simon and Schuster, 1991); and D. M. Lewis et al., eds., *The Cambridge Ancient History*, vol. 5: *The Fifth Century* B.C. 2nd. ed. (Cambridge: Cambridge University Press, 1992). Strauss and Ober, *Anatomy of Error*, ch. 2, also is useful.

8. See M. I. Finley, *The Ancient Greeks* (London: Penguin, 1966; first pub. 1963), ch. 3; C. M. Bowra, *Periclean Athens* (London: Penguin, 1974; first pub. 1971); Russell Meiggs, *The Athenian Empire* (Oxford, Clarendon Press, 1972); P. J. Rhodes, *The Athenian Empire*, Greece and Rome, New Surveys in the Classics No. 17 (Oxford: Clarendon Press, 1985); Malcolm F. McGregor, *The Athenians and Their Empire* (Vancouver: University of British Columbia Press, 1987); and Anton Powell, *Athens and Sparta: Constructing Greek Political and Social History from 478* B.C. (London: Routledge, 1988).

9. Finley, *Ancient Greeks*, p. 85.

10. Thucydides, *Peloponnesian War*, pp. 62–63.

11. Kagan, *Outbreak of the Peloponnesian War*, p. 87.

12. "Pseudo-Zenophon," quoted in William Scott Ferguson, *Greek Imperialism* (Boston: Houghton Mifflin, 1913), p. 67.

13. On the possibility that a lasting victory was beyond the strength of Athens to secure, see Finley, *Ancient Greeks*, pp. 68–70. The strategic critique of Pericles in Henderson, *Great War between Athens and Sparta*, ch. 2, is interesting, given the 1914–18 context of his analysis.

14. See D. M. Lewis, "The Archmidamian War" in Lewis et al., eds., *Cambridge Ancient History*, vol 5, p. 382.

15. Ibid., pp. 431–32.

16. See Peter Garnsey, *Famine and Food Supply in the Graeco-Roman World: Responses to Risk and Crisis* (Cambridge: Cambridge University Press, 1988), ch. 8.

17. Kagan, *Fall of the Athenian Empire*, p. 423.

18. Thucydides, *Peloponnesian War*, p. 212.

19. J. F. C. Fuller, *The Decisive Battles of the Western World and Their Influence upon History*, vol. 1: *From the Earliest Times to the Battle of Lepanto* (London: Eyre and Spottiswoode, 1954), p. 74.

20. See Lionel Casson, *The Ancient Mariners: Seafarers and Sea Fighters of the Mediterranean in Ancient Times* (Princeton, N.J.: Princeton University Press, 1991), pp. 94–95; and A. Andrews, "The Peace of Nicias and

the Sicilian Expedition," in Lewis et al., eds., *Cambridge Ancient History*, vol. 5, pp. 458–59.

21. See Charles D. Hamilton, *Sparta's Bitter Victories: Politics and Diplomacy in the Corinthian War* (Ithaca, N.Y.: Cornell University Press, 1979). The Athenian strategic response to defeat in the Peloponnesian War is treated interestingly in Josiah Ober, *Fortress Attica: Defense of the Athenian Land Frontier, 404–322 B.C.* (Leiden [Neths.]: E. J. Brill, 1985).

22. See Brian Caven, *The Punic Wars* (London: Weidenfeld and Nicolson, 1980), p. 292 (also see p. 56).

23. Strauss and Ober, *Anatomy of Error*, ch. 5, is insightful.

24. William V. Harris, *War and Imperialism in Republican Rome, 327–70 B.C.* (Oxford: Clarendon Press, 1985; first pub. 1979), p. 53 (also see p. 254).

25. But see Chester G. Starr, *The Beginnings of Imperial Rome: Rome in the Mid-Republic* (Ann Arbor, Mich.: University of Michigan Press, 1980), ch. 5.

26. See Alfred Thayer Mahan, *The Influence of Sea Power upon History, 1660–1783* (Boston: Little, Brown, 1918; first pub. 1890), p. 49.

27. Caven, *Punic Wars*, p. 27.

28. On the building of the Roman fleet, see Rodgers, *Greek and Roman Naval Warfare*, pp. 270–74. Roman attitudes toward sea power are well described in F. E. Adcock, *The Roman Art of War Under the Republic* (Cambridge, Mass.: Harvard University Press, 1940), ch. 2.

29. Starr, *Influence of Sea Power on Ancient History*, p. 57.

30. C. R. M. F. Cruttwell, *The Role of British Strategy in the Great War* (Cambridge: Cambridge University Press, 1936), p. 3.

31. Mahan, *Influence of Sea Power upon History, 1660–1783*, pp. vi–vii, 14–21.

32. Rodgers, *Greek and Roman Naval Warfare*, pp. 320–21.

33. Caven, *Punic Wars*, p. 292. A helpful discussion of Roman war aims, with particular reference to Polybius's not always consistent claim that Rome was bidding for universal empire, is Harris, *War and Imperialism in Republican Rome, 327–70 B.C.*, pp. 107–17. See also M. I. Finley, *Ancient History: Evidence and Models* (New York: Viking Penguin, 1986; first pub. 1985), ch. 5.

34. The image of the fugitive is Mahan's. See *Influence of Sea Power upon History, 1660–1783*, p. 138.

35. See H. H. Scullard, *Scipio Africanus: Soldier and Politician* (Ithaca, N.Y.: Cornell University Press, 1970).

36. Chester G. Starr, Jr., *The Roman Imperial Navy, 31 B.C.–A.D. 324* (Westport, Conn.: Greenwood Press, 1975; first pub. 1941), p. 167.

37. See Peter Brown, *The World of Late Antiquity* (New York: Harcourt Brace Jovanovich, 1971), p. 200. Also see Introduction to J. R. Tanner, C. W. Previté-Orton, and Z. N. Brooke, eds., *The Cambridge Medieval History*, vol. 4: *The Eastern Roman Empire (717–1453)* (Cambridge: Cambridge University Press, 1927), pp. ix–x.

38. See Geza Perjes, *War and Society in East Central Europe*, vol. 26: *The Fall of the Medieval Kingdom of Hungary: Mohacs 1526–Buda 1541*. East European Monographs No. 255 (Highland Lakes, N.J.: Atlantic Research and Publications, 1989), p. 44.

39. On the strategic significance of Constantinople, see Edwin Pears, *The Fall of Constantinople: Being the Story of the Fourth Crusade* (New York: Harper and Brothers, 1886); Steven Runciman, *The Fall of Constantinople, 1453* (Cambridge: Cambridge University Press, 1965); Michael Maclagan, *The City of Constantinople* (New York: Frederick A. Praeger, 1968); H. St. L. B. Moss, "The Formulation of the East Roman Empire, 330–717," in J. M. Hussey, ed., *The Cambridge Medieval History*, vol. 4: *The Byzantine Empire*, pt. I. *Byzantium and Its Neighbours* (Cambridge: Cambridge University Press, 1966), pp. 6–10; and George Ostrogorsky, *History of the Byzantine State* (New Brunswick, N.J.: Rutgers University Press, 1969; first pub. 1940), p. 45.

40. For example, see Speros Vryonis, Jr., "The Byzantine Legacy and Ottoman Forms," in *Dumbarton Oaks Papers, Nos. 23 and 24* (Washington, D.C.: Dumbarton Oaks Center for Byzantine Studies, 1969–70), p. 275.

41. The maritime history of the empire is traced usefully in Archibald R. Lewis, *Naval Power and Trade in the Mediterranean, A.D. 500–1100* (Princeton, N.J.: Princeton University Press, 1951); and Archibald R. Lewis and Timothy J. Runyan, *European Naval and Maritime History, 300–1500* (Bloomington, Ind.: Indiana University Press, 1985), ch. 2.

42. For an outstanding, brief strategic analysis see C. E. Stevens, "Constantine the Great and the Christian Capital—A.D. 324–527," in Philip Whitting, ed., *Byzantium: An Introduction*, rev. ed. (Oxford: Basil Blackwell, 1981), esp. pp. 7, 10–13.

43. See Romilly Jenkins, *Byzantium: The Imperial Centuries, A.D. 610–1071* (Toronto: University of Toronto Press [for Medieval Academy of America], 1987; first pub. 1966), p. 312.

44. Hans Delbrück, *History of the Art of War Within the Framework of Political History*, vol. 3: *The Middle Ages* (Westport, Conn.: Greenwood Press, 1982), p. 195.

45. See Charles Oman, *A History of the Art of War in the Middle Ages,* vol. 2: *1278–1685* (London: Methuen, 1978; first pub. 1898), pp. 357–59; and Runciman, *Fall of Constantinople, 1453.*

46. See Lord Kinross, *The Ottoman Centuries: The Rise and Fall of the Turkish Empire* (New York: Morrow Quill Paperbacks, 1979; first pub. 1977), p. 100.

47. See Norman H. Baynes, *Byzantine Studies and Other Essays* (Westport, Conn.: Greenwood Press, 1974; first pub. 1955), pp. 248–60.

48. See Walter Emil Kaegi, Jr., *Byzantium and the Decline of Rome* (Princeton, N.J.: Princeton University Press, 1968).

49. Brown, *World of Late Antiquity,* pp. 200–202.

50. Valuable case studies are Donald M. Nicol, *Byzantium and Venice: A Study in Diplomatic and Cultural Relations* (Cambridge: Cambridge University Press, 1988); and Gerald W. Day, *Genoa's Response to Byzantium, 1155–1204: Commercial Expansion and Factionalism in a Medieval City* (Urbana, Ill.: University of Illinois Press, 1988).

51. Lewis and Runyan, *European Naval and Maritime History, 300–1500,* pp. 19–20.

52. Steven Runciman, *A History of the Crusades,* vol. 1: *The First Crusade and the Foundation of the Kingdom of Jerusalem* (Cambridge: Cambridge University Press, 1951), p. 20.

53. See Bozeman's superb brief analysis of Byzantine diplomacy in *Politics and Culture in International History,* pp. 326–40. Also see the "diplomacy" entry in Alexander P. Kazhdan, ed., *The Oxford Dictionary of Byzantium,* vol. 1 (New York: Oxford University Press, 1991), pp. 634–635.

54. See Philip K. Hitti, *History of the Arabs: From the Earliest Times to the Present* (New York: St. Martin's Press, 1970; first pub. 1937), ch. 18. See also William Ledyard Rodgers, *Naval Warfare Under Oars, 4th to 16th Centuries: A Study of Strategy, Tactics and Ship Design* (Annapolis, Md.: Naval Institute Press, 1986; first pub. 1940), ch. 2.

55. This theme is central to Prior, *Geography, Technology and War.*

56. See R. C. Smail, *Crusading Warfare, 1097–1193* (Cambridge: Cambridge University Press, 1972; first pub. 1956), p. 27. For the full story, see Runciman, *History of the Crusades;* and Kenneth M. Setton (series editor), *A History of the Crusades,* 5 vols. (Madison, Wis.: University of Wisconsin Press, 1969–85).

57. Speros Vryonis, Jr., *The Decline of Medieval Hellenism in Asia Minor and the Process of Islamization from the Eleventh through the Fifteenth Century* (Berkeley: University of California Press, 1971), is the standard treatment.

58. E. W. Brooks, "The Struggle with the Saracens (717–867)," in Tanner, Previté-Orton, and Brooke, eds., *Cambridge Medieval History,* 4:118–119.

59. See Jenkins, *Byzantium,* p. 235.

60. An outstanding study of the radically shifting security condition of the empire in the eleventh and twelfth centuries is Michael Angold, *The Byzantine Empire, 1025–1204: A Political History* (London: Longmans, 1984). Also see Nicol, *Byzantium and Venice.*

61. See Lewis and Runyan, *European Naval and Maritime History, 300–1500,* pp. 36–39.

62. Warren Treadgold, *The Byzantine Revival, 780–842* (Stanford, Cal.: Stanford University Press, 1988), p. 260.

63. See Prior, *Geography, Technology and War,* ch. 7.

64. For the course of Venetian history, I have relied upon Frederic C. Lane, *Venice: A Maritime Republic* (Baltimore: Johns Hopkins University Press, 1973); M. E. Mallett and J. R. Hale, *The Military Organization of a Renaissance State: Venice c. 1400 to 1617* (Cambridge: Cambridge University Press, 1984); William H. McNeill, *Venice: The Hinge of Europe, 1081–1797* (Chicago: University of Chicago Press, 1986; first pub. 1974); Nicol, *Byzantium and Venice;* and Louise Buenger Robbert, "Venice and the Crusades", in Norman P. Zacour and Harry W. Hazard (Kenneth M. Setton, rev. ed.), *A History of the Crusades* vol. 5: *The Impact of the Crusades on the Near East* (Madison, Wis.: University of Wisconsin Press, 1985), pp. 379–651. Frederic C. Lane, *Venice and History: The Collected Papers of Frederic C. Lane* (Baltimore: Johns Hopkins Press, 1966), also is valuable, as are the popular histories: John Julius Norwich, *A History of Venice* (New York: Alfred A. Knopf, 1982), and Jan Morris, *The Venetian Empire: A Sea Voyage* (London: Penguin, 1990; first pub. 1980).

65. The population was recorded by census to have peaked at 168,000 in 1563. McNeill, *Venice,* p. 132.

66. Venetian statecraft is described well in Bozeman, *Politics and Culture in International History,* pp. 457–77.

67. Lane, *Venice,* p. 27.

68. Ibid., p. 235.

69. See R. Cessi, "Venice to the Eve of the Fourth Crusade," in Hussey, ed., *Cambridge Medieval History,* vol. 4, pt. 1, pp. 288–89.

70. Lane, *Venice,* pp. 42–43; and D. M. Nicol, "The Fourth Crusade and the Greek and Latin Empires, 1204–61," in Hussey, ed., *Cambridge Medieval History,* vol. 4, pt. 1, pp. 288–89.

71. Lane, *Venice,* p. 229.

CHAPTER 5:   SEA POWER IN THE AGE OF SAIL

1. M. S. Anderson, "Eighteenth-Century Theories of the Balance of Power," in Ragnhild Hatton and M. S. Anderson, eds., *Studies in Diplomatic History: Essays in Memory of David Bayne Horn* (London: Longman, 1970), p. 196.

2. R. B. Wernham, "Elizabethan War Aims and Strategy," in S. T. Bindoff, J. Hurstfield, and C. H. Williams, eds., *Elizabethan Government and Society: Essays Presented to Sir John Neale* (London: Athlone Press, 1961), p. 345.

3. G. J. Marcus, *A Naval History of England: I, The Formative Centuries* (Boston: Little, Brown, 1961), p. 68.

4. See Kenneth R. Andrews: *Elizabethan Privateering* (Cambridge: Cambridge University Press, 1964), and *Trade, Plunder and Settlement: Maritime Expertise and the Genesis of the British Empire, 1480–1630* (Cambridge: Cambridge University Press, 1984), ch. 6.

5. Colin Martin and Geoffrey Parker, *The Spanish Armada* (London: Hamish Hamilton, 1988), p. 84.

6. See Felipe Fernandez-Armesto, *The Spanish Armada: The Experience of War in 1588* (Oxford: Oxford University Press, 1989), p. 88.

7. See Geoffrey Parker, *The Army of Flanders and the Spanish Road, 1567–1659: The Logistics of Spanish Victory and Defeat in the Low Countries' Wars* (Cambridge: Cambridge University Press, 1972), p. 57.

8. Marcus, *Naval History of England, I,* pp. 70–71.

9. Parker, *Army of Flanders,* p. 77.

10. For example, ibid., p. 250.

11. Fernandez-Armesto, *Spanish Armada,* p. 80.

12. See J. H. Parry, *The Spanish Seaborne Empire* (London: Hutchinson, 1966), pp. 133–35.

13. A particularly fine treatment is Julian S. Corbett, *Drake and the Tudor Navy* (Aldershot [U.K.]: Temple Smith, 1988; first pub. 1898), 2:chs. 1–2.

14. Parry, *Spanish Seaborne Empire,* is indispensable (for the post-Armada maritime defense *system*, see esp. pp. 256–57). J. H. Elliott, *Imperial Spain, 1469–1716* (London: Penguin, 1970; first pub. 1963); and John Lynch, *Spain under the Habsburgs,* 2 vols. (New York: New York University Press, 1984; first pub. 1964–1969), also are excellent.

15. Alberto Coll, "England and Spain, 1567–1604," in Colin S. Gray and

Roger W. Barnett, eds., *Seapower and Strategy* (Annapolis, Md.: Naval Institute Press, 1989), p. 155.

16. Fernandez-Armesto, *Spanish Armada,* p. 273.

17. See Geoffrey Parker's speculative essay, "If the Armada Had Landed," in Parker, *Spain and the Netherlands, 1559–1659: Ten Studies* (London: Fontana, 1990; first pub. 1979), pp. 135–47. A variant of the essay is in Martin and Parker, *Spanish Armada,* pp. 265–77.

18. See Marcus, *Naval History of England, I,* p. 16. But see also the discussion of "The Birth of the Royal Navy," in W. L. Warren, *King John* (London: Eyre Methuen, 1978; first pub. 1961), pp. 120–25; as well as the excellent treatment of naval issues in Christopher Allmand, *The Hundred Years War: England and France at War c. 1300–c. 1450* (Cambridge: Cambridge University Press, 1988), pp. 82–90.

19. See Paul Kennedy, *The Rise and Fall of the Great Powers: Economic Change and Military Conflict from 1500 to 2000* (New York: Random House, 1987), ch. 2. Also relevant are R. A. Stradling, *Europe and the Decline of Spain: A Study of the Spanish System, 1580–1720* (London: George Allen and Unwin, 1981); and J. H. Elliott's masterpiece, *The Count-Duke of Olivares: The Statesman in an Age of Decline* (New Haven, Conn.: Yale University Press, 1986).

20. See Fernandez-Armesto, *Spanish Armada,* pp. 74–80.

21. See Wallace T. MacCaffrey, *Queen Elizabeth and the Making of Policy, 1572–1588* (Princeton, N.J.: Princeton University Press, 1981), ch. 6.

22. Herbert Richmond, *Statesmen and Sea Power* (Oxford: Clarendon Press, 1946), p. 19. For a different view, less critical of Elizabeth, see Stephen Roskill, *The Strategy of Sea Power: Its Development and Application* (London: Collins, 1962), pp. 29–32; Marcus, *Naval History of England, I,* pp. 113–22; and Paul Kennedy, *The Rise and Fall of British Naval Mastery* (New York: Charles Scribner's Sons, 1976), pp. 32–35.

23. Corbett, *Drake and the Tudor Navy,* 1:ix.

24. M. Oppenheim, *A History of the Administration of the Royal Navy and of Merchant Shipping in Relation to the Navy: From 1509 to 1660 with an Introduction Treating of the Preceding Period* (Hamden, Conn.: Shoe String Press, 1961; first pub. 1896), p. 115.

25. R. B. Wernham, "Elizabethan War Aims and Strategy," *Before the Armada: The Growth of English Foreign Policy, 1485–1588* (London: Jonathan Cape, 1966), *The Making of Elizabethan Foreign Policy, 1558–1603* (Berkeley: University of California Press, 1980), and *After the Armada: Elizabethan England and the Struggle for Western Europe, 1588–1595* (Oxford: Clarendon Press, 1984).

26. For example, see Andrews, *Trade, Plunder and Settlement,* p. 236.

NOTES

27. Corbett, *Drake and the Tudor Navy,* 1: ix.

28. Gerald S. Graham, *Tides of Empire: Discursions on the Expansion of Britain Overseas* (Montreal: McGill–Queen's University Press, 1972), ch. 1. Also see J. Holland Rose, *Man and the Sea: Stages in Maritime and Human Progress* (Cambridge: W. Heffer and Sons, 1935), pp. 105–22; and Parry, *Spanish Seaborne Empire.*

29. See Wernham, *After the Armada,* p. 563.

30. Martin and Parker, *Spanish Armada,* p. 264.

31. Ibid., p. 277.

32. Ibid., pp. 88–89.

33. Note the ironical title to J. S. Bromley, "The Second Hundred Years War," in Bromley, *Corsairs and Navies, 1660–1760* (London: Hambledon Press, 1987), pp. 495–503. J. R. Jones, "Limitations of British sea power in the French Wars, 1689–1815," in Jeremy Black and Philip Woodfine, eds., *The British Navy and the Use of Naval Power in the Eighteenth Century* (Leicester [U.K.]: Leicester University Press, 1988), pp. 33–49, also implicitly is very critical of the concept of a Second Hundred Years' War. The opposite point of view may be located in David French, *The British Way in Warfare, 1688–2000* (London: Unwin Hyman, 1990), p. 122, and remains well represented by Arthur H. Buffington, *The Second Hundred Years War, 1689–1815* (Westport, Conn.: Greenwood Press, 1975; first pub. 1929).

34. Carl von Clausewitz, *On War,* trans. Michael Howard and Peter Paret (Princeton, N.J.: Princeton University Press, 1976; first pub. 1832), pp. 88–89.

35. Correlli Barnett, *Britain and Her Army, 1509–1970: A Military, Political and Social Survey* (London: Penguin, 1970), pp. 187–88.

36. See Bernard Capp, *Cromwell's Navy: The Fleet and the English Revolution, 1648–1660* (Oxford: Clarendon Press, 1989), p. 88.

37. As is made plain in Joseph Martray, *La Destruction de la marine française par la Révolution* (Paris: Editions France-Empire, 1988).

38. See Brian Lavery, *The Ship of the Line,* vol. 1: *The Development of the Battlefleet, 1650–1850* (Annapolis, Md.: Naval Institute Press, 1983), pp. 116–17. The best comprehensive description of the mature Royal Navy in the age of sail is Brian Lavery, *Nelson's Navy: The Ships, Men and Organization, 1793–1815* (Annapolis, Md.: Naval Institute Press, 1989).

39. See William Maltby, "Politics, Professionalism, and the Evolution of Sailing-Ship Tactics, 1650–1714," in John A. Lynn, ed., *Tools of War: Instruments, Ideas, and Institutions of Warfare, 1465–1871* (Urbana, Ill.: University of Illinois Press, 1990), p. 68; and C. Northcote Parkin-

son, *Britannia Rules: The Classic Age of Naval History, 1793–1815* (London: Book Club Associates, 1977), p. 13.

40. Anderson, "Eighteen-Century Theories of the Balance of Power," p. 183.

41. See the superb treatment in John Creswell, *British Admirals of the Eighteenth Century: Tactics in Battle* (London: George Allen and Unwin, 1972).

42. Daniel A. Baugh, *British Naval Administration in the Age of Walpole* (Princeton, N.J.: Princeton University Press, 1965), p. 2. Emphasis added.

43. See G. J. Marcus, *Heart of Oak: A Survey of British Sea Power in the Georgian Era* (London: Oxford University Press, 1975), ch. 9; and N. A. M. Rodger, *The Wooden World: An Anatomy of the Georgian Navy,* (Annapolis, Md.: Naval Institute Press, 1986), ch. 3.

44. John Creswell, *Naval Warfare: An Introductory Study,* 2d. ed. (London: Sampson, Low, Marston, 1942; first pub. 1936), pp. 5–6.

45. See Wayne P. Hughes, Jr., *Fleet Tactics: Theory and Practice* (Annapolis, Md.: Naval Institute Press, 1986), p. 52; and J. R. Jones, "The Dutch Navy and National Survival in the Seventeenth Century," *International History Review* 10, no. 1 (February 1988): 18–32.

46. Julian S. Corbett, *Fighting Instructions, 1530–1816* (London: Navy Records Society, 1905), pp. 99–104, "Commonwealth Orders, 1653."

47. See Julian S. Corbett, *England in the Mediterranean: A Study of the Rise and Influence of British Power within the Straits, 1603–1713,* 2d. ed. (London: Longmans, Green, 1917; first pub. 1903), 2:569–80, "Appendix: The Origin of the Line of Battle;" and Creswell, *British Admirals of the Eighteenth Century,* ch. 1.

48. Michael Lewis, *The Navy of Britain: A Historical Portrait* (London: George Allen and Unwin, 1948), p. 481. Emphasis in original.

49. Ibid.

50. Helmut Pemsel, *A History of War at Sea: An Atlas and Chronology of Conflict at Sea from Earliest Times to the Present* (Annapolis, Md.: Naval Institute Press, nd; first pub. 1975), p. 73.

51. A superior tactical analysis is Creswell, *British Admirals of the Eighteenth Century,* ch. 12.

52. See Hughes, *Fleet Tactics,* p. 52.

53. See Julian S. Corbett, *The Campaign of Trafalgar* (London: Longmans, Green, 1910). John Terraine, *Trafalgar* (New York: Mason/Charter, 1976), also has merit in a much overwritten field.

54. See French, *British Way in Warfare, 1688–2000,* p. xvi.

55. A point made forcefully in Jeremy Black, "Naval Power and British Foreign Policy in the Age of Pitt the Elder," in Black and Woodfine, eds., *British Navy and the Use of Naval Power in the Eighteenth Century,* p. 98.

56. Paul Fregosi, *Dreams of Empire: Napoleon and the First World War, 1792–1815* (London: Hutchinson, 1989), p. 51.

57. See W. Mediger, "Great Britain, Hanover and the Rise of Prussia," in Hatton and Anderson, eds., *Studies in Diplomatic History,* pp. 199–213.

58. John Brewer, *The Sinews of Power: War, Money and the English State, 1688–1783* (New York: Alfred A. Knopf, 1989), p. 114. See the graphical tracing of the "Growth of the National Debt, 1691–1785," p. 115.

59. The playwright Richard Sheridan, quoted in C. E. Callwell, *Military Operations and Maritime Preponderance: Their Relations and Interdependence* (Edinburgh: William Blackwood and Sons, 1905), pp. 177–78. Also see Michael Duffy, *Soldiers, Sugar and Seapower: The British Expeditions to the West Indies and the War against Revolutionary France* (Oxford: Clarendon Press, 1987), ch. 1.

60. Brewer, *Sinews of Power,* passim.

61. An excellent discussion is P. G. M. Dickson, "War Finance, 1689–1714," in J. S. Bromley, ed., *The New Cambridge Modern History,* vol. 6: *The Rise of Great Britain and Russia, 1688–1715/25* (Cambridge: Cambridge University Press, 1970), pp. 284–315.

62. Callwell, *Military Operations and Maritime Preponderance,* p. 63.

63. See David G. Chandler, *The Campaigns of Napoleon* (London: Weidenfeld and Nicolson, 1967), p. 601.

64. J. S. Bromley and A. N. Ryan, "Navies" in Bromley, ed., *New Cambridge Modern History,* 6:795.

65. Julian S. Corbett, *England in the Seven Years' War: A Study in Combined Strategy* (London: Longmans, Green, 1918; first pub. 1907) 1: ch. 1.

66. Ibid., p. 804.

67. Buffington, *Second Hundred Years War,* p. 40. He quoted the claim, implicitly with approval.

68. See C. Northcote Parkinson, *War in the Eastern Seas, 1793–1815* (London: George Allen and Unwin, 1954).

311

CHAPTER 6:   SEA POWER IN THE FIRST WORLD WAR

1. By far the most persuasive treatment, amid a huge literature, is Marc Trachtenberg, "The Coming of the First World War: A Reassessment," in Trachtenberg, *History and Strategy* (Princeton, N.J.: Princeton University Press, 1991), pp. 47–99. Also useful are the essays by Samuel R. Williamson, Jr. ("The Origins of World War I") and Charles S. Maier ("Wargames: 1914–1919") in Robert I. Rotberg and Theodore K. Rabb, eds., *The Origin and Prevention of Major Wars* (Cambridge: Cambridge University Press, 1989), pp. 225–48, 249–79 respectively; H. W. Koch, ed., *The Origins of the First World War: Great Power Rivalry and German War Aims*, 2d ed. (London: Macmillan, 1984); James Joll, *The Origins of the First World War* (London: Longman, 1984); and A. Lentin, *Lloyd George,Woodrow Wilson and the Guilt of Germany: An Essay in the Pre-History of Appeasement* (Baton Rouge: Louisiana State University Press, 1985; first pub. 1984). The landmark works of German revisionism are Fritz Fischer: *Germany's Aims in the First World War* (New York: W. W. Norton, 1967), and *War of Illusions: German Policies from 1911 to 1914* (New York: W. W. Norton, 1975).

2. B. H. Liddell-Hart, *Strategy: The Indirect Approach,* 4th ed. (London: Faber and Faber, 1967), p. 366.

3. Jutland has been a source of endless fascination. Helpful analyses at different levels of detail include: Julian S. Corbett, *History of the Great War, Naval Operations* (London: Longmans, Green, 1923), 3:chs. 16–21; C. R. M. F. Cruttwell, *A History of the Great War 1914–1918* (Oxford: Clarendon Press, 1934), chs. 18–19; Donald Macintyre, *Jutland* (London: Pan, 1960; first pub. 1957); Correlli Barnett, *The Swordbearers: Studies in Supreme Command in the First World War* (London: Eyre and Spottiswoode, 1963), pp. 107–97; H. H. Frost, *The Battle of Jutland* (Annapolis, Md.: United States Naval Institute, 1964; first pub. 1936); Arthur J. Marder, *From the Dreadnought to Scapa Flow, The Royal Navy in the Fisher Era, 1904–1919*, vol. 3: *Jutland and After (May 1916–December 1916)* (London: Oxford University Press, 1966); John Campbell, *Jutland: An Analysis of the Fighting* (Annapolis, Md.: Naval Institute Press, 1986); and John Keegan, *The Price of Admiralty: The Evolution of Naval Warfare* (New York: Viking, 1988), pp. 97–155.

4. Basil Liddell-Hart, *History of the First World War* (London: Pan, 1972; first pub. 1930), p. 460. Emphasis added.

5. Basil Liddell-Hart, *The British Way in Warfare* (London: Faber and Faber, 1932). Also see Michael Howard, *The Continental Commitment: The Dilemma of British Defence Policy in the Era of the Two World Wars* (London: Temple Smith, 1972), ch. 5; and Brian Bond, *British Military Policy between the Two World Wars* (Oxford: Clarendon Press, 1980), chs. 8–9.

6. See Alan Clark, *The Donkeys* (London: Hutchinson, 1961).

7. See James E. Edmonds, *History of the Great War, Military Operations, France and Belgium, 1914* (Woking [U.K.]: Shearer Publications, 1984; reprint of 1933 ed.), 1:1–14; and John Gooch, *The Plans of War: The General Staff and British Military Strategy, c. 1900–1916* (London: Routledge and Kegan Paul, 1974), ch. 9.

8. L. C. F. Turner, "The Significance of the Schlieffen Plan," in Paul Kennedy, ed., *The War Plans of the Great Powers, 1880–1914* (London: George Allen and Unwin, 1979), p. 200.

9. See Zara S. Steiner, *Britain and the Origins of the First World War* (London: Macmillan, 1977); Joll, *Origins of the First World War;* and Michael Brock, "Britain Enters the War," in R. J. W. Evans and Hartmut Pogge von Strandmann, eds., *The Coming of the First World War* (Oxford: Clarendon Press, 1988), pp. 145–78.

10. Howard, *Continental Commitment,* p. 45.

11. Quoted in ibid., p. 42.

12. See Michael Howard, "Men Against Fire: Expectations of War in 1914," *International Security* 9, no. 1 (Summer 1984):41–57.

13. P. M. Kennedy, "The Development of German Naval Operations Plans against England, 1896–1914," in Kennedy, ed., *War Plans of the Great Powers,* p. 189.

14. See Julian S. Corbett, *Some Principles of Maritime Strategy* (Annapolis, Md.: Naval Institute Press, 1988; first pub. 1911), pp. 183–208.

15. Gordon A. Craig, "The Political Leader as Strategist," in Peter Paret, ed., *Makers of Modern Strategy: From Machiavelli to the Nuclear Age* (Princeton, N.J.: Princeton University Press, 1986), p. 486. Bill Jackson and Dwin Bramall, *The Chiefs: The Story of the United Kingdom Chiefs of Staff* (London: Brassey's, 1992), chs. 3–4, is useful.

16. David French, "The Meaning of Attrition, 1914–1916," *English Historical Review* 103, no. 407 (April 1988): 385–405, is a superb overview of the debate on military strategy.

17. Michael Howard does not confuse causes and effects in his insightful essay, "The Edwardian Arms Race," in Howard, *The Lessons of History* (New Haven, Conn.: Yale University Press, 1991), pp. 81–96.

18. On just how shaky were the pillars of excellence for French fighting power, see Douglas Porch, *The March to the Marne: The French Army, 1871–1914* (Cambridge: Cambridge University Press, 1981).

19. See Samuel R. Williamson, *The Politics of Grand Strategy: Britain and France Prepare for War, 1904–1914* (Cambridge, Mass.: Harvard University Press, 1969), ch. 8.

20. James E. Edmonds, *History of the Great War, Military Operations, France and Belgium, 1914* (London: Macmillan, 1925), 2:465.

21. Quoted in Howard, *Continental Commitment,* p. 57. Howard proceeds to observe plausibly that "it was with that decision that the total commitment of British resources to the Western Front really began."

22. French, "Meaning of Attrition," p. 389. Also see David French, *British Strategy and War Aims, 1914–1916* (London: Allen and Unwin, 1986), particularly ch. 6.

23. French, "Meaning of Attrition," p. 389.

24. See Julian S. Corbett, *England in the Seven Years' War: A Study in Combined Strategy* (London: Longman, Green, 1918; first pub. 1907), 2:12–15.

25. See C. F. Aspinall-Oglander, *History of the Great War, Military Operations, Gallipoli,* 2 vols. (London: William Heinemann, 1929–32); C. E. Callwell, *The Dardanelles* (London: Constable, 1924); Winston S. Churchill, *The World Crisis,* 2 vols. (London: Odham's Press, 1938), 1:461–689, 2:750–931; Cruttwell, *History of the Great War,* pp. 204–7; Trumbull Higgins, *Winston Churchill and the Dardanelles: A Dialogue in Ends and Means* (Westport, Conn.: Greenwood Press, 1977; first pub. 1963); Alan Moorehead, *Gallipoli* (Annapolis, Md.: Nautical and Aviation Publishing Company of America, 1982; first pub. 1956); Robert Rhodes James, *Gallipoli* (London: Pan, 1984; first pub. 1965); and Eliot A. Cohen and John Gooch, *Military Misfortunes: The Anatomy of Failure in War* (New York: Free Press, 1990), ch. 6.

26. Frederick Maurice, *British Strategy: A Study of the Application of the Principles of War* (London: Constable, 1929), p. 78 (also see pp. 76–77).

27. The impact of the course of the war upon British politics is treated superbly in John Turner, *British Politics and the Great War: Coalition and Conflict, 1915–1918* (New Haven, Conn.: Yale University Press, 1992.

28. John Terraine, *Douglas Haig: The Educated Soldier* (London: Hutchinson, 1963), p. 72. Emphasis in original.

29. Ibid., pp. 72–73.

30. See Corbett, *England in the Seven Years' War,* 1: ch. 8.

31. See John Gooch, *The Prospect of War: Studies in British Defence Policy, 1847–1942* (London: Frank Cass, 1981), pp. 124–25.

32. See Norman Gibbs, "British Strategic Doctrine, 1918–1939," in Michael Howard, ed., *The Theory and Practice of War* (London: Cassell, 1965), particularly pp. 191–92, 210; and David French, *The British Way in Warfare, 1688–2000* (London: Unwin Hyman, 1990), pp. 232–33.

33. A point made appropriately in French, *British Way in Warfare, 1688–2000*, p. 51.

34. C. R. M. F. Cruttwell, *The Role of British Strategy in the Great War* (Cambridge: Cambridge University Press, 1936), p. 42. Emphasis added.

35. See James E. Edmonds, *History of the Great War, Military Operations, France and Belgium, 1916* (Woking [U.K.]: Shearer Publications, 1986; first pub. 1932), 1:4–10.

36. For an excellent biography see Richard Holmes, *The Little Field-Marshal, Sir John French* (London: Jonathan Cape, 1981).

37. First-class studies in English of the war on the Eastern Front are not plentiful, but prominent among their small number are: Winston S. Churchill, *The Unknown War: The Eastern Front* (New York: Charles Scribner's Sons, 1931); Norman Stone, *The Eastern Front, 1914–1917* (London: Hodder and Stoughton, 1975); and for a racy but still useful treatment of the Russian experience, W. Bruce Lincoln, *Passage Through Armageddon: The Russians in War and Revolution, 1914–1918* (New York: Simon and Schuster, 1986). Keith Neilson, *Strategy and Supply: The Anglo-Russian Alliance, 1914–17* (London: Allen and Unwin, 1984), also is relevant.

38. Edmonds, *Military Operations, France and Belgium, 1916*, 1:5.

39. See the contrasting judgments in Turner, "Significance of the Schlieffen Plan," p. 212; and Martin van Creveld, *Supplying War: Logistics from Wallenstein to Patton* (Cambridge: Cambridge University Press, 1977), p. 121.

40. See Larry H. Addington, *The Blitzkrieg Era and the German General Staff, 1865–1941* (New Brunswick, N.J.: Rutgers University Press, 1971), pp. 12–22; and Creveld, *Supplying War*, pp. 109–41.

41. See Martin van Creveld, *Command in War* (Cambridge, Mass.: Harvard University Press, 1985), pp. 148–55.

42. See Cruttwell, *History of the Great War*, ch. 9.

43. For a scalding commentary, see Barnett, *Swordbearers*, p. 195.

44. Michael Howard, "British Grand Strategy in World War I," in Paul Kennedy, ed., *Grand Strategies in War and Peace* (New Haven, Conn.: Yale University Press, 1991), p. 40.

45. For very different treatments of the Battle of the Somme, see Liddell-Hart, *History of the First World War*, pp. 231–53; John Terraine, *The First World War, 1914–1918* (London: Leo Cooper, 1983; first pub. 1965), pp. 114–23; and Tim Travers, *The Killing Ground: The British Army, the Western Front and the Emergence of Modern Warfare, 1900–1918* (London: Allen and Unwin, 1987), pt. 3.

46. See John Terraine, *Business in Great Waters: The U-Boat Wars, 1916–1945* (London: Leo Cooper, 1989), p. 55.

47. See Ernest Fayle, *History of The Great War, Seaborne Trade,* vol. 3: *The Period of Unrestricted Submarine Warfare* (London: John Murray, 1924), statistical diagrams 12–13. John Terraine: *White Heat: The New Warfare, 1914–18* (London: Sidgwick and Jackson, 1982), p. 260, and *Business in Great Waters,* pp. 85–92, also are useful.

48. Terraine, *First World War,* p. 156.

49. General Ludendorff, *My War Memories, 1914–1918,* 2d ed. (London: Hutchinson, n.d. [written in 1918–19]), 2:537.

50. See John Terraine, *To Win a War: 1918, the Year of Victory* (Garden City, N.Y.: Doubleday, 1981; first pub. 1978), p. 22. In addition to such modern studies as Timothy T. Lupfer, *The Dynamics of Doctrine: The Changes in German Tactical Doctrine During the First World War,* Leavenworth Papers No. 4 (Ft. Leavenworth, Ks.: Combat Studies Institute, U. S. Army Command and General Staff College, July 1981), and Bruce I. Gudmundsson, *Stormtroop Tactics: Innovation in the German Army, 1914–1918* (New York: Praeger, 1989), see the contemporary analyses: Wilhelm Balck, *Development of Tactics—World War* (Ft. Leavenworth, Ks.: General Service Schools Press, 1922), and Pascal M. H. Lucas, *The Evolution of Tactical Ideas in France and Germany During the War of 1914–1918* (Paris: Berger-Levrault, 1925; first pub. 1923). Also useful is G. C. Wynne, *If Germany Attacks: The Battle in Depth in the West* (Westport, Conn.: Greenwood Press, 1976; first pub. 1940).

51. See Georg Bruckmüller, *The German Artillery in the Breakthrough Battles of the World War* (Ft. Sill, Okla.: U.S. Army Field Artillery School, n.d.).

52. See James E. Edmonds, *History of the Great War, Military Operations, France and Belgium, 1918* (London: Macmillan, 1935), 1:chs. 7–18; and Martin Middlebrook, *The Kaiser's Battle, 21 March 1918: The First Day of the German Spring Offensive* (London: Penguin, 1983; first pub. 1978).

53. Churchill, *World Crisis, 1911–1918,* 2:915–16.

54. See Fischer, *Germany's Aims in the First World War,* ch. 15.

55. Cruttwell, *History of the Great War,* p. 338.

56. An excellent discussion of "The Rule of War of 1756" and related issues in their historical context is G. J. Marcus, *Heart of Oak: A Survey of British Sea Power in the Georgian Era* (London: Oxford University Press, 1975), ch. 4. Marcus writes: "What was in fact at issue were two conflicting interpretations of international law: for while the Dutch and certain others claimed that enemy goods in neutral ships were immune

from capture, the British maintained that enemy goods were lawful prize everywhere at sea" (p. 63).

57. Viscount Grey of Fallodon, *Twenty-Five Years, 1892–1916* (New York: Frederick A. Stokes, 1925), 2:107. Emphasis added.

58. Fayle, *Seaborne Trade,* 3:404.

59. C. Northcote Parkinson, *Britannia Rules: The Classic Age of Naval History, 1793–1815* (London: Book Club Associates, 1977), p. 155.

60. See French, *British Strategy and War Aims, 1914–1916,* pp. 45–46, 80–82; and David Stevenson, *The First World War and International Politics* (Oxford: Oxford University Press, 1988), pp. 124–26.

61. See Churchill, *World Crisis,* 2:930.

62. Quoted in Henry Newbolt, *History of the Great War, Naval Operations* (London: Longmans, Green, 1931), 5:207.

63. See Marder, *Dreadnought to Scapa Flow,* 3:166–75.

64. Barnett, *Swordbearers,* p. 125.

65. Quoted in Arthur J. Marder, *From the Dreadnought to Scapa Flow, The Royal Navy in the Fisher Era, 1904–1919,* vol. 5: *Victory and Aftermath (January 1918–June 1919)* (London: Oxford University Press, 1970), p. 298.

CHAPTER 7:   FROM WAR TO WAR: SEA POWER AND THE CRISIS OF 1940

1. See Albert Seaton, *The Russo-German War, 1941–45* (New York: Praeger, 1970), p. 586.

2. A point made abundantly clear in Kenneth J. Hagan, *This People's Navy: The Making of American Sea Power* (New York: Free Press, 1991).

3. See Charles Webster and Noble Frankland, *The Strategic Air Offensive Against Germany, 1939–1945,* vol. 1: *Preparation* (London: HMSO, 1961), p. 372.

4. See D. Clayton James, "American and Japanese Strategies in the Pacific War," in Peter Paret, ed., *Makers of Modern Strategy: From Machiavelli to the Nuclear Age* (Princeton, N. J.: Princeton University Press, 1986), p. 712.

5. Robert Graves and Alan Hodge, *The Long Week-End: A Social History of Great Britain, 1918–1939* (London: Faber and Faber, 1941).

6. Napoleonic Wars—C. R. M. F. Cruttwell, *The Role of British Strategy in the Great War* (Cambridge: Cambridge University Press, 1936), p. 2; First World War—John Terraine, *The First World War, 1914–18* (Lon-

don: Leo Cooper, 1985; first pub. 1965), p. 198; Second World War—R. Ernest Dupuy and Trevor N. Dupuy, *The Encyclopedia of Military History: from 3500 B.C. to the Present,* 2d rev. ed. (New York: Harper & Row, 1986), p. 1198.

7. C. Ernest Fayle, *History of the Great War, Seaborne Trade,* vol. 3: *The Period of Unrestricted Submarine Warfare* (London: John Murray, 1924), p. 458. Emphasis added.

8. John Gooch, *The Prospect of War: Studies in British Defence Policy, 1847–1942* (London: Frank Cass, 1981), p. 142.

9. On the intensity of French pressure on Britain for a continental commitment, see N. H. Gibbs, *History of the Second World War, Grand Strategy,* vol. 1: *Rearmament Policy* (London: HMSO, 1976), pp. 492–502.

10. See ibid., p. 504, for the determined way in which the Chiefs of Staff chose to evade this issue in the winter of 1938–39.

11. Ibid., pp. 501–2.

12. Ibid., pp. 657–67.

13. David French, *The British Way in Warfare, 1688–2000* (London: Unwin Hyman, 1990), p. 194.

14. See Williamson Murray, *The Change in the European Balance of Power, 1938–1939: The Path to Ruin* (Princeton, N.J.: Princeton University Press, 1984).

15. The outstanding treatments of the fighting on the Western Front in 1940 are Gregory Blaxland, *Destination Dunkirk: The Story of Gort's Army* (London: The Military Book Society, 1973); and Robert Allan Doughty, *The Breaking Point: Sedan and the Fall of France* (Hamden, Conn.: Archon Books, 1990). For a more sweeping view, Telford Taylor, *The March of Conquest: The German Victories in Western Europe, 1940* (Baltimore: The Nautical and Aviation Publishing Company of America, 1991; first pub. 1958), has worn remarkably well.

16. A theme well argued in Paul Kennedy, "Why Did the British Empire Last So Long," in Kennedy, *Strategy and Diplomacy, 1870–1945: Eight Studies* (London: George Allen and Unwin, 1983), pp. 197–218. Aaron L. Friedberg, *The Weary Titan: Britain and the Experience of Relative Decline, 1895–1905* (Princeton, N.J.: Princeton University Press, 1988), also is useful.

17. Christopher Hall, *Britain, America and Arms Control, 1921–37* (New York: St. Martin's Press, 1987), needs to be balanced by Robert Gordon Kaufman, *Arms Control During the Pre-Nuclear Era: The United States and Naval Limitation Between the Two World Wars* (New York: Columbia University Press, 1990). The scene is well set in John Robert

Ferris, *Men, Money, and Diplomacy: The Evolution of British Strategic Policy, 1919–26* (Ithaca, N.Y.: Cornell University Press, 1989).

18. Quoted in Gibbs, *Grand Strategy*, 1:256. A first-rate extended treatment of British dilemmas is Anthony Clayton, *The British Empire as a Superpower, 1919–39* (Athens, Ga.: University of Georgia Press, 1986).

19. See Wesley K. Wark, *The Ultimate Enemy: British Intelligence and Nazi Germany, 1933–1939* (Ithaca, N.Y.: Cornell University Press, 1985), particularly pp. 65–69; and Paul Kennedy, "British 'Net Assessment' and the Coming of the Second World War," in Williamson Murray and Allan R. Millett, eds., *Calculations: Net Assessment and the Coming of World War II* (New York: Free Press, 1992), pp. 19–59.

20. See W. N. Medlicott, *History of the Second World War: The Economic Blockade* (London: HMSO, 1959), 2:631.

21. On German intentions toward the Soviet Union, see Norman Rich, *Hitler's War Aims,* **vol. 1:** *Ideology, The Nazi State, and the Course of Expansion* (New York: W. W. Norton, 1973), ch. 18, and vol. 2: *The Establishment of the New Order* (New York: W. W. Norton, 1976), ch. 11.

22. The occupation of Norway had been a principal recommendation of naval theorist Vice-Admiral Wolfgang Wegener, writing in the 1920s. See Wegener, *The Naval Strategy of the World War* (Annapolis, Md.: Naval Institute Press, 1989; first pub. 1929), pp. 26, 73–76, 98; and Herbert Rosinski, *The Development of Naval Thought* (Newport, R.I.: Naval War College Press, 1977), pp. 59–63.

23. François Kersaudy, *Norway 1940* (London: Collins, 1990; first pub. 1987), is superb.

24. Winston S. Churchill, *The Second World War,* vol. 1: *The Gathering Storm* (London: Guild Publishing, 1985; first pub. 1948), p. 592. Also see the tally of losses and the commentary in Correlli Barnett, *Engage the Enemy More Closely: The Royal Navy in the Second World War* (New York: W. W. Norton, 1991), pp. 138–39.

25. Peace terms were debated heatedly in Cabinet on May 26–28, 1940. See David Reynolds, *The Creation of the Anglo-American Alliance, 1937–1941: A Study in Competitive Co-operation* (Chapel Hill, N.C.: University of North Carolina Press, 1982; first pub. 1981), pp. 103–8; and Christopher Hill, *Cabinet Decisions on Foreign Policy: The British Experience, October 1938–June 1941* (Cambridge: Cambridge University Press, 1991), ch. 6.

26. Quoted in Michael Howard, *The Continental Commitment: The Dilemma of British Defence Policy in the Era of the Two World Wars* (London: Temple Smith, 1972), p. 143.

CHAPTER 8: SEA POWER IN THE SECOND WORLD WAR

1. See F. H. Hinsley et al., *History of the Second World War, British Intelligence in the Second World War*, vol. 1: *Its Influence on Strategy and Operations* (London: HMSO, 1979), ch. 14.

2. See Hinsley et al., *British Intelligence in the Second World War*, vol. 2: (1981), p. 169; John Terraine, *Business in Great Waters: The U-Boat Wars, 1916–1945* (London: Leo Cooper, 1989), ch. 4; and Marc Milner, "The Battle of the Atlantic," *Journal of Strategic Studies* 13, no. 1 (March 1990): 45–66.

3. Charles Burdick and Hans-Adolf Jacobson, *The Halder War Diary, 1939–1942* (Novato, Cal.: Presidio Press, 1988), p. 227, is telling on this point.

4. See David Irving, *Hitler's War, 1939–1942* (London: Macmillan, 1983; first pub. 1977), p. 142.

5. See Gerhard Schreiber, "The Mediterranean in Hitler's Strategy in 1940. 'Programme' and Military Planning," in Wilhelm Deist, ed., *The German Military in the Age of Total War* (Dover, N.H.: Berg Publishers, 1985), pp. 240–81.

6. Quoted in F. H. Hinsley, *Hitler's Strategy* (Cambridge: Cambridge University Press, 1951), p. 37.

7. Telford Taylor, *The Breaking Wave: The Second World War in the Summer of 1940* (New York: Simon and Schuster, 1967), p. 43. Emphasis in original.

8. John Keegan, *The Second World War* (London: Hutchinson, 1989), p. 219.

9. For example, John Ellis, *Brute Force: Allied Strategy and Tactics in the Second World War* (New York: Viking, 1990), overstates a good case.

10. Quoted in Norman Rich, *Hitler's War Aims*, vol. 1: *Ideology, The Nazi State, and the Course of Expansion* (New York: W. W. Norton, 1973), p. 246.

11. See Robert W. Coakley and Richard M. Leighton, *United States Army in World War II: The War Department, Global Logistics and Strategy, 1943–1945* (Washington, D.C.: GPO, 1968), pp. 10–24 and passim.

12. Roland G. Ruppenthal, *United States Army in World War II: The European Theater of Operations, Logistical Support of the Armies*, vol. 1: *May 1941–September 1944* (Washington, D.C.: GPO, 1953), pp. 268–82.

13. C. R. M. F. Cruttwell, *The Role of British Strategy in the Great War* (Cambridge: Cambridge University Press, 1936), p. 3.

14. See David M. Glantz, *The Role of Intelligence in Soviet Military Strategy in World War II* (Novato, Cal.: Presidio Press, 1990), pp. 221–27.

15. Julian S. Corbett, *England in the Seven Years' War: A Study in Combined Strategy* (London: Longmans, Green, 1918; first pub. 1907), 1:7.

16. Hew Strachan, *European Armies and the Conduct of War* (London: George Allen and Unwin, 1983), p. 176.

17. I am indebted to Correlli Barnett, *Engage the Enemy More Closely: The Royal Navy in the Second World War* (New York: W. W. Norton, 1991), p. 440.

18. George W. Baer, "U.S. Naval Strategy, 1890–1945," *Naval War College Review* 44, no. 1 (Winter 1991):21.

19. Gordon A. Harrison, *United States Army in World War II: The European Theater of Operations, Cross-Channel Attack* (Washington, D.C.: GPO, 1951), appendix G, p. 671.

20. Reprinted as appendix D in ibid., p. 464. Emphasis added.

21. Albert Seaton, *The Russo-German War, 1941–45* (New York: Praeger, 1970), p. 396.

22. See T. H. Vail Motter, *United States Army in World War II: The Middle East Theater, the Persian Corridor and Aid to Russia* (Washington, D.C.: GPO, 1985; first pub. 1952), appendix A, pp. 481–83.

23. Seaton, *Russo-German War*, p. 589. See the careful balanced analysis in Hubert P. van Tuyll, *Feeding the Bear: American Aid to the Soviet Union, 1941–1945* (Westport, Conn.: Greenwood Press, 1989).

24. See Larry H. Addington, *The Blitzkrieg Era and the German General Staff, 1865–1941* (New Brunswick, N.J.: Rutgers University Press, 1971), p. 215.

25. Seaton, *Russo-German War*, pp. 589–90.

26. See Williamson Murray, *Luftwaffe* (Baltimore: Nautical and Aviation Publishing Company of America, 1985; first pub. 1983), pp. 153, 177, 232.

27. See Kent Roberts Greenfield, *American Strategy in World War II: A Reconsideration* (Baltimore: Johns Hopkins Press, 1963), pp. 24–28.

28. Mark Skinner Watson, *United States Army in World War II: The War Department, Chief of Staff, Prewar Plans and Preparations* (Washington, D.C.: GPO, 1979; first pub. 1950), p. 344.

29. Greenfield, *American Strategy in World War II*, p. 68.

30. Michael Howard, *The Mediterranean Strategy in the Second World War* (London: Weidenfeld and Nicolson, 1968), p. 23. Emphasis in original.

31. See Ronald H. Spector, *Eagle Against the Sun: The American War with Japan* (New York: Free Press, 1985), p. 543.

32. See Corbett, *England in the Seven Years' War*, 1:148, for quotations from Frederick the Great's proposal for the coordination of continental and peripheral, or raiding, strategies.

33. Maurice Matloff, "Allied Strategy in Europe, 1939–1945," in Peter Paret, ed., *Makers of Modern Strategy: From Machiavelli to the Nuclear Age* (Princeton, N.J.: Princeton University Press, 1986), p. 691.

34. John Ellis, *Cassino, The Hollow Victory: The Battle for Rome, January–June 1944* (New York: McGraw-Hill, 1985), p. 2.

35. See Dan van der Vat, *The Pacific Campaign, World War II: The U.S.-Japanese Naval War, 1941–1945* (New York: Simon and Schuster, 1991), p. 81.

36. On the approach of the Pacific War, see Herbert Feis, *The Road to Pearl Harbor: The Coming of the War Between the United States and Japan* (Princeton, N.J.: Princeton University Press, 1950); Louis Morton, *United States Army in World War II: The War in the Pacific, Strategy and Command: The First Two Years* (Washington, D.C.: GPO, 1962), chs. 2, 4–5; Nobutaka Ike, ed., *Japan's Decision for War: Records of the 1941 Policy Conferences* (Stanford, Cal.: Stanford University Press, 1967); Jonathan Utley, *Going to War with Japan, 1937–1941* (Knoxville, Tenn.: University of Tennessee Press, 1985); Akira Iriye, *The Origins of the Second World War in Asia and the Pacific* (London: Longman, 1987); Michael A. Barnhard, *Japan Prepares for Total War: The Search for Economic Security, 1919–1941* (Ithaca, N.Y.: Cornell University Press, 1987); and Scott D. Sagan, "The Origins of the Pacific War," *Journal of Interdisciplinary History* 18, no. 4 (Spring 1988), pp. 893–922.

37. Barnhart, *Japan Prepares for Total War*, pp. 240–41. The debate in the early summer of 1941 is presented admirably in Alvin D. Coox, "Japanese Net Assessment in the Era Before Pearl Harbor," in Williamson Murray and Allen R. Millett, eds., *Calculations: Net Assessment and the Coming of World War II* (New York: Free Press, 1992), pp. 258–98.

38. Sagan, "Origins of the Pacific War," pp. 905–6. The freezing of Japanese assets was in response to the Japanese military occupation of virtually the whole of (Vichy-) French Indochina.

39. Admiral Nagano Osami, Chief of Staff of the Imperial Navy, quoted in ibid., p. 917.

40. See Morton, *Strategy and Command: The First Two Years*, pp. 24–44; Michael Vlahos, "Wargaming, an Enforcer of Strategic Realism: 1919–1942," *Naval War College Review* 39, no. 2 (March–April 1986); 7–22;

and Edward S. Miller, *War Plan Orange: The U.S. Strategy to Defeat Japan* (Annapolis, Md.: Naval Institute Press, 1991).

41. For example, Spector, *Eagle Against the Sun,* pp. 245–46, 560.

42. See the outstanding essay by Eliot A. Cohen, "Churchill and Coalition Strategy in World War II," in Paul Kennedy, ed., *Grand Strategies in War and Peace* (New Haven, Conn.: Yale University Press, 1991), pp. 43–67.

43. For a penetrating analysis of a classic case in point, Williamson Murray, "Attrition and the Luftwaffe," *Air University Review* 34, no. 3 (March–April 1983): 66–77.

44. For the effect of Nazi ideology on the German Army in the field, see the pioneering work by Omer Bartov, *Hitler's Army: Soldiers, Nazis, and War in the Third Reich* (New York: Oxford University Press, 1991).

45. John W. Dower, *War Without Mercy: Race and Power in the Pacific War* (New York: Pantheon Books, 1986), is a landmark study.

CHAPTER 9: THE COLD WAR: SEA POWER IN THE NUCLEAR AGE

1. Greg Herken, *Counsels of War* (New York: Alfred A. Knopf, 1985), p. 5.

2. Bernard Brodie: *Sea Power in the Machine Age* (Princeton, N.J.: Princeton University Press, 1941), and *A Layman's Guide to Naval Strategy* (Princeton, N.J.: Princeton University Press, 1942).

3. Alfred Thayer Mahan, *The Influence of Sea Power upon History, 1660–1783* (Boston: Little, Brown, 1918; first pub. 1890), p. 22.

4. Edward N. Luttwak, "An Emerging Postnuclear Era?" *Washington Quarterly* 11, no. 1 (Winter 1988): 5–15, is powerfully suggestive.

5. See David Alan Rosenberg, "The Origins of Overkill: Nuclear Weapons and American Strategy, 1945–1960," *International Security* 7, no. 4 (Spring 1983): 3–71.

6. See Christopher Donnelly, *Red Banner: The Soviet Military System in Peace and War* (Alexandria, Va.: Jane's Publishing, 1988), ch. 13; Gary L. Guertner, "Flexible Response: Soviet Style," *Journal of Soviet Military Studies* 1, no. 4 (December 1988): 417–50; and Steven R. Covington, "The Soviet Military: Prospects for Change," *Journal of Soviet Military Studies* 3, no. 2 (June 1989): 241–65.

7. Paul K. Huth, *Extended Deterrence and the Prevention of War* (New Haven, Conn.: Yale University Press, 1988), is an excellent scholarly treatment.

8. See Robert Jervis, *The Meaning of the Nuclear Revolution: Statecraft and the Prospect of Armageddon* (Ithaca, N.Y.: Cornell University Press, 1989).

9. See David N. Schwartz, *NATO's Nuclear Dilemmas* (Washington, D.C.: Brookings Institution, 1983).

10. See Samuel P. Huntington, "National Policy and the Transoceanic Navy," U.S. Naval Institute *Proceedings* 80, no. 5 (May 1954): 483–93; and Michael A. Palmer, *Origins of the Maritime Strategy: American Naval Strategy in the First Postwar Decade,* Contributions to Naval History No. 1 (Washington, D.C.: Naval Historical Center, Department of the Navy, 1988).

11. For a geopolitical analysis, see Colin S. Gray, *The Geopolitics of Super Power* (Lexington, Ky.: University Press of Kentucky, 1988).

12. W. D. Puleston, *The Influence of Sea Power in World War II* (New Haven, Conn.: Yale University Press, 1947), p. 16.

13. A point properly emphasized in Joel J. Sokolsky, *Seapower in the Nuclear Age: The United States Navy and NATO, 1949–80* (Annapolis, Md.: Naval Institute Press, 1991).

14. See James D. Watkins et al., *The Maritime Strategy,* U.S. Naval Institute *Proceedings, Supplement* (January 1986); John B. Hattendorf, "The Evolution of the Maritime Strategy," *Naval War College Review* 41, no. 3 (Summer 1988): 7–28; Norman Friedman, *The U.S. Maritime Strategy* (London: Jane's Publishing, 1988); and Frederick H. Hartmann, *Naval Renaissance: The U.S. Navy in the 1980's* (Annapolis, Md.: Naval Institute Press, 1990).

15. See Paul H. Nitze and Leonard Sullivan, Jr., *Securing the Seas: The Soviet Naval Challenge and Western Alliance Options* (Boulder, Colo.: Westview Press, 1979), ch. 13, and Eric Grove, *Maritime Strategy and European Security* (London: Brassey's [U.K.]: 1990). Malcolm J. Kennedy and Michael J. O'Connor, eds., *Safety by Sea* (Lanham, Md.: University Press of America, 1990), provides a Pacific perspective.

16. See the close scrutiny provided in Donald C. F. Daniel, "The Soviet Navy and Tactical Nuclear War at Sea," *Survival* 29, no. 4 (July–August 1987): 318–35.

CHAPTER 10: LEVERAGE FOR VICTORY

1. See Colin S. Gray, *Maritime Power and Space Strategy* (Fairfax, Va.: National Security Research, 1991); and Peter Anson and Dennis Cummings, "The First Space War: The Contribution of Satellites to the Gulf War," *RUSI Journal* 136, no. 4 (Winter 1991): 45–53.

2. See Correlli Barnett: *The Collapse of British Power* (Gloucester [U.K.]: Alan Sutton Publishing, 1984; first pub. 1972), and *The Audit of War: The Illusion and Reality of Britain as a Great Nation* (London: Macmillan, 1986).

3. James E. Edmonds, *History of the Great War, Military Operations, France and Belgium, 1914* (London: Macmillan, 1925), 2:1. Emphasis added.

4. For illustration of the all but insular position of the Dutch, see Philippe Masson, *De la Mer et de sa stratégie* (Paris: Tallandier, 1986), p. 343.

5. See Andrew W. Lambert, *The Crimean War: British Grand Strategy, 1853–56* (Manchester [U.K.]: Manchester University Press, 1990). Basil Greenhill and Ann Gifford, *The British Assault on Finland, 1854–1855: A Forgotten Naval War* (London: Conway Maritime Press, 1988), also is excellent.

6. In Halford J. Mackinder, *Democratic Ideals and Reality* (New York: W. W. Norton, 1962; first pub. 1942), the key essay, "The Geographical Pivot of History," dates from 1904. Also see J. R. Seeley, *The Expansion of England* (Chicago: University of Chicago Press, 1971), ch. 7, which dates from 1881–82.

7. See Arthur J. Marder, *From the Dreadnought to Scapa Flow: The Royal Navy in the Fisher Era, 1904–1919,* vol. 1: *The Road to War, 1904–1914* (London: Oxford University Press, 1961), pp. 386–94.

BIBLIOGRAPHY

Adcock, F. E. *The Roman Art of War Under the Republic*. Cambridge, Mass.: Harvard University Press, 1940.

————. *The Greek and Macedonian Art of War*. Berkeley, Cal.: University of California Press, 1957.

Addington, Larry H. *The Blitzkrieg Era and the German General Staff, 1865–1941*. New Brunswick, N.J.: Rutgers University Press, 1971.

Allmand, Christopher. *The Hundred Years War: England and France at War c. 1300–c. 1450*. Cambridge: Cambridge University Press, 1988.

Anderson, M. S. "Eighteenth-Century Theories of the Balance of Power." In Ragnhild Hatton and M. S. Anderson, eds., *Studies in Diplomatic History: Essays in Memory of David Bayne Horn*, pp. 183–98. London: Longmans, 1970.

Andrews, Kenneth R. *Elizabethan Privateering*. Cambridge: Cambridge University Press, 1964.

————. *Trade, Plunder and Settlement: Maritime Expertise and the Genesis of the British Empire, 1480–1630*. Cambridge: Cambridge University Press, 1984.

Angold, Michael. *The Byzantine Empire, 1025–1204: A Political History*. London: Longmans, 1984.

Anson, Peter, and Dennis Cummings. "The First Space War: The Contribution of Satellites to the Gulf War." *RUSI Journal* 136, no. 4 (Winter 1991): 45–53.

Aspinall-Oglander, C. F. *History of the Great War, Military Operations, Gallipoli*. 2 vols. London: William Heinemann, 1929–32.

Baer, George W. "U.S. Naval Strategy, 1890–1645." *Naval War College Review* 44, no. 1 (Winter 1991): 6–33.

Balck, Wilhelm. *Development of Tactics—World War*. Ft. Leavenworth, Ks.: General Service Schools Press, 1922.

Ball, Desmond. "Nuclear War at Sea." *International Security* 10, no. 3 (Winter 1985–86): 3–31.

Barnett, Correlli. *The Swordbearers: Studies in Supreme Command in the First World War*. London: Eyre and Spottiswoode, 1963.

327

———. *Britain and Her Army, 1509–1970: A Military, Political and Social Survey.* London: Penguin, 1970.

———. *The Collapse of British Power.* Gloucester (U.K.): Alan Sutton Publishing, 1984; first pub. 1972.

———. *The Audit of War: The Illusion and Reality of Britain as a Great Nation.* London: Macmillan, 1986.

———. *Engage the Enemy More Closely: The Royal Navy in the Second World War.* New York: W. W. Norton, 1991.

Barnhart, Michael A. *Japan Prepares for Total War: The Search for Economic Security, 1919–1941.* Ithaca, N.Y.: Cornell University Press, 1987.

Bartov, Omer. *Hitler's Army: Soldiers, Nazis, and War in the Third Reich.* New York: Oxford University Press, 1991.

Baugh, Daniel A. *British Naval Administration in the Age of Walpole.* Princeton, N.J.: Princeton University Press, 1965.

———. "Why Did Britain Lose Command of the Sea during the War for America?" In Jeremy Black and Philip Woodfine, eds., *The British Navy and the Use of Naval Power in the Eighteenth Century.* pp. 149–60. Leicester (U.K.): Leicester University Press, 1988.

Baynes, Norman H. *Byzantine Studies and Other Essays.* Westport, Conn.: Greenwood Press, 1974; first pub. 1955.

Beatty, Jack. "In Harm's Way." *Atlantic* (May 1987), 37–46, 48–49, 52–53.

Bekker, Cajus (pseud). *Hitler's Naval War.* New York: Zebra Books, 1985; first pub. 1971.

Bennett, Geoffrey. *Naval Battles of the First World War.* London: B. T. Batsford, 1968.

Best, Geoffrey. *War and Society in Revolutionary Europe, 1770–1870.* London: Fontana, 1982.

Black, Jeremy. *Natural and Necessary Enemies: Anglo-French Relations in the Eighteenth Century.* London: Gerald Duckworth, 1986.

———. "Naval Power and British Foreign Policy in the Age of Pitt the Elder." In Jeremy Black and Philip Woodfine, eds., *The British Navy and the Use of Naval Power in the Eighteenth Century*, pp. 91–107. Leicester (U.K.): Leicester University Press, 1988.

Blaxland, Gregory. *Destination Dunkirk: The Story of Gort's Army*, London: The Military Book Society, 1973.

328

Blumenson, Martin. "Of Landpowers and Seapowers." In George E. Thibault, ed., *The Art and Practice of Military Strategy*, pp. 36–41. Washington, D.C.: National Defense University, 1984.

Bond, Brian. *British Military Policy between the Two World Wars.* Oxford: Clarendon Press, 1980.

Bond, Gordon C. *The Grand Expedition: The British Invasion of Holland in 1809.* Athens, Ga.: University of Georgia Press, 1979.

Bowra, C. M. *Periclean Athens.* London: Penguin, 1974; first pub. 1971.

Bozeman, Adda B. *Politics and Culture in International History.* Princeton, N.J.: Princeton University Press, 1960.

Brewer, John. *The Sinews of Power: War, Money and the English State, 1688–1783.* New York: Alfred A. Knopf, 1989.

Brock, Michael. "Britain Enters the War." In R. J. W. Evans and Hartmut Pogge von Strandmann, eds., *The Coming of the First World War.* Oxford: Clarendon Press, 1988.

Brodie, Bernard. *Sea Power in the Machine Age.* Princeton, N.J.: Princeton University Press, 1941.

———. *A Layman's Guide to Naval Strategy.* Princeton, N.J.: Princeton University Press,1942.

Bromley, J. S. *Corsairs and Navies, 1660–1760.* London: Hambledon Press, 1987.

———, and A. N. Ryan. "Navies." In J. S. Bromley, ed., *The New Cambridge Modern History.* Vol. 6: *The Rise of Great Britain and Russia, 1688–1715/25,* pp. 790–833. Cambridge: Cambridge University Press, 1970.

Brooks, E. W. "The Struggle with the Saracens (717–867)." In J. R. Tonner, C. W. Previté-Orton, and Z. N. Brooke, eds., *The Cambridge Medieval History.* Vol. 4: *The Eastern Empire (717–1453),* pp. 119–38. Cambridge: Cambridge University Press, 1927.

Brown, Peter. *The World of Late Antiquity.* New York: Harcourt Brace Jovanovich, 1971.

Bruckmüller, Georg. *The German Artillery in the Breakthrough Battles of the World War.* Ft. Sill, Okla.: U.S. Army Field Artillery School, n.d. [early 1920s].

Bryant, Arthur. *Samuel Pepys: The Saviour of the Navy.* London: Panther, 1985; first pub. 1938.

Buffington, Arthur H. *The Second Hundred Years War, 1689–1815.* Westport, Conn.: Greenwood Press, 1975; first pub. 1929.

Burdick, Charles, and Hans-Adolf Jacobson. *The Halder War Diary, 1939–1942.* Novato, Cal.: Presidio Press, 1988.

Bush, George. *National Security Strategy of the United States.* Washington, D.C.: GPO, March 1990.

Butler, J. R. M. *History of the Second World War, Grand Strategy.* Vol. 2: *September 1939–June 1941.* London: HMSO, 1957.

Callwell, Charles E. *The Effect of Maritime Command on Land Campaigns since Waterloo,* Edinburgh: William Blackwood and Sons, 1897.

———. *Military Operations and Maritime Preponderance: Their Relations and Interdependence.* Edinburgh: William Blackwood and Sons, 1905.

———. *The Dardanelles.* London: Constable, 1924.

Campbell, John. *Jutland: An Analysis of the Fighting.* Annapolis, Md.: Naval Institute Press, 1986.

Capp, Bernard. *Cromwell's Navy: The Fleet and the English Revolution, 1648–1660.* Oxford: Clarendon Press, 1989.

Casson, Lionel. *The Ancient Mariners: Seafarers and Sea Fighters of the Mediterranean in Ancient Times.* Princeton, N.J.: Princeton University Press, 1991.

Caven, Brian. *The Punic Wars.* London: Weidenfeld and Nicolson, 1980.

Cessi, R. "Venice to the Eve of the Fourth Crusade." in J. M. Hussey, ed., *The Cambridge Medieval History.* Vol. 4: *The Byzantine Empire, Part I, Byzantium and Its Neighbours,* pp. 250–74. Cambridge: Cambridge University Press, 1966.

Chandler, David. *The Campaigns of Napoleon.* London: Weidenfeld and Nicolson, 1967.

Childers, Erskine. *The Riddle of the Sands: A Record of Secret Service.* London: Collins, 1953; first pub. 1903.

Churchill, Winston S. *The Unknown War: The Eastern Front.* New York: Charles Scribner's Sons, 1931.

———. *The World Crisis, 1911–1918.* 2 vols. London: Odham's Press, 1938.

———. *The Second World War.* Vol. 1: *The Gathering Storm.* London: Guild Publishing, 1985; first pub. 1948.

———. *The Second World War.* Vol. 5: *Closing the Ring.* London: Guild Publishing, 1985; first pub. 1952.

Clark, Alan. *The Donkeys.* London: Hutchinson, 1961.

Clausewitz, Carl von. *On War.* Translated by Michael Howard and Peter Paret. Princeton, N.J.: Princeton University Press, 1976; first pub. 1832.

Clayton, Anthony. *The British Empire as a Superpower, 1919–39.* Athens, Ga.: University of Georgia Press, 1986.

Coakley, Robert W., and Richard M. Leighton. *United States Army in World War II: The War Department, Global Logistics and Strategy, 1943–1945.* Washington, D.C.: GPO, 1968.

Cohen, Eliot A. *Commandos and Politicians: Elite Military Units in Modern Democracies.* Cambridge, Mass.: Center for International Affairs, Harvard University, 1978.

————, and John Gooch. *Military Misfortunes: The Anatomy of Failure in War.* New York: Free Press, 1990.

————. "Churchill and Coalition Strategy in World War II." In Paul Kennedy, ed., *Grand Strategies in War and Peace,* pp. 43–67. New Haven, Conn.: Yale University Press, 1991.

Coll, Alberto. "England and Spain, 1567–1604." In Colin S. Gray and Roger W. Barnett, eds., *Seapower and Strategy,* pp. 132–58. Annapolis, Md.: Naval Institute Press, 1989.

Colomb, P H. *Naval Warfare: Its Ruling Principles and Practice Historically Treated.* London: W. H. Allen, 1891.

Coox, Alvin D. "Japanese Net Assessment in the Era Before Pearl Harbor." In Williamson Murray and Allan R. Millett, eds., *Calculations: Net Assessment and the Coming of World War II,* pp. 258–98. New York: Free Press, 1992.

Corbett, Julian S. *Fighting Instructions, 1530–1816.* London: Navy Records Society, 1905.

————. *The Campaign of Trafalgar.* London: Longmans, Green, 1910.

————. *England in the Mediterranean: A Study of the Rise and Influence of British Power within the Straits, 1603–1713.* 2 vols. 2d ed. London: Longmans, Green, 1917; first pub. 1903.

————. *England in the Seven Years' War: A Study in Combined Strategy.* 2 vols. London: Longmans, Green, 1918; first pub. 1907.

————. *History of the Great War, Naval Operations.* Vol. 1. London: Longmans, Green, 1920.

————. *History of the Great War, Naval Operations.* Vol. 3. London: Longmans, Green, 1920.

————. *Some Principles of Maritime Strategy.* Annapolis, Md.: Naval Institute Press, 1988; first pub. 1911.

————. *Drake and the Tudor Navy.* 2 vols. Aldershot (U.K.): Temple Smith, 1988; first pub. 1898.

Covington, Steven R. "The Soviet Military: Prospects for Change." *Journal of Soviet Military Studies* 2, no. 2 (June 1989): 241–65.

Craig, Gordon A. "The Political Leader as Strategist." In Peter Paret, ed., *Makers of Modern Strategy: From Machiavelli to the Nuclear Age,* pp. 481–509. Princeton, N.J.: Princeton University Press, 1986.

Creswell, John. *Naval Warfare: An Introductory Study.* 2d ed. London: Sampson, Low, Marston, 1942; first pub. 1936.

——. *British Admirals of the Eighteenth Century: Tactics in Battle.* London: George Allen and Unwin, 1972.

Creveld, Martin van. *Supplying War: Logistics from Wallenstein to Patton.* Cambridge: Cambridge University Press, 1977.

——. *Command in War.* Cambridge, Mass.: Harvard University Press, 1985.

Crowhurst, Patrick. *The Defence of British Trade, 1689–1815.* Folkestone (U.K.): William Dawson and Sons, 1977.

Cruttwell, C. R. M. F. *A History of the Great War, 1914–1918.* Oxford: Clarendon Press, 1934.

——. *The Role of British Strategy in the Great War.* Cambridge: Cambridge University Press, 1936.

Daniel, Donald C. F. "The Soviet Navy and Tactical Nuclear War at Sea." *Survival* 29, no. 4 (July–August 1987): 318–35.

Daveluy, Rene. *The Genius of Naval Warfare, I: Strategy.* Annapolis, Md.: U.S. Naval Institute, 1910; first pub. 1905.

Day, Gerald W. *Genoa's Response to Byzantium, 1155–1204: Commercial Expansion and Factionalism in a Medieval City.* Urbana, Ill.: University of Illinois Press, 1988.

Delbruck, Hans. *History of the Art of War Within the Framework of Political History.* Vol. 3: *The Middle Ages.* Westport, Conn.: Greenwood Press, 1982.

Dickson, P. G. M. "War Finance, 1689–1714." In J. S. Bromley, ed., *The New Cambridge Modern History.* Vol. 6, *The Rise of Great Britain and Russia, 1688–1715/25,* pp. 284–315. Cambridge: Cambridge University Press, 1970.

Donnelly, Christopher. *Red Banner: The Soviet Military System in Peace and War.* Alexandria, Va.: Jane's Publishing, 1988.

Doughty, Robert Allan. *The Breaking Point: Sedan and the Fall of France, 1940.* Hamden, Conn.: Archon Books, 1990.

——, and Harold E. Raugh, Jr. "Embargoes in Historical Perspective." *Parameters* 21, no. 1 (Spring 1991): 21–30.

Dower, John W. *War Without Mercy: Race and Power in the Pacific War.* New York: Pantheon Books, 1986.

Duffy, Michael. *Soldiers, Sugar and Seapower: The British Expeditions to the West Indies and the War against Revolutionary France.* Oxford: Clarendon Press, 1987.

Dull, Paul S. *A Battle History of the Imperial Japanese Navy (1941–1945).* Annapolis, Md.: Naval Institute Press, 1978.

Dupuy, R. Ernest, and Trevor N. Dupuy. *The Encyclopedia of Military History: From 3500 B.C. to the Present.* 2d rev. ed. New York: Harper & Row, 1986.

Edmonds, James E. *History of the Great War, Military Operations, France and Belgium, 1914.* Vol. 1. Woking (U.K.): Shearer Publications, 1984; reprint of 1933 ed.

———. *History of the Great War, Military Operations, France and Belgium, 1914.* Vol. 2. London: Macmillan, 1925.

———. *History of the Great War, Military Operations, France and Belgium, 1916.* Vol. 1 Woking (U.K.): Shearer Publications, 1986; first pub. 1932.

———. *History of the Great War, Military Operations, France and Belgium, 1918.* Vol. 1. London: Macmillan, 1935.

Elliot, J. H. *Imperial Spain, 1469–1716.* London: Penguin, 1970; first pub. 1963.

———. *The Count-Duke of Olivares: The Statesman in an Age of Decline.* New Haven, Conn.: Yale University Press, 1986.

Ellis, John. *Cassino, The Hollow Victory: The Battle for Rome, January–June 1944.* New York: McGraw-Hill, 1985.

———. *Brute Force: Allied Strategy and Tactics in the Second World War.* New York: Viking, 1990.

Falls, Cyril. Introduction to Kent Roberts Greenfield, ed., *Command Decisions,* pp. ix–xiv. London: Methuen, 1960; first pub. 1959.

Fayle, Ernest. *History of the Great War, Seaborne Trade.* 3 vols. London: John Murray, 1920–24.

Feis, Herbert. *The Road to Pearl Harbor: The Coming of the War Between the United States and Japan.* Princeton, N.J.: Princeton University Press,1950.

Ferguson, William Scott. *Greek Imperialism.* Boston: Houghton Mifflin, 1913.

Fernandez-Armesto, Felipe. *The Spanish Armada: The Experience of War in 1588.* Oxford: Oxford University Press, 1989.

Ferris, John Robert. *Men, Money, and Diplomacy: The Evolution of British Strategic Policy, 1919–26.* Ithaca, N.Y.: Cornell University Press, 1989.

Finley, M. I. *The Ancient Greeks.* London: Penguin, 1966; first pub. 1963.

———. *Ancient History: Evidence and Models.* New York: Viking Penguin, 1986; first pub. 1985.

Fischer, Fritz. *Germany's Aims in the First World War.* New York: W. W. Norton, 1967.

———. *War of Illusions: German Policies from 1911 to 1914.* New York: W. W. Norton, 1975.

Fregosi, Paul. *Dreams of Empire: Napoleon and the First World War.* London: Hutchinson, 1989.

French, David. *British Strategy and War Aims, 1914–1916.* London: Allen and Unwin, 1986.

———. "The Meaning of Attrition, 1914–1916." *English Historical Review* 103, no. 407 (April 1988): 385–405.

———. *The British Way in Warfare, 1688–2000.* London: Unwin Hyman, 1990.

Friedberg, Aaron L. *The Weary Titan: Britain and the Experience of Relative Decline, 1895–1905.* Princeton, N.J.: Princeton University Press, 1988.

Friedman, Norman. *The U.S. Maritime Strategy.* London: Jane's Publishing, 1988.

Frost, H. H. *The Battle of Jutland.* Annapolis, Md.: United States Naval Institute, 1964; first pub. 1936.

Fuller, J. F. C. *The Decisive Battles of the Western World and Their Influence upon History.* Vol. 1: *From the Earliest Times to the Battle of Lepanto.* London: Eyre and Spottiswoode, 1954.

Garnsey, Peter. *Famine and Food Supply in the Graeco-Roman World: Responses to Risk and Crisis.* Cambridge: Cambridge University Press, 1988.

Gates, David. *The Spanish Ulcer: A History of the Peninsular War.* New York: W. W. Norton, 1986.

Gibbs, Norman. "British Strategic Doctrine, 1918–1939." In Michael Howard, ed., *The Theory and Practice of War,* pp. 185–212. London: Cassell, 1965.

———. *History of the Second World War, Grand Strategy.* Vol. 1: *Rearmament Policy.* London: HMSO, 1976.

Gilbert, Martin. *Winston S. Churchill*. Vol. 6: *Finest Hour, 1939–1941*. Boston: Houghton Mifflin, 1983.

Glantz, David M. *The Role of Intelligence in Soviet Military Strategy in World War II*. Novato, Cal.: Presidio Press, 1990.

Glover, Richard. *Britain at Bay: Defence against Bonaparte, 1803–14*. New York: Barnes and Noble, 1973.

Goldrick, James, *The King's Ships Were at Sea: The War in the North Sea, August 1914–February 1915*. Annapolis, Md.: Naval Institute Press, 1984.

Gooch, John. *The Plans of War: The General Staff and British Military Strategy, c. 1900–1916*. London: Routledge and Kegan Paul, 1974.

———. *The Prospect of War: Studies in British Defence Policy, 1847–1942*. London: Frank Cass, 1981.

Graham, Gerald S. *Tides of Empire: Discursions on the Expansion of Britain Overseas*. Montreal: McGill–Queen's University Press, 1972.

Graves, Robert, and Alan Hodge. *The Long Week-End: A Social History of Great Britain, 1918–1939*. London: Faber and Faber, 1941.

Gray, Colin S. *The Geopolitics of Super Power*. Lexington, Ky.: University Press of Kentucky, 1988.

———. *Maritime Power and Space Strategy*. Fairfax, Va.: National Security Research, 1991.

———., ed. *Special Operations: What Succeeds and Why? Lessons of Experience*. Fairfax, Va.: National Institute for Public Policy, May 1992.

Gray, G. Buchanan. "The Foundation and Extension of the Persian Empire." In J. B. Bury, S. A. Cook, and F. E. Adcock, eds., *The Cambridge Ancient History*. Vol. 4: *The Persian Empire and the West*, pp. 1–25. Cambridge: Cambridge University Press, 1964; first pub. 1926.

Greenfield, Kent Roberts. *American Strategy in World War II: A Reconsideration*. Baltimore: Johns Hopkins Press, 1963.

Greenhill, Basil, and Ann Gifford. *The British Assault on Finland, 1854–1855: A Forgotten Naval War*. London: Conway Maritime Press, 1988.

Grey of Fallodon, Viscount. *Twenty-Five Years, 1892–1916*. 2 vols. New York: Frederick A. Stokes, 1925.

Grove, Eric. *Maritime Strategy and European Security*. London: Brassey's, 1990.

Gudmundsson, Bruce I. *Stormtroop Tactics: Innovation in the German Army, 1914–1918*. New York: Praeger, 1989.

Guertner, Gary L. "Flexible Response: Soviet Style." *Journal of Soviet Military Studies* 1, no. 4 (December 1988): 417–50.

Guilmartin, John Francis, Jr. *Gunpowder and Galleys: Changing Technology and Mediterranean Warfare at Sea in the Sixteenth Century.* Cambridge: Cambridge University Press, 1974.

Hagan, Kenneth J. *This People's Navy: The Making of American Sea Power.* New York: Free Press, 1991.

Hall, Christopher. *Britain, America and Arms Control, 1921–37.* New York: St. Martin's Press, 1987.

Hamilton, Charles D. *Sparta's Bitter Victories: Politics and Diplomacy in the Corinthian War.* Ithaca, N.Y.: Cornell University Press, 1979.

Harris, William V. *War and Imperialism in Republican Rome, 327–70 B.C.* Oxford, Clarendon Press, 1985; first pub. 1979.

Harrison, Gordon A. *United States Army in World War II: The European Theater of Operations, Cross-Channel Attack.* Washington, D.C.: GPO, 1951.

Hartmann, Frederick H. *Naval Renaissance: The U.S. Navy in the 1980's.* Annapolis, Md.: Naval Institute Press, 1990.

Hasebroak, Johannes. *Trade and Politics in Ancient Greece.* Chicago: Ares Publishers, 1978.

Hattendorf, John B. "The Evolution of the Maritime Strategy, 1977–1987." *Naval War College Review* 41, no. 3 (Summer 1988): 7–28.

Heckscher, Eli F. *The Continental System: An Economic Interpretation.* Gloucester, Mass.: Peter Smith, 1964; first pub. 1922.

Henderson, Bernard E. *The Great War Between Athens and Sparta: A Companion to the Military History of Thucydides.* London: Macmillan, 1927.

Herken, Greg. *Counsels of War.* New York: Alfred A. Knopf, 1985.

Herodotus, *The Persian Wars.* Translated by George Rawlinson. New York: Modern Library, 1942.

Hess, Andrew C. *The Forgotten Frontier: A History of the Sixteenth-Century Ibero-African Frontier.* Chicago: University of Chicago Press, 1978.

Higgins, Trumbull. *Winston Churchill and the Dardanelles: A Dialogue in Ends and Means.* Westport, Conn.: Greenwood Press, 1977; first pub. 1963.

Hill, Christopher. *Cabinet Decisions on Foreign Policy: The British Experience, October 1938–June 1941.* Cambridge: Cambridge University Press, 1991.

Hinsley, F. H. *Hitler's Strategy*. Cambridge: Cambridge University Press, 1951.

Hinsley, F. H., et al. *History of the Second World War, British Intelligence in the Second World War: Its Influence on Strategy and Operations.* Vols. 1–3. London: HMSO, 1979–88.

Hitti, Philip K. *History of the Arabs: From the Earliest Times to the Present.* New York: St. Martin's, 1970; first pub. 1937.

Holmes, Richard. *The Little Field-Marshal, Sir John French.* London: Jonathan Cape, 1981.

Howard, Michael. *The Mediterranean Strategy in the Second World War.* London: Weidenfeld and Nicolson, 1968.

———. *The Continental Commitment: The Dilemma of British Defence Policy in the Era of the Two World Wars.* London: Temple Smith, 1972.

———. "Men Against Fire: Expectations of War in 1914." *International Security* 9, no. 1 (Summer 1984): 41–57.

———. *The Causes of Wars and Other Essays.* London: Unwin Paperbacks, 1984; first pub. 1983.

———. "British Grand Strategy in World War I." In Paul Kennedy, ed., *Grand Strategies in War and Peace,* pp. 31–41. New Haven, Conn.: Yale University Press, 1991.

———. *The Lessons of History.* New Haven, Conn.: Yale University Press, 1991.

Hughes, Wayne P., Jr. *Fleet Tactics: Theory and Practice.* Annapolis, Md.: Naval Institute Press, 1986.

Huntington, Samuel P. "National Policy and the Transoceanic Navy." U.S. Naval Institute *Proceedings* 80, no. 5 (May 1954): 483–93.

Huth, Paul K. *Extended Deterrence and the Prevention of War.* New Haven, Conn.: Yale University Press, 1988.

Ike, Nobutaka, ed. *Japan's Decision for War: Records of the 1941 Policy Conferences.* Stanford, Cal.: Stanford University Press, 1967.

Iriye, Akira. *The Origins of the Second World War in Asia and the Pacific.* London: Longmans, 1987.

Irving, David. *Hitler's War, 1939–1942.* London: Macmillan, 1983; first pub. 1977.

Isely, Jeter A., and Philip A. Crowl. *The U.S. Marines and Amphibious Warfare: Its Theory and Practice in the Pacific.* Princeton, N.J.: Princeton University Press, 1951.

337

Jackson, Bill, and Dwin Bramall. *The Chiefs: The Story of the United Kingdom Chiefs of Staff*. London: Brassey's, 1992.

James, D. Clayton. "American and Japanese Strategies in the Pacific War." In Peter Paret, ed., *Makers of Modern Strategy: From Machiavelli to the Nuclear Age*, pp. 703–32. Princeton, N.J.: Princeton University Press, 1986.

Jenkins, Romilly. *Byzantium: The Imperial Centuries, A.D. 610–1071*. Toronto: University of Toronto Press (for Medieval Academy of America), 1987; first pub. 1966.

Jervis, Robert. *The Meaning of the Nuclear Revolution: Statecraft and the Prospect of Armageddon*. Ithaca, N.Y.: Cornell University Press, 1989.

Joll, James. *The Origins of the First World War*. London: Longmans, 1984.

Jones, J. R. *Britain and the World, 1649–1815*. London: Fontana, 1980.

———. "Limitations of British Sea Power in the French Wars, 1689–1815. In Jeremy Black and Philip Woodfine, eds., *The British Navy and the Use of Naval Power in the Eighteenth Century*, pp. 33–49. Leicester (U.K.): Leicester University Press, 1988.

———. "The Dutch Navy and National Survival in the Seventeenth Century." *International History Review* 10, no. 1 (February 1988): 18–32.

Kaegi, Walter Emil, Jr. *Byzantium and the Decline of Rome*. Princeton, N.J.: Princeton University Press, 1968.

Kagan, Donald. *The Outbreak of the Peloponnesian War*. Ithaca, N.Y.: Cornell University Press, 1969.

———. *The Archidamian War*. Ithaca, N.Y.: Cornell University Press, 1974.

———. *The Peace of Nicias and the Sicilian Expedition*. Ithaca, N.Y.: Cornell University Press, 1981.

———. *The Fall of the Athenian Empire*. Ithaca, N.Y.: Cornell University Press, 1987.

———. *Pericles of Athens and the Birth of Democracy: The Triumph of Vision in Leadership*. New York: Simon and Schuster, 1991.

Kaufman, Robert Gordon. *Arms Control During the Pre-Nuclear Era: The United States and Naval Limitation Between the Two World Wars*. New York: Columbia University Press, 1990.

Kazhdan, Alexander P., ed. *The Oxford Dictionary of Byzantium*. 3 vols. New York: Oxford University Press, 1991.

Keegan, John. *The Price of Admiralty: The Evolution of Naval Warfare*. New York: Viking, 1988.

338

———. *The Second World War*. London: Hutchinson, 1989.

Kennedy, Malcolm J., and Michael J. O'Connor, eds. *Safely by Sea*. Lanham, Md.: University Press of America, 1990.

Kennedy, Paul. *The Rise and Fall of British Naval Mastery*. New York: Charles Scribner's Sons, 1976.

———. "The Development of German Naval Operations Plans against England, 1896–1914." In Paul Kennedy, ed., *The War Plans of the Great Powers, 1880–1914*, pp. 171–98. London: George Allen and Unwin, 1979.

———. *The Realities Behind Diplomacy: Background Influences on British External Policy, 1865–1980*. London: Fontana, 1981.

———. *The Rise of the Anglo-German Antagonism, 1860–1914*. London: George Allen and Unwin, 1982; first pub. 1980.

———. *Strategy and Diplomacy, 1870–1945: Eight Studies*. London: George Allen and Unwin, 1983.

———. *The Rise and Fall of the Great Powers: Economic Change and Military Conflict from 1500 to 2000*. New York: Random House, 1987.

———. "British 'Net Assessment' and the Coming of the Second World War. In Williamson Murray and Allan R. Millett, eds., *Calculations: Net Assessment and the Coming of World War II*, pp. 19–59. New York: Free Press, 1992.

Kersaudy, François. *Norway 1940*. London: Collins, 1990; first pub. 1987.

Kinross, Lord. *The Ottoman Centuries: The Rise and Fall of the Turkish Empire*. New York: Morrow Quill Paperbacks, 1979; first pub. 1977.

Knox, Dudley W. *The Naval Genius of George Washington*. Boston: Houghton Mifflin, 1932.

Koch, H. W., ed. *The Origins of the First World War: Great Power Rivalry and German War Aims*. 2d ed. London: Macmillan, 1984.

Lane, Frederic C. *Venice and History: The Collected Papers of Frederic C. Lane*. Baltimore: Johns Hopkins University Press, 1966.

———. *Venice: A Maritime Republic*. Baltimore: Johns Hopkins University Press, 1973.

Lavery, Brian. *The Ship of the Line*. Vol. 1: *The Development of the Battlefleet, 1650–1850*. Annapolis, Md.: Naval Institute Press, 1983.

———. *Nelson's Navy: The Ships, Men and Organization, 1793–1815*. Annapolis, Md.: Naval Institute Press, 1989.

Lentin, A. *Lloyd George, Woodrow Wilson and the Guilt of Germany: An Essay in the Pre-History of Appeasement*. Baton Rouge, La.: Louisiana State University Press, 1985; first pub. 1984.

Lewin, Ronald. *Ultra Goes to War*. New York: McGraw-Hill, 1978.

Lewis, Archibald R. *Naval Power and Trade in the Mediterranean, A.D. 500–1100*. Princeton, N.J.: Princeton University Press, 1951.

——— and Timothy Runyan. *European Naval and Maritime History, 300–1500*. Bloomington, Ind.: Indiana University Press, 1985.

Lewis, D. M., et al., eds. *The Cambridge Ancient History*. Vol. 5: *The Fifth Century B.C.* 2d ed. Cambridge: Cambridge University Press, 1992.

Lewis, Michael. *The Navy of Britain: A Historical Portrait*. London: George Allen and Unwin, 1948.

Liddell-Hart, B. H. *The British Way in Warfare*. London: Faber and Faber, 1932.

———. *Strategy: The Indirect Approach*. 4th ed. London: Faber and Faber, 1967.

———. *History of the First World War*. London: Pan, 1972; first pub. 1930.

———. "Marines and Strategy." *Marine Corps Gazette* 64, no. 1 (January 1980): 23–31.

Lincoln, W. Bruce. *Passage Through Armageddon: The Russians in War and Revolution, 1914–1918*. New York: Simon and Schuster, 1986.

Lloyd, Christopher. *The Capture of Quebec*. New York: Macmillan, 1959.

Lucas, Pascal M. H. *The Evolution of Tactical Ideas in France and Germany During the War of 1914–1918*. Paris: Berger-Levrault, 1925; first pub. 1923.

Ludendorff, General. *My War Memories*. 2d ed. 2 vols. London: Hutchinson, n.d. [written in 1918–19].

Lupfer, Timothy T. *The Dynamics of Doctrine: The Changes in German Tactical Doctrine During the First World War*. Leavenworth Papers No. 4. Ft. Leavenworth, Ks.: Combat Studies Institute, U.S. Army Command and General Staff College, July 1981.

Luttwak, Edward N. "An Emerging Postnuclear Era?" *Washington Quarterly* 11, no. 1 (Winter 1988): 5–15.

Lynch, John. *Spain under the Habsburgs*. 2 vols. New York: New York University Press, 1984; first pub. 1964–69.

MacCaffrey, Wallace T. *Queen Elizabeth and the Making of Policy, 1572–1588*. Princeton, N.J.: Princeton University Press, 1981.

McGregor, Malcolm F. *The Athenians and Their Empire*. Vancouver: University of British Columbia Press, 1987.

McKiernan, Patrick L. "Tarawa: The Tide That Failed." In Merrill L. Bartlett, ed., *Assault from the Sea: Essays on the History of Amphibious Warfare*, pp. 210–18. Annapolis, Md.: Naval Institute Press, 1983.

Mackinder, Halford J. *Democratic Ideals and Reality*. New York: W. W. Norton, 1962; first pub. 1942.

Maclagan, Michael. *The City of Constantinople*. New York: Frederick A. Praeger, 1968.

McLynn, Frank. *Invasion: From the Armada to Hitler, 1588–1945*. London: Routledge and Kegan Paul, 1987.

McNeill, William H. *Venice: The Hinge of Europe, 1081–1797*. Chicago: University of Chicago Press, 1986; first pub. 1974.

Mahan, Alfred Thayer. *The Influence of Sea Power upon the French Revolution and Empire, 1793–1812*. 2 vols. Boston: Little, Brown, 1898; first pub. 1892.

———. *The Influence of Sea Power upon History, 1660–1783*. Boston: Little Brown, 1918; first pub. 1890.

Maier, Charles S. "Wargames: 1914–1919." In Robert I. Rotberg and Theodore K. Rabb, eds., *The Origin and Prevention of Major Wars*, pp. 249–79. Cambridge: Cambridge University Press, 1989.

Mallett, M. E., and J. R. Hale. *The Military Organization of a Renaissance State: Venice c. 1400 to 1617*. Cambridge: Cambridge University Press, 1984.

Maltby, William. "Politics, Professionalism, and the Evolution of Sailing-Ship Tactics, 1650–1714." In John A. Lynn, ed., *Tools of War: Instruments, Ideas, and Institutions of Warfare, 1465–1871*, pp. 53–73. Urbana, Ill.: University of Illinois Press, 1990.

Marcus, Geoffrey. *Quiberon Bay: The Campaign in Home Waters, 1759*. London: Hollis and Carter, 1960.

———. *A Naval History of England, I: The Formative Centuries*. Boston: Little, Brown, 1961.

———. *The Age of Nelson: The Royal Navy, 1793–1815*. New York: Viking, 1971.

———. *Heart of Oak: A Survey of British Sea Power in the Georgian Era*. London: Oxford University Press, 1975.

Marder, Arthur J. *From the Dreadnought to Scapa Flow: The Royal Navy in the Fisher Era, 1904–1919*. 5 vols. London: Oxford University Press, 1961–70.

341

———. *The Anatomy of British Sea Power: A History of British Naval Policy in the Pre-Dreadnought Era, 1880–1905.* Hamden, Conn.: Archon Books, 1964; first pub. 1940.

———. *From the Dardanelles to Oran: Studies in the Royal Navy in War and Peace, 1915–1940.* London: Oxford University Press, 1974.

———. *Old Friends, New Enemies: The Royal Navy and the Imperial Japanese Navy, Strategic Illusions, 1936–1941.* Oxford: Clarendon Press, 1981.

Martin, Colin, and Geoffrey Parker. *The Spanish Armada.* London: Hamish Hamilton, 1988.

Martray, Joseph. *La Destruction de la marine française par la Révolution.* Paris: Editions France–Empire, 1988.

Masson, Philippe. *De la Mer et de sa stratégie.* Paris: Tallandier, 1986.

Matloff, Maurice. "Allied Strategy in Europe, 1939–1945." In Peter Paret ed., *Makers of Modern Strategy: From Machiavelli to the Nuclear Age,* pp. 677–702. Princeton, N.J.: Princeton University Press, 1986.

Maurice, Frederick. *British Strategy: A Study of the Application of the Principles of War.* London: Constable, 1929.

Mearsheimer, John J. "A Strategic Misstep: The Maritime Strategy and Deterrence in Europe." *International Security* 11, no. 2 (Fall 1986): 3–57.

Mediger, W. "Great Britain, Hanover and the Rise of Prussia." In Ragnhild Hatton and M. S. Anderson, eds., *Studies in Diplomatic History: Essays in Memory of David Bayne Horn,* pp. 199–213. London: Longmans, 1970.

Medlicott, W. N. *History of the Second World War, The Economic Blockade.* 2 vols. London: HMSO, 1952.

Meiggs, Russell. *The Athenian Empire.* Oxford: Clarendon Press, 1972.

Middlebrook, Martin. *The Kaiser's Battle, 21 March 1918: The First Day of the German Spring Offensive.* London: Penguin, 1983; first pub. 1978.

Miller, Edward S. *War Plan Orange: The U.S. Strategy to Defeat Japan.* Annapolis, Md.: Naval Institute Press, 1991.

Milner, Marc. "The Battle of the Atlantic." *Journal of Strategic Studies* 13, no. 1 (March 1990): 45–66.

Milward, Alan S. *War, Economy, and Society, 1939–1945.* London: Penguin, 1987; first pub. 1977.

Moorehead, Alan, *Gallipoli.* Annapolis, Md.: Nautical and Aviation Publishing Company of America, 1982; first pub. 1965.

Morris, Jan. *The Venetian Empire: A Sea Voyage*. London: Penguin, 1990; first pub. 1980.

Morrison, J. S., and J. F. Coates. *The Athenian Trireme: The History and Reconstruction of an Ancient Greek Warship*. Cambridge: Cambridge University Press, 1986.

Morton, Louis. *United States Army in World War II: The War in the Pacific, Strategy and Command: The First Two Years*. Washington, D.C.: GPO, 1962.

Moss, H. St. L. B. "The Formation of the East Roman Empire, 330–717." In J. M. Hussey, ed., *The Cambridge Medieval History*. Vol. 4: *The Byzantine Empire. Pt. 1: Byzantium and Its Neighbours*, pp. 1–41. Cambridge: Cambridge University Press, 1966.

Motter, T. H. Vail. *United States Army in World War II: The Middle East Theater, the Persian Corridor and Aid to Russia*. Washington, D.C.: GPO, 1985; first pub. 1952.

Murray, Williamson. "Attrition and the Luftwaffe." *Air University Review* 34, no. 3 (March–April 1983): 66–77.

———. *The Change in the European Balance of Power, 1938–1939: The Path to Ruin*. Princeton, N.J.: Princeton University Press, 1984.

———. *Luftwaffe*. Baltimore: Nautical and Aviation Publishing Company of America, 1985; first pub. 1983.

Neilson, Keith. *Strategy and Supply: The Anglo-Russian Alliance, 1914–17*. London: Allen and Unwin, 1984.

Newbolt, Henry. *History of the Great War, Naval Operations*. Vol. 5. London: Longmans, Green 1931.

Nicol, D. M. "The Fourth Crusade and the Greek and Latin Empires, 1204–61." In J. M. Hussey, ed., *The Cambridge Medieval History*. Vol. 4: *The Byzantine Empire. Pt. 1: Byzantium and Its Neighbours*, pp. 275–330. Cambridge: Cambridge University Press, 1966.

———. *Byzantium and Venice: A Study in Diplomatic and Cultural Relations*. Cambridge: Cambridge University Press, 1988.

Nitze, Paul H., and Leonard Sullivan, Jr. *Securing the Seas: The Soviet Naval Challenge and Western Alliance Options*. Boulder, Colo.: Westview Press, 1979.

Norwich, John Julius. *A History of Venice*. New York: Alfred A. Knopf, 1982.

Ober, Josiah. *Fortress Attica: Defense of the Athenian Land Frontier, 404–322 B.C.* Leiden: E. J. Brill, 1985.

343

Oman, Charles. *A History of the Art of War in the Middle Ages.* 2 vols. London: Methuen, 1978; first pub. 1898.

Oppenheim, M. *A History of the Administration of the Royal Navy and of Merchant Shipping in Relation to the Navy: From 1509 to 1660 with an Introduction Treating of the Preceding Period.* Hamden, Conn.: Shoe String Press, 1961; first pub. 1896.

Ostrogorsky, George. *History of the Byzantine State.* New Brunswick, N.J.: Rutgers University Press, 1969; first pub. 1940.

Padfield, Peter. *Dönitz, the Last Führer: Portrait of a Nazi War Leader.* New York: Harper & Row, 1984.

Palmer, Michael A. *Origins of the Maritime Strategy: American Naval Strategy in the First Postwar Decade.* Contributions to Naval History No. 1. Washington, D.C.: Naval Historical Center, Department of the Navy, 1988.

Parker, Geoffrey. *The Army of Flanders and the Spanish Road, 1567–1659: The Logistics of Spanish Victory and Defeat in the Low Countries' Wars.* Cambridge: Cambridge University Press, 1972.

———. *The Dutch Revolt.* London: Penguin, 1979; first pub. 1977.

———. *Spain and the Netherlands, 1559–1659: Ten Studies.* London: Fontana, 1990; first pub. 1979.

Parker, W. H. *Mackinder: Geography as an Aid to Statecraft.* Oxford, Clarendon Press, 1982.

Parkinson, C. Northcote. *War in the Eastern Seas, 1793–1815.* London: George Allen and Unwin, 1954.

———. *Britannia Rules: The Classic Age of Naval History, 1793–1815.* London: Book Club Associates, 1977.

Parry, J. H. *The Spanish Seaborne Empire.* London: Hutchinson, 1966.

———. *Trade and Dominion: The European Overseas Empires in the Eighteenth Century.* New York: Praeger, 1971.

Pears, Edwin. *The Fall of Constantinople: Being the Story of the Fourth Crusade.* New York: Harper and Brothers, 1886.

Peden, G. C. *British Rearmament and the Treasury, 1932–1939.* Edinburgh: Scottish Academic Press, 1979.

Pensel, Helmut. *A History of the War at Sea: An Atlas and Chronology of Conflict at Sea from Earliest Times to the Present.* Annapolis, Md.: Naval Institute Press, n.d.; first pub. 1975.

Perjes, Geza. *War and Society in East Central Europe.* Vol. 26: *The Fall of the Medieval Kingdom of Hungary: Mohacs 1526–Buda 1541.* East

European Monographs No. 245. Highland Lakes, N.J.: Atlantic Research and Publications, 1989.

Plehwe, Friedrich-Karl von. "Operation Sealion 1940." *RUSI Journal* 118, no. 1 (March 1973): 47–53.

Porch, Douglas. *The March to the Marne: The French Army, 1871–1914.* Cambridge: Cambridge University Press, 1981.

Posen, Barry R. "Inadvertent Nuclear War? Escalation and NATO's Northern Flank." *International Security* 7, no. 2 (Fall 1982): 28–54.

Powell, Anton. *Athens and Sparta: Constructing Greek Political and Social History from 478 b.c.* London: Routledge, 1988.

Prior, John G. *Geography, Technology and War: Studies in the Maritime History of the Mediterranean, 649–1571.* Cambridge: Cambridge University Press, 1988.

Puleston, W. D. *The Influence of Sea Power in World War II.* New Haven, Conn.: Yale University Press, 1947.

Quinn, D. B., and A. N. Ryan. *England's Sea Empire, 1550–1642.* London: George Allen and Unwin, 1983.

Ranft, Brian. "The Protection of British Seaborne Trade and the Development of Systematic Planning for War, 1860–1906." In Brian Ranft, ed., *Technical Change and British Naval Policy, 1860–1939,* pp. 1–22. London: Hodder and Stoughton, 1977.

Reynolds, Clark G. "The Continental Strategy of Imperial Japan." U.S. Naval Institute *Proceedings* 109, no 8 (August 1983): 65–71.

Reynolds, David. *The Creation of the Anglo-American Alliance, 1937–1941: A Study in Competitive Cooperation.* Chapel Hill, N.C.: University of North Carolina Press, 1982; first pub. 1981.

———. "Churchill and the British 'Decision' to Fight On in 1940: Right Policy, Wrong Reasons." In Richard Langhorne, ed., *Diplomacy and Intelligence during the Second World War: Essays in Honour of F. H. Hinsley,* pp. 147–67. Cambridge: Cambridge University Press, 1985.

Rhodes, P. J. *The Athenian Empire.* Greece and Rome, New Surveys in the Classics No. 17. Oxford: Clarendon Press, 1985.

Rich, Norman. *Hitler's War Aims: I, Ideology, the Nazi State, and the Course of Expansion.* New York: W. W. Norton, 1973.

———. *Hitler's War Aims: II, The Establishment of the New Order.* New York: W. W. Norton, 1976.

Richmond, Herbert W. *Imperial Defence and Capture at Sea in War.* London: Hutchinson, 1932.

——. *The Invasion of Britain: An Account of Plans, Attempts and Counter-measures from 1586–1918.* London: Methuen, 1941.

——. *Statesmen and Sea Power.* Oxford: Clarendon Press, 1946.

Ritter, Gerhard. *The Schlieffen Plan: Critique of a Myth.* London: Oswald Wolff, 1958; first pub. 1956.

Robertson, Esmonde E. "German Mobilization Preparations and the Treaties between Germany and the Soviet Union of August and September 1939." In Robert Boyce and Esmonde Robertson, eds., *Paths to War: New Essays on the Origins of the Second World War,* pp. 330–66. Basingstoke (U.K.): Macmillan Education, 1989.

Rodger, N. A. M. *The Wooden World: An Anatomy of the Georgian Navy.* Annapolis, Md.: Naval Institute Press, 1986.

Rodgers, William Ledyard. *Greek and Roman Naval Warfare: A Study of Strategy, Tactics, and Ship Design from Salamis (480 B.C.) to Actium (31 B.C.).* Annapolis, Md.: Naval Institute Press, 1983; first pub. 1937.

——. *Naval Warfare Under Oars, 4th and 16th Centuries: A Study of Strategy, Tactics and Ship Design.* Annapolis, Md.: Naval Institute Press, 1986; first pub. 1940.

Ropp, Theodore. "Continental Doctrines of Sea Power." in Edward Meade Earle, ed., *Makers of Modern Strategy: Military Thought from Machiavelli to Hitler,* pp. 446–56. Princeton, N.J.: Princeton University Press, 1941.

Rose, J. Holland. *Napoleonic Studies.* London: George Bell and Sons, 1906; first pub. 1904.

——. "The Continental System, 1809–14." In A. W. Ward, G. W. Prothero, and Stanley Leathes, eds., *The Cambridge Modern History.* Vol. 9: *Napoleon,* pp. 361–89. New York: Macmillan, 1934; first pub. 1906.

——. *Man and the Sea: Stages in Maritime and Human Progress.* Cambridge: W. Heffer and Sons, 1935.

——. *The Indecisiveness of Modern War and Other Essays.* Port Washington, N.Y.: Kennikat Press, 1968; first pub. 1927.

Rosenberg, David Alan. "The Origins of Overkill: Nuclear Weapons and American Strategy, 1945–1960." *International Security* 7, no. 4 (Spring 1983): 3–71.

Rosinski, Herbert. *The Development of Naval Thought.* Newport, R. I.: Naval War College Press, 1977.

Roskill, S. W. *History of the Second World War: The War at Sea, 1939–1945.* Vol. 1: *The Defensive.* London: HMSO, 1954.

346

———. *The Strategy of Sea Power: Its Development and Application*. London: Collins, 1962.

Rothenberg, Gunther E. *The Art of Warfare in the Age of Napoleon*. Bloomington, Ind.: Indiana University Press, 1980; first pub. 1978.

Runciman, Steven. *A History of the Crusades*. 3 Vols. Cambridge: Cambridge University Press, 1951–54.

———. *The Fall of Constantinople, 1453*. Cambridge: Cambridge University Press, 1965.

Ruppenthal, Roland G. *United States Army in World War II: The European Theater of Operations, Logistical Support of the Armies*. Vol. 1: *May 1941–September 1944*. Washington, D.C.: GPO, 1953.

Sagan, Scott D. "The Origins of the Pacific War." *Journal of Interdisciplinary History* 18, no. 4 (spring 1988): 893–922.

Schreiber, Gerhard. "The Mediterranean in Hitler's Strategy in 1940. 'Programme' and Military Planning." In Wilhelm Deist, ed., *The German Military in the Age of Total War*, pp. 240–81. Dover, N.H.: Berg Publishers, 1985.

Schwartz, David N. *NATO's Nuclear Dilemmas*. Washington, D.C.: Brookings Institution, 1983.

Scullard, H. H. *Scipio Africanus: Soldier and Politician*. Ithaca, N.Y.: Cornell University Press, 1970.

Seaton, Albert. *The Russo-German War, 1941–45*. New York: Praeger, 1970.

Seeley, J. R. *The Expansion of England*. Chicago: University of Chicago Press, 1971.

Setton, Kenneth M. (rev. ed.). *A History of the Crusades*. 5 vols. Madison, Wis.: University of Wisconsin Press, 1969–85.

Sherwig, John M. *Guineas and Gunpowder: British Foreign Aid in the Wars with France, 1793–1815*. Cambridge, Mass.: Harvard University Press, 1969.

Smail, R. C. *Crusading Warfare, 1097–1193*. Cambridge: Cambridge University Press, 1972; first pub. 1956.

Sokolsky, Joel J. *Seapower in the Nuclear Age: The United States Navy and NATO, 1949–80*. Annapolis, Md.: Naval Institute Press, 1991.

Spector, Ronald. *Eagle Against the Sun: The American War with Japan*. New York: Free Press, 1985.

Starr, Chester G., Jr.. *The Roman Imperial Navy, 31 B.C.–A.D. 324*. Westport, Conn.: Greenwood Press, 1975; first pub. 1941.

————. *The Beginnings of Imperial Rome: Rome in the Mid-Republic*. Ann Arbor, Mich.: University of Michigan Press, 1980.

————. *The Influence of Sea Power on Ancient History*. New York: Oxford University Press, 1989.

Ste. Croix, G. E. M de. *The Origins of the Peloponnesian War*. London: Gerald Duckworth, 1972.

Steiner, Zara S. *Britain and the Origins of the First World War*. London: Macmillan, 1977.

Stevens, C. E. "Constantine the Great and the Christian Capital—A.D. 324–527." In Philip Whitting, ed., *Byzantium: An Introduction*, pp. 1–14. Rev. ed. Oxford: Basil Blackwell, 1981.

Stevenson, David. *The First World War and International Politics*. Oxford: Oxford University Press, 1988.

Stone, Norman. *The Eastern Front, 1914–1917*. London: Hodder and Stoughton, 1975.

Strachan, Hew. *European Armies and the Conduct of War*. London: George Allen and Unwin, 1983.

Stradling, R. A. *Europe and the Decline of Spain: A Study of the Spanish System, 1580–1720*. London: George Allen and Unwin, 1981.

Strauss, Barry S., and Josiah Ober. *The Anatomy of Error: Ancient Military Disasters and Their Lessons for Modern Strategists*. New York: St. Martin's Press, 1990.

Taylor, Telford. *The Breaking Wave: World War II in the Summer of 1940*. New York: Simon and Schuster, 1967.

————. *The March of Conquest: The German Victories in Western Europe, 1940*. Baltimore: Nautical and Aviation Publishing Company of America, 1991; first pub. 1958.

Terraine, John. *Douglas Haig: The Educated Soldier*. London: Hutchinson, 1963.

————. *Trafalgar*. New York: Mason/Charter, 1976.

————. *The Road to Passchendaele: The Flanders Offensive of 1917, a Study in Inevitability*. London: Leo Cooper, 1977.

————. *To Win a War: 1918, The Year of Victory*. Garden City, N.Y.: Doubleday, 1981; first pub. 1978.

————. *White Heat: The New Warfare, 1914–18*. London: Sidgwick and Jackson, 1982.

————. *The First World War, 1914–1918*. London: Leo Cooper, 1983; first pub. 1965.

———. *Business in Great Waters: The U-Boat Wars, 1916–1945*. London: Leo Cooper, 1989.

Thucydides. *The Peloponnesian War*. Translated by Rex Warner. London: Cassell, 1962.

Trachtenberg, Marc. *History and Strategy*. Princeton, N.J.: Princeton University Press, 1991.

Travers, Tim. *The Killing Ground: The British Army, the Western Front and the Emergence of Modern Warfare, 1900–1918*. London: Allen and Unwin, 1987.

Treadgold, Warren. *The Byzantine Revival, 780–842*. Stanford, Cal.: Stanford University Press, 1988.

Tuchman, Barbara. *The Guns of August*. New York: Macmillan, 1962.

Turner, John. *British Politics and the Great War: Coalition and Conflict, 1915–1918*. New Haven, Conn.: Yale University Press, 1992.

Turner, L. C. F. "The Significance of the Schlieffen Plan." In Paul Kennedy, ed., *The War Plans of the Great Powers, 1880–1914*, pp. 199–221. London: George Allen and Unwin, 1979.

Tuyll, Hubert P. van. *Feeding the Bear: American Aid to the Soviet Union, 1941–1945*. Westport, Conn.: Greenwood Press, 1989.

Utley, Jonathan. *Going to War with Japan, 1937–1941*. Knoxville, Tenn.: University of Tennessee Press, 1985.

Vlahos, Michael. "Wargaming, an enforcer of Strategic Realism: 1919–1942." *Naval War College Review* 39, no. 2 (March–April 1986): pp. 7–22.

Vyronis, Speros, Jr. "The Byzantine Legacy and Ottoman Forms." In *Dumbarton Oaks Papers, Nos. 23 and 24*. Washington, D.C.: Dumbarton Oaks Center for Byzantine Studies, 1969–1970.

———. *The Decline of Medieval Hellenism in Asia Minor and the Process of Islamization from the Eleventh through the Fifteenth Century*. Berkeley, Cal.: University of California Press, 1971.

van der Vat, Dan. *The Pacific Campaign, World War II: The U.S.-Japanese Naval War, 1941–1945*. New York: Simon and Schuster, 1991.

Wallach, Jehuda L. "The Sea Lion That Did Not Roar: Operation *Sea Lion* and Its Limitations." In John B. Hattendorf and Malcolm H. Murfett, eds., *The Limitations of Military Power: Essays Presented to Professor Norman H. Gibbs on His Eightieth Birthday*, pp. 173–202. Basingstoke (U.K.): Macmillan, 1990.

Wark, Wesley K. *The Ultimate Enemy: British Intelligence and Nazi Germany, 1933–1939*. Ithaca, N.Y.: Cornell University Press, 1985.

Warner, Philip. *Invasion Road.* London: Cassell, 1980.

Watkins, James D., et al. *The Maritime Strategy.* U.S. Naval Institute *Proceedings, Supplement* (January 1986).

Watson, Mark Skinner. *United States Army in World War II: The War Department, Chiefs of Staff, Prewar Plans and Preparations.* Washington, D.C.: GPO, 1979; first pub. 1950.

Webster, Charles, and Noble Frankland. *History of the Second World War: The Strategic Air Offensive Against Germany, 1939–1945.* 4 vols. London: HMSO, 1961.

Wegener, Wolfgang. *The Naval Strategy of the World War.* Annapolis, Md.: Naval Institute Press, 1989; first pub. 1929.

Weigley, Russell F. *The Age of Battles: The Quest for Decisive Warfare from Breitenfeld to Waterloo.* Bloomington, Ind.: Indiana University Press, 1991.

Wernham, R. B. "Elizabethan War Aims and Strategy." In S. T. Bindoff, J. Hursfield, and C. H. Williams, eds., *Elizabethan Government and Society: Essays Presented to Sir John Neale,* pp. 340–68. London: Athlone Press, 1961.

———. *Before the Armada: The Growth of English Foreign Policy, 1485–1588.* London: Jonathan Cape, 1966.

———. *The Making of Elizabethan Foreign Policy, 1558–1603.* Berkeley, Cal.: University of California Press, 1980.

———. *After the Armada: Elizabethan England and the Struggle for Western Europe, 1588–1595.* Oxford: Clarendon Press, 1984.

Wight, Martin. *Power Politics.* New York: Holmes and Meier, 1978.

Williamson, Samuel R. *The Politics of Grand Strategy: Britain and France Prepare for War, 1904–1914.* Cambridge, Mass.: Harvard University Press, 1969.

———. "The Origins of World War I." In Robert I. Rotberg and Theodore K. Rabb, eds., *The Origin and Prevention of Major Wars,* pp. 225–48. Cambridge: Cambridge University Press, 1989.

Willmott, H. P. *Sea Warfare: Weapons, Tactics and Strategy.* Chichester (U.K.): Antony Bird Publications, 1981.

———. *Empires in the Balance: Japanese and Allied Pacific Strategies to April 1942.* Annapolis, Md.: Naval Institute Press, 1982.

———. *The Barrier and the Javelin: Japanese and Allied Pacific Strategies, February to June 1942.* Annapolis, Md.: Naval Institute Press, 1983.

Wilson, H. W. "The Command of the Sea, 1803–15." In A. W. Ward, G. W.

Prothero, and Stanley Leathes, eds., *The Cambridge Modern History.* Vol. 9: *Napoleon,* pp. 208–43. New York: Macmillan, 1934; first pub. 1906.

Wynne, G. C. *If Germany Attacks: The Battle in Depth in the West.* Westport, Conn.: Greenwood Press, 1976; first pub. 1940.

ACKNOWLEDGMENTS

My friend Seth Cropsey, then Deputy Under Secretary of the Navy, was the inspiration for me to explore the strategic leverage of sea power in this book. The historical approach adopted and the judgments developed are, of course, solely my responsibility.

I am in the debt of my friend and colleague Captain Roger Barnett, USN (Ret.), who has contributed extensively to my understanding of things maritime. Such errors as the book contains are certainly no fault of his. Dr. Michael Vlahos of the Center for Naval Analyses and Professor Ken Hagan of the U. S. Naval Academy offered excellent advice, for which I am grateful. I thank the editor and publishers of *Naval Forces*, who have allowed me to use in Chapter 10 a later variant of a portion of my article, "The Wartime Utility of Seapower: Part I—The Historical Record," from their Vol. 11. In addition I thank my long-suffering editor at the Free Press, Joyce Seltzer, whose patience and good advice have seemed inexhaustible. Finally, I thank my wife, Valerie, who has endured with more good nature than I deserve the protracted family costs of my writing about the leverage of sea power.

INDEX

371